W9-BZG-555

Dance Teaching Methods and Curriculum Design

Gayle Kassing, PhD
Human Kinetics

Danielle M. Jay, PhD
Northern Illinois University

Human Kinetics

Library of Congress Cataloging-in-Publication Data

Kassing, Gayle.
Dance teaching methods and curriculum design / Gayle Kassing, Danielle M. Jay
p. cm.
Includes bibliographical references and index.
ISBN 0-7360-0240-5
1. Dance--Study and teaching--Handbooks, manuals, etc. 2. Dance teachers--Training of--Handbooks, manuals, etc. 3. Lesson planning--Handbooks, manuals, etc. I. Jay, Danielle M. (Danielle Mary), 1947- II. Title.
GV1589 .K37 2003
792.6'2'071--dc21

2002012685

ISBN: 0-7360-0240-5

The Web addresses cited in this text were current as of November 2002, unless otherwise noted.

Acquisitions Editor: Judy Patterson Wright, PhD; **Developmental Editor:** Joanna Hatzopoulos Portman; **Managing Editor:** Amy Stahl; **Assistant Editors:** Derek Campbell and Sandra Merz Bott; **Copyeditor:** Jan Feeney; **Proofreader:** Pam Johnson; **Indexer:** Marie Rizzo; **Permission Manager:** Dalene Reeder; **Graphic Designer:** Nancy Rasmus; **Graphic Artist:** Kathleen Boudreau-Fuoss; **Photo Manager:** Leslie A. Woodrum; **Cover Designer:** Andrew Tietz; **Photographer (cover):** George Tarbay; **Photographer (interior):** George Tarbay; **Art Manager:** Kelly Hendren; **Illustrators:** Tom Roberts, Brian McElwain, Kathleen Boudreau-Fuoss, and Kristin Darling; **Printer:** Sheridan Books

Printed in the United States of America 10 9 8 7 6 5 4 3 2 1

Human Kinetics
Web site: www.HumanKinetics.com

United States: Human Kinetics
P.O. Box 5076, Champaign, IL 61825-5076
800-747-4457
e-mail: humank@hkusa.com

Canada: Human Kinetics
475 Devonshire Road Unit 100, Windsor, ON N8Y 2L5
800-465-7301 (in Canada only)
e-mail: orders@hkcanada.com

Europe: Human Kinetics
107 Bradford Road, Stanningley, Leeds LS28 6AT, United Kingdom
+44 (0) 113 255 5665
e-mail: hk@hkeurope.com

Australia: Human Kinetics, 57A Price Avenue, Lower Mitcham, South Australia 5062
08 8277 1555
e-mail: liahka@senet.com.au

New Zealand: Human Kinetics
P.O. Box 105-231, Auckland Central
09-523-3462
e-mail: hkp@ihug.co.nz

To Dr. Aileene Lockhart,
for envisioning dance education
in the future and in our futures.

To Dr. Judy Patterson Wright,
for sharing your expertise, support, and guidance
throughout the process of writing this book,
which is a merging of our experiences
and love of dance.

To our families,
who have supported us through this journey.

Gayle Kassing
Danielle M. Jay

"To Dance: it is a discipline of all hours, of all days,
but it is also a pleasure of all of life."

— Source unknown
quoted by Katerina Fernandez—translated by Web master of the Ballet Web

"It takes an athlete to dance, but an artist to be a dancer."

— Shanna La Fleur

FANTASY: "I got the JOB!"
SURVIVAL: The empty classroom
MASTER (or breathe): "I know the content; I can deliver the content."
IMPACT: In-depth learning or AHA!

— Unknown

Contents

Part II Implementing Dance Pedagogy: What You Need to Do to Create a Dance Curriculum

Preface

Two students apply for a high school dance teaching position: one student with a major in a dance education certification program, and one student with a major in dance performance. Each is a skilled dancer, but only one is prepared to teach dance. The dance education student is able to answer the principal's questions regarding methods, teaching styles, lesson plans, and curriculum design. He gets the job because he communicates to the principal the value of dance as an educational medium and the role of dance in the school's curriculum. After the teacher's first year at the school, the principal is satisfied with the new dance teacher's work, and the dance teacher is content yet challenged in his position.

As a dance educator, you must know how to communicate with people who have no background in dance. You must be prepared to explain dance's role in education and its relationship to other disciplines in the curriculum. The old adage "If you're going to talk the talk, you'd better walk the walk" applies; but it also works conversely: To effectively perform the feats, you have to know the subject, "the talk."

Preparing for a dance education profession requires you to practice a variety of skills beyond dancing. This book addresses the content, the skills, and the supporting knowledge a dance teacher uses in public education.

Dance teaching involves sharing knowledge about dance, caring about students' learning of the art of dance, and teaching dance technique. As dancers we typically strive to communicate nonverbally; but as dance educators we must strive to verbally communicate effectively with students, educators in other disciplines, administrators, members of the community, and school and government agencies at all levels.

Mission

To become a dance educator, you need to be dedicated to promoting dance as an art and as an educational medium. This book presents a conceptual model of dance education that embraces dance as an art form and disseminates it through learning experiences in dancing, dance making, and dance appreciation. Dance education requires an understanding of content in relation to the learner, the environment, and current education theories.

Dance Teaching Methods and Curriculum Design is unique in its compilation of a variety of resources. Through this book, you will gain an understanding of your students, the educational setting in which you teach, and the dance content that is appropriate for the students and the environment. You will learn not only the appropriate methods and strategies for teaching dance in educational settings but also the appropriate circumstances in which to use them. The particular methods and strategies depend on your experience and knowledge; the particular dance form to be taught; your students' skill, age, and knowledge base; and the environment. Dance education must extend its perspective beyond teaching dance technique to incorporate education theories to meet state and national arts standards; these education theories and standards are the basis of presenting the content to students. This book is a guide for those that need answers to the questions about the *who, what, when, where,* and *why* of dance education.

Audience

Dance Teaching Methods and Curriculum Design works as a foundational resource for dance education students, dance educators, and physical educators who teach in public or private schools. Drama and music teachers and those who teach dance in collaboration with another art will also benefit from the information in this book. You will find sample units for 10 dance forms: creative movement and creative dance, folk dance, square dance, contra dance, social dance, ballet, modern dance, jazz, tap, and aerobic dance. The 10 different dance forms are divided into four categories: creative movement and dance, recreational dance, concert dance, and aerobic dance (dance fitness).

In addition, you will find practical applications of appropriate dance education methods and curriculum design for students in preschool through high school.

If you are a dancer with some teaching background, you must become familiar with dance forms that you have never studied and also learn about teaching different age groups and abilities within a variety of settings. If you are a teacher with dance experience but little choreographic experience, you must acquire this knowledge and expand it to include teaching your students how to view a dance. Dance teachers come from various backgrounds and diverse experiences. When using this book, you can select information that pertains to your teaching setting and philosophy.

Organization

Dance Teaching Methods and Curriculum Design is divided into two parts. **Part I** (chapters 1 through 8) covers information specific to teaching dance and understanding learners in preschool through high school. **Chapter 1** is an overview of dance education; it provides a model for the teaching and learning process in dance, which guides you through the book. **Chapter 2** organizes dance knowledge into seven cross-disciplinary categories that you must know to teach dance. **Chapter 3** helps you develop observation skills in the dance class. **Chapter 4** explains how students learn dance and provides methods for constructing the parts of the dance class. **Chapter 5** presents the methods and strategies for teaching dance. **Chapter 6** imparts ways to organize and manage the dance class and students' behavior. **Chapter 7** studies the age groups of learners and their relation to the school and community. **Chapter 8** explores the four categories of dance forms and considers the artistic demands of dancing and producing dance performances.

Part II (chapter 9 through the epilogue) emphasizes the application of dance knowledge to teaching, developing a curriculum, and dance programming. You will learn how to create learning experiences, then lesson plans, then unit plans, and finally a curriculum. A culminating curriculum portfolio project integrates all of the theory and application into a practical product that you can present to a prospective employer. In addition, you will find sample unit plans for 10 dance forms taught in public schools. The unit plans provide an outline for teaching these beginning dance units.

Chapter 9 guides you in developing the lesson plan by explaining learning domains and the parts of an objective for the lesson. **Chapter 10** gives you assessment tools that apply to dance teaching. **Chapter 11** provides instruction on writing the lesson plan and prepares you to teach and analyze your implementation of the lesson plan. **Chapter 12** leads you through the process of developing a unit plan and creating a curriculum. **Chapter 13** provides sample unit plans for 10 dance forms. **Chapter 14,** the culminating portfolio project, prepares you for creating a curriculum guide. The **epilogue** presents the model as a compilation of all its parts that you have explored throughout this book.

Special Features

This book contains many special features that will help you access important information quickly:

- **A model** for the teaching and learning process in dance
- **Chapter objectives and summaries**
- **Tables** that compile information about different topics
- **Highlight boxes** that contain specific information that is easy to access
- **Self-check lists** that provide you with a quick way to understand a process or help you learn a new concept
- **It's Your Turn** exercises that provide practical, interactive experiences in dance
- **Forms** for lesson plans, teaching evaluations, unit plans, scope and sequence, and block time plans
- **Sample unit plans** for 10 different dance forms, each containing a three-week unit of 15 progressive sessions
- **An extensive list of selected resources** for each dance unit
- **Icons** for movement, choreographic, and aesthetic principles as they apply to each dance form
- **Beyond technique** exercises that provide additional learning activities in dance mak-

ing and dance appreciation in each sample unit plan

- **A culminating portfolio project** that synthesizes all of the elements explored in the book

Dance education students should read parts I and II in sequence. Part I presents a rationale for dance education in its various settings and its relationship to the national mandates for educational reform; part II offers possibilities for unit and curriculum development, design, and evaluation. This book will serve as your main resource after you earn your degree. For the current dance educator, the sample unit plans presented in chapter 13 will be the first place to peruse. This chapter provides quick access to content for teaching 10 dance forms. Part I may serve as a review or provide new information about teaching strategies and education theories that apply to the teaching of dance.

If you are a dance educator or student involved in a methods course, you will benefit from this book because it provides a course of study. You will come to understand the profession of the dance educator and feel comfortable with the responsibilities of this new role.

It is our hope that *Dance Teaching Methods and Curriculum Design* will help you to assess and meet the needs of your students and provide effective learning experiences in dance, dance making, and dance appreciation.

Acknowledgments

Thanks to the following principals, who allowed us to arrange the photo shoots: Robert Allison at Wildrose Elementary School in St. Charles, Illinois; Tammy Prentiss at Stratford Middle School in Bloomingdale, Illinois; Jan Borja at New Trier High School in Northfield, Illinois. Nancy La Cursia, head of kinetic wellness at New Trier High School in Northfield, Illinois, helped us coordinate this project with the other campus at New Trier High School.

Thanks to the dance educators who were responsible for organizing and recruiting students for the photo shoot: Becky Sleutem at Wildrose Elementary School, Jamie Kindl-O'Conner at Stratford Middle School, and Maureen Maher (our main organizer), Christine Bauer, and Christopher Rutt at New Trier High School. Thanks to all the students from Northern Illinois University, Wildrose Elementary School, Stratford Middle School, and New Trier High School for modeling for the photos.

Randall Newsom, from the theatre and dance department at Northern Illinois University, supplied students and costumes. George Tarbay from Northern Illinois University was our wonderful photographer.

Thanks to Dr. Judith Bischoff, former chair of the department of kinesiology and physical education at Northern Illinois University, for her support. Thanks to Dean Sorensen from Northern Illinois University for her support.

Jill Heintz helped to keep us organized during the photo shoot, and Denise Nakaji helped in checking our photos.

Special thanks to all the teachers who made their students available at Wildrose Elementary School, Stratford Middle School, and New Trier High School. And thanks to all the parents who permitted their children to participate in this project.

Special thanks to Melissa Hebert.

PART I

Dance Pedagogy: What You Need to Know About Teaching and Learning Dance

Teaching dance requires a firm grounding in the art and science of dance, dance pedagogy, and teaching methodology. As a professional dance educator, you must gain an expanded view of the many components that contribute to enriching the art and supporting the science of teaching dance. This book is a guide for your personal journey in dance pedagogy and dance education. The chapters in the first part of the book help you in gaining pedagogical content knowledge for dance.

Chapter 1, Envisioning Dance Education, is an overview of dance education. In it we define dance and dance education and describe the differences between the dancer and the dance educator. In public schools, dance functions as an academic discipline and as arts education and is required for meeting established standards. Three types of overall learning experiences that constitute dance education are dancing, dance making, and dance appreciation. A teaching and learning process model in dance encompasses the teacher, the dance content, and the learner within the context of public education.

Chapter 2, Teaching Dance and Cross-Disciplinary Knowledge, focuses on identifying seven cross-disciplinary categories of knowledge sources. Both the student and the teacher share some of these cross-disciplinary categories in the teaching and learning situation.

In **chapter 3, Observing and Analyzing the Teaching and Learning Situation,** you learn observational strategies applicable to the dance class. After reading this chapter, you will practice observing dance classes, and you will write an observation report.

Chapter 4, Guiding Students in Learning Dance, explores the ways in which students learn dance, the stages of motor learning, and connections between language and movement. This sets the stage for constructing exercises, figures, and combinations for the dance class.

Chapter 5, Understanding Dance Teaching Methods, covers teaching methods and strategies applied to dance. This chapter introduces presentational methods, teaching strategies, and the use of music and accompaniment in the dance class.

In **chapter 6, Organizing and Managing the Dance Class,** you will learn to create a positive learning atmosphere in which to communicate effectively with your dance students. Managing the dance class requires that you organize the class so that you can focus on teaching the students. In the dance class, you will encounter various students' behaviors that you must control. Several approaches for managing students' behavior are discussed.

Chapter 7, Analyzing the Learner and the Learning Environment, aids in determining the characteristics of different age groups, children with special needs, and personal and group development through dance. The learner as part of the school environment is a part of the larger community and its values.

Chapter 8, Categorizing Dance Forms and Their Artistic Demands, begins with ways of acquiring dance knowledge for teaching. The dance forms taught in public education are comprised of four dance form categories: creative dance, recreational dance, concert dance, and aerobic dance (dance fitness). Underlying the dance form categories are movement, choreographic, and aesthetic principles. Many of the dance forms have artistic demands that involve understanding various styles of the dance form, producing dance, and performing attributes.

These eight chapters address the pedagogical knowledge that you need in teaching and learning dance. We invite you to take a journey with us to discover things about yourself in relation to the art, the science, and the profession of teaching dance.

CHAPTER

Envisioning Dance Education

Chapter Objectives

By the end of this chapter, you should be able to do the following:

- Describe differences between dance and dance education.
- Identify the three types of learning experiences in dance and how they relate to the National Dance Standards.
- Understand the teaching and learning process model in dance.

Envisioning dance education involves understanding dance from different points of view to gain new perspectives. This chapter will help you develop an awareness of what a dance educator does, what dance education is in public schools and how it relates to dance standards, and the difference between a dancer and a dance educator. A model representing the teaching and learning process in dance provides ways of looking at how the dance education process works. The components of the model include the types of experiences that activate dance teaching and learning.

Defining Dance and Dance Education

Dance as a profession and as a discipline are internally joined. Dance becomes the nucleus that supports dance education as an artistic and educational medium. Dance education can be defined as educating the learner through the media of dance, dance making, and dance appreciation. On the surface, this definition seems simple, but in its simplicity lies also its complexity. Dance education is not as simple as putting dance and education together.

Dance means different things to different peoples and cultures. Often it is difficult to separate the dancer from the dance. Defining dance provides a basis on which to build an understanding of dance education.

Defining Dance

Simply defined, dance is the human body rhythmically moving through space and time with energy or effort. Dance engages the dancer's physical, mental, and spiritual attributes to perform a dance form as a work of art, a cultural ritual, a social recreation, and an expression of the person. A dance form initiates from physical movement, rhythm, content, style, aesthetics, traditions, and mental and spiritual meanings that may be social, cultural, or religious.

Dance as an art is a conduit of expression and communication—the message and the medium. It provides a structure that may be intricate, precise, casual, or personal through which the dancer expresses movement, style, and aesthetics. Dance is what entices the dancer in a continuous quest for knowledge about himself in his changing relationship to the dance.

Dance can transport us from the studio, the gym, or the dance space to the theater or other performance spaces and on to the larger arena of life. It is a part of society and academia and an important component of arts education. In one form or another, dance can be our lifelong partner that will enrich and fulfill us as human beings. Dance affords countless rewards to the audiences who watch performances, to the students we teach, and to the profession through the research we pursue. Whatever role we assume, the dance is nothing without the dancer, and neither can exist without dance education.

Defining Dance Education

To define dance education, we need to explore dance in its many roles. Without the passing of knowledge of the dance forms from one person to another and from one generation to the next, dance could not have survived as a discipline and as an art form. Our dance heritage is vast; the forms range from authentic to classical. Dance education has taken many forms in educational settings; it has been used for many purposes; and it is often viewed as inferior to other disciplines. Exploring dance and its functions in education provides a better perception of the expanse of dance education.

Understanding Dance in Educational Settings

The discipline of dance in educational settings concentrates on process with performances that come out of the process rather than the goal of producing performance after performance.

Dance as an educational modality enriches the child, the adolescent, the adult, and the senior citizen in a variety of ways. It educates physically, socially, emotionally, and intellectually. Although there are many benefits of dance in education, it remains the least understood and developed of the arts in education.

Ideally, dance education should begin with the preschool student. Dance is a lifelong learning-enrichment activity. A variety of educators deliver dance programs in kindergarten through high school: dance educators, physical educators, classroom teachers, and other arts educators such as music or drama teachers.

In elementary, middle, and high school, physical educators often teach dance. In magnet school programs, a dance specialist teaches dance. The dance specialist may be a certified dance educator, a resource teacher, or an adjunct teacher with dance experience. The adjunct teacher often comes from a dance studio background.

The purposes of dance in the elementary school encompass those for general education and dance as arts education. In the ideal situation, the elementary dance program effectively funnels into a middle school program that in turn sends the student into a high school program. As a graduate of a high school program, the student may enter the profession or a college program. Through these programs, dance functions as both a separate discipline and a component of arts education.

Understanding Historical Functions of Dance in Education

Dance functions as an essential component of education and as a partner with physical education, other academic subjects, and arts education. Dance first had to gain acceptance as a separate discipline. At the beginning of the 20th century, dance was taught in physical education as either folk dance for boys and girls or aesthetic dance, an exclusively female activity. Throughout much of the 20th century, dance was a viable part of the physical education curriculum. The continued efforts of dance artists and educators led to the definition of dance as a separate discipline. Dance separated from its physical education roots and often joined other arts disciplines in the fine arts or became recognized as a singular discipline that developed as a dance program or department. Regardless of the positioning of dance within the public school and college setting that prepares dance educators for teaching in K-12 public education, the focus remains on the study of dance.

Understanding Dance As a Discipline of Study

For any subject to be considered a discipline of study, it must contain content knowledge of facts, concepts, principles, and theories. Dance is a discipline of study, just like other subjects such as science, music, language arts, and physical education. Content knowledge is information focused on the subject matter; thus, it is distinguished from other subjects. Dance content knowledge includes information about dance forms through the learning experiences of dancing, dance making, and dance appreciation. As with any discipline of study, dance does not exist in an isolated state. Drawing knowledge from other fields of study to support dance as a discipline is embracing cross-disciplinary knowledge, which expands, enriches, and supports the content knowledge of the discipline. Cross-disciplinary knowledge in dance provides background, scientific evidence, educational foundations, and psychological support for dance content and teaching methods. Dance has earned additional credibility as a separate identity and value as a subject for study in educational settings as a component of arts education.

Understanding Dance As Arts Education

During the second half of the 20th century, dance joined arts education as a key player in educational reform. Professional organizations representing the visual arts, music, dance, and drama asserted the importance of arts in education. As a unified voice supported by educational research and state mandates, the arts gained national recognition as a viable tool for learning and therefore gained a place in the educational reform movement. Arts education builds the case that each of the arts contributes to a person's development as a productive member of society.

Educational theories developed by Howard Gardner about multiple intelligences (1983) gave pivotal support to the importance of arts education. One of Gardner's theories suggests that the arts use other forms of intelligence to reach students beyond the traditional linguistic and logical/mathematical learning paradigms. Students who participate in the arts use different intelligences to learn, understand, and perform tasks. Research has provided much data regarding the effect of arts education programs on students. These studies show that arts education

- gives students opportunities to achieve in the arts as well as in other disciplines,
- gives students opportunities to learn about human nature and culture,
- develops self-discipline and persistence,
- prepares students for the workplace,
- provides access to learning for students who do not respond to traditional methods, and
- has a positive effect on students' motivation and academic performance.

Dance has many roles within the parameters of dance education. Dance can range from simple, exploratory experiences in an elementary school to professional-level performance in an arts magnet high school. Dance can be learning folk dances as part of a social studies unit about Greece, or it can be a way to integrate the study of the four phases of a butterfly in science. The richness and diversity of dance and its appropriateness to so many situations give it a magnitude of options that are suited to many students and situations.

Literacy in the arts has become an important attribute of becoming educated as a well-rounded person in 21st-century society. Dance teachers have been aware of the benefits that students derive from participating in and studying dance. The dancer and dance educator occupy distinct roles in the teaching and learning process.

Distinguishing Between Dancers and Dance Educators

There are innate similarities in being a dancer and a dance educator; many differences exist as well. These differences are what lead us to ask some important questions that will, in turn, help define certain parameters within dance. Quite often, dance and dance education are viewed as indistinguishable. Consequently, dancers and dance educators are thought of as doing many of the same things. The reason for this misconception is that no clear-cut distinctions exist between these two interrelated parts of the profession. Dispelling some of the confusion about the differences between a dancer and a dance educator begins by identifying what each of them does.

What a Dancer Does

To be a good dancer you have to observe, listen, practice, perfect, and perform. Being a good dancer does not necessarily make you a good teacher. However, being a thinking, feeling, questioning, understanding dancer is a prerequisite to teaching. You must formulate questions about why something is done a certain way, comprehend how to separate tradition from scientific knowledge, aspire to teach others to bring out their best as dancers and as arts-educated people in our society, and share your art form with others. You must love dance with your body, your mind, and your spirit. These attributes are equally essential to becoming a dance educator and to understanding the profession.

What a Dance Educator Does

As a dance educator, you are multitalented. You must first gain competency as a dancer. You master the skills and develop technique and knowledge of one or more dance forms. As your dancing improves, you acquire style in performing the dance form.

You must perform several roles in your function as an educator. Some roles revolve around dance and teaching dance; other roles broaden your capabilities professionally and personally. Being an educator requires that you function as a professional in your field by demonstrating certain behaviors and qualities. You have a role as an expert in the field of dance in the school and community and as a participant in professional organizations. Although many of these roles blend into one another, the dance teacher's profession centers on students in the dance studio classroom.

A dance educator is foremost a teacher but also an instructional strategist, a mentor, a curriculum planner, and administrator. Other roles include choreographer and director of dance activities such as extracurricular dance clubs, orchesis, or dance companies. Many of these roles intertwine with one another, which make them difficult to separate as you shift from one to the other effortlessly to solve a problem, support an outcome, or fulfill a responsibility associated with being a dance educator:

- Teacher
- Mentor
- Choreographer
- Director
- Curriculum planner
- Administrator
- Assessor and evaluator

All of these roles are part of your everyday work as a dance teacher. As an educator, you concentrate your work into three types of dance learning experiences.

Learning Experiences in Dance

Dance can be categorized into three types of learning experiences: dancing, dance making, and dance appreciation. These types of learning experiences, or modes of learning, encompass distinct areas of dance as a discipline, yet they interconnect and support one another as the basis of dance education. The modes are processes that students experience in dance education and that teachers use to teach dance. In the following list, each type of learning experience is defined in relation to the material in this book:

- Dancing involves learning the skills to perform and using movement principles that are universal to dance and specific to the form as shown in the following photos.

Dancing in elementary school using creative movement and dance.

Middle school dancers doing a line dance.

High school dancers executing a jazz pull-back.

Elementary school dancers doing a square dance.

Middle school dancers showing the elbow swing in contra dance.

High school dancers doing aerobic dance.

- Dance making involves creating dances (directed either by the teacher or student) and using choreographic principles that culminate in either informal or formal production as the following photos show.

Dance making in elementary school: groups talking, creating, and moving.

Dance making in middle school: putting together movement sequences in social dance.

Dance making in high school: using a computer-generated choreography program.

- Dance appreciation is viewing, perceiving, and responding to dance using aesthetic principles that are universal to dance and specific to the form. Students participate in dance appreciation activities as shown in the following photos.

Dance appreciation in elementary school: children watching their classmates perform a ribbon dance in the dance space.

Dance appreciation in middle school: students watching a dance video.

Dance appreciation in high school: students observing a student performance on stage.

The scope of each of these learning experiences in any dance education setting depends on the students, the experiences of the teacher, and the educational values of the school. However, in a larger context, the scope of any one public school relates to district, state, and national standards for education.

Relating National Standards for Dance to Dance Education

The National Standards for Arts Education are voluntary and provide the achievement standards for each of the art forms; but they delegate specific curriculum and instructional activities to states, local school districts, and teachers to achieve these standards (National Standards for Arts Education 1994). Using the National Standards for Arts Education as a basic framework, some states have adopted, adapted, expanded, modified, and changed them to create their own dance standards. As a general curriculum framework for dance, the National Standards provide guidelines on what students in dance should study and achieve. The National Standards as well as state and district standards provide the curriculum frameworks for teachers in dance education. Before the inception of the National Standards, state and national involvement in educational reforms and the Secretary's Commission on Achieving Necessary Skills (SCANS) Report (U.S. Department of Labor 1991) authenticated some of the most compelling reasons for dance education.

Goals 2000: Educate America

The Goals 2000: Educate America Act grew out of the SCANS Report. Goals 2000 examines the world of work and its implications for changes in student learning. The SCANS Report designated competencies and foundations of skills and personal qualities that are required for effective job performance. The report identified five competencies and a three-part foundation of skills (U.S. Department of Labor 1991). The fine and performing arts became core content for Goal 3 of Goals 2000. Overall, the Goals 2000 document identified thinking skills, personal qualities, and abilities for the work force that can be realized through dance learning. The Goals 2000 provide a broad foundation of learning outcomes that support the National Standards for Arts Education (Goals 2000: Educate America Act H.R. 1804).

The skills and competencies required by Goals 2000 are necessary for pursing a dance career as a professional dance educator. These foundational competencies create a well-rounded person who could be successful in dance or in another career in the 21st-century workplace. With dance acknowledged as one of the arts education disciplines absorbed into the educational reform movement, it gained increased recognition as a constituent of arts education and the development of the National Standards for Arts Education.

Exploring the National Standards for Dance

The standards outline cumulative skills and knowledge expected of students engaging in dance activities. The expectations created by the Consortium for National Arts Education Associations are that students will demonstrate higher skills than the National Standards dictate. The standards for grades 9 through 12 establish both a proficient and advanced achievement for that level. In the National Standards for Arts Education, the expectation is that every student will achieve the proficient level in at least one arts discipline by the time of graduation from high school (Consortium of National Arts Education Associations [The Dance Standards Task Force] 1994).

The National Standards for Dance consist of two types of standards: content and achievement. Content standards specify "what students should know and be able to do in the arts disciplines" (Consortium of National Arts Education Associations [The Dance Standards Task Force] 1994, p. 18). In dance this covers three modalities of learning: dancing, dance making, and dance appreciation. Students enrich these modalities by using critical thinking, understanding aesthetics, and employing historical and cultural studies to enhance communication and creative activities in dance as an art form or participate in dance as part of a healthy physical activity.

The National Standards for Dance and Arts Education consolidate the body of knowledge that dance encompasses. The standards categorize knowledge by age and by what is developmentally appropriate. Students are expected to attain the benchmarks identified at the completion of grades 4, 8, and 12 (Consortium of National Arts Education Associations [The Dance Standards Task Force] 1994, p. 17).

The National Standards for Dance amplify these modalities through seven content standards.

1. Identify and demonstrate movement elements and skills in performing dance.
2. Understand choreographic principles, processes, and structures.
3. Understand dance as a way to create and communicate meaning.
4. Apply and demonstrate critical- and creative-thinking skills in dance.
5. Demonstrate and understand dance in various cultures and historical periods.
6. Make connections between dance and healthful living.
7. Make connections between dance and other disciplines.

National Dance Standards 1–7 (pp. 6–9). These quotes are reprinted from the *National Standards for Arts Education* with permission of the National Dance Association (NDA), an association of the American Alliance for Health, Physical Education, Recreation and Dance. The source of the National Dance Standards *(National Standards for Dance Education: What Every Young American Should Know and Be Able to Do in Dance)* may be purchased from: National Dance Association, 1900 Association Drive, Reston, VA 20191-1599; or telephone 703-476-3421.

Connecting the National Standards and your state standards to your work in the classroom will enable you to become part of a network of participating teachers, thereby validating your work as a dance educator and as part of arts education. This information can become a guide for lesson and unit plans and curriculum development. The dance standards apply to all dance forms.

Dance Education in Relation to the Standards

Each of the national initiatives highlights the role of the arts and dance within education and educational reform. It is often part of our mission as dance educators to explain, defend, and advocate the importance of dance to a child, an organization, the community, or the state. Goals 2000, the

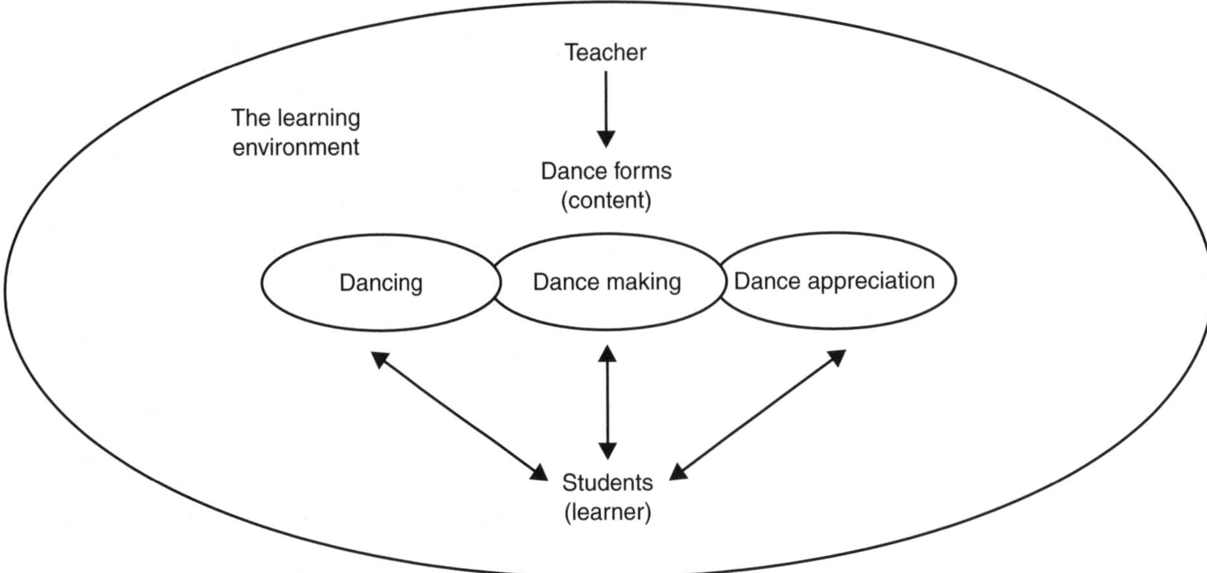

Figure 1.1 The teaching and learning process model in dance.

National Standards for Dance Education, and current arts and education literature provide information that enables you to communicate the importance of dance as a means of personal development. Standards provide a focus for many of the benefits that dance educators have long believed about the discipline of dance in education. Using standards makes your dance program viable, legitimate, and defendable.

Standards provide a blueprint for content presented in public education. The dance teacher implements the appropriate content for the learner, which is identified in the dance standards as foundational steps in learning dance. To guide you through the teaching and learning process, we have developed a model (see figure 1.1) that identifies components in dance education to meet the teaching and learning goals.

Understanding the Teaching and Learning Process Model in Dance

The teaching and learning process model in dance provides a new way of looking at dance education. The model includes the following components: the teacher, the dance form, the learner, and the learning experiences in dance.

The teacher must know the following:

- Content for various dance forms
- The dance forms and other disciplines that support dance learning
- Teaching and class management strategies to deliver, assess, and build the dance curriculum
- How to choose content to develop learning experiences that are appropriate for the learners and for the public school setting

Students learn through the processes of dancing, dance making, and dance appreciation. The dance teacher builds an appropriate curriculum based on the needs of the learners and the parameters of the teaching environment. The components of the teaching and learning process model can be interpreted from two different views. In one view, the model begins with the teacher and ends with the learner in the traditional dance education teaching process. Conversely, the model begins with the learner and what he has to learn to become a teacher. At present, the teaching and learning process model is an outline for all of the knowledge that you will acquire throughout this book.

Summary

Dance is the human body's rhythmic movement through space and time with energy. The learner experiences dance education through the media of dancing, dance making, and dance appreciation. These media convey the National Dance Standards. To understand dance education, we must understand the teaching and learning model in dance, which focuses on the teacher, the dance form, the learner, and the learning experiences.

References

Consortium of National Arts Education Associations (The Dance Standards Task Force). 1994. *National Standards for Arts Education.* Reston, VA: The Music Educators National Conference (MENC). (The National Standards for Dance Education: What Every Young American Child Should Know and Be Able to Do in Dance and the Opportunity to Learn. Standards for Dance Education are available from the National Dance Association, 1900 Association Drive, Reston, VA 20191; telephone 703-476-3421. The complete National Arts Education Standards and additional materials relating to the Standards are available from MENC—The National Music Educators Association, 1806 Robert Fulton Drive, Reston, VA 20191; telephone 800-336-3768.)

Gardner, H. 1983. *Frames of mind: The theory of multiple intelligences.* New York: Basic Books.

Goals 2000: Educate America Act H.R. 1804, January 25, 1994. [Goal 3: Student Achievement in Citizenship]. www.negp.gov/page3.htm.

National Standards for Arts Education. 1994. Music Educators National Conference. Reston, VA, 1994.

U.S. Department of Labor. 1991. *What work requires of schools. Secretary's Commission on Achieving Necessary Skills (SCANS) Report on America 2000.* Washington, DC: U.S. Department of Labor. http://wdr.doleta.gov/SCANS.

It's Your Turn

1. Identify your strengths and challenges as a dancer and as a teacher.
2. Obtain copies of your state and national dance standards. Write a one-page comparison of the state and national standards.
3. Describe where you are in relation to the components of the teaching and learning dance model.

CHAPTER

2

Teaching Dance and Cross-Disciplinary Knowledge

Chapter Objectives

By the end of this chapter, you should be able to do the following:

- Identify and describe the seven cross-disciplinary categories relevant to teaching dance.
- Understand the various knowledge categories as they apply to dance.

You have to have more than a basic knowledge of dance to teach it. You must acquire a broad knowledge base from which to select relevant information for the dance form you plan to teach. This chapter will help you organize dance information into a series of categories to create a comprehensive knowledge base for teaching dance. Once you create this knowledge base, you as the dance teacher can easily understand and access it to support the teaching and learning of various dance forms. The first step is to distinguish the cross-disciplinary categories of dance knowledge.

Identifying the Seven Cross-Disciplinary Categories of Dance Knowledge

A cross-disciplinary category is a series of interdisciplinary subjects that contribute to a discipline. An adaptation of this concept is derived from the work of Joan Vickers (1987) to align the cross-disciplinary categories for dance into seven distinct, yet interconnected, categories:

1. Supportive knowledge encompasses defining the dance form, vocabulary, history and culture, attire and etiquette, teaching environment, class format, equipment, national standards, dance books, notation, and media (which includes technology resources).
2. Physiological training and conditioning, or dance science, comprises the general components of fitness, types of activity, training factors, principles of exercise, nutrition, and weight control.
3. Technique and choreography comprise the vocabulary, teaching progressions, music and accompaniment, and teacher- and student-created choreography.
4. Teaching methods and management comprise presentation methods, observation skills, types of feedback, teaching strategies, classroom management, motor learning, and assessment strategies.
5. Education theories explore sensory and student-centered learning; critical-thinking skills; metacognitive skills; multiple, emotional, and everyday intelligence; brain/mind principles; and interdisciplinary (integrated) learning.
6. Psychosocial development focuses on conduct and expectations in the classroom, personal development of the student, communication with the teacher, and group collaboration.
7. Artistic development covers aesthetic principles, artistic demands of the dance form, production, performance, and attributes of the dancer striving to develop artistry.

These seven cross-disciplinary categories give credence to dance as an academic discipline. Much of the content in each of the categories is applicable to all dance forms. The cross-disciplinary categories become a basis for any of the dance forms taught from preschool through high school.

To teach dance, the instructor needs to experience the dance form and know its content. The teacher must be cognizant of what students will learn so that she can develop specific lesson and unit plans. The dance educator must realize the depth and breadth of knowledge that students need about a dance form. She develops dance content that will meet the requirements of the students, their technical development, and the teaching environment. The dance content places demands on the learner as well as on the instructor, but some of the requirements for the dancers are different than those for the instructor. Five of the seven cross-disciplinary categories for dance focus on the learner:

- Supportive knowledge
- Physiological training and conditioning (dance science)

- Technique and choreography (psychomotor skills)
- Psychosocial development
- Artistic development

Becoming acquainted with the student's dance content and learning the categories within the content are only the first steps for the dance teacher. The dance content determines what the instructor will teach during the time allocated to the dance classes. Thus, the teaching process becomes a balancing act of continuous planning and revising to meet students' needs and their abilities to absorb the content.

Learners in the beginning dance class focus on the techniques or skills being taught; they don't see much of the underlying pedagogy that the teacher uses to teach the class. Because the teacher uses this information routinely, it goes unnoticed in teaching and managing the class.

Dance Content for the Teacher

For the teacher, the dance content encompasses all of the components for the student and includes two additional categories. The teacher's dance content requires more in-depth understanding of all of the student's cross-disciplinary categories and these additional specific categories:

- Teaching methods and management
- Education theories

As a teacher, you must select what you will teach and implement elements from all of the cross-disciplinary categories into your instruction. Figure 2.1 organizes the seven cross-disciplinary categories. Some of the categories will be discussed in this chapter; others will be addressed in depth in later chapters. To examine the dance content for the teacher, begin on the left-hand side of the chart with "Supportive knowledge."

Supportive Knowledge and Other Knowledge

Under the cross-disciplinary category of supportive knowledge, the subcategory is other knowledge. This encompasses many other types of knowledge that are necessary for the teacher to present dance content in the class: a definition of the dance form, vocabulary, history and culture, the teaching environment, the equipment necessary to teach, the format of the class specific to the dance form, national standards in arts education for dance, dance books and notation, and dance technology (which includes media and computer-interactive resources) and somatic techniques. The other types of knowledge collectively weave through the dance content, giving it richness and meaning for students.

Definition

A definition gives a brief explanation of the dance form, its purpose, unique characteristics, and the artistic nature of the dance form. The definition for a specific dance form and other supporting knowledge combines to create a complete picture of the dance form. The vocabulary of the dance form is an important part of its structure.

Vocabulary

Vocabulary is the written and spoken terms for the exercises, steps, positions, poses, figures, and concepts that constitute a dance form. The following are aspects of vocabulary:

- It is shared by more than one dance form and, for the most part, has the same meaning; for example, demi-plié is a "half bend" that is part of ballet, modern dance, jazz, and tap dance.
- It uses precise terminology or possesses generic or open-ended meanings that leave room for different interpretations.
- It connects the written and spoken communication used to the cross-disciplinary category of technique.
- It provides a means for dancers and dance educators to teach or talk and write about a dance form.
- It is linked to a historical period and to a specific culture and uses a variety of languages to express the meaning.

Dance vocabulary readily establishes a connection with the culture in which the dance form developed.

Supportive knowledge	Physiological training and conditioning (dance science)	Technique and choreography (psychomotor skills)	Teaching methods and management	Education theories	Psychosocial development	Artistic development
Other knowledge • Definition of dance form • Vocabulary • History and culture • Teaching environment • Equipment • Class format for specific dance forms • National Standards • Dance books • Notation • Technology • Somatic techniques	Dance-specific exercise principles • Overload • Individuality • Overuse Nutrition and weight control	Vocabulary • Exercises, steps, positions, poses, figures, and combinations • Dances Teaching progressions • Legs • Legs and arms • Legs, arms, and head Music and accompaniment • Music theory • Music specific to dance form • Music history and styles • Improvisational or semi-structured • Sound collage Teacher-created choreography • Progression of simple to complex combinations • Styles and repertory Student-created choreography • Problem solving • Improvisational form	Presentational methods • Whole–part • Part–whole–part • Add-on (linked) Observation skills • Technique • Applied kinesiology • Artistic aspects • performance quality Types of feedback • Verbal and nonverbal • Acknowledgment • Perspective • Corrective • Negative • Guided manipulation Teaching strategies • Cueing • Imagery • Movement—language connection • Methods specific to the dance form Classroom management • Teaching styles • Safety • Class organization • Time management • Individualized learning Motor learning • Verbal-cognitive • Motor • Autonomous Assessment strategies • Formative and summative evaluation • Performance evaluation • Authentic assessment • Writing exercises and written tests	Learning theories and styles • Sensory learning • Student-centered learning • Individualized learning • Critical-thinking skills • Metacognitive skills • Multiple intelligences • Emotional intelligence • Everyday intelligence • Brain/mind principles • Interdisciplinary, interrelated, integrated approaches	Psychosocial aspects • Classroom behavior and expectations • Personal development of students and teacher • Group development (cooperation, respect)	Artistic demands of dance form • Styles • Schools • Performance • Choreography Production and performance • Professional attitude • Technical proficiency • Artistry

Figure 2.1 Dance content knowledge for the teacher.

History and Culture

History and culture provide background and traditions of the dance form to support it as a viable endeavor or subject worthy of study and a context for presenting the dance form. Presenting the historical or cultural significance of a dance or dance form is often important in the teaching of dance courses. The history and culture of a dance form serve as a conduit to multiculturalism because dance provides insight into the customs, traditions, and mores of the people.

The subcategories of definition, vocabulary, and historical and cultural information are supportive knowledge unique to each dance form. They expand the students' knowledge about the dance form they are studying and give meaning to the techniques studied. The teacher must master the knowledge in these subcategories to impart dance within a larger context of meaning that provides the student with a rich experience.

The next set of subcategories under supportive knowledge is often imperceptible to the student. These subcategories are the resources the teacher uses when preparing to teach the class.

Teaching Environment

Teaching environment refers to the setting in which the dance teacher instructs. Within the environment, the following factors must be considered:

- The age of the students
- The skill level of the students
- The length of the class, unit, or program
- The physical nature of the studio
- The expectations, or mission, of the organization or educational institution
- The demographics of the community

In the teaching environment, the teacher determines some important factors of teaching the dance form. The teacher has to possess a complete picture of what he has in equipment to support his teaching the dance class.

Equipment

Equipment comprises the items the teacher uses to conduct the dance class. These include music equipment (record player, cassette or compact disc player, piano, records, cassettes, compact discs, sheet music), barres, floors, mirrors, mats, carpet squares, props, and other items used in classroom instruction. Prioritizing the equipment in terms of importance to the class supports organizational and budgeting requirements for purchasing it. Another teaching consideration is determining the format of the class within the teaching environment and selecting the appropriate equipment for the format of the class.

Class Format

The dance form determines the format of the class. The form gives the teacher an outline of elements to be included in a complete and balanced class. The different class formats for each dance form will be addressed in chapter 8. Class content is derived from personal and educational experiences and information from dance literature, notation, and technology sources.

Dance Literature

Books and dance notation scores constitute much of the literature for a given dance form. Dance books contain different aspects of dance content and cross-disciplines. Dance notation offers wonderful supplemental materials for the teacher and the student to study. Learning how to read and write dance notation and then re-creating a dance from a notation score are challenging and exciting experiences. Dance literature sources are further enhanced through dance technology.

Dance Technology

Broadly defined, dance technology includes media such as video, interactive computer-assisted programs, and the Internet. Dance videos are essential to the training and development of the dancer and dance teacher. Computer-assisted programs developed for dance and Internet research have become important tools for gaining knowledge about all forms of dance. Subjects related to dance as supporting or other knowledge include a variety of somatic techniques.

Somatic Techniques

Somatic techniques enable the dancer to sense or feel the body kinesthetically. Using somatic techniques, the person does specific movements that require less effort for more efficient movement results. These techniques help to retrain, rehabilitate, strengthen, or maintain the body's ability to move. The techniques attune people to their spiritual, physical, and mental selves. Somatic techniques include Bartenieff Fundamentals, Pilates, Body-Mind Centering (BMC), the Feldenkrais Method, the Alexander Technique, and Ideokinesis.

Bartenieff Fundamentals, developed by Irmgard Bartenieff, is a system that trains and reeducates the body in movement. The system focuses on using functional movement and directing intentions with the use of shifts of weight, awareness of space, sequential muscle movement, breathing rhythm, and the relationship of body parts. This technique improves alignment, ease of movement, efficiency, and expressiveness.

Pilates, or the physical mind method devised by Joseph Pilates, emphasizes economy of movement and produces strong, lean bodies without weight training or aerobics. It uses strengthening and stretching, which involve stress-free and nonimpact movement. The Pilates method uses an inside–outside approach that incorporates kinesthetic monitoring through balancing muscular innovation.

Body-Mind Centering, founded by Bonnie Bainbridge Cohen, is an all-encompassing educational and therapeutic approach to movement. It releases the stress, fear, pain, restrictive behaviors, and perceptions that prevent a person from performing in the best way possible. This movement-centering study requires the learner to focus on a physical problem area. BMC uses a variety of methods: hands-on work, movement, guided imagery, developmental repatterning, and props (large balls, stretch bands, music, and videos).

The Feldenkrais Method, created by Moshe Feldenkrais, relies on integrating the body and the mind through movement awareness. It is a learning process that innervates and reeducates the nervous system through deliberate communication to the senses. The mind, body, and senses are integrated to support correct movement. A Feldenkrais practitioner leads a group through highly structured movement experiences.

The Alexander Technique, formulated by Frederick Alexander, emphasizes balance in the head-neck relationship, which is referred to as the *primary control* area of the body. Proper positioning of the head on top of the spine culminates in maximal lengthening of the spine and fluid movement. Repetitive experience helps to stimulate a person's kinesthetic sense. The intent of the Alexander Technique is to change habitual patterns that lead to tightening of muscles.

Ideokinesis, developed by Lulu E. Sweigard, is an approach to neuromuscular reeducation that uses mental imagery to change motor patterns. The main purpose of Ideokinesis is to direct the nervous system and coordinate postural alignment, muscular patterns, and skeletal use. Visualizing the lines of movement that travel through the body in a constructive rest position transforms a person's body shape, flexibility, tone, strength, and endurance.

The supportive knowledge category amplifies the teacher's knowledge about a specific dance form. The physiological training and conditioning of the dancer is the scientific aspect of dance and dance teaching.

Physiological Training and Conditioning

Dancers have been viewed as highly trained athletes, and some athletes such as Michael Jordan (a team sport athlete), Michelle Kwan, and Tiger Woods (individual sport athletes) have been deemed artists. Much of the dancer's physiological training for specific dance forms has developed through tradition, such as in ballet. Certain dance forms evolved from a choreographer's viewpoint (such as the Graham technique in modern dance). Some dance forms have examined their techniques and modified them based on the emergence of dance science.

Physiological training and conditioning of the dancer is an important cross-disciplinary category of the student and the teacher's dance content. Teachers must be able to train and condition dancers by applying this information to effectively develop dancers' technique, prevent injury, and promote good health. Some of this information applies to all dance forms. Specific training and conditioning information is contained in the aerobic dance (dance fitness) sample unit in chapter 13.

Dance Exercise Principles

Exercise principles impart practical guidelines to the training process. In the various forms of dance, many training practices have been transmitted from teacher to student and have become traditions in dance training. The advent of dance science has brought about exercise principles to maintain and guide the training of dance students according to physiological facts supported by research. The principles of overload, overuse, and individuality apply to the training of dancers.

Overload

Overload means placing a demand on the body greater than that to which it is accustomed. According to this principle, a dancer must experience slight discomfort while exercising to obtain a training effect. A dancer or athlete can achieve overload by manipulating the intensity, the length, and the frequency of a workout. The maximum recommendation for obtaining a training effect requires a person to work in at least the 60 percent heart rate range (HRR) for 20 minutes, three times per week. Over time, the body will adapt to the new stress level. A person must increase the frequency, intensity, or length of exercise to gain improvement. When a person goes beyond a sensible training regimen, the benefits decrease and the likelihood of injury increases.

Overuse

Overuse refers to the overtraining of a person. If one does not have sufficient rest between workouts, exercise produces a reverse effect. Fatigue, injury, illness, or an overall feeling of fruitlessness are signs of overuse. Often a dancer experiences a plateau effect and sometimes seems to perform steps or an activity worse instead of better.

A traditional concept of dance training is that the more times a skill is performed, the better it will be. In most cases, the opposite is true—less is more—if the skill is performed correctly. This does not mean that practice and rehearsal are unnecessary; rather, a balanced and sensible approach is best. A dancer only has one body, and the best way to take care of it is through the practice of sound physiological training.

Classes and rehearsals are often demanding. As a result, the dancer experiences muscle soreness. Delayed-onset muscle soreness, or DOMS, usually occurs 24 to 48 hours after strenuous exercise. This is caused by microscopic damage to or inflammation of the muscle cell infrastructure from excessive muscle force. Stretching before and after each class helps prevent or relieve muscle soreness.

Individuality

Individuality refers to the uniqueness of every person. No two bodies are physiologically the same. Dance students learn from individual as well as general class corrections from teachers. Students know that reminders and feedback aimed at an entire class may not apply to each student, but the general class corrections are reminders that keep students on the right track as self-checks in preventing bad habits. Each dancer's talents and achievements are hers alone, and her progress toward becoming better can be fulfilling and challenging. It is important for dancers to compare the self with the self instead of with other dancers. Each person is the best judge of her own physiological limits.

Nutrition and Weight Control

A proper balance of diet and exercise helps in developing a strong, athletic dancer. A varied diet of carbohydrates, proteins, and fats should include breads, pasta, rice, and beans as well as fresh fruits and vegetables. Meats, fish, and fowl are also part of a well-balanced diet but in lesser quantities. The control of fat intake stabilizes a dancer's weight. Dancers should avoid high-calorie, unhealthful food and beverages. Water is essential in preventing dehydration from exercise and is instrumental in keeping body functions regular. Proper nutrition promotes good health, weight control, and peak conditioning for performance.

Technique and Choreography

Technique and choreography are the core of dance and of the teacher's training. Of all the cross-disciplinary categories, the dual-strand category of technique and choreography is the primary focus leading to artistic development. Many of the subcategories are interwoven into methods of teaching dance.

Dancer's Technique

Technique is the dancer's skill in execution. In some dance forms, technique is extremely important, whereas in other forms, technique is less important than other aspects. The dancer starts by learning the vocabulary of a dance form. From there, the dancer acquires technique through executing the exercises, steps, positions, poses, and figures while applying movement principles to the dance vocabulary.

Vocabulary comprises the movements specific to a dance form and includes exercises, specific elements of the dance form, principles, and concepts. Positions and poses can be unique to a specific form, or several forms may share them. Using the vocabulary of dance, the teacher designs the class format and creates choreography.

Teacher-Created Choreography

The teacher creates movement combinations that become the basis for choreographing dances for performance in and out of the classroom. The teacher relies on his knowledge of styles and specific dances that exist within a dance form to create variety in choreography and to provide students with a well-rounded dance experience.

The teacher builds classroom combinations based on the components and progressions for each level of the chosen dance form. These combinations progress from one-step, two-step, and three-step combinations to more complex and extended combinations. The extended combinations serve as studies in styles of the dance form.

Each dance form contains one or more styles. The teacher must have knowledge and performance experience in at least one of the styles that pertain to the dance form he is teaching. Instructors study styles in conjunction with technique and vocabulary of the dance form. Some styles reflect the teacher's point of view; others are inherent to the dance form. Certain styles are incorporated into the dance form, and they appear and disappear within decades or other time frames. In the dance classroom, students emulate the teacher's style of choreography. The teacher becomes the reference for students as they learn to dance and take their first steps in composing dances.

Student-Created Choreography

Students create choreography under a teacher's guidance. In student-created choreography, the following steps are taken:

1. The teacher poses a movement problem that the student or a group of students must solve.
2. The teacher gives the students the parameters for solving the problem.
3. The dancers explore and discover ways of solving the problem.
4. The students select movement elements and manipulate them into a study or dance.
5. The students develop the dance, rehearse and perfect the work, then perform it for peers in the classroom.
6. After the performance, the teacher may ask the students to further refine their work.

This process is used in creative movement classes and other dance forms. Through improvisation, the body explores movement by playing with the elements of the dance form. Improvisation uses unstructured movement—movement made up or formed in the moment—rather than a series of predetermined steps. In contact improvisation, dance partners or groups interact to create movements using the forces of motion. These processes become the source for new movement material for choreography. Another form of improvisation is structured improvisation. In this form, after the dancers improvise movement, they select and rehearse the movements into a semistructured choreographic form.

Choreography and technique are visible products of the process of learning dance. To move effectively through these processes, the teacher uses a variety of teaching methods and management tools. The next cross-disciplinary category is teaching methods and management. This category is vital in dance instruction and is addressed in great detail in subsequent chapters.

Education theories form the foundation of dance teaching and management. Those teaching in the public school setting must understand and apply these theories in their instruction.

Applying Education Theories in the Dance Class

Education theories enrich the content and its delivery in the class setting. Current educational research offers different ways for students to learn and become excited about what they are learning. These theories also validate dance as a discipline in public education settings.

Correlating Learning Dance Theories

Education has undergone an immense change in response to the skill requirements in the 21st-century workplace. In this restructured view of education, sensory, student-centered, and individualized learning; critical thinking; metacognitive, multiple, emotional, and everyday intelligence; and brain/mind principles play an important part in the teaching and learning process in dance.

Sensory Learning

Sensory learning focuses on using the senses to acquire information about a subject. Dance is a natural means of activating our kinesthetic, visual, and auditory sensory learning skills. These are the primary senses with which we learn dance. In turn, using these sensory learning modalities triggers other learning processes. (Sensory learning's relationship to motor learning is discussed further in chapter 4.) Using sensory learning to progress continually reinforces a student's innate abilities to process information.

Student-Centered Learning

In student-centered learning, teachers devise activities and projects that engage students in the teaching and learning process. Student-centered learning enables dancers to become actively involved in gathering and presenting information about dance or interpreting or staging a dance of a particular time period. Student-centered learning projects transfer easily into the traditional choreographic, technical, and teaching processes. This theory focuses on students' accomplishments. During the process, students become more responsible for their own learning and assessment of their work. Using practical and authentic assessment tools, students and the teacher evaluate their projects. These strategies are explained in chapter 10 on assessment related to student-centered learning and individualized learning.

Individualized Learning

A class of 30 students is a class of 30 individuals. Each student in the class has individual needs and learns in a slightly different way than other students learn. The dance teacher must accommodate these learning differences while attending to the instruction of the entire class. Individualized learning requires that the teacher adopt a multifocus view to provide appropriate instruction for each person in the class.

Through teaching methods, class management, and integration of education theories, the dance teacher has options for accommodating each student's needs. In learning dance technique and choreography and dance appreciation activities, students are challenged through the use of critical-thinking skills.

Critical-Thinking Skills

Critical, or higher-level, thinking is an approach to learning that uses the high-level cognitive skills of analyzing, synthesizing, and evaluating. The dance student who uses critical-thinking skills strengthens her ability to come up with creative solutions in assignments and choreography projects.

Lower-level cognitive skills include comprehending, identifying, and describing. In many situations, dancers focus on these skills: They regurgitate facts, translate movement into written or spoken terminology, and provide yes-or-no answers to questions.

In dance, the process of thinking can be both a performing and a creative art. Choreography uses higher-level thinking skills, as does technique. Students have the responsibility to learn and then assess their own progress. Learners are challenged with problems to which they respond through written reports or oral presentations. The following are some situations that allow learners to develop and practice critical-thinking skills (Wiggins 1999):

- Reading strengthens comprehension and analytical skills.
- Writing helps learners organize thoughts, determine similarities and differences, and trace relationships for the purpose of communicating clearly.
- Reasoning skills are inherent in both reading and writing and are required for discussion.
- Oral presentations involve discussion of logical statements, justification, and explanations.

The fundamental concepts of critical thinking are apparent in a model developed by Larry Lavender for critiquing a dance work in a choreography class. In his book *Dancers Talking Dance* (1996), Lavender refers to J.G. Kurfiss (1988), who noted that discovery and justification must be present for the development of critical-thinking skills. The discovery phase consists of observing, previewing, and assessing a dance work. In the justification phase, one's observations are presented as evidence in defending through argument one's assessment of what is actually seen in the dance.

In his book, Lavender devised the ORDER approach, which consists of observation, reflection, discussion, evaluation, and revision. Observation is the careful examination of a dance work—truly seeing what is actually there, not what we interpret. Reflection consists of writing observations of what you actually see. Discussion includes vocally sharing with others what one has observed and formulated in a written report. Evaluation is the stage in which judgments about the work are posed and debated. Revision depends on the choices the choreographer makes from the class members' suggestions for improving the work. The final step takes place when the revised dance is performed again.

Lavender's book describes critical thinking as it applies to teaching composition and choreography, but much more can be done to develop critical-thinking skills in a dance class, regardless of whether it is applied to dance technique or theory. In dance technique class, you evaluate your execution of combinations for the upcoming performance test. Then you practice the combinations applying your refinements to fine-tune your work. In methods of teaching dance class, you synthesize a variety of teaching strategies you observe or read about into your teaching behaviors. You select what you determine is the best strategy and adapt it to your specific situation.

Margaret H'Doubler (1940), an early 20th-century dance educator, wrote about the "thinking dancer" in her book *Dance: A Creative Art Experience.* H'Doubler's philosophy of dance education and the emerging role of dance educators called upon dance teachers to develop their art and profession in academic circles. She wanted dance teachers to analyze the art and theory of dance in education to give it credence equal to other arts and academic disciplines in public and higher education settings.

Metacognitive Skills

Aligned with critical-thinking skills are metacognitive skills. Metacognition is thinking about how we and others think and being able to distinguish between *what we know* and *what we don't know.* Teachers and students use metacognitive skills in developing a repertoire of thinking processes for ongoing, in-depth understanding (dance styles), problem solving (in choreography), and communication skills (in teaching). Metacognitive processes are important for dance teachers because their role is to make knowledge acquisition easy for the learner (Scruggs, Mastropieri, Monson, and Jorgenson 1985).

The following are two strategies for developing metacognitive behaviors:

1. Identify *what you know* and *what you don't know* about a topic. This is the starting point for active research: Students use the two statements to verify, clarify, and expand their information with more accurate information.

2. Talk about thinking. During brainstorming, planning, and problem-solving situations, a teacher should think aloud so students can follow his thinking processes. While modeling and discussing, the teacher should develop labels for the thinking processes and steps to promote student understanding. The following are several examples of how to implement metacognitive processes.

   - Engage in paired problem solving in improvisation or composition class. In this strategy, which is similar to reciprocal teaching, one student talks through a problem by describing his thinking processes to his partner. The partner listens and then asks questions to clarify thinking.

- Play the teacher. In small groups, students take turns in the role of teacher by asking questions and clarifying and summarizing the material being studied.
- Keep a thinking journal or learning log in dance technique or choreography class. In the journal, the learner reflects on her thinking, noting awareness of ambiguities and inconsistencies and commenting on how she resolved certain issues or difficulties (Palinscar, Ogle, Jones, Carr, and Ransom 1986).

If every lesson is planned well, it is difficult for students to become self-directed in their learning. To accomplish these goals, the teacher creates a flexible environment, providing adequate materials for students to explore and create. The teacher assigns students planning and problem-solving activities within a time frame. Likewise, the students generate criteria for evaluation of projects as they proceed through the activity phases. After the students complete the projects, the teacher leads a debriefing session to ascertain the thinking processes that occurred during the project. This session helps students develop awareness of strategies that can be applied to other learning situations.

Improving metacognitive and critical-thinking skills is essential for living and working. Multiple intelligences provide the instruments with which to attain these thinking skills.

Applying Multiple Intelligences to Dance Instruction

The theory of multiple intelligences, developed by educational psychologist Howard Gardner (1983), expands the concept of intelligence. Traditionally, intelligence has been measured by verbal and mathematical abilities. Gardner's paradigm expands intelligence to include bodily-kinesthetic, musical, spatial, logical-mathematical, linguistic, interpersonal, intrapersonal, and naturalist abilities.

Dance uses the following primary forms of intelligence: bodily-kinesthetic (movement of the body or bodies), spatial (use of space in place and through space), musical (rhythm, tempo, texture, accompaniment), interpersonal (how one relates to other people), and intrapersonal (how one perceives oneself). The other multiple intelligences—logical-mathematical, linguistic, and naturalistic—support dance when it is translated choreographically, vocally, or into written form. The dance teacher uses naturalist intelligence in classifying dance content into categories and establishing learning progressions for steps or progressions in a dance form; in recognizing cross-disciplinary similarities and differences; or in charting relationships among several dance forms, techniques, or theories. Continued research may reveal other intelligences and understandings, such as the existential understanding that relates to developing a philosophy.

Using bodily-kinesthetic intelligence, the dancer moves and employs movement memory. Dancing to music or some kind of accompaniment engages musical intelligence. As a dancer moves through space, the movement evolves into spatial patterns. Intrapersonal intelligence is what gives dancers the confidence and security to perform, which allows them to evaluate themselves realistically and set reasonable goals. Interpersonal intelligence is the ability to relate physically, mentally, and socially with others in dance. Being able to cooperate with others is vital to performing dance as well as to gaining the sense of ensemble. In everyday interactions, dancers and dance educators should cultivate awareness, sensitivity, flexibility, and the ability to compromise in their work.

Under Gardner's theory of multiple intelligences, the arts become a conduit for learning that permeates into the academic curriculum. This relationship between the arts and academic subjects expands through the multiple intelligences that provide a variety of learning pathways for all students. The conscious implementation of teaching through multiple intelligences in the dance classroom enriches the experience for all students, building on strengths and intelligences that are under development. Multiple intelligences coupled with emotional intelligences educate intellectually and emotionally. These two educational theories interface easily with dance education and its mission to develop the person spiritually, emotionally, physically, and intellectually.

Maximizing Emotional Intelligence for Teaching Dance

Emotional intelligence (Goleman 1995) examines the awareness and understanding of our emotions of rage, fear, passion, and joy. Emotional intelligence, shaped early in life, attunes us to learning about behavior that may be self-destructive or counterproductive. As children develop emotional intelligence, they gain control of their impulses and insight into others' feelings. This form of intelligence nurtures the ability to handle relationships without trauma. It enables people to cope with their environment and provides tools that make life more fulfilling, pleasurable, and rewarding.

Emotional intelligence, like multiple intelligences, is a different kind of "smartness." Research has shown that IQ, at best, contributes to about 20 percent of the factors related to life success. Emotional intelligence uses emotional messages sent and received in the brain. People develop emotional intelligence by acquiring skills through five dimensions: self-awareness, managing emotions, motivation, empathy, and social skills (Pool 1997).

Dance teachers encounter many different types of people in their work. Students and teachers often come with their own baggage or negative ways of dealing with others. Dance teachers should be nurturing, fair, and understanding while giving feedback to every student in the class. Often the dance teacher's spoken communication and actions in the classroom will make or break a person's desire to dance. Some students have the ability to irritate and infuriate the teacher. Regardless, the teacher's response should be to the student's behavior, not to the student. It is imperative that the teacher control this behavior and know when and how to use or harness rage, fear, passion, and joy appropriately.

The following five dimensions of emotional intelligence are important personal and professional attributes for the dance teacher and are to be cultivated in the dance student:

1. Self-awareness applies to both verbal and nonverbal communication.
2. Managing emotions is the responsibility of the student and is within the teacher's scope in managing the class.
3. Motivation to make the right decision about one's actions and their results helps in attaining one's goals.
4. Empathy for others builds understanding and compassion.
5. Social skills learned in dance class parallel the common courtesies applied and practiced in everyday life.

The dance class is a laboratory of both verbal and nonverbal human interaction; it provides the materials with which to learn and practice emotional intelligence skills. To implement methods for younger students to become aware of and use their emotional intelligence, post a paper stoplight—circles of red, yellow, and green paper aligned vertically—as a visual reminder. When student behavior requires intervention, use the stoplight system. Stop (red) the interaction. Ask students to think (yellow) of their options for resolving the situation. If necessary, count to 10! If that doesn't work, count to 20! Go (green) with the decision you think is best, and learn from its consequences (Goleman 1998).

Learning to cope with your emotions and creating relationships with others in the classroom are important attributes and the basis for gaining a professional attitude that moves with you from the classroom to the stage and into your professional dance career. Cultivating awareness of yourself and others emotionally is an important aspect of teaching and managing the dance class.

Everyday Intelligence

Everyday intelligence, as defined by Robert Sternberg (1985), has three parts that form a triarchy: experiential, contextual, and componential. Experiential learning involves accessing information through active participation and use of learning styles. Exercising experiential learning, the dancer uses visual, auditory, and kinesthetic senses to access knowledge about the topic explored. Executing dances of a particular period or culture provides a wealth of information about the people who danced; their capabilities; and especially their interaction with the history, society, and culture of their time.

The contextual part of everyday intelligence provides the learner with three ways to adapt to a given situation:

1. Fit yourself into the situation.
2. Change the situation to fit your needs.
3. Find another situation.

Componential intelligence provides a basis for problem solving. It enables the investigation of a hypothesis or research question and adjusts it through participation in active research. Dance teachers conduct active research on an ongoing basis as they learn and refine new ways to teach movement.

By solving problems, students gain a better understanding of problem-solving techniques. This is everyday intelligence at work: real-life experience; analysis; and application of theories, concepts, and principles. In dance, problem solving is learning how to use the tools of the art form in a functional and then aesthetic manner to communicate what the dancer or choreographer holds as deep meaning about a subject.

Using everyday intelligence, students acquire tacit feelings. These intuitive feelings become embedded in the process and are often inexplicable. They are part of a deep understanding that becomes the basis for making decisions that "feel right." In dance, using these intuitive feelings interfaces with brain/mind principles that bring life to an artistic work.

Brain/Mind Principles

Brain/mind principles focus on acquiring perceptual or dynamic knowledge that is deep, or felt, meaning (Caine and Caine 1999). Felt meaning is more than intellectual understanding; it is the synthesis of thoughts, ideas, sensations, and impressions that create a larger insight, an "Aha!" Deep meanings come from the social, emotional, intellectual, and spiritual parts of our lives. When brain/mind principles are used in teaching to expand dynamical knowledge, the learner has to meet three requirements:

1. Having a state of relaxed alertness. This is achieved as a combination of low threat, high challenge when the nervous system is relaxed and rested.
2. Being immersed in complex experiences. The activity or project should be orchestrated to contain multiple rich experiences similar to those found in our lives.
3. Processing the experience. While engaged in the process, the learner searches for patterns and meanings. All of these requirements are easily accessed during the dance class (Caine and Caine 1999).

Brain/mind principles synthesize research about how people learn from many disciplines and incorporates the education theories already explored in this chapter. Brain/mind principles provide ways to interconnect many aspects of how we learn into deep or felt meaning experiences through dance, choreography, and dance appreciation experiences. Integrated and interdisciplinary approaches in dance activities and projects promote thinking that synthesizes technique, principles, and concepts.

Interdisciplinary, Interrelated, and Integrated Approaches to Learning

Interdisciplinary, interrelated, and integrated approaches overlap, often confuse, and contain shades of meaning that are determined by circumstances and points of view. These approaches describe the roles that dance plays in relation to other academic subjects taught within a curriculum. With these approaches, dance interfaces either as the primary modality for teaching another subject, a collaborative modality, or a supportive one.

Interdisciplinary Approach

Interdisciplinary learning is an educational process in which two or more subject areas are integrated with the goal of fostering enhanced learning in each area (Cone, Werner, Cone, and Woods 1998). The interdisciplinary approach relates dance to other academic subject areas: social studies, science, math, language arts, foreign language, and health and physical education. In this approach, students learn basic concepts in academic subjects through dance. Crossover activities make experiences more memorable and meaningful. Using an interdisciplinary approach, the dancer and student are more apt to retain the dance concepts presented within different academic contexts. For instance, concepts presented in exercises might use counting, subtraction, gravity, weather, geography, culture, and other topics.

Interdisciplinary activities inspire a better understanding of the subject matter with which dance connects. This approach makes learning more interesting and fun. For example, when teaching a folk dance, a teacher might include the customs, culture, geography, mores, and other art forms of the country. In creative dance, the children make letter shapes with their bodies or create shapes with other children to form letters or words. The more connections we can have in this compartmentalized world, the better. Another approach is using one art to teach another.

Interrelated Arts

Interrelated arts demonstrate the commonalities in different art forms: space, time, force, line, rhythm, texture, and other concepts. An important aspect of this theory is that it helps a person understand and appreciate other art forms by focusing on their commonalities and differences.

Some arts are collaborative, such as music, dance, and drama. A dancer often uses music and self-accompaniment (vocal, self-accompaniment, or sound). The dancer accompanies herself by spoken words, sound, and/or rhythmic instrument. Dance interrelates with the visual arts when the dancer or dancers create designs in space and carve pathways through space with their bodies. Drama and dance are synergetic arts: Movement communicates in a nonverbal way, either in an interpretive or abstract manner. The arts and dance provide powerful conduits for integration with other disciplines in the curriculum.

Integrated Arts

Integrated arts refer to using arts, their tools, and processes as a way to teach or support learning in other academic subjects. Through integrated activities or projects, learners gain both content knowledge and conceptual understanding. Students respond favorably to participating in integrated learning projects and, through their work, show development of team spirit and improvement of attitudes and work habits.

Integrated curriculums create higher expectations for students, requiring their involvement in more complex problem solving that relates the subjects in the real world. An integrated curriculum relates fragmented learning experiences into a combined experience (Kase-Polisini and Scott-Kassner 1996).

All of the education theories explored provide many ways to support dance learning. The next cross-disciplinary category, psychosocial development, focuses on the learner in his personal development as an individual, and his interaction within the dance class. The psychosocial development category is further discussed in chapter 7, which addresses the environment and the learner.

The final cross-disciplinary category is the artistic development of the dancer. This category is paramount to the process of learning dance, performing it as an art form, and meeting the artistic and performance demands of the particular dance form. Artistic development is linked to dance forms and discussed in chapter 8.

Summary

This chapter identifies and describes the seven cross-disciplinary categories relevant to dance teaching and learning: supportive knowledge, physiological training and conditioning, technique and choreography, teaching methods and management, education theories, psychosocial development, and artistic development. The dance teacher uses the seven cross-disciplinary categories as content knowledge for teaching dance. Five of the categories relate directly to what students learn in the dance class or the student knowledge base. The other two categories specifically support the teacher (teaching methods and management and education theories). The dance teacher incorporates education theories into her dance class that, in turn, support dance education as a viable educational subject taught in public schools.

References

Caine, R.N., and G. Caine. 1999. Brain/mind learning principles. www.cainelearning.com.

Cone, T.P., P. Werner, S.L. Cone, and A.M. Woods. 1998. *Interdisciplinary teaching through physical education.* Champaign, IL: Human Kinetics.

Gardner, H. 1983. *Frames of mind: The theory of multiple intelligences.* New York: Basic Books.

Goleman, D. 1995. *Emotional intelligences.* Port Chester, NY: National Professional Resources.

Goleman, D. 1998. *Emotional intelligences with Daniel Goleman.* Washington, DC: WETA.

H'Doubler, M. 1940. *Dance: A creative art experience.* New York: F.S. Crofts & Co.

Kase-Polisini, J., and C. Scott-Kassner, eds. 1996. *Interconnecting pathways to human experience: Teaching the arts across the disciplines.* Orlando, FL: Arts for Complete Education.

Kurfiss, J.G. 1988. *Critical thinking theory: Theory, research, practice and possibilities.* Washington, DC: Association for the Study of Higher Education.

Lavender, L. 1996. *Dancers talking dance: Critical evaluation in choreography class.* Champaign, IL: Human Kinetics.

Palinscar, A.S., D.S. Ogle, B.F. Jones, E.G. Carr, and K. Ransom. 1986. *Teaching reading as thinking.* Alexandria, VA: Association for Supervision and Curriculum Development.

Pool, C.R. 1997. Up with emotional health. *Educational Leadership* 54 (2): 12-14.

Scruggs, T.E., M.A. Mastropieri, J. Monson, and C. Jorgenson. 1985. Maximizing what gifted students can learn: Recent findings of learning strategy. *Research Gifted Child Quarterly* 29 (4): 181-185.

Sternberg, R.J. 1985. *Beyond IQ: A triarchic theory of human intelligence.* New York: Cambridge University Press.

Vickers, J. 1987. *Instructional design for teaching physical activities.* Champaign, IL: Human Kinetics.

Wiggins, G. 1999. Multiple intelligence approach to assessment. In *Solving the assessment conundrum,* edited by D. Lazear. Tucson, AZ: Zephyr.

It's Your Turn

1. In one or two paragraphs, give four examples of four different dance forms and how they connect with specific cross-disciplinary categories. For example, "My most familiar dance form is ballet. It connects with the following specific cross-disciplinary categories: technique (vocabulary is in French), supportive knowledge (ballet is from 17th-century French court), artistic development (it is performed in a classical style), and education theories (it uses sensory learning modes in the classroom)."
2. Select one of the education theories and describe how it applies to a dance or dance form.
3. Select a book and a video on any dance form. Read and view the two sources, then write a summary paragraph on them, highlighting the most obvious cross-disciplinary categories used. Support your answers with examples.

CHAPTER

3

Observing and Analyzing the Teaching and Learning Situation

Chapter Objectives

By the end of this chapter, you should be able to do the following:

- Understand the different observation strategies used by teachers.
- Use an observation sheet to identify the dance dynamics of the class.
- Become aware of the appropriate observation protocols.

Learning to see the dance class through the teacher's eyes requires skills in observation. Throughout the dance class the teacher continually observes and analyzes students' learning. Observation during the dance class provides an enormous amount of information. The teacher continually sifts through the information, discerning what is important and applicable in the situation and to the development of a specific student. This chapter will help you learn what and how to observe in the dance class. Participating in observation experiences allows you to see teaching and management strategies in action. Observation gives you a view of the teacher's changing roles during the class, his interaction with the students, and the teacher's use of strategies that will be discussed in this chapter.

Understanding Observation Techniques in the Dance Class

During the dance class, the teacher receives a constant stream of visual, auditory, and kinesthetic information through watching, listening, and feeling the movement and behaviors of the students. What the teacher observes during the class becomes part of the pool of knowledge from which she selects her strategies for teaching the class.

The teacher memorizes students' movement responses and behaviors. She sorts out the information for immediate use and records it, mentally and sometimes in writing, for future classes. Much of the observation information is not always communicated when it is seen; rather, it is often reflected on, stored, synthesized, and delivered when the time is right or when it is necessary to make an opportunity for a teachable moment. As classes progress, the teacher collects information for each student in a mental file that contains the student's physical attributes, movement profile, and personality. Constant classroom observation provides the teacher with information for student feedback, teaching strategies, classroom management, and formative and summative evaluation of each student in the class.

In many cases, a teacher's observation skills develop to the point that they become intuitive. To reach this stage of using observation skills, one has to have taught many years and observed dance educators teach a variety of dance forms in different settings. Observation skills develop over time, so you must be patient in learning to observe. The many details that the teacher observes in the dance class can be classified into three categories of observation: general observation, technical observation, and applied kinesiology observation.

General Observation

General observation covers everything that goes on before, during, and after the dance class. The minute the teacher enters the dance class, she begins her constant observing and analyzing. One aspect of general observation is awareness of the general mood of the class and each student's disposition in the class that day. Before and during the class, the teacher observes the class as a group as well as each individual student. This observation gives the teacher information about the students in the class and their response to the material presented. Observing students' reactions gives the teacher information so that she can be flexible within the teaching and learning process of the day's lesson. Her observation of individuals and groups alerts her to implement the appropriate management strategies for individuals and the class. The use of general observation is akin to the teacher's turning on a radar sweep over the

Teacher watches children dance.

class; it provides ongoing information that she processes as the students move through the day's lesson.

Another aspect of general observation information is spatial awareness of the dancers before they begin executing an exercise, combination, or dance. For some dance forms, such as concert dance forms, it is important to notice the feet position or which foot is in front *before* the students begin dancing. In recreational dance forms, it is important to notice the direction the dancer faces or his relation to his partner and the group. General observation continues throughout the class as the teacher concentrates on presenting the exercises and skills.

Dance Technique and Observation Skills

Observing technique comes from watching the execution of the movement to see whether it is correct. This type of observation requires the teacher to read the student's movement. By doing this, the teacher gains extensive information about what techniques or skills are correct, which need attention, and which skills are lacking. For each dance form, the teacher establishes criteria for correct performance for each level of study. Teachers acquire technical and skill information through these means:

- Observing technique or skill by watching the execution of movements to analyze whether they meet the criteria of correct performance, application of principles, and rules of the dance form
- Listening to the music and watching the students' movements to gain information about their rhythmic competency and musicality
- Checking the movement qualities and emotions students express as they dance to give insight into the depth and variety of qualities they can exemplify
- Assessing student performance for synthesis of technique, artistic, and stylistic requirements

Both the teacher and the student use this technical information. For each dance form, the teacher establishes a series for expectations for performance at each level of study. Using observation, the dance teacher is able to provide corrections and plan the class effectively. The dancer becomes aware of his movements by gaining observation skills. Technical observation is paramount

Teacher observes a student leading her peers in middle school.

Teacher leads high school dancers as student teacher observes.

for the dancer to gain technique and increase skill to move from the beginning to the intermediate and then advanced levels of technique. Student teachers and dance education students gain insights by attending public school dance classes.

Many exercises and steps are part of several different dance forms. For example, a demi-plié in ballet is the same demi-plié in modern dance or jazz dance though it may not use the turnout of the feet. It is a movement used throughout all dance forms—creative, concert, and recreational. Anytime a dancer performs a jump, leap, or hop, a demi-plié begins and ends each movement.

The dance form determines the amount of technique required to execute that particular form. The teacher must know the parameters for each dance form: the principles, rules for correct performance of the skills in a dance form, and the applied kinesiology.

Applied Kinesiology Observation

Applied kinesiology is the practical application of kinesiology to dance technique. It encompasses structural anatomy, laws of physics, planes, and levers that affect movement as they apply to dance.

As students execute steps, combinations, and dances, the teacher watches for technically correct execution and applied kinesiological principles (Fitt 1988). If the applied kinesiology is inaccurate, the teacher gives the student instruction on proper form to avoid injury or strain. The teacher and the dancer must know and understand the following summary of applied kinesiology principles (Fitt 1988):

- The action of the muscle is to pull, not to push.
- The contraction occurs in the center of the muscle. The contraction pulls on both sides equally.
- The attachment and the path of the muscle determine the action of the muscle on a joint.
- The muscles oppose gravity to produce a movement or maintain a position.

The following practical applications of kinesiology are significant aspects of dance technique. These include jumping, pointing, turning, spotting, relevé, falling and rising techniques, contraction and release, ankle and foot articulation, and isolation techniques.

Jumping Technique

Jumping technique is the mechanics involved in a dancer's execution of a jump, hop, or leap. Because hops and leaps are part of the general category of jumps, in this section they will be collectively referred to as *jumps.*

Each jump begins and ends in a demi-plié. The knees must demi-plié (half-bend) before the ascent and at the end of the descent from the jump. After the dancer performs the demi-plié, the foot disengages from the floor sequentially: heel, ball of the foot (metatarsals), and toes. The legs usually fully extend during the air moment. As the dancer descends to the floor, the foot lands: toes, ball (metatarsals), and heel followed by the demi-plié.

The heels remain on the floor during the demi-plié for the takeoff and landing. The demi-plié engages the quadriceps and calf muscles, which enable the dancer to push off from the floor. It also provides a shock absorber during the landing of the jump.

During a jump, the torso is aligned, with leg and feet positions that are maintained. The principles of counterpull and counterbalance may come into play depending on the step and the dance form.

Pointing Technique

Pointing the foot involves using the muscles of the foot to stretch it into an arched shape. The foot begins in a full-foot position, or the foot flat on the floor. The working foot either brushes or lifts off the floor. The brush or lift off is referred to as *articulation of the foot.* In the brushing technique, the foot slides to a pointed position releasing from the heel, the metatarsals (ball of the foot), and the toes so that only the tips of the toes remain on the floor or the entire foot points in the air. The foot returns and slides with the opposite action (i.e., toes lead, then the ball and heel follow) to the same or another position of the feet.

In the lift from the floor, used in the relevé and jumping technique, the foot begins to lift sequentially from the heel through the metatarsals for the three-quarter relevé position. In jumping, this action continues through the toes and into the air. On the return from relevé or the pointed position off the floor, the foot presses sequentially into the floor with resistance back to the full-foot position and into demi-plié.

Turning Technique

Turns are important movements that encompass almost all dance forms: concert, recreational, and creative. A turn in place consists of a circular motion performed inward (toward the supporting leg) or outward (away from the supporting leg) on the supporting foot as the body rotates around a central axis, the supporting leg.

To successfully turn, the dancer must possess a strong supporting leg, which is straight or bent. The turn is performed either on full foot or in relevé (rising to three-quarter point) or full point, vertically rising and descending. The complete shift of body weight from two feet onto the supporting leg and the power of the relevé are principal elements in a turn. During the turn, the arms and legs usually pull in toward the center of the body via centripetal force. The dancer generally uses a spotting technique, which focuses the eyes on a spot or an object.

Spotting Technique

Spotting is a technique the dancer uses while executing turns through space, during pirouettes, or in one place. The dancer focuses slightly higher than eye level on a spot in space or an object in the direction he is facing or moving. The dancer's eyes remain focused on the spot while the body begins the turn. Then the head quickly turns around independently of the body. At the end of the turn, the body returns to the starting position first, followed by the head snapping around to focus on the selected spot. The head moves on a plane parallel to the floor. The head and eyes are the last part to return to the designated point in space, the spot. A good spotting technique prevents the dancer from becoming dizzy or losing balance while performing a turn or multiple turns in place or while moving through space.

Relevé Technique

To effectively rise to three-quarter relevé, the dancer must have correct body alignment or a stable and balanced body position in other positions. If the dancer is rising from the full-foot position to three-quarter relevé on two feet or one foot, the ankle and foot positions are critical. The ankle joint fully extends so that the foot attains the three-quarter relevé position. All five toes remain on the floor; if the little toe is short, the first four toes remain on the floor and the fifth toe reaches for the floor. In the three-quarter relevé position, the weight shifts from the foot triangle of the full foot to the ball of the foot (Kassing and Jay 1998). Simultaneously, the body centered over the foot triangle as a unit lifts as the feet shift from full foot to three-quarter relevé. If the dancer rises on one foot to three-quarter relevé, the body's center of gravity slightly shifts the weight toward the ball of the supporting foot. Before the relevé, the dancer executes a demi-plié. During the demi-plié, the dancer vertically centers the body weight over the foot triangle to execute the relevé. For most relevés, this shift of weight initiates the dancer's move vertically up and down with ease.

On relevé, the dancer's legs and torso are lifted to make the rising and balance appear effortless. The return from three-quarter relevé is as important as the rising phase. On the return, the dancer maintains the lift to resist and control the descent and shift of weight back to full foot. This effort maintains the illusion of effortlessness. The feet articulate from the three-quarter relevé position through full foot, which generally is followed by demi-plié.

Falling and Rising Technique

Falling and rising techniques, associated with modern and jazz dance, use momentum to move the body in forward, backward, and sideward paths and with a spiraling motion to the floor and back to a standing or other upright position, such as kneeling. The movement connects and flows in a logical, sequential motion through the torso and its limbs to attain safe, effective, and efficient movement.

During a fall, energy is released so that the movement is continuous. In a basic fall, the body propels itself upward in space before descending to the floor (falling) and then ascending from the floor (rising). Bony parts, such as knees, elbows, head, spine, hipbones, or tailbone, should not take the weight and hence crash into the floor. The more padded parts (such as buttocks and hands) absorb most of the weight during the movement through the fall and recovery. Arm movements complement the action and initiate the hands' acceptance of weight. Proper breathing techniques are vital to correct energy use and proper execution of a fall and recovery. The dancer inhales on the fall and exhales on the rise.

Contraction and Release Technique

Contraction and release techniques are trademarks of modern and jazz dance forms. Different types of contractions occur in the chest and shoulders, at the waist, and in the pelvis. In a contraction, the head usually stays in the same place while the torso alters its shape. Not all contractions are the same; some reflect a particular style, such as Horton or Graham techniques. In contrast, the release from a contraction returns the dancer to a neutral, beginning, or aligned position.

These techniques emphasize the body's three-dimensional quality and also change the shape of the torso. Contractions and releases often heighten the expressiveness of the movement. Breathing is an important aspect of both of these movements. In performing a contraction, the dancer exhales; on the release, the dancer inhales. The contraction and release technique is analogous to the inflating and deflating of a balloon.

Breathing Techniques

Breathing techniques are integral to dance performance. Correct breathing enables the dancer to use her body to regulate and enhance movement. The dancer uses her body and respiratory system synergetically. For example, performing a relevé, she inhales on the rise and exhales on the descent. The elements of moving and breathing work together so that an individual can work efficiently.

Holding the breath is neither effective nor efficient because it can hamper the movement. Breathing or breath phrases coincide with the movement or movement phrases. Breath phrases enhance the dynamics of a dancer's movement, which is apparent to the audience viewing the dance.

Ankle and Foot Articulation

Ankle and foot articulation technique is important in all dance forms. Tap dance uses articulation extensively to produce specific sounds with various parts of the foot: toe, toe tip, flat heel, heel edge, ball of the foot. Foot and ankle articulation are interdependent. If the ankle is loose and pliable, it allows the foot added range for effortless movement. This is particularly important as tempo and number of sounds increase.

Leading and Following

In social, ballroom, folk, and square dance, good leading and following techniques are paramount. In the closed dance position, the leader uses a slight pressure from his hands to direct the path of his partner. The follower follows by paying attention to these signals the leader gives. The couple moves together at the same speed and with the same length of steps. There must be a synergy between the two dancers so that the couple performs as a single dancer responding to the music or the calls.

Isolation Techniques

Isolation techniques are used in jazz and tap dance. Using isolation, one body part initiates the movement while all other parts remain still. Often multiple body parts together or in sequence create a movement effect. The dancer most often incorporates this technique in the movement of the head, shoulders, hips, rib cage, hands, wrists, elbows, toes, heels, and ankles.

The muscles and the joints perform different types of movements that are known as *movement pairs*. The movement pairs in the following box relate to isolation.

Movement Pairs Relating to Isolation

- Elevation refers to lifting the scapula up, and depression refers to pressing the scapula down.
- Flexion lessens the angle between two bones, and extension increases the angle between two bones.
- Abduction moves the body part away from the midline of the body, and adduction moves the part toward the midpoint of the body.
- Plantarflexion is pointing of the foot, and dorsiflexion is flexion of the ankle.
- Eversion is lifting of the outside of the foot, and inversion is lifting of the inside of the foot.
- Supination is facing the palm upward, and pronation is facing the palm downward.
- Hyperextension goes beyond extension.
- Rotation or circumduction rotates or pivots around a central axis.

Isolations are determined and restricted by the structure of the joint. The six types of joints are listed in the following box.

Six Types of Joints in the Body

1. Pivot permits rotaion about the long central axis of the body part (radio-ulnar).
2. Gliding moves in all directions (cervical, thoracic, lumbar, vertebral).

(continued)

(continued)

3. Hinge moves only in one plane of motion (elbow), modified hinge (knee).
4. Condyloid allows movement in two planes (wrist).
5. Saddle moves in two planes of motion. One bone sits in an articular surface of another (thumb).
6. Ball and socket has a range of motion in three planes. This joint has a concave shape in which the ball-shaped head of another bone inserts (hip, shoulder).

Knowing these types of joints and their actions, the dancer and the teacher become aware of the strengths and limitations of each type of joint and how it moves. Relating this information to isolations, the dancer becomes more accurate in her execution of isolations. Isolations in jazz dance accentuate the movement. Often movement isolations reflect the rhythm of the accompanying music or percussion.

From observing students' execution of movement, the teacher creates a checklist for changes or improvements in performance. These changes or improvements may be technical, kinesiological, or artistic qualities to the class work. Following the route from observing to giving student feedback leads to learning and later assessment. It is this circuit that makes the teaching and learning process successful. All of these observation techniques—general, technical, and applied kinesiology—fuse together in the acquisition of observation skills.

Developing Observation Skills

Seeing the movement as it is performed by the students is crucial to being a good dance teacher. Observation skills develop over time, so be patient as you learn to observe. As a student in the class, you can begin to watch the teacher's methods of delivering content and managing the class. As a class member, you cannot concentrate fully on observing, so you should study teachers as an observer in their classes so that you can focus entirely on the teacher in the class. There are preparations and protocols for observing and specific things to watch for while observing a class.

Using Observation Protocols in the Dance Class

As an observer in a dance class, you are a visitor. At least a day or two in advance, contact the teacher and ask for permission to observe a specific class. This courtesy of asking permission to observe is equally important for attending master classes. Talking with the teacher before the class will ensure that the class you plan to observe is the type you want to observe. Some dance classes may be devoted to group work on a project, performance testing, or written examinations, and they may not provide you with the type of experience you want. For first observation experiences, general classes in a concert, creative, fitness, or recreational dance form are most appropriate. Certain protocols apply for visits to the class.

Arrive before the class begins so that you can introduce yourself to the teacher or let her know you will be observing the class. During this conversation, ask the teacher where she would like you to sit to observe the class. Arriving after the class begins is unconscionable. Stay for the entire class; leaving early is not an option. After the class, thank the teacher for allowing you to visit. In academic situations, present the observation form to the teacher for his signature at the end of class. As an observer, you must be as unobtrusive as possible; attend to the class without talking. All of the attention is directed to what is happening in class. To effectively observe, you have to do advance preparation.

Preparing to Observe Effectively

Before arriving at the class, read or review the dance class observation form (see form 3.1). Having in mind what you will be observing during the class gives you the mind-set to gain as much knowledge as possible about the dance class, the students, and the teacher's role in the learning environment.

Practice observation etiquette during the class. Effective observation in the dance class requires you to *see* the dancers' movements, facial expressions, errors and corrections; and the teacher's demonstration of combinations, her mannerisms, and her hands-on corrections of students' posi-

FORM 3.1

Dance Class Observation Form

Observe one dance class in concert, creative, recreational, or aerobic dance form. Have the classroom instructor sign the report form at the end of the class period. Hand in the report on the following class period. LATE REPORTS WILL NOT BE ACCEPTED. The classroom observation report must be typed in narrative form. The report should include, but is not limited to, the following items:

The Dance Class

Date

Day of class

Time of class

Teacher

School or organization

The Dance Form

Level of class and motor learning levels of students in the class

Grade or ages of students

Observable concepts, focus or theme, or objectives of the class

Description of the Class

1. Format of the class:
   A. List the components of the class in the order they are presented. Record the approximate time spent for each component of the class.
   B. Write a summary describing the exercises, combinations, and dances and their progressions during the class.
2. Identify whether the construction of exercises, combinations, problems, and dances are appropriate for the ages of the students and their motor learning levels.

Teaching Methods and Strategies

1. Presentational methods:
2. Teaching styles:
3. Teaching strategies (cueing, imagery, assessment techniques):
4. Accompaniment/music (teacher's techniques, appropriateness for students, variety of selections):
5. Organization and management

   Time management, pacing:

   Teacher's management style, feedback, student behavior management:
6. Teacher's observation techniques (general, technical, applied kinesiology, performance qualities, artistic aspects):
7. Summary of the class

   Overall impressions about the class:

tions. You are also expected to *hear* the teacher's words and cues, the accompaniment and its beat, and the students' movements on the floor (e.g., the brushing of grand battements). You use your *kinesthetic sense* to correlate these perceptions to the items specified on the observation form. At your first observation, you may not be able to take in all of the events and information presented during a dance class. This is why practicing your observation skills by viewing many teachers and dance classes enhances your abilities. If possible, your observation experiences should include a recreational dance class, a dance fitness class, and a creative movement or a concert dance class so that you can understand each form's similarities and differences.

During the first class observation, you may notice some of the variables only once. If possible, look at some of the items several times during the class because they may change for different exercises, combinations, or parts of the class. The items may depend on what the teacher asks the student to observe. The following are specific pedagogical and class variables to observe:

- Structure of the class in relation to the dance form
- General teaching methods
- Feedback
- Combination construction
- Teacher's class management

All of these items are general observations to make about the class. To look at the class using these perspectives, read the brief descriptions of each of the components to examine their application during the class. After observing, reflect on the experience: Analyze the components of the dance class and store what you have learned for future use. This gives you choices when you teach dance.

Writing the Observation Report

Writing about the event engages your critical-thinking skills. But often after a first observation, you feel overwhelmed because there were so many things to see and take into account. Take time to digest what you saw in the class before you start to write the report, but write the report within 24 hours of viewing the class to keep a clear sense of the event. Envision the class from the beginning to end. Put what you saw into words and describe the sequence of events. Before you write the report, take time to reflect on the experience:

- Read the observation form and your notes to identify and analyze situations.
- Translate what you saw using appropriate dance and education vocabulary (so that you become accustomed to using the terminology).
- Report on paper what you observed.
- If possible, discuss and evaluate the situation with others who observed the same class.
- Consider what you would have done in the same circumstances if you were the teacher in the same situation.

After analyzing the class, sit back and reflect on the class in its entirety.

Overall View of the Class

After analyzing individual elements of the class, you must also reflect on the class as an entity. Taking an overall view of the class synthesizes its various parts. From this view, the following questions provide a starting point for other observations that can be made about the class:

- Was the material of interest to the students? Did the students enjoy the class? Did the class fall within the expectations and mission of the organization?
- Was the class planned carefully? Was the teacher prepared for the class? Was she flexible in meeting students' needs and did she have alternative plans and solutions prepared? Was she able to anticipate problems and resolve them before they became big problems?
- Did the teacher allow practice time for students to learn the exercises, steps, combinations, or dances? Did the teacher allow students sufficient time to work through the movement individually and practice it with music?
- Did the teacher allow time for students to respond to an idea, feeling, or quality of the dance movement?

- Did the combinations have energy?
- Was the teacher sufficiently involved with the students' learning and did she give feedback to students?
- Was it an atmosphere that was open yet required students to attend to the instruction?

How did each of these items and others that become apparent to you influence the students, the teacher, and the class? When you capture the essence of the class, write it down as a summary or conclusion of your observation.

In a first observation, look at the teacher and the students in the class. Subsequent observation experiences can include more or all of the items listed on the observation sheet after these variables are discussed in future chapters.

Learning to observe is an important component in developing teaching skills. Using the observation sheet for future observation experiences will be useful in learning dance content, teaching, and using management strategies for the dance class. If an unusual situation occurs while observing a class, write a brief commentary on how the teacher solved the problem, and then write how you would have solved it.

Observation is a continuing learning experience for the dance teacher. This facet of continuing education involves observing a variety of teachers and the skills they use in different technique levels of classes, age groups, and dance forms. Teachers notice the adjustments, cues, explanations, and analogies that other teachers use in their classes. After some time, observing becomes an automatic process from which you continually acquire information that you apply to planning, teaching, and assessing dance.

Summary

Acquiring observation skills is imperative for success as a dance teacher. A teacher's observation skills become activated as he enters the classroom to ascertain the mood of the students, to support his style of teaching, to give feedback, and to manage the class. The dance teacher uses various observation techniques: general, technical, and applied kinesiological. These observation techniques develop over time and must be practiced. When observing dance classes, students practice certain protocols and focus on particular aspects of the dance class and report them on an observation form. Vital to the process of observation is the ability to isolate and observe parts of the class. Observing the class and classroom dynamics helps to hone the observation skills and prepare the student to write the observation report.

References

Fitt, S.H. 1988. *Dance kinesiology*. New York: Schirmer.

Kassing, G., and D.M. Jay. 1998. *Teaching beginning ballet technique.* Champaign, IL: Human Kinetics.

It's Your Turn

1. Visit a dance class, select any three dancers to observe, and use the items on the observation form (form 3.1) to evaluate the students.
2. Visit another dance class (ideally where you do not know the teacher), observe the teacher, and fill out the items on the observation form.
3. Visit another type of dance class, observe, and fill in the observation form.
4. Visit two different age groups taking the same dance form class, observe, and compare their performances.

CHAPTER

4

Guiding Students in Learning Dance

Chapter Objectives

By the end of this chapter, you should be able to do the following:

- Describe the three stages of learning and how they apply to dance.
- Understand the movement–language connection when teaching dance.
- Construct exercises, steps, combinations, and figures across three stages of learning.

Learning movement is different from learning other academic subjects. This chapter will help you gain an understanding of how students learn movement. By using sensory learning styles and the movement–language connection, students progress through the three stages of motor learning as they apply to dance. With this knowledge about student learning, the teacher can construct appropriate exercises, combinations, and other components of the dance class that will meet each student's needs and goals for the class.

Understanding How Students Learn Movement

Understanding how students learn movement and dance is central to teaching. The teacher must know her students, their learning styles, and their abilities so that she can make decisions about the dance content and appropriate assignments for their continued success and progress. Analysis of these components begins with examining styles of student learning in the dance class.

Three Styles of Student Learning

In the dance class the students learn using three senses: visual, auditory, and kinesthetic. Dance is primarily a kinesthetic sensory learning experience reinforced by visual and auditory learning. Each student relies on one sense as a primary medium while the other two senses support the primary sense at various times and to different degrees.

Dancers use the kinesthetic sense predominantly. They learn by doing the movement. Dancers develop kinesthetic memories of movement, dance vocabulary, individual dances, and a repertory of dances. Dancers often keep a kinesthetic repertory of works in their memory. Kinesthetic memory is a powerful tool for the dancer. It is the means for memorizing and remembering movement, patterns or figures, musical cues, breath phrasing, partnering movements, and style of one dance or even a repertory of dances in a variety of styles and forms. A dancer's kinesthetic memory is prodigious; it is a resource often unacknowledged but rich in literacy of our tradition as dancers.

Dancers are very visual learners. They watch the teacher and replicate movements. They can watch a videotape of a piece and imitate the movement, attempting to capture its style, nuances, and symbolism attached to it. Dancers translate visual images into their interpretation of the movement. If students see another dancer's or teacher's movement, for example, they take that image and put it into their own rendition of the movement. Or, they can take something not related to dance and translate that into a movement interpretation. Using either type of translation of a visual image, the teacher is responsible for clarifying the dancer's interpretation of the movement so that it meets the technical and stylistic properties of the choreography. Dancers record dances through the use of their visual and auditory sensory learning.

Some dancers use the auditory sense to remember the music and attach the movement to the music. These learners have a clear, deep understanding and sensitivity to music theory and styles. Often the movement and music become one for the dancer and provide the foundation or impetus for the movement. Auditory learners are excellent listeners. They connect music with movement in such a way as to exhibit and magnify the musicality of a dance work.

Generally in the dance teaching and learning process, the teacher says the name of the step or action while performing the movement, first without music and then with music. Beginning students watch the teacher perform the movements while they listen to a description of the movements and the names of the steps before they attempt to perform them. This teaching and learning process may be too complex to be effective for some learners. One dance scholar, Phyllis Weikart (1998), purports that the teacher should explain the movement, then execute it. Using this method, the teacher presents information in one sensory modality at a time for the learner.

While learning movement, some students have to execute the movement to remember it. Other students watch movement and then replicate it sometimes without executing it with the teacher. Certain learners require a vocal explanation or the music to replicate movement. When teaching movement, the dance teacher focuses on accommodating all three of these sensory learning styles and combinations of them when creating learning experiences, exercises, and combinations. The teacher analyzes the motor learning level in coordination with the learning styles of each person in the class.

Three Stages of Motor Learning

Learning movement and dance depends on the processes used in motor learning. In these processes practice or experiences cause changes that permanently alter a student's learning capacity and performance of skilled dance movements. Often these processes are undetectable because the changes take place in the central nervous system. As these changes grow in number and subtlety, they become permanent and stable as part of the dancer's increased capacity for skilled performance. Motor learning has three distinct stages (Schmidt and Wrisberg 2000) through which the teacher guides students: the verbal-cognitive stage, motor stage, and autonomous stage.

Verbal-Cognitive Stage

In the verbal-cognitive stage of learning dance, the dance instructor demonstrates the exercise, step, or movement, verbalizing the cues and instructions using action words or dance terminology without, and then with, the music to make the movement–language connection for the students. The teacher breaks down the exercise into segments by using cues and instructions to guide the students through the sequence of movements. Then students execute the movements, exercises, or steps by repeating them in the same way or through practice. During the next several classes the teacher must engage students in repetitive practice of the exercise in a consistent manner so that the students learn it.

At the verbal-cognitive stage, the dancer engages his observational skills and learning styles, physically practicing the movement sequence of an exercise. Beginning dancers learn basic exercises, steps, or movements and execute them with limited ability. Students visually identify exercises, steps, or movements and correlate them to action words and later to dance terminology, thereby starting a visual memory of dance vocabulary connected to dance terminology.

During the verbal-cognitive stage the dancer must be motivated to learn these exercises, steps, or movements. One reason may be the dancer's desire to be promoted to a higher level or that he admires more advanced dancers and wants to emulate them.

The use of feedback reinforces the learning process at this stage of motor learning. The teacher corrects specific elements in a student's execution using a pinpointing technique. The dancer needs feedback about the sequence of the movement (knowledge of performance). Feedback must be positive and encouraging (prescriptive). To maximize success in the verbal-cognitive stage of learning movement, the teacher focuses on the following goals:

- ☐ Teaching the simplest elements of the dance form vocabulary and having students perform the exercises and steps at a rudimentary skill level
- ☐ Using different techniques to motivate the students (films, observing advanced classes, and attending dance concerts)
- ☐ Giving instruction and demonstration that are simple, clear, and concise
- ☐ Having dancers observe the step and then execute it while the teacher explains the movements, then break the step or combination into parts
- ☐ Using frequent feedback that focuses on identifying problem areas (pinpointing) and correcting errors (knowledge performance)

Children exploring different shapes.

Dancers regress to the verbal cognitive stage when learning new vocabulary and dance forms. Previous experiences in the dance form or in other dance forms make this experience shorter and easier to assimilate into their visual memory. Adequate preparation at the verbal-cognitive level is necessary for making a smooth transition to the motor stage of learning.

Motor Stage

The second phase of learning movement is the motor stage. At this stage, the teacher uses fewer cues and focuses more on specific problems and ways of executing the movement and its variations, transitions, qualities, phrasing, musicality, and artistry. Constant guidance at this level of learning is detrimental to long-term retention. The teacher uses cues to remind students about important aspects of performing a combination of steps. Students learn how to perform self-checks to become more responsible for their progress through analyzing their work. The teacher presents feedback to each student by targeting prominent problems and prescribing a way for the student to execute the exercise correctly (also known as error detection). The teacher shows the dancer relationships between similar steps, such as a relevé on both feet (rising onto the toes and ball of the foot) and a sauté (jump into the air with the legs fully extended and feet pointed) in ballet. The sashay in contra dance (a dance performed in two parallel lines with the dancers facing each other) is similar to the slide and the chassé (which means to chase) in jazz or modern dance.

During the motor stage, the dancer learns to perform the exercise or step in its various ways. Exercises and steps are varied in terms of time (fast, moderate, or slow) and space (direction, level, dimension, pathway). For example, in a modern dance class, the dancer performs a leap with straight legs or with such variations as the front développé (the front leg unfolds on the rise to the top of the leap), or in attitude (front or back leg bent) or both legs in attitude. Constant practice enables the student to perfect the step variations. The student becomes more proficient in executing the steps or exercises and gains the ability to remember and perform them correctly every time.

Random practice is another factor important to this stage. This promotes long-term retention. Often the teacher uses this technique in intermediate and advanced classes. She gives different combinations in each class to test the students' knowledge of vocabulary and ability to execute the exercises and steps correctly.

Imagery becomes more important at this stage of learning. It enhances the dancer's understanding of the quality and phrasing of the steps in a combination or ability to generalize information about two steps when performing them together.

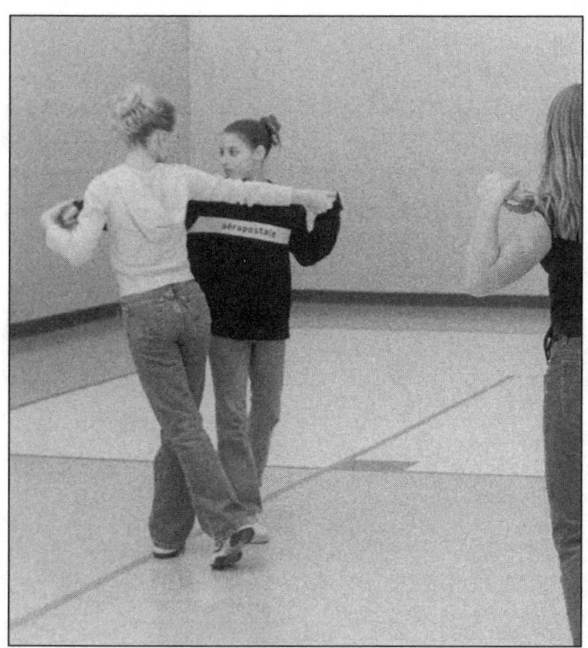

Middle school dancers practicing a dance step.

The teacher encourages the student to use mental practice that enhances learning at this stage. Often by going through the combination mentally, the student is able to work out the trouble spots in the step or combination before actually performing it.

At this level, students become more responsible for learning and perfecting their performance. To maximize success in the motor stage of learning, the teacher focuses on the goals listed in the following box.

Goals for Maximizing Success in the Motor Stage

- Reviewing exercises and steps once they are learned
- Varying these exercise and steps according to time and space
- Using prescriptive feedback
- Refraining from giving too much feedback and guidance
- Using random practice (new combinations using the step)
- Encouraging students to mentally practice the execution of steps and combinations
- Selecting imagery to heighten performance and artistry

At the motor stage, the student becomes more responsible for analyzing his performance for correctness while adding other variables such as quality, musicality, and artistry in preparation for the autonomous stage.

Autonomous Stage

The last stage of motor learning is the autonomous stage. This stage occurs when the teacher presents the combination with vocal cues or with limited teacher demonstration. In practice, the teacher breaks down combinations into sections, sometimes isolating transitions for further study. At this stage of learning, the dancer's kinesthetic sense and motor memory enable him to perform the exercises and steps accurately and automatically as phrases, figures, or combinations without thinking about each movement. This automatic process is faster than the controlled processes of the earlier motor stages. Working toward this stage, students practice performing dances.

The development of mental and psychological skills is part of this stage. The teacher encourages and promotes specific techniques, such as positive attitude, confidence, and self-talk, to ensure the dancer's success. Psychological techniques include trust in the unconscious mind to perform the combination. Likewise, imagery and mental practice enable the dancer to rehearse the dance in her mind, to review and solve trouble spots, to focus, and control nerves and emotions before performance.

At this level, the student is responsible for learning and perfecting his performance. The teacher remains an outside eye that guides him to refinement of his work. To maximize success in the student's autonomous stage of learning, the teacher focuses on the following goals:

- ❑ Practicing combinations automatically to reduce the influence of outside stimuli or attention demands
- ❑ Using whole–part–whole practice (The teacher performs the entire dance. Then she teaches each step of the dance separately. She and the students put the steps in the sequential order they occur in the dance. Finally, the dancers execute the entire dance.)
- ❑ Applying imagery, mental practice, and other psychological techniques

High school students practicing for a student dance performance.

- ❑ Promoting personal excellence, positive attitude, confidence, and self-talk

Students experience one or more of these stages as they learn new exercises and steps, refine those they have already learned, and perfect those steps they have executed for a long time. Understanding the stages of motor learning is paramount to teaching and assessment (see table 4.1).

Table 4.1 presents the overview of the three stages of motor learning as applied to dance: verbal-cognitive, motor, and autonomous. Each stage of learning has three phases:

1. Progression is the moving phase that identifies the appropriate amount and complexity of the movement for that stage of learning.
2. Motor memory is the remembering and executing of the movement phase that progresses through learning, perfecting, and automatically performing movement with artistry.
3. Assessment criteria use the appropriate movement for that particular stage of learning to assess learning phases of the student.

Although dance is a nonverbal art, the *teaching* of dance is a verbal process. The teacher is the communicator in the classroom. He guides students through the infinite paths of learning dance. The movement–language connection in dance is important for effective teaching of beginning students.

Movement–Language Connection in Dance

Movement–language connections result from the action words that the teacher uses as the movement is performed. Choosing the appropriate words and dance terminology and using them consistently reinforce the learning of movement through cues.

Dance terminology for exercises, steps, poses, positions, figures, and principles is usually in the language in which the dance form was originally taught. However, there are exceptions. Ballet terminology uses the French language. Folk dances

Table 4.1 Learning Stages Applied to Dance

Early: verbal-cognitive	Middle: motor	Late: autonomous
Progression		
Move one body part, add other body parts, and increase number of body parts moving 1. feet 3. head 2. arm 4. all	Combine 3 to 4 different steps together	Do the step without thinking about it
Motor memory		
• Associated with learning the dance vocabulary and movement • Practice and review from the beginning, using the add-on (linked) method	• Know the step and execute it • Think ahead to connect movement and transitions, and add some quality to the step	Focus on quality, style, projection, and artistry
Assessment criteria		
Repeat with the same number of steps as done in the example	• Focus on execution and developing quality • Perform with arms, feet, and head together • Emphasis on execution and rhythm quality	• Focus on total movement • Know the movements • Execute the movement correctly • Rhythm • Carriage of the body • Qualities of movements
Example		
• 4 skips to the left; 4 skips to the right • 2 skips to the left; 2 skips to the right • 1 skip to the left; 1 skip to the right • 1 skip to the left; 1 skip to the right	• 4 skips to the left; 4 skips to the right • 2 jumps to the left; 2 jumps to the right • 1 step–hop to the left; 1 step–hop to the right	2 skips; 2 jumps; 1 step–hop right; 1 step–hop left; 2 jumps
Performance criterion checklist		
• Performs same movements • Uses different directions	• Performs four different movements • Executes movement with correct rhythm	• Knows steps, arms, and head • Quality of skip, using a light and airy manner • Arms extended and in opposition • Legs are straight in the air; toes are pointed on skips, jumps, and hops • Executes movement correctly and qualities of movements

may contain lyrics that are part of the performance of the dance. For example, in the *Doudlebska Polka,* the dancers sing "tra-la-la-la." Square dance and contra dance use patter songs, calls, and phrases to command the dancers to execute certain movements and figures.

The teacher is responsible for knowing the movement vocabulary. In the dance classroom, the teacher must be prepared to perform the movement, say the term for the movement, and write the terminology on the board or present a written or typed handout of the terminology for the students. This movement–language connection reinforces the learning of dance skills and the different ways for students to learn: kinesthetic, visual, auditory, and linguistic.

The movement–language connection has an additional feature. After a teacher explains concepts and principles of a movement, she can synthesize it into a catchphrase. She uses this catchphrase to check or apply the concept or principles of that movement. For example, in square dancing, the teacher says, "Square the set" as a phrase for everyone to get in the beginning formation to start the dance. In a concert dance form, the teacher says, "Check your beginning position" to tell the student to self-check for alignment, weight distribution, and correct foot and arm positions. In creative dance, the teacher says, "Do you have a movement sentence?" She is asking whether the movement sequence has a beginning, a middle, and an end. In social dance, the teacher says, "Who is leading whom?" She is asking whether the man (or leader) is leading and whether he is giving proper cues to the lady (or follower). In aerobic dance, the teacher says, "Keep moving." She is reminding students to continue moving while she demonstrates the new step.

Acquiring competency in the movement of a dance form and its terminology is the first step in being able to talk about it, read it, and understand its fundamentals. The movement–language connection is an essential tool for the dance teacher and the dance student.

One of the biggest changes that occurs when the student becomes the teacher is becoming not only a movement guide but also a verbal guide in demystifying the art of dance. Movement is the primary language the dancer learns so that he can communicate and express himself eloquently. Describing the movement and explaining what to do, how to do it, and when to do it are at the heart of teaching. Understanding the student's acquisition of dance through sensory movement, the stages of motor learning, and the movement–language connection becomes the basis for constructing a dance class. These components influence the type of construction the teacher uses for exercises, combinations, and figures.

Constructing the Dance Class

Among all of the duties the dance educator has, constructing the dance class is the driving force for acquiring the vocabulary and skills necessary for training the competent dancer. The dance teacher appraises his students' stages of learning in relation to the components and the class. This information helps him determine the methods of construction for the exercises, steps, combinations, figures, and dances so that they are appropriate for the students in the class.

Effective teaching is built on constructing exercises and combinations that progressively develop the dancer's techniques and skills that lead the beginning dancer to become the intermediate and then the advanced dancer. To achieve these goals, the teacher constructs appropriate exercises, combinations, and figures that combine age and developmental factors, levels of motor learning, and vocabulary of the dance form for a specific level. But a teacher must also be realistic. A student's skills, coordination, and maturity may not correspond to his chronological age.

To construct exercises and combinations, a teacher must analyze several aspects of students' movement. Usually the teacher does this the first day that students dance in class. She develops a set of exercises that meet the expectations for that level of performance. She carefully observes the students to ascertain what they do and do not know about the material. This first class becomes the basis for determining the next exercise, step, transition, or concept to be taught. Creating a progression in the dance form content requires that the teacher understand the capabilities of her students. A journal of students' successes and challenges with the class content is a gauge for determining how fast or slow to go in presenting material in the class.

An advanced dancer finds it easy to develop and teach advanced classes because the dancers know the dance form and are able to use its vocabulary fluently as a language. Advanced exercises and combinations are inappropriate for beginning and intermediate students. These skills are beyond their dance experience and too difficult for them to accomplish correctly. For example, a student teacher instructing a beginning jazz class expected the students to perform double pirouettes, which was incongruous with the students' knowledge and abilities. Rather, the student teacher should have focused on the elements of the pirouette: the demi-plié, relevé, balance, and close. The dancers can build on strong foundational skills to make the pirouette a natural outcome rather than a frustrating step that requires the coordination of too many factors performed incorrectly.

If the student does not learn the step correctly, he will perpetually execute it incorrectly. This situation then requires that the student undergo remedial learning. It is harder to relearn the step correctly because the student has to retrain his muscle memory. During the retraining, the student who automatically performed the step must now consciously monitor each part of the step and make the appropriate changes in its execution. It is difficult for the student to break the flow of movement to solve each problematic element. Remedial learning can take up the teacher's time in the intermediate and even advanced classes.

Teaching correct execution of exercises and steps is important to the efficient development of dancers. Moreover, the dance educator sifts through many interpretations and variations of steps to select a stylistic preference appropriate for her students. Constructing interesting, meaningful, appropriate, and relevant exercises and combinations for beginning and intermediate students is a challenge. The following methods guide the student dancer from simple to complex combinations in a dance form.

Combinations

A combination is a series of three or four different steps that join together into a movement phrase. The student should have some traditional phrases of movement in his repertoire. In ballet, temps levé, tombé, pas de bourrée, glissade is a movement phrase that works as a transition in a petit allegro or grand allegro combination. In recreational, creative movement and dance, and aerobic dance forms, combinations are often linked together to form longer movement sequences that ultimately constitute the dance.

The basis for good construction of exercises and combinations is presenting them in a logical progression with small increments of challenge. This allows students to execute each step correctly and precisely before joining it to others. If this process is rushed, the movement becomes blurred, sloppy, and, in some cases, unrecognizable as the dance form vocabulary.

One-, Two-, and Three-Step Exercises and Combinations

This method works well with a limited dance vocabulary. By using this method, the beginning student practices the movement or the step repeatedly to master it and then join it with another step and then another. For the beginning student, the combination of three steps into a series is appropriate.

Figure Construction

In recreational forms such as square, contra, and social dance, the teacher constructs his series of figures and progressions based on the learner's abilities. Depending on the learning level of the student, the figures can range from 8 to 32 counts of movement. The teacher strives to be creative so that students are successful.

Add-On (Linked) Combinations

This method of construction uses the addition of steps and combinations to build a longer combination or dance. For example, in both concert and recreational dance forms such as jazz dance and folk dance, the student learns the first step and practices it. Then she learns the second step and masters it. The student combines the first and second step and practices them together until they are mastered. This progression continues until she learns the entire dance.

Diversity in Combinations

Diversifying combinations adds interest to the choreography and demands students' awareness and thought. Changing direction, partners, formations, and relationships and adding levels are some of the variables you may choose. Diversification of the material allows you to provide simple to complex levels of performance for the range of abilities in the class. These types of combinations give a student options of performance levels to choose from and motivates the dancer to expand his movement skills.

Another way to expand combinations is through the block method. This method permits the teacher to devise dances that use combinations in a repetitive yet interesting way to provide variety and balance. The block method is most effectively used in large dance production works, musicals, or ballets. The choreographer constructs several combinations, repeats them by adding elements to diversify them, and arranges the combinations into a dance. The arrangement uses choreographic tools such as variations in the number of dancers performing the combination, the contrast of one combination with another, and the use of two groups to mirror the combination.

Creating Options in Combinations

Within each dance class, students' abilities range from below average to above average within a level. Sometimes, students' abilities cross levels in certain skills and especially in different dance forms. You may be an intermediate ballet dancer but an advanced jazz dancer. You may be an advanced folk dancer but a beginning tap dancer. In each dance class, the teacher must create for each student a movement ability profile defining his strengths and challenges.

To meet all of the students' needs in a dance class, develop options for increased or decreased ability within the exercises and combinations. To create optional combinations, begin by constructing a combination geared toward the students who are in the middle range of the class. Or you can create a basic combination that meets the goal you have identified for the class; then decide how you can increase or decrease the difficulty one level above or below. Try these two methods to find your way of working and to find the most effective method for the students in your class. The goal is for all students to feel successful and challenged to extend themselves in gaining skills appropriate to their level. The following list notes ways you can accomplish increasing and decreasing difficulty in a combination:

Do the following to increase difficulty in a combination:

Increase the tempo of the music.

Include directional changes of steps.

Add relevé (rise), fondu (demi-plié on one leg).

Beat certain steps.

Increase number of pirouettes or turns.

Turn while executing the step.

Jump into the air or through the air.

Add two or more of the previous elements.

Do the following to decrease difficulty in a combination:

Execute the combination using two measures for the step instead of one.

Practice the first step and use the add-on method to learn the entire combination.

Do the step on full foot instead of on relevé.

Execute the step facing one direction.

Break the step into parts.

Practice only one section of the step.

Mark it without a jump.

Although the options are often determined through the construction of the combination, the teacher decides how she allows the options to be used. She may set options for certain students. Or she may tell the students the options available when she presents the combination, and they may choose the ones to add to the combination. If you set the options for students, you are challenging them. If the student sets his options, he is challenging himself. At times, you must temper a student's choices so that he gains clarity of execution in the step. "Danny, this time, can you execute one clean jazz pirouette that finishes in position?" Or "Kendra and Julio, change the skip to a walk back to your place in the square so that you can get there on time."

An aerobic dance combination presents several opportunities for increasing difficulty in the movement. In a combination, the dancers can perform:

1. Grapevine step (step side, step behind, step side, touch) twice (to right side and then to left side)
2. Step, touch alternating sides four times (right, left, right, left)
3. Step, kick alternating sides four times (right, left, right, left)
4. Repeat step, touch alternating sides four times (right, left, right, left)

First, students perform the combination. To increase the difficulty, the dancers perform the combination on the balls of their feet (relevé). To further increase the difficulty, ask them to execute the movements adding hops and leaps. For example, the grapevine becomes a leap side (instead of step), leap behind, leap side, hop, touch.

Extending the size of the leap in the grapevine will help you get off the ground easier.

Teaching Progressions

Teaching progressions requires a teacher to analyze the difficulty of combinations and steps to determine when the students are ready to learn them. The teacher may break the exercise or step down into its smallest movement parts and then put the parts back together into the step or combination. During this process, the teacher focuses on specific body parts separately, then gradually adds them into the performance of the step or combination. First, focus on teaching the leg gestures. Then teach the arm gestures or combine the legs and the arms while executing the movement. Finally, add the head movement or other body parts to the step or combination to make the movement complete. For more information, see *Teaching Beginning Ballet Technique* (Kassing and Jay 1998).

Summary

To teach dance, one must understand how students learn. Students learn through the senses: visual, auditory, and kinesthetic. Learning styles support the teaching of dance, but more important are the three stages of motor learning: verbal-cognitive, motor, and autonomous. The teacher uses the movement–language connection to unite the cognitive and physical aspects of teaching dance. As a dance teacher you must keep in mind sensory learning, motor learning, and the movement–language connection when constructing your class. While constructing appropriate yet challenging dance classes for students, the teacher considers every exercise and combination in relation to the students' technique and development as dancers. Appropriate teaching progressions of exercises and combinations enrich the student's learning experience.

References

Kassing, G., and D. Jay. 1998. *Teaching beginning ballet technique*. Champaign, IL: Human Kinetics.

Schmidt, R.A., and C.A. Wrisberg. 2000. *Motor learning: A problem-based approach,* 2nd ed. Champaign, IL: Human Kinetics.

Weikart, P.S. 1998. *Teaching movement and dance: A sequential approach to rhythmic movement,* 3rd ed. Ypsilanti, MI: The Highscope.

It's Your Turn

1. Observe a dance class and identify at least one student in each stage of learning dance. Describe the characteristics of each learner. Categorize the learner's performance according to the three stages of learning and support your answer with examples.
2. Create an 8-count combination. Teach it to a small group by describing each movement using appropriate dance vocabulary. Connect the movement with each count.
3. Teach a combination, short dance, or figures using the add-on method.

CHAPTER

5

Understanding Dance Teaching Methods

Chapter Objectives

By the end of this chapter, you should be able to do the following:

- Identify and describe presentational methods.
- Identify and describe teaching strategies as they apply to dance.
- Understand how to use accompaniment effectively in dance class.

Being a dance teacher requires a multidimensional focus. This chapter will help you understand the tools and strategies the teacher uses in presenting dance content in the lesson. The teacher chooses presentational methods for the dance content and selects the music, teaching styles, and strategies to teach the movement. All of these tasks are accomplished in a warm, firm, efficient, and professional manner.

Teaching methods and strategies are the procedures that present the content of the dance form. Teaching methods in dance have been handed down from teacher to student through a verbal tradition. But, as dance education professionals, we can no longer rely on the standard of "what worked for my teacher will work for me." Rather, we must embrace teaching methods and strategies that are most appropriate for teaching movement and dance. Presentational methods, observation skills, and feedback play an important part in the kinesthetic, visual, auditory, interpersonal, and intrapersonal aspects of the dance class. The strategies the teacher employs are equally important to the teaching and learning process of a dance form.

Choosing a Presentational Method

Presentational methods are distinctive ways of presenting dance content. The three methods are whole–part, part–whole–part, and add-on (or linked). These presentational methods produce the desired results based on the dance content, the level of the students, and the different stages of learning.

Whole–Part Method

In this method the teacher performs the entire combination or exercise and then breaks it down into parts. In tap dance a basic combination is shuffle, hop, step. The teacher performs the step. Then he breaks the combination down into its three parts: 1) shuffle, 2) hop, 3) step. He observes as students practice each part before connecting the parts to form the whole combination. This presentational method is effective for teaching new vocabulary.

Part–Whole–Part Method

The teacher demonstrates and explains the parts of the exercise or combination and then puts the entire movement sequence together. The teacher may practice sections or select the parts that require specific or more intense instruction. He breaks down the troublesome part for the students to practice or demonstrates a complicated movement. Then he repeats the entire combination. This presentational method is effective for combining steps into combinations of vocabulary that students have already learned. For example, in a square dance class, the teacher introduces each part of the dance and then students practice it. The teacher executes the various figures and calls, then students perform them. When students learn all the parts, they perform the entire square dance. Then the teacher refines certain transitions or particular steps by asking the students to practice them.

Add-On (Linked) Method

In the add-on method, the teacher presents the first part of the exercise or combination. The students practice it. Then the teacher demonstrates the second part, and the students perform the first and second parts. The teacher shows the third part, and the students perform the first, second, and third part, and so on. For example, in folk dance, the teacher would present the following steps:

Step 1: Step, together; step, touch two times (right and left)

Teacher and a student perform a step, standing in an optimal place so that the class can observe them.

Step 2: Step, touch four times (right, left, right, left)

Step 3: Step, hop four times (right, left, right, left)

Step 4: Repeat step, together; step, touch two times (right and left)

Step 5: Combine steps 1, 2, 3, 4 together.

The add-on method of presentation is appropriate for teaching combinations and dances. After the students have learned the first combination, the teacher adds another combination, and so on to create either an extended combination or an entire dance. This type of presentation has many uses at any instructional level in concert, recreational, and aerobic dance classes. Underlying the presentational methods are teaching strategies.

Teaching Strategies in the Dance Classroom

Teaching strategies used in the dance class may be predetermined by the dance form, traditions, and personality of the teacher. In dance, teaching strategies have traditionally been teacher-centered. One strong underlying reason is the oral tradition of passing dance content knowledge from teacher to students. Teaching strategies from other academic disciplines have enhanced dance teaching and support student-centered learning. These strategies include teaching styles, cueing, imagery, and specific methods for the dance forms.

Teaching Styles

Teaching styles are the various methods the teacher uses to instruct students. Styles range from teacher-centered to student-centered learning situations. The teaching styles come from the work of Mosston and Ashworth (1986). To understand these teaching styles, picture a continuum. Teacher-centered teaching styles are on the left and student-centered styles are on the right of the continuum. From left to right the teaching styles are command, practice, reciprocal, self-check, inclusive, guided discovery, and divergent. In teacher-centered teaching styles the teacher is the central focus and source of learning. In student-centered teaching styles, the student initiates and takes responsibility for his learning while the

Teacher watches as students perform an aerobic dance.

Students mirror the teacher's movement.

teacher acts as a mentor in the learning process. All of the teaching styles are applicable to dance teaching.

Command Style

The command style is traditionally used in dance instruction. The teacher plans the class, demonstrates the exercises, and corrects the dancers' execution. The teacher makes all of the decisions about subject matter, etiquette, discipline, and motivation. For example, in tap dance, the teacher says, "Execute 8 Time Steps."

Practice Style

The practice style is slightly less teacher-centered than the command style. This style provides the

Practice teaching style in social dance.

dancer with the time to practice an exercise during the class. In this teaching style, the teacher plans exercises and allots time for students to practice the exercises during the class period. The practice may be either new, recently learned, or a review of exercises. Students practice without music at first, and then they practice the movement with the music. This teaching style is used in conjunction with the command style. For example, the teacher says, "Practice the 4-count transition of moving from the parallel passé to the layout in second position. In a few minutes, we will practice it with the music."

Reciprocal Style

The teacher implements reciprocal teaching into the dance class. This style involves an observer and a performer. First the teacher creates the criteria for executing exercises. These criteria can be presented in the form of a checklist. The students are grouped into pairs. The observer watches the performer execute the combination. Then the observer writes a check or minus for each criterion. The observer discusses his criteria-based observations in a constructive manner with the performer. Then, the observer and performer reverse roles.

An alternative method for creating the criteria checklist involves a collaborative effort between

Reciprocal teaching style used in high school.

the teacher and the students. In this method, the teacher and dancers create the checklist based on their discussion. As you can see, the reciprocal teaching style requires student involvement and is more student-centered than the command and practice styles. This teaching style also works when one couple observes another couple. Reciprocal teaching is also referred to as peer teaching. For example, Jami says, "Nicole, your leap was great! If you can push off and stretch your back leg even more, it will help you stay in the air even longer. Want to try it?"

Self-Check Style

The self-check teaching style moves even further toward student-centered teaching. In this style the teacher develops a checklist of criteria for execution of an exercise. Or, the dancer can self-check using the teacher's cues for executing the movement. During a self-check, the dancer observes while he executes combinations. Then the student self-evaluates his performance using the established criteria checklist or the teacher's cues. The method is more effective when a student has at least an intermediate level of proficiency in executing the movement. Here is an example of a student's use of the self-check method: Carlos thinks to himself after observing his performance of an assemblé, *My supporting leg needs to be perpendicular to the floor during the jump. I need to think about that before and during the takeoff for the step.*

Inclusive Style

The inclusive teaching style allows the student to choose the degree of challenge to her abilities. The teacher provides different levels of expectations for execution of a combination. These levels of expectations include difficulty, speed, number of turns, or addition of beaten steps. In this style the teacher arranges the dancers into groups. These groups perform the combination at various levels of difficulty. For example, in ballet, a more difficult variation involves performing a combination on relevé instead of on full foot or with beats on jumps. This style gives the dancers options to adjust their levels of performance to a lesser degree or to challenge their abilities by pressing the boundaries. The teacher presents these options to the class as a whole or a specific student, thereby individualizing learning. For example, the teacher says, "The group on the left will perform the combination using two measures for each step and concentrate on performing each step and ending in position. Then the group on the right will perform the combination at standard tempo. You can perform a double pirouette and alter the changement to a royale if you wish."

Guided Discovery Style

Guided discovery is a student-centered teaching style. The teacher poses questions or provides statements that elicit a specific response from the student. The teacher may create a problem that has only one answer that results in the development of convergent thinking. In convergent thinking, the student is guided by the teacher's questioning to finding one answer to a question.

Creative movement readily uses guided discovery. Although not used as frequently in ballet, modern, jazz, tap, folk, square, and social dance, this teaching style is suitable for these dance forms. For example, the dance instructor in the ballet class asks, "Is your leg straight in arabesque? Are your shoulders and hips square? Do you have a beginning, middle, and end in your dance?" These types of questions require the student to analyze his movement and then to add this information to his personal checklist.

Divergent Style

The divergent teaching style promotes problem solving. The teacher poses a problem to a group of dancers. She sets the boundaries for the elements that may be used in solving the problem. Within these set boundaries there may be a number of ways to solve this problem. So as long as the group adheres to the parameters of the problem, the group will achieve success. In this structure, the group may find many solutions. This teaching style is basic to teaching creative movement, improvisation, and choreography. Divergent teaching as student-centered learning also provides experiences that are applicable beyond the dance studio. Students' creative and higher-level thinking skills are enhanced in divergent teaching environments. For example, in the creative movement class the teacher says, "How would you move if you were the wind . . . blowing dandelion puffs on a hot summer afternoon? . . .

blowing leaves from a tree in autumn? . . . during a violent thunderstorm? . . . during a hurricane? Look at how Jessica is floating across the space. . . . Look at Chin whipping and spiraling to the floor. . . . Look at Mutakeem's slashing and sharp movements as he jumps and darts through the space. . . . Look at Maria as she whirls faster and faster and stops, and then she starts again." Teaching strategies, such as cueing and imagery, support teaching styles.

Cueing

Cueing tells the dancers the what, when, and where of a movement. The teacher uses cues to remind students about how they do the movement and what they will do next. Cues also prompt students' movement through a difficult part. The various cues include action words, directional words, counting, singing, voice augmentation, clapping, nonsense syllables, parts of phrases (or word omissions), and signals.

• Action words describe the physical action of the movement, such as "step, kick." Anatomical words are often used as action words. For example, in "kick, ball–change," the word *ball* refers to the ball or metatarsals of the foot.

• Directional cues indicate whether the dancer moves right or left, up or down, front or back, forward, or backward. Directional cues for the waltz clog are right (step), left (shuffle), left (ball), right (change).

• Counting cues indicate the meter and rhythm when a movement is executed to the music. Counts are assigned to each part of the movement. The teacher counts the music while she or the students perform the exercise. For example, the teacher says for the waltz clog, "1 & 2 & 3":

1	&	2	&	3
step	shuf-	fle	ball–	change

• Singing cues are the action words either said or sung in time with the music. These cues emphasize the relationship between the movement and the music. For example, the waltz clog step is in a 3/4 meter; the step has a lilting quality with the singing cues: "step, shuffle, ball–change."

• Voice augmentation uses high and low pitches that give emphasis to a movement phrase or part of the step. You may use a high-pitch or a low-pitch voice, depending on the effect you want to achieve.

high pitch	medium	low
step	shuffle	ball–change

Your voice rises on the first beat to emphasize the beginning of a measure. This helps the student to remember each movement's place within the sequence. Also, it can make them smile!

• Clapping cues establish the rhythm of the movement. A clapping cue is helpful for introducing a new step or clarifying a learned step. The teacher claps the rhythm of the step.

clap	clap	clap	clap	clap
step	shuf-	fle	ball–change	
1	&	2	&	3

• Nonsense syllable cues vocally mirror the rhythm or quality of the step using nonwords. The waltz clog could sound like "Yah, da–da, ra–ra."

1	& 2	& 3
(step)	(shuf-)(fle)	(ball–change)
yah	da–da	ra–ra

• Part of a phrase (or word omission) refers to skipping some of the action word cues to emphasize the important cue word for the movement. You usually use this type of cueing after the dancer has a sufficient mastery of the step.

For example, on count one, teacher says, "Step." On count two, the teacher says nothing. On count three, the teacher says, "Ball–change."

• Signal cues convey meaning through gestures for such actions as stop, quiet, and change of direction or position. Predetermined signals keep movement continuing smoothly and groups moving easily during the dance class. An example of a signal cue is pointing to the right or to the left.

Often the teacher combines one or more of these cueing methods. He may say the name of the step followed by the count. In jazz dance, this would be "Step, 7; pivot, 8," or vice versa, "7, step; 8, pivot."

When you are introducing a new step, you will need to use many cues. Action words clarify the movement or sequence. The teacher and dancers can say the action words and do it at the same time. Counting all the time does not communicate the movement and its quality; it is meaningless if the dancers do not know the movement. Dancers need to remember the movement and then its relation to the counts. The better the dancer knows the movement, the less you will need to cue.

Imagery

Imagery adds greatly to the teaching and learning process; it enriches the experience and stimulates the dancer's imagination and feelings. It connects the unfamiliar with the familiar. Imagery enhances the process that inspires the dancer's feeling of the movement and expands his imagination in conveying a feeling, emotion, or idea through movement.

Choose your images with care so that they are appropriate for your students' age. For young students realistic imagery is necessary, whereas for older students more abstract images are suitable. Many types of imagery are applied to dance: visual, kinesthetic, anatomical, and pictorial.

- Visual images describe an action of a familiar object that is similar to the movement. "When performing a backward fall, imagine your body moving as a pendulum: Move upward on the hop, swing down and backward, rise upward and forward."
- Kinesthetic images give the dancer a physical representation of what is happening in the body. "When performing a front layout in jazz dance, can you feel your torso and arms extending in the hinge position, stretching forward in opposition and unfolding your leg to the side?"
- Anatomical images focus on the structure of the body and the muscle movement. "In a grand battement derrière the hips strive to be square, but after the leg reaches 15 degrees the pelvis tilts downward and forward."
- Pictorial images are mental pictures that become a memory that connects to the physical performance of movements. In creative movement, for example, the children can glide like a bird over a meadow, then soar over a mountain and swoop low through a valley.

Different types of imagery help dancers to see with the mind's eye. Ultimately the image translates into the appropriate body movement. The teacher uses a variety of images to communicate the essence of the movement. Some images may be more successful than others and relate better to one person than to another. Images aid in muscle memory of movements, concepts, and principles throughout the teaching and learning process.

Teaching strategies are the means by which you communicate the dance content to the students. Specific dance forms use additional teaching methods.

Teaching Methods for Specific Dance Forms

Each dance form uses general teaching methods, and some methods are specific to one dance form. Specific methods for a dance form pertain to meeting the requirements of executing the dance form, the format of the class, the skill level of the class, and the traditions associated with teaching the dance form.

As the teacher, you must be willing and flexible to try a variety of methods to accomplish the goals that you set for the dance class. Remember that what is successful in one class may not be successful in another class. Keep a record of teaching tips that work for you. Some methods focus on teaching strategies for groups and individuals and others are related to specific dance forms.

Recreational Dance Forms

In recreational dance forms, it is more difficult for students to distinguish correct foot and arm movements when the class is taught in a circle. Ask students to face the front of the classroom so that they can follow your movements without thinking about transposing the left or right side. They can be in staggered lines so that everyone can see you and your movements. As the teacher, you will face the students and mirror their movements. If the movement is difficult, face the mirror so that students can follow the movement as you teach it. This method of facing the front of the classroom is applicable in recreational, concert, and fitness dance forms.

In folk and social dance classes, students may learn the movement as a group in lines but practice the movement in couples. Teach square and contra dance figures in the couple positions because these dance forms are based on figures. In square and contra dance, you will teach by walking the students slowly through the calls and figures. As the teacher or caller in square dance, you constantly give vocal instructions during the class. In social dance class you present the steps of the dance and may ask the students to arrange them in their own sequence.

Tap Dance

Tap dance requires that students listen to the rhythm of the steps while you demonstrate them. The students stand quietly to hear this. Break down the parts of the combination for the students. The students practice these parts individually and in combination without and then with the music. In a tap class, you may not always cue the movement.

Ballet

You will need a barre for the first part of the class. Barres may be installed along the wall or walls of the studio. Portable barres may be placed in the center of the studio. You will say and demonstrate the exercises while facing all of the students. For the center portion of the class, the portable barres are moved to the side or back of the studio so that students can move in the center or across the floor. For center work, you will face the students, and they will mirror your movement. As in other dance forms, if the movement is complicated, you will turn and face the mirror to demonstrate the movement and have the students follow using the same leg and arm movements. This facing allows you to view students' progress in the mirror while you teach the combination.

Creative Movement or Dance

Creative movement or dance uses a circle as a beginning, gathering, and ending place for students. In the circle, everyone faces one another. The circle provides a method of control in moving in personal and general space. You can easily define general space, or the dance space, by taping the perimeter of the space in which the children move safely. Standing in a line or lines is a progression to more structure in the movement. Students can move through the general space or in lines crossing the dance space; each is equally appropriate for locomotor and brief movement sequences.

Aerobic Dance (Dance Fitness)

You can begin the class in a circle or in staggered lines. Stand in the center of the circle with the students surrounding you, or stand in front of the class while the students form staggered lines. You will demonstrate the movement first and then ask the students to join in the movement. Later, you can ask a student to lead the step or aerobic dance so that you are able to move through the class and give corrections and help students if they are having trouble with the movement. Turning and facing different walls for steps or combinations adds fun and increases the challenge for the students in the class. Teaching on the move and having students continue to move by marching in place while you demonstrate a step are unique to aerobic dance. Enthusiasm and the selection of appropriate music are vital to the success of the aerobic dance class.

Understanding Music and Accompaniment in the Dance Class

A dance teacher must have a fundamental understanding of music theory and terminology, the ability to count the music, and knowledge of its structure. (See figure 5.1 to self-check your knowledge of music and note values.) The teacher knows music specific to the dance forms that he teaches. Studying music history and styles acquaints the teacher with unlimited choices for choreography. A variety of accompaniment, sound collage, text, improvisational, and semistructured forms provide additional sources from which the teacher and choreographer can choose. As a dancer you are usually acquainted with many of these musical components through participation in dance forms. But as a teacher, you must transfer your musical awareness and further expand your musical knowledge to support teaching one or many dance forms.

The primary task to address is the collaboration between music and dance. Appropriate, inspiring music is the key to a successful dance class and provides a meaningful learning experience for students. Choose a variety of music to expand students' knowledge of music. A basic

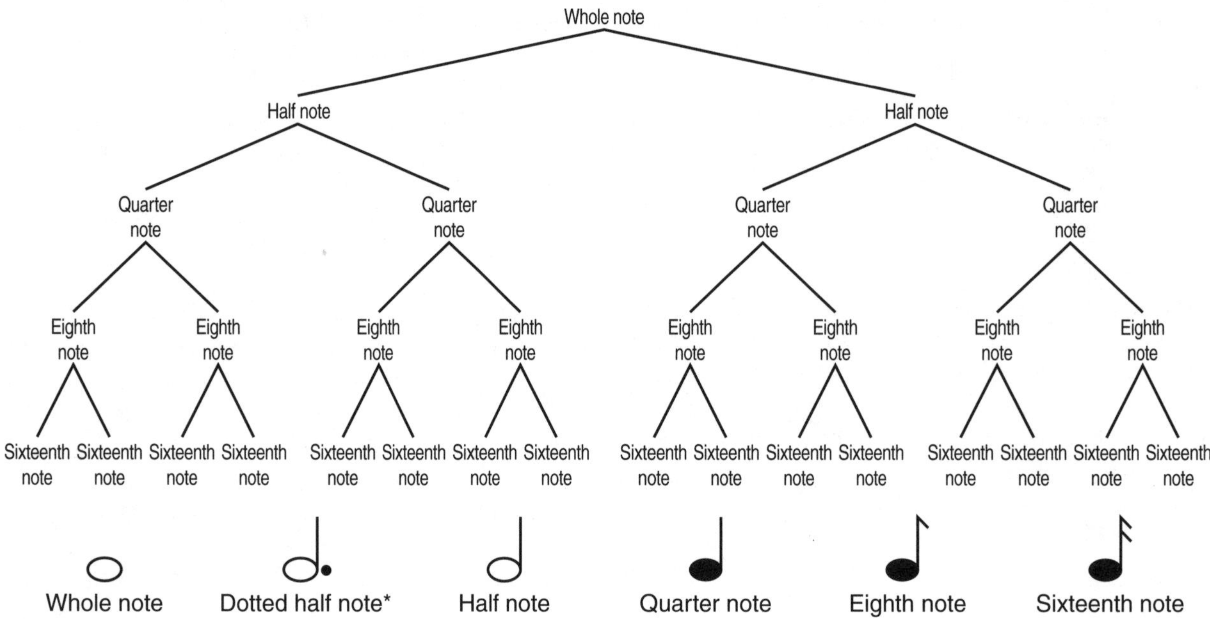

*A dot placed on the right side of the note head lengthens the time value by one half. For example a dotted half note is equal to three quarter notes or beats.

Figure 5.1 Note values and their relationships.

understanding of music begins with note values (see figure 5.1).

In a 4/4 meter, there are 4 beats to a measure: A whole note receives 4 beats, a half note receives 2 beats, a quarter note receives 1 beat, an eighth note gets half a beat, and a sixteenth note receives a quarter of a beat.

In a 3/4 meter, there are three beats to a measure: A dotted half note receives 3 beats, a half note receives 2 beats, a quarter note receives 1 beat, an eighth note receives half a beat, and a sixteenth note receives a quarter of a beat. Basic knowledge of music involves knowing note values and their relation to meters.

Basic Musical Knowledge

A basic knowledge of music entails

- hearing the beat and distinguishing notes and their values,
- knowing the rhythmic pattern,
- recognizing the time signature and counting the music effectively, and
- discerning a musical phrase and the structure of the music.

Dance teaching requires both a general knowledge of music and music specific to dance forms. Because dance relies on music or accompaniment to set the rhythm of the movement, teachers must have a basic knowledge of music to use it correctly in conjunction with teaching dance.

Music Specific to the Dance Form

You must develop a working knowledge of the type of music that accompanies each dance form you teach. Expand your musical resources for a dance form to provide variety and new experiences for your students. The sample units in chapter 13 will provide you with a starting point of music to accompany each of the dance forms.

Music History and Styles

Understanding music history and styles of music opens up even greater resources for each dance form. The music of a certain era often relates to the dance style of that era. Styles of music within a genre provide variety and possibilities for the teacher and the choreographer to explore through movement.

Music Structures

A musical structure is both the internal and external framework of the music. Musical structures often correspond and translate into choreographic structures. An understanding of musical forms and the ability to read a score enable you to communicate effectively with a conductor and musicians for dance. Other musical forms include other compositional techniques.

Improvisational and Semistructured Forms

Often music of a historical era or within a style does not fit the needs of certain choreography. For example, in creative movement and dance, modern, or jazz dance classes, musicians create improvisational compositions. These compositions may be improvised and change with each performance. Or, the improvisation may become a semistructured form with predetermined musical signposts at which both the musicians and the dancers meet. These are interactive musical and movement cues between the musicians and the dancers. Improvisational or semistructured forms add a degree of immediacy for all involved in performing the work. These musical forms or text provide a soundscape for dancers to use as a springboard or background for movement exploration using both musical and movement devices.

Sound Collage

A sound collage is recorded sounds that become the background accompaniment for dance. The dancers may create these sounds while moving, or they may record the sound collage and then create a dance to its accompaniment. Sounds from everyday life, sounds created on instruments, and synthesized scores cover the range of elements in a sound collage. Sound collages use many different sounds, sometimes with random timing, to create sound-scapes.

Effective dance teachers and choreographers select appropriate music that is not overpowering yet can stand by itself as an art form. The accompaniment for any dance form is complementary, contrasting, supportive, and atmospheric.

Harmonizing Accompaniment With Movement

Accompaniment and movement in the dance class work in concert for the success of the dance class and the instructor. Using recorded music (compact discs, tapes, or records), the teacher selects the accompaniment as she constructs the exercises or reviews the dances for the class. At this time, the teacher questions whether the selection meets the criteria for her class.

If the music in the class is provided by a musician for dance, the process is somewhat different than the selection process for recorded music played on a sound system. Ideally, the musician for dance and the teacher confer before the dance class to review the day's lesson and the music selections. Hectic schedules sometimes inhibit this process. Sometimes these conferences take place several times during the term as different types of music are needed in the class. The fortunate teacher is one who works with a musician for dance who has a broad repertoire of music selections and knows how music and the dance form work together.

Before the dance teacher and the musician for dance work together, they have to establish some musical prompts to indicate introductions for exercises. For example, if a preparation for an exercise is a 4-count bar introduction, the musician for dance plays a 4-count bar lead-in to prepare the students for the exercise. For beginning students, the 4-count bar introduction of "5, 6, 7, 8" is appropriate to prepare them to start the exercise. A 2-count bar introduction of "7, 8" is often used for intermediate and advanced students. When working with inexperienced musicians for dance, the teacher may need to count "1, 2, 3, 4" to set the tempo, then the musician begins the musical introduction of "5, 6, 7, 8."

Before each exercise, the teacher communicates to the musician for dance a clear indication of the time signature, tempo, and quality of the music necessary for the exercise. She listens to the choice of music of the musician for dance and

The teacher operates the sound system for class.

evaluates whether the selection meets the criteria for quality, student needs, and performance. This is one of the most important working relationships a dance teacher can cultivate. The partnership between the musician for dance and the teacher is what makes the class work!

During class, the dance teacher and the musician for dance communicate both verbally and nonverbally. The teacher demonstrates the movement at a spot where the musician for dance can see and hear her. The teacher and musician for dance should establish verbal and nonverbal cues to ensure a proper start to exercises or combinations. The musician for dance should be able to hear the teacher in the event that added instructions are required. For example, a teacher might say, "Brian, extend the balancé for another 8 counts." Or the teacher increases or decreases the tempo of a combination by counting or using hand signals to cue the musician for dance for this change.

An important attribute of the dance educator is competency in rhythmic techniques. These techniques include rhythmic literacy (knowing the time signature), knowledge of the form of the musical work, and the ability to count the music and the movement in their relation to each other. The teacher counts the movement in relation to the music to construct the combinations and to ensure that all the students perform the same movement on the same counts. Knowledge of the time signature and musical form is required for constructing exercises consistent with musical phrasing and creating choreography. When selecting music for the different exercises and activities of the dance class, the teacher analyzes it for the learners' skill level and for its effect in providing variety in the class.

Appropriate Music

Students have to dance to the music, so the music must be appropriate for the class content and skill level. The following are aspects to consider in the selection of music for the dance class.

- Can the students count it? If they can't count it, don't use it. Students, not the teacher, should be responsible for counting the music. If you continually count the music and movement, you are unable to teach it effectively.
- Is the tempo too fast or too slow for the movement? Set and check the tempo with students to meet their needs and to ensure quality performance. If the tempo is too fast, the movement looks scrambled, and that is what the students will learn. The tempo must allow students to complete and finish all of the movements.

If the steps, figures, or movements are complicated, students may not be able to coordinate all of these components immediately. A device used in ballet is known as *cut time.* The student does a step in one measure and holds the position for the second measure. This device is especially appropriate for the beginning dancer because it gives him time to complete all parts of the movement and think ahead to the next movement. Then the tempo is adjusted so that the student completes the step in one slow measure; then the tempo gradually increases to standard tempo as the students are able to perform the movement faster.

Practicing the combination or dance while increasing tempo allows students to process the movement information at a faster rate. A compact disc player, cassette player, or record player with speed control allows the teacher to adjust the tempo of the music. Changing the tempo should not be so extreme that the music becomes distorted or offensive.

Dance and music complement each other in most dance forms. In modern dance, the choreographer's intent may be to contrast or provide counterpoint between the music and dance. The quality of the music supports the quality of the movement or provides initiatives for dancers to explore and enhance their movement qualities. The selection of music for this purpose depends on what the teacher envisions, his intuition, and the ability of the musician for dance to play and improvise. The teacher chooses descriptive words and uses music vocabulary to get the proper quality of music for a combination. The best test of this criterion is to dance the combinations to the music and do a movement quality check.

Variety of Music

Variety is an important ingredient in giving students exposure and practice in working with music. When students hear the same music class after class, they become bored and mechanical in their movement. Using a variety of music in the class stimulates students to think about what they are doing and challenges their musicality.

Teaching the dance form content effectively to music that supports and enhances it is the heart of dance training and education. Interwoven in this process are the teaching styles and strategies that the teacher uses to progress through the day's lesson.

Summary

Teaching dance is a complex skill with many facets that encompass presentational methods, teaching strategies, and integration of musical accompaniment. Specific presentational methods include whole–part, part–whole–part, and the add-on methods. Teaching styles (command, practice, reciprocal, self-check, inclusive, guided discovery, and divergent) focus on different ways the dance teacher facilitates students' learning of dance. Teaching strategies comprise a variety of ways of communicating to enhance students' movement. A teaching strategy uses types of cueing (action and directional words, counting, singing, voice augmentation, clapping, nonsense syllables, part of a phrase or word omission, and signals) that augment and reinforce learning of movement. Imagery (anatomical, pictorial, visual, and kinesthetic images) aids in the visualization of movement, which enables the dancer to improve his physical and artistic performance. The teacher uses general teaching methods as well as specific methods for particular dance forms.

Music is an essential part of the creation and instruction of a dance class. A knowledge of music theory and various styles of music and accompaniment is necessary because of the close relationship between dance and music. Careful selection of the appropriate music is vital to the successful teaching of the dance class.

Reference

Mosston, M., and S. Ashworth. 1986. *Teaching physical education*, 3rd ed. Columbus, OH: Merrill.

It's Your Turn

1. Observe a dance class and identify the teaching methods, strategies, and accompaniment used in the class. Fill out form 3.1 on page 41.
2. Create an 8- or 16-count combination or figure. Cue it three different ways and present it to a small group.
3. Develop an 8- or 16-count combination or figure. Present it at least two different ways to a partner. Then ask your partner to tell you what method was more effective.

CHAPTER

6

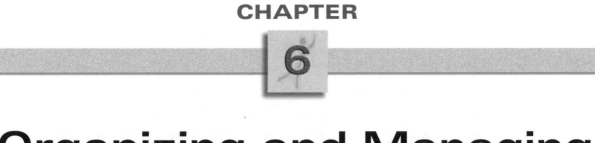

Organizing and Managing the Dance Class

Chapter Objectives

By the end of this chapter, you should be able to do the following:

- Understand the benefits of creating a positive learning atmosphere.
- Use classroom management strategies and develop a management style.
- Apply various types of learner feedback used in the dance class.
- Utilize organization and time management effectively in a dance class.
- Deal with a variety of students' behavior in the dance class.
- Understand how teaching and managing a dance class help in developing a philosophy of teaching.

Effective teaching depends on a teacher's ability to organize and manage the dance class. This chapter will help you create a positive learning atmosphere and understand organization and management strategies for the dance class. Dealing with students' behavior in the dance class and giving appropriate feedback to students are additional management strategies. Teaching strategies mesh with classroom organization and management. The teacher uses management strategies to direct behaviors befitting a viable learning environment. As the dance teacher, you must attain and execute this multitask focus throughout each class. These skills and strategies support a rich teaching and learning environment. Using teaching and management strategies effectively contributes to your development of a philosophy of teaching dance. The foundation for effective management of the dance class begins with establishing a positive learning atmosphere for students.

Creating a Positive Learning Atmosphere

A positive learning atmosphere is conducive to learning and effective teaching and management of the class. The teacher is the catalyst in the dance classroom and sets the level of freedom for the students and the atmosphere for learning. If you are a new teacher, expect the students to test you to see where you set your boundaries. Know those boundaries and expectations before you enter the classroom. It is easier to set boundaries in advance than to try to incorporate or adjust them later. A firm set of guidelines will enable you to attend more to instruction than to management. After your first year of teaching dance, current students will communicate your expectations for classroom conduct to new students so that these students will know your expectations before beginning the course. After several years, your guidelines become easier to implement in the classroom. Your students will know the boundaries and the expectations you have set. Selecting classroom expectations that mirror expected professional dance conduct supports you as a practicing professional dance educator.

Positive approaches in behavior management strategies for dance inspire and challenge students and incite a positive atmosphere and actions in the studio.

The following box is a list of positive approaches taken from *Positive Behavior Management Strategies of Physical Education* by Lavay, French, and Henderson (1997). These items are applicable to the dance studio classroom environment.

Positive Approaches in Behavior Management Strategies for Dance

- Catch students being good. Focus on the appropriate actions; this reinforcement of positive behavior makes students feel good about themselves. Be truthful about these behaviors.
- Expect dancers to follow instructions. Give the instructions once or twice; if you repeat them too many times, students will tend to depend on your instructions and not think for themselves. Continually monitor

Polyspots designate boundaries of the dance space.

whether students are on task. It does not make sense to give instructions and never check to see whether students are accomplishing them.

• Keep your cool and address problems quickly. Control your own behavior as a teacher and act quickly when problems arise. Use positive methods to motivate the dancers. Often practicing a group ritual can dispel problems before they get out of hand.

• Focus on the behavior that is to be corrected, not the person. Be specific with your corrections so that dancers know what they are not doing and what is expected of them.

• Be consistent. Know what students expect from you and you expect from them. Make sure your "yes" means yes, and do not keep changing your mind about what you want. Make sure you respond in the same way every time. If you correct a person's behavior one day, you need to repeat it in the same manner the next time. Also, do not respond differently to other people in the group; try to be fair. Implement these constants into the dance class to ensure a smooth process so that you can spend time on teaching dance rather than managing the class.

Expectations for the Dance Classroom

The teacher implements similar expectations and management strategies to teach each age group. Classroom expectations are the ground rules for the learners' behavior. The teacher clearly communicates these expectations at the first class meeting and they are often posted in the dance classroom. The number and intensity of the ground rules depends largely on the age group and teaching setting. Students who adhere to these ground rules develop discipline and motivation, which are necessary for acquiring a correct performance attitude. Another aspect that gives uniformity to the members of the class and supports discipline is wearing proper attire to class.

Attire

What do you wear in dance class? The dance form and setting generally determine the attire. For example, a teacher in a creative movement and dance class in elementary school wears a T-shirt and pants or similar attire that will allow her to move freely. Your choice of dance attire and grooming habits speaks loudly of your commitment and regard for your profession. Be specific about the type of attire you want your students to wear to class. Your students become a reflection of you, your school, and the profession.

Children sit back to back in threes, listening to the teacher.

Children sit on lines facing the teacher while she gives directions.

Children sit against the wall watching a group perform while waiting their turn to perform.

Discipline

Discipline is students' self-control to meet the expectations of the teaching environment, the dance form, and the attitude and actions associated with the dance profession. Discipline in the class may be a result of the dance form or teacher's management of the class, or the students may initiate their own discipline.

Motivation

Motivation is the impetus to try a new thing and the drive to follow through and to achieve it. Motivation is either internal (initiated by the student's goals for improvement) or external (the student's desire to please the teacher or to pass the course). Students have many motives for taking a dance class, such as personal fitness, enjoyment, passing a required course, greater technical ability, and preparation for a career. Self-motivation leads students to set their personal goals and self-check their progress toward their goals. The teacher's attitude and demeanor in her relationship with the student are central to the student's continued motivation and success. The extent of a student's motivation from the teacher hinges on the teacher's observation, communication, feedback, and love of dance that are imparted through her management strategies.

Developing a Teaching Management Style

Teaching management style is your demeanor as a teacher. Your management style reflects how you relate to students. How do you speak to students? Do your volume and tone encourage or frighten students? Think before you speak. What you say and how you say it set the tone in the class. Your interaction with students creates the atmosphere for learning. Are they able to ask questions? How do you deal with confrontations? Think about ways you would handle these and other situations before you enter the dance class.

Your teaching management style and intensity correspond to the level of the dance class, the age of the dancers, the dance form, and the setting. Becoming a successful class manager is sometimes a juggling act. Analyze what you did in a specific situation, and mentally file your plan for the next time something similar happens. The more you do it, the easier it becomes. An excellent management style involves acquiring observation and communication skills.

Communication Skills

You have a prodigious job to communicate in a nonverbal, symbolic language, dance, to students who may or may not know the language. The teacher must execute the exercises fluently and have the following traits:

- A command of the dance form vocabulary
- Knowledge of the dance form's internal structure to explain its technical and artistic demands to students in such a way as to motive them
- The ability to provide feedback and guide students through positive and successful learning experiences

The teacher notices everything, deals with the most important issues, and thinks of new ways to motivate students to be responsible and responsive dancers. When communicating with the dancer, the teacher uses several forms of feedback.

Three Types of Feedback

The three main types of feedback are verbal, nonverbal, and guided manipulation. Verbal feedback has three types of positive feedback: acknowledgment, prescriptive, and corrective. Negative feedback is either verbal or nonverbal in nature. Nonverbal feedback involves gestures and facial expressions. Guided manipulation, although primarily nonverbal, is reinforced with vocal cues. The dance teacher uses guided manipulation as a means of communicating posture or movement changes to students. The teacher's choice of feedback sets the atmosphere of the class.

Verbal Feedback

The teacher's statements and vocal inflections to the student constitute verbal feedback. For the most part, verbal feedback is positive and motivates and engages students in the learning process. Verbal feedback provides a dancer with constructive criticism and praise for his performance efforts. Pinpointing gives specific instruction. Hold back on using negative feedback until it is absolutely necessary.

- Acknowledgment refers to giving the dancer information about his performance in a positive way. "You did two clean pirouettes without losing balance. Now try three clean pirouettes." Acknowledgment can be either verbal or nonverbal communication with the student.
- Prescriptive feedback directs the dancer to perform correctly. "Remember to keep your shoulders and hips squared at the beginning of a pirouette."
- Corrective feedback indicates the error that the student made and presents a solution to correct it. "When you perform a pirouette, your shoulders and hips are not square, and your body weight is shifted back during the relevé."
- Pinpointing is a feedback technique that clarifies the trouble zones that students encounter. After explaining and showing the movement sequence, the teacher observes how well the students understand the specific components and requirements to successfully perform the movement.

An effective example of pinpointing is to choose two or more students to demonstrate the correct execution of the movement and then point out their correct positions or transitions. This method calls attention to the expectations of the step. Select students who are neither the most nor least experienced in the class. This gives them positive reinforcement on their performance of this particular aspect of the step (Graham 1992).

- Negative feedback points out the student's attitude or action that must be changed. This type of feedback should be used sparingly and only as a last resort. What you say may influence the dancer's attitude about his confidence and himself. Dancers are often their own harshest critics. If negative feedback is necessary, say it to the class in general or to the person by himself after class.

Nonverbal Feedback

Nonverbal feedback is a facial expression or gesture such as a smile, nod, quizzical look, touch, or eye contact with the student as well as the physical distance to the student. This type of feedback engages the student, acknowledges his work as verbal feedback does, and may inspire and motivate students to move, improve, and strive for excellence.

You should be aware of your facial expression during the class so that you do not communicate something that you do not want the students to see. Students should not be able to read your thoughts as you read their movement and form your feedback. Therefore, maintain a pleasant but neutral facial expression so that the nonverbal feedback you give has an effect by itself or reinforces your verbal comments.

Guided Manipulation

Guided manipulation is the teacher's physical handling of a student's body or body parts. The teacher may guide the student through the steps of an exercise. You should bring up this topic at the first class and ask whether any student feels uncomfortable with the idea of someone else touching her. When you engage in guided manipulation with a student, quietly ask her permission before touching the student or moving a body part. Always tell the student what you will be doing before you actually do it to avoid any surprises.

Guided manipulation is often most effective in one-on-one feedback sessions. Often the teacher can explain how to place or move a body part, and then the student can try to make this change without the teacher's physical help. Dance is physical in nature, so guided manipulation to achieve and feel the correct movement is an important type of feedback in the dance classroom.

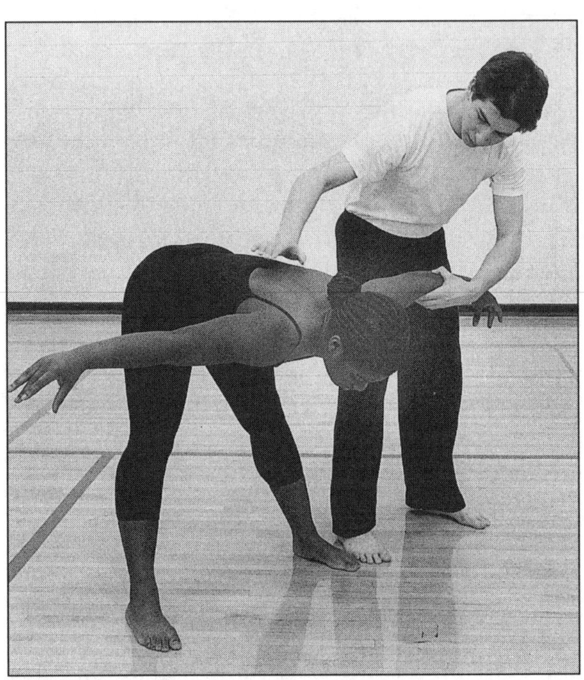

Students using guided manipulation.

Effective feedback is part of the strategies the teacher uses in presenting the class content. Each type of feedback pertains to the entire class as well as to individual students. Everyone deserves some type of feedback in each dance class. All communication (verbal and nonverbal) must be clear, concise, consistent, fair, positive, and constructive. As teachers we help students develop lifelong skills. Success in the dance class gives a person confidence and a feeling of self-worth, which emanate from his responsible and motivated behavior. You must understand your personality and management abilities as a teacher in the dance class. These attributes will largely determine your interaction with students and their behavior in the class.

Managing the Dance Classroom

To manage a dance class effectively, you must decide on many classroom management issues before you begin teaching. Make it a priority to understand your students and their skill levels, the dance form, the setting, and the resources you use to teach the class. Some of the classroom management decisions are inherent in your teaching assignment and the school setting. Before you enter the classroom, gather information about those factors that affect your teaching setting.

Gathering Information About the Teaching Setting

The setting for dance instruction in the school may be a dance studio, a gymnasium, a classroom, a stage, or a cafeteria. Evaluate the dance studio or room for its size and layout, flooring, ventilation, lighting, and equipment (mirrors, barres, and audio equipment). Familiarize yourself with the dance space in relation to rest rooms, dressing rooms, entrances, and exits to the space and the building.

Become acquainted with the custodian of the facility. He has the keys and is responsible for opening and closing the room or the building. Know where thermostats are located and who is responsible for turning on the heat and air conditioning. Also find out whom to call if something is not working. Ask the administrator or building supervisor whether there are specific rules regarding the use of the classroom or building.

Locate the sound equipment for teaching the class. Is the equipment located in the dance space or somewhere else? Will you share the equipment with other teachers or programs? Most important, is there adequate and appropriate music for the dance forms that you will teach? Other music questions surface if you will be working with an accompanist. Is the accompanist trained to play for dance and the specific dance forms you will be teaching? Is sheet music available? Who is responsible for purchasing the sheet music—you, the musician for dance, or the organization?

Acquiring information about the teaching space and its operations will help you to become comfortable in the school setting. The next strategy is to consider the organization of the class.

Organizing the Dance Class

Organizing each class begins with a plan for the course. Make an overall plan of what you will teach and when you will teach it. The first considerations are the age and skill level of your students. During the first several classes, conduct an assessment of the skills your students can perform. A student's number of years of training does not always reflect his level of competence. The key to your success is to plan, overplan, and be flexible in managing each class.

The dance form determines the format of the class. All dance classes follow a common format: warm-up; development of techniques; introduction, development, or review of movement material or dances; cool-down; and closing.

Within the format of the class, students move into different formations for instruction. If the class involves a barre, establish each person's place at the barre. For center instruction, stagger the lines so that each person can see the teacher and the teacher is able to see each student. In creative movement classes, identify each child's place in either a circle or on lines for the warm-up.

In dance class, students execute combinations in the center of the dance space. Dancers perform movement as a class or divide into groups. The class or groups spread out across the dance space, staggering the lines so each person has adequate space in which to perform. After group 1 performs

Standing at the barre with adequate space between each person.

Dancers stand in staggered lines in the dance space.

the movement or combination one or more times, they exit usually to a side of the room quickly. At the same time, group 2 comes into their staggered lines in the center, ready to start executing the combination.

For movements or combinations performed across the floor, the dancers may divide into groups of usually two, three, or four people. Single dancers or a group move in lines across the floor. Sometimes the group moves in a formation such as three dancers in a triangle or four dancers in two staggered lines. Dancers move either from side to side or on a diagonal from corner to corner in the dance space.

The folk or contra dance teacher finds it easiest to teach students in lines. This allows the teacher to check the students' movement before going into the formation of the dance. The teacher walks the students through the figures so that the partners know the movements, sequence of the figures, and with whom they will be dancing. Regardless of the dance form you are teaching, efficiently moving students from one part of the class to the other requires time management skills.

Managing Time

Time management is an integral part of class planning. In some beginning classes, you may spend more time in acquisition of vocabulary and skills than in other parts of the class. For example, in a beginning ballet class, the barre exercises will take more time than the work in the center, but as the course progresses these two parts of the class shift into equal parts.

Teacher sits in the circle with children.

Teacher demonstrates movement while children sit in lines and watch.

Dancers move across the floor in a diagonal path with a delay of 4 to 8 counts between dancers.

A balanced class is essential in any dance form. Students are in the class to learn, to train, and to dance. You are responsible for warming up the class, but do not spend an inordinate amount of time preparing them to move. Let them dance—that is where learning takes place! In some settings, you may teach 40- to 50-minute dance classes. Getting all the dance content into a 40- or 50-minute class format sometimes is difficult, but it is possible.

Pacing

Establish an effective pace to get all of the work accomplished during the class. A well-paced class requires you to move groups of people into new formations quickly. Keep the class focused and progressing through the class work in a timely fashion to attain the goal for the class. If class periods are short, effective time management becomes even more important. To properly pace the class, consider the following:

- Be punctual in starting and ending classes.
- Make students responsible for signing in or checking in for roll.
- Set places at the barre or in the center for students to stand or move across the floor.
- Combine exercises and steps to save time with the additional benefit of increasing variety.
- Give feedback to students while they are dancing. When necessary, stop them and give feedback, but try to avoid distracting them from the exercise.
- Be available for student conferences in the studio before and after class.

An important consideration in time management for any class is allowing adequate time for the assessment of students. Assessment may take one or two class periods depending on the size of the class and experience of the students. Prepare the students beforehand for assessment, making sure they understand the criteria by which they will be evaluated. Good organization skills make the evaluation process efficient and less stressful for both students and the teacher.

Safety

The dance teacher is responsible for monitoring the students' safety. The space must be large enough to accommodate the number of students in the class so that they can move without invading others' personal space. Children should not be allowed to climb or hang on barres. At the beginning of the term, the teacher instructs her students in studio safety so that everyone can share the space to enjoy dancing. These are the most important factors:

- The space is free of obstacles.
- The floor is clean.
- The temperature of the studio is conducive to moving.

All of these classroom organization and management strategies contribute to creating an effective learning environment for all students.

Dealing With Student Behaviors in the Dance Classroom

Some of the most common student behaviors in the dance class involve noise, echo effect, commotion, requests to use the rest room, traffic jams, distractions, loss of focus, and refusal to participate (see table 6.1).

When you encounter these behaviors in the dance class, you must consistently communicate the rules, expectations, and responsibilities to the class. Be prepared with a plan to resolve these behaviors efficiently and effectively so that you and the class can get on with learning dance. A disciplined, trustful, and caring environment helps students enjoy dance and develop lifelong behaviors. If they follow the rules and meet the expectations set out for them, they become responsible and accountable for their actions.

Ridicule and threats are not constructive ways of dealing with disruptive behavior. Be constructive with your criticism. Always be consistent and fair in your criticism. Listen to and understand the student's side of the issue before addressing the situation. Personal verbal attacks, such as "You are stupid," are never effective. But you can say you are not pleased with the person's behavior or attitude: "Please do not talk while you are dancing because it is a sign that you're not concentrating." Sometimes you must remind the student that he is responsible for his behavior and there will be consequences

Table 6.1 Student Behaviors in the Classroom

Problem	Solution	Example	Caution
Noise is expected if dancers work in groups or projects. In a technique class, noise is counter-productive, disrespectful, and not permitted.	• Make sure students know that they are in class to dance. • Remind the students that talking and making noise in class take away from everyone's concentration.	• Using humor may get their attention. In middle and high school classes, "Please keep it down to to a dull roar" or "Dance is nonverbal art" or "In dance class, express yourself with your body" might remind them that their voices are getting too loud.	• Try not to let the noise get out of hand.
Echo effect occurs when one person starts to giggle and it leads to everyone giggling.	• Allowing the students to laugh helps them to stop laughing.	• In a creative dance class, you can incorporate a laugh time.	• If giggling persists, children lose their concentration.
Commotion ensues when what you are doing in class is not working.	• Go on to something completely different to stop the commotion.	• "Let's go on to something else."	• If allowed to erupt, chaos is unproductive and unfulfilling for the teacher and students.
Needing the rest room is a situation usually related to young dancers.	• Ask everyone as they enter the studio if they need to go to the bathroom before class begins.	• When one child asks to go to the bathroom, all children will ask to leave.	• Discern whether the child might not want to do what the class is doing or the child has a weak bladder.
Traffic jams happen in any dance class and usually are a result of a teacher's lack of complete ideas or direction. Other causes involve a few students who become excited and enthusiastic, or even a change in the weather. Collisions are frightening and can be dangerous in the dance class.	• Use a predetermined sign for "freeze" or "melt down" exercise if you feel the situation has become electric in your class. • Do some relaxation exercises before the group resumes dancing.	• "Freeze. Now begin to slowly melt and relax into the floor." If there is music, turn it off and let everyone become very still. Do some breathing exercises and slowly stand and return to work. • Use a musical or drum signal to get the students' attention. Then sort out what has happened.	• Collisions can happen in almost any dance classes; try to foresee the possibilities when setting up the groups for center or across-the-floor work.
Distractions vary from sights and sounds outside the windows of the dance classroom to fire sirens or other unforeseen events. If these things persist, the teacher finds a way to resolve the situation to ensure the classroom remains quiet.	• Defuse the situation by talking about what has happened. • Find out what is happening and inform the students about the situation.	• "Students, I need your cooperation. Please be quiet and patient while I find out what is happening." • "Students, don't move. Just sit down and get comfortable until I can find out why the lights went out."	• If something is not done to ease the students' minds, they will become frightened and agitated.

(continued)

Table 6.1 *(continued)*

Problem	Solution	Example	Caution
In another world occurs when a person focuses inwardly and has difficulty attending to what is done and said in the classroom. This person is easily distracted, has trouble concentrating, exhibits a short attention span, and appears to be in another world often because of a learning disability, lack of sleep, poor nutrition, medication, or abuse.	• Talk with the dancer about his actions in the class. The student is often unaware of his problem. • Be kind, helpful, and patient. • Find mutually stimulating subject matter to incorporate into the dance class. • The student needs order and a well-defined structure.	• If the child is consistently daydreaming in class or appears to be in another world, this is probably a result of pervasive fantasy.	• If this condition persists, the student's lack of interest in what you are doing or the material being taught can spread to others in the class.
"We won't do it" attitude stems from lack of interest in the subject or is instigated by disruptive, uncooperative members of the class that the students admire or follow.	• Talk with specific students or the entire group about the focus of the class. • Establish a dialogue to create a compromise or reiterate the process or rules.	• In a creative dance class, ask the students to suggest a topic for dancing.	• If you do not ask what the problem is, you cannot fix it.

for his bad behavior. If you do remind the student, list the consequences again and follow up on them to show consistency in discipline and to maintain group control.

Even with its inherent structure, a dance class is often neither a quiet nor an orderly atmosphere. You may encounter a variety of behaviors that you have to stop on the spot to maintain order in the class and to continue the lesson.

Discipline Problems

The structure of a dance class establishes natural parameters for the students. These parameters are built-in support systems that the teacher uses to dissipate discipline problems. Although dance as an art instills self-discipline in students, the teacher must maintain order in the classroom so that effective teaching and learning can take place. She must be ready to resolve discipline problems in a constructive manner.

In educational settings, the teacher sets the guidelines for students' behavior and responsibilities. In some settings, student expectations are less formal. The teacher tells the class about her expectations either at the beginning of the course or when it becomes necessary. The teacher may post the rules for the dance class in the dance space for easy reference.

Some discipline problems arise that neither the teacher nor the school administration can handle. In this case, parents must be notified. When the parents have little interest or involvement in the child's education, the school's administration becomes the entity for disciplining and mentoring, and for providing role models.

Appropriate discipline strategies range from minimal to maximal interaction with students. Because each student is different, a variety of strategies are used to diffuse discipline problems (see table 6.2). These strategies include waiting in silence, dealing with nonparticipation, giving a time out, separating the child from the class, exhibiting self-control, reminding the child of who is in charge, revoking privileges, and other extreme situations. The strategies are adapted from Sue Stinson's *Dance for Young Children* (1988).

It is worth the extra effort to learn ways to deal with students' behaviors before they occur in the classroom. The teacher has several options in managing behavior.

Table 6.2 Defusing Discipline Problems

Strategy	Example	Caution
Waiting in silence is a technique to get the dancer's attention. • Inform students beforehand so that they will be aware of what you do in a noisy, chaotic situation.	• If the noise in the class has gotten out of control or you are unable to get the students' attention, stop and stand very quietly; do not say a word; wait until everyone is quiet. • Use a gesture such as raising your hand, a verbal signal, or a predetermined drum phrase, to stop what the students are doing.	• Be patient and do not say anything until everyone is quiet and you have their full attention.
Opposite of waiting in silence is identifying the behavior immediately. In some settings this technique is necessary. • Clearly describe the appropriate action or attitude expected.	• If there is a disagreement between two children, take care of this immediately.	• If you do not immediately address the students' actions or attitude, it will escalate or other students will imitate the inappropriate actions.
Nonparticipation problems often solve themselves when the teacher does nothing. • If the child is shy or embarrassed, let him watch the class. • If the child moves closer or mimics the movement from a distance, you or the group move closer to the child and try to make him feel like part of the group. This also makes the child physically nearer to the group and shows the class cares.	• Encourage the child by saying, "We really need you. Please come and dance with us."	• Be patient, but actively find a way to bring the student into the dance class as soon as possible.
Explain time-out at the beginning of the course. If a child is aggressive, combative, or just acting out, he may need a quiet time away from the group. Time-out is a way to extinguish undesirable behavior. Time may vary from 1 to 5 minutes.	• The child may watch or the child may face the wall, which prevents him from seeing what the class is doing.	• Use your own judgment. • Be aware the child can manipulate the situation by acting out or not cooperating because he does not like doing flexibility exercises or whatever activity the class is doing at the moment. • Use this technique only when needed or it will lose its effect.
Separate the child from the class in some cases of classroom disruption. • In a school setting, send her to the office.	• If the child is being disruptive and has already been cautioned, separate the child from the group.	• Try to find a way out of the situation before it gets out of hand. • Being singled out in class is not constructive.

(continued)

Table 6.2 (continued)

Strategy	Example	Caution
Exhibit self-control if attitude or self-control is continually a problem and disruptive to the class; you and the child need to find a way out of the situation. • Individual conferences with the child away from other class members opens communication about the problem so that you can understand it and work toward a resolution. These conferences work to preserve the child's dignity.	• When a child constantly interrupts, the child needs to be aware of how to wait her turn.	• Be consistent and vigilant in your corrections and feedback. • Instill responsibilities in students.
Be in charge and don't allow the child to engage in a power struggle. Be aware of and address these situations before they escalate into a power struggle.	If a student does not want to dance: • Talk with the student and tell her about your perception and expectations. • Face the problem; try to develop mutual trust and understanding through the process. • Allow the student to voice her point of view, contribute to the discussion, and plan to alleviate the problem.	• Do not engage in a power struggle. • No one wins; you both need to save face. • Don't argue with the child. • Be consistent with your classroom rules and remind the children of these rules.
Losing privileges is a disciplinary method used when a dancer is irresponsible. If a dancer has been given an appropriate number of warnings about his behavior, then implement other solutions. • Write the expectations of the class in your syllabus or discuss them in class. • Make the dancer accountable for his own actions.	• Continually talk with other students, then transfer the student to another place in the class or to work with another group. • Missing a rehearsal without explanation or prior notification is more serious. If this behavior repeats, decide whether to eliminate the student from the dance or performance.	• If the dancer continues to engage in undesirable behaviors after being warned, reduce or deny credit for the assignment or replace the person in the performance. • Carefully consider the consequences of the action from the viewpoint of the dancer, other dancers, and the performance. The decision and how you communicate it sends a message to all students. • Be consistent in your decisions.
Irresolvable situations are extreme situations that cannot be resolved by the teacher, parents, or the school. • Encouragement by both parents and teacher in a supportive environment is the key for the child to participate willingly. This allows him to focus on the benefits of dance as a physical challenge and other benefits derived from the situation.	• A student brings a gun or a knife to school.	• Your awareness of the boundaries of the student's disciplinary actions, the school's disciplinary options, and the administrative chain of command helps control the student's behavior and attitude in the classroom. • Become acquainted with the organization's operations and procedures.

Strategy	Example	Caution
• If a student continually acts out or does not want to participate, an administrator puts constraints on the student, such as loss of privileges (not participating in the next basketball game, not graduating with the credit for the course) or a reduction of the student's grade for the class.		

Behavioral Approach

The behavioral approach begins with defining the desirable behavior that you expect from dancers before you begin the class, exercise, or combination. To implement this approach use the steps found in the following box.

Four Steps in the Behavioral Approach

1. Select and define the behavior. For example, "Line up in three rows. Make sure the lines are staggered. Be able to see yourself and me (the teacher) in the mirror; otherwise I will not be able to see you and correct you." Keep your comments clear and concise.
2. Observe and record behavior. Look and write down or mentally make a note of what is happening. Did they understand your instructions? Do you have to alter and reword what you said? Monitoring your verbal and nonverbal behavior enables you to check the effectiveness of your instruction.
3. Implement behavior intervention. This is reinforcement of the desired behavior. "You did a nice job of working and cooperating with others in rehearsing the dance, so you will be able to perform the dance in the concert."
4. Evaluate whether the behavior intervention is working to produce appropriate behavior. Is the students' behavior a result of the intervention or not? Use a frequency recording chart or keep track of the behavior in a log or journal to give you a specific idea of the students' behavior progress.

Different types of positive reinforcement are used to maintain and increase appropriate student behavior. Primary reinforcement deals with a person's eating, drinking, and sleeping habits. Secondary reinforcement happens when the student learns to perform a step correctly and feels good about himself. It usually involves a physical reward (see the following box).

Four Types of Secondary Reinforcements That Aid in Activating the Desired Behavior

1. Social reinforcement is a smile or a touch on the shoulder.
2. Positive verbal reinforcement is a compliment. "Your jazz leap was well done! Your legs were extended and toes were fully pointed."
3. Tangible reinforcement uses material objects the student wants, such as stickers or awards.
4. Physical reinforcement allows students time to perform dances, combinations, or chants. The teacher may also award privileges or free dance time during the class for the students who like to create and perform their own dances.

Secondary reinforcements help the teacher to mold students' behavior, implement behavior intervention, and assess students' behavioral progress. The dance educator models and teaches expectations, attitudes, and attributes that filter into other disciplines and everyday life. These types of reinforcement allow the teacher to achieve order and discipline in the dance class. Another method of molding behavior uses the psychodynamic approach, which centers on the student's choices.

Psychodynamic Approach

The psychodynamic approach (Lavay, French, and Henderson 1997) stems from responsibility models. This approach involves becoming responsible through taking care of ourselves, others, and our surroundings. The teacher guides students to become more responsible through the activities and interactions that take place in the dance class. The following box contains the four components of the psychodynamic approach.

Four Components of the Psychodynamic Approach

1. Teacher's talk requires the teacher to be mindful of her use of language and aware that her message is positive and helpful for students.
2. Student's talk helps him become responsible for his actions. The statement of "He made me do it" changes to " I was responsible for my actions." The teacher monitors student communication to reinforce responsibility.
3. Teacher's actions include designing activities that build responsibility. This is accomplished in two steps. First the teacher establishes what responsibility means. Then she explains why responsibility is important. Be specific about what behaviors are responsible, then ask the dancer to list these behaviors so that he is willing to exert his responsibility.
4. Student's actions depend on the teacher to create activities that encourage responsibility for the student's action. For example, students cooperatively work to choreograph a dance. The teacher provides activities that require dancers to demonstrate mutual support or use conflict resolution skills to constructively handle conflict through communication and compromise.

Inherent to the psychodynamic approach is learning to take responsibility for one's talk and actions. The psychodynamic approach indicates levels of student responsibility. The six levels of responsibility are noted in the following box (Hellison and Templin 1991).

Six Levels of Responsibility

1. Level 0 is irresponsibility. The person at this level displays behavior that is undisciplined. He discriminates against or makes fun of others, makes excuses, and blames others. The person may interrupt, intimidate, manipulate, or physically and verbally abuse others.
2. Level 1 is respect. The person at this level possesses self-control, wants peaceful resolution of conflict, accepts differences of opinion, and wants to negotiate and resolve problems.
3. Level 2 refers to participation. The person at this level incorporates into everyday life the skills learned through dance participation. In addition, the dancer understands expectations of the profession, such as showing up to class, improving his own technique, dancing with others, and being a leader.
4. Level 3 is self-direction. The dancer is responsible for his own choices and makes connections to his self-identity. At level 3, the dancer exhibits self-control, works on his own without direct supervision, and takes responsibility for his choices and actions. He holds responsibility for learning a dance. The teacher can correct, coach, and encourage, but the responsibility for improvement and mastery is on the dancer.
5. Level 4 is caring. The dancer demonstrates his capacity to reach out to others to help, support, cooperate, and show concern. If one dancer is having trouble with a step, the other dancer helps the student learn it.
6. Level 5 happens outside the dance studio. This is the ability to use the skills learned in levels 1 through 4 in everyday situations. The dancer learns about self-control, responsibility for choices, self-identity, self-direction, motivation, and caring about others and the environment. He then puts these attributes into practice in everyday living.

When using the level of responsibility scale, the dance teacher explains the purpose of the levels of responsibility and how they can be incorporated into students' own lives. Additionally, the teacher can provide students with ways of communicating with others. These are called *awareness paths* (Hellison and Templin 1991), which create opportunities for experiences and include reflection time, decision making, and group meetings. Reflection time gives dancers time to write in a journal, set goals, or fill out a checklist. Individual decision making provides dancers the opportunities to negotiate and to make choices. What actions do they want to improve? Group meetings offer dancers a chance to voice opinions, feelings, concerns, and ideas. These meetings dissipate misunderstandings and serve as informal counseling sessions.

Another venue for communicating is one-on-one talks between the teacher and a student about her behavior and how she interacts with others in the class. Set realistic goals for each class, each age group, and each setting. Students should work to develop skills in developing self-control of actions and emotions and cooperating with group and class members. These attributes enhance a person's quality of life, communication skills, social skills, maturity, and lifelong learning.

Contingency Contract

A contingency contract is either a vocal or written contract that makes reinforcement contingent on a learner's performance. It is also another example of the psychodynamic approach. If the student passes a performance proficiency exam in ballet, modern, jazz, and tap dance, he will be in the concert. Also, he must attend all rehearsals and performances unless something dire happens. These circumstances must be communicated to the artistic director of the concert. A contingency contract is a method of ensuring everyone's commitment. If the student doesn't meet the expectations, he is accountable for the consequences. In the dance class, as in any class, the student is responsible for his actions. The teacher is a driving force in keeping the student on track and supporting him through the organization and management of the class. A teaching philosophy stems from a teacher's management and organization of the dance class.

Developing a Philosophy of Teaching Dance

As an educator you will develop a philosophy of teaching, a point of view. Your philosophical approach to teaching is an evolving process and is influenced by your personal training, experience, and personality. This philosophy may change as your knowledge of teaching expands and your experience grows. Certain portions of your philosophy may change, but your overall approach is likely to remain consistent. At times you may alter your philosophical approach because of the teaching situation, students, or what you learn about yourself and dance pedagogy. The organization that employs you may partially shape your teaching philosophy and expectations. Your philosophy is directly related to your responsibilities as a dance educator.

You must be aware of your attributes as both a dancer and a teacher. What do you consider important characteristics of proper dance training? What do you believe about teaching dance? What are your beliefs about dance education? What do you think the issues are in dance as a profession? Your philosophy should be grounded with a love of dance, a dedication to teaching, and a passion to share dance in all its wealth and diversity with others.

Summary

Creating a positive learning environment fosters the teaching and learning process in dance. Classroom expectations, discipline, and motivation aid in the development of this positive atmosphere. The teacher develops a management style based on her personality and background. Her management style regulates how she communicates with dance students and gives them feedback. The types of feedback used in the dance classroom include verbal, nonverbal, and guided manipulation. Acknowledgment, prescriptive, and corrective feedback are positive forms of feedback; negative feedback is used sparingly. Nonverbal feedback involves the teacher's expressions and gestures. Management strategies depend on the teaching setting, organization of the class, time management, pacing, and safety concerns.

Organization and management of the dance class begin with the establishment of a positive learning environment. Teachers must set parameters and be consistent in decisions to deal with students' behavior. Classroom management strategies and style enable the teacher to mold students' behavior through feedback. Organization and time management contribute to an effective dance classroom. Students' discipline problems are defused with the use of various techniques. Students learn responsible behavior through the teacher's use of three approaches (behavioral, psychodynamic, and contingency contract) that are effective and useful in the dance class. Overall, teaching and management strategies provide the basis for developing a personal philosophy of teaching dance. Your philosophy reflects your background, training, and often the settings in which you have taught.

References

Graham, G. 1992. *Teaching children physical education: Becoming a master teacher.* Champaign, IL: Human Kinetics.

Hellison, D.R., and T. Templin. 1991. *A reflective approach to teaching physical education.* Champaign, IL: Human Kinetics.

Lavay, B.W., R. French, and H. Henderson. 1997. *Positive behavior management strategies of physical education.* Champaign, IL: Human Kinetics.

Stinson, S. 1988. *Dance for young children: Finding the magic in movement.* Reston, VA: American Alliance for Health, Physical Education, Recreation and Dance.

It's Your Turn

1. Observe a dance class and notice the teacher's management and organization techniques. Fill out form 3.1 on page 41.
2. Assume you are teaching a middle school social dance unit that involves couples. You've heard from other teachers that these students don't particularly want to hold hands or touch in partner positions. How would you handle this situation? What specifically would you do? Write one or two paragraphs on how you would solve this problem.
3. These questions are adapted from Lavay, French, and Henderson (1997). The following is a checklist of how well you influence a positive learning atmosphere:

❑ Am I turned on? Do I

- keep aware of what is going on at all times?
- act immediately to inhibit or extinguish misbehavior or act before it gets out of hand?

❑ Am I enthusiastic? Do I

- like the dance subject matter?
- spread the joy of dance to others?
- communicate a positive, nurturing class atmosphere?

❑ Am I flexible? Do I

- think on my feet?
- adjust to the students and situation?
- make personal contact with a student if necessary?

❑ Am I personable? Do I

- know the names of all students in the class?
- give positive comments in some way to acknowledge each dancer in each class?

CHAPTER

7

Analyzing the Learner and the Learning Environment

Chapter Objectives

By the end of this chapter, you should be able to do the following:

- Understand how community values, cultural diversity, and the school environment affect your dance class.
- Identify the characteristics of different ages of learners and how to meet their needs.
- Understand the special considerations necessary for including learners with special needs.

Teaching in the new millennium presents many challenges. This chapter will help you develop an understanding of the interconnectedness of learners, their learning environment, the community, and its values. Good dance instruction involves understanding learners of different age groups and meeting their needs in the dance class. The dance class and the school are both learning environments that support the student population they serve and the roles of the school within the community. The learner and the school are part of the community that is characterized by its demographics and values. The learner, the school environment, and the community influence and interact with one another to facilitate dance instruction in public education.

Since the mid-1970s, our culture has changed significantly. Humans seem to mature more quickly physically, mentally, sociologically, and sexually. Some contributing factors to these cultural changes include inadequate parental support and guidance, diet, lack of respect for authority, reluctance to take responsibility for one's own actions, violence, little drive to achieve, and impatience in achieving success. In this environment, strong male and female role models are essential. If parents are not good role models, then children need mentors and teachers to help them develop trust and self-confidence to become productive human beings in society.

The cultural, racial, and religious preconceptions formed by society nurture prejudice; teachers and students must understand this so that they can break down barriers and constructively live with one another. The following are some of the issues that teachers have to resolve and cope with in the classroom:

- Language and differences in communication
- Rural, urban, and suburban community life differences
- Street smarts for the environment or knowing how to avoid potentially dangerous situations
- Community values
- Cultural identity and diversity
- Psychosocial problems of abuse and violence
- Global accessibility or seeing and knowing about events immediately may impact how you interpret them

The dance educator can be influential in our global community. The arts bring people together by fostering understanding, appreciation, and hope. Dance serves as a universal creative, expressive, physical, and emotional outlet that nurtures commonalities across many cultures. This era brings unfamiliar experiences and exciting possibilities for us to embrace, celebrate, and explore through dance. Dance teachers have many opportunities in and out of the classroom to interact with and influence students in a positive way. Your students reflect the values of their parents, upbringing, and community. An awareness of the world and all its problems and joys contributes to your success as a dance educator.

Students are the focal point of all your work as a dance educator. They are the reason you teach and want to share your love of learning and knowledge of dance. To accomplish these goals, you must have a clear understanding of each age group.

Understanding the Learner

Each age group you teach has certain characteristics and behaviors. You must acquire the necessary information about your student population so that you can develop age-appropriate dance content. Teaching dance as an art, educational medium, or leisure-time activity is appropriate for students of all ages. Some dance forms are more appropriate for certain age groups, depending on the person's physical development, the complexity of the form, and social behaviors required to perform the dance form.

A great deal has been written about child development but little is in relation to the dance setting. Dance educators need useful guidelines for students in specific dance forms and age groups. The National Standards for Arts Education: Dance published voluntary guidelines that divide students into three specific age groups: grades kindergarten through 4, grades 5 through 8, and grades 9 through 12 (National Standards for Arts Education 1994). These standards establish outcome expectations for student achievement in dance for each of these age groups.

Practical information about the learner aids the teacher in conducting a class for a specific age group and developing appropriate lesson plans. The next section is a synthesis of many sources and provides a basis for you to learn about each of these age groups. Observing and teaching students will aid in defining and characterizing these age groups. With both the Standards and practical information in mind, we have further divided the age groups to represent pre-K, lower elementary, upper elementary through middle school, and high school students. Key concepts about students for each age group are *distinguishing general characteristics, learns by, needs to have, relates to, motor skills, dance activities,* and *dance forms* (see tables 7.1-7.4).

General Characteristics of Three- to Five-Year-Olds

Three- to five-year old children are inquisitive, exuberant, emotional, erratic, easily distracted, self-involved, moving beings. They have a short attention span (they usually focus for less than 20 minutes) and have trouble separating from a parent. Children in this age group tire easily. Their bones are growing, and they are unable to distinguish between right and left.

General Characteristics of Six- to Eight-Year-Olds

Children in the primary grades have the ability to concentrate 20 minutes or longer on a single activity. They love to move, and they thrive on vigorous activities that use the large muscles of the arms and legs. Children in this age group are able to distinguish between the right and left side. They want adult attention, like to have their own way, and test boundaries given by the teacher. In this stage friendships develop, vocabulary heightens, and understanding of concepts increases. They can follow instructions and have a knowledge of rules and safety.

General Characteristics of 9- to 14-Year-Olds

Children in upper elementary school through middle school are physically more apt in gross and fine motor skills, are interested in rules and regulations, and are intense and emotional. They rely on the group for approval. The attention span lengthens. They develop time management skills and understand causal relationships. Boys are physically stronger than girls; girls are more flexible than boys. Complex physical and emotional changes take place at this stage. Boys and girls act out and fight verbally and physically. Between the ages of 10 and 12, learners may be uncoordinated, awkward, clumsy, inhibited, and insecure because of sporadic growth. Differences in interests and personality are more apparent. A wide range of levels of development and maturity is common within this and the next age group.

General Characteristics of 15- to 18-Year-Olds

Students in high school have improved motor coordination. Their bones continue to grow, and they usually complete puberty by the end of high school. They participate in prolonged activities, solve problems and use critical thinking, form personal identity, identify with peers, and display an awareness of sexuality. Students at this stage are critical of adults and people in power. Their emotions and behaviors can be volatile.

Tables 7.1 through 7.4 present a total picture of the distinguishing characteristics of students in different age groups.

Learners With Special Needs

Students with special needs and disabilities are part of public education populations. In the 1980s,

Table 7.1 Distinguishing Characteristics of 3- to 5-year-olds

Learn by	Need to have	Relate to	Motor skills	Dance activities	Dance forms
• imitation • following • leading • manipulating • watching and listening • exploring and discovering the elements of the dance • using senses (taste, touch, hearing, seeing, feeling) • practicing respect for property and equipment	• structure in the class • repeated practice with following instructions • repetition of the activity • praise (positive reinforcement) • smiles • short activities balanced with rest periods • gross motor activity (arms and legs) • class work as a group	• lively music • stories and tales • bright colors • familiar objects • people and occupations • animals • machines • songs • chant songs • fantasy • pretending • props, ribbons, scarves, yarn balls	• locomotor movements: walk, run, jump, gallop • nonlocomotor movements: bend, stretch, twist, turn, jump in place, fall	• body awareness • spatial awareness • discovery and exploration dances • dance making (know that there is a beginning, middle, and end of a dance)	• creative movement and dance • preballet • tap dance • acrobatics

Table 7.2 Distinguishing Characteristics of 6- to 8-year-olds

Learn by	Need to have	Relate to	Motor skills	Dance activities	Dance forms
• imitation • watching • listening • exploring (elements of dance) • creating (improvising and short dance making) • working as a group, later in partners • problem solving through group activities in which children take turns	• short activities • rest periods • vigorous activities (gross motor) • body awareness • personal space • instructions for 3 to 4 steps • adult attention and approval • structure • prop manipulation • repetition • new challenges • short skill practice • self-discipline • cooperation	• animal movements • modes of transportation • environments: zoo, farm, forest, jungle, • variety of music • self-expression • movement exploration using dance vocabulary • performing steps • props	• horizontal and vertical jumps • hop • slide • skip • gallop • leap • directional movements and steps • physical fitness (leg strength, flexibility, and abdominal strength)	• nonlocomotor • locomotor • body awareness • spatial awareness • use of space • quality of movement • relationship of body to other objects • dance making • dance performing • dance appreciation	• creative movement and creative dance • preballet • tap dance • folk dance

Table 7.3 Distinguishing Characteristics of 9- to 14-year-olds

Learn by	Need to have	Relate to	Motor skills	Dance activities	Dance forms
• exploring • movement–language connections • executing • performing • creating • observing	• peer activities • listening and observation skills to contribute to activities • interest in topic • action, enthusiasm, and opportunities to participate fully • emotional outcomes met or will not participate • respect, fairness, and understanding of responsibility to feel mature • praise and reinforcement • problem-solving situations	• variety of learning activities • motivation to learn • dance making • developing and practicing skills and steps • variety of music and props • personal appearance • peers	• locomotor • nonlocomotor • training concepts (conditioning) • develop upper-body strength • agility, balance, and speed	• perfecting steps, dance patterns, and combinations • dance making in small groups • choreography (teacher and student) • performing dances • dance class for fun, enjoyment, personal development, or enrichment • dance as a career • dance as education • interest in attending performances and learning about dance • dance appreciation	• ballet • tap dance • modern dance • beginning jazz dance • folk dance • square dance • social dance

Table 7.4 Distinguishing Characteristics of 15- to 18-year-olds

Learn by	Need to have	Relate to	Motor skills	Dance activities	Dance forms
• observing • exploring • improvising • creating dances • executing and performing • discussing, evaluating, and developing aesthetics	• skills and creative problem-solving situations • emotional support • accommodation for differences in maturity and development • structure in class • encouragement and positive feedback • a part in decision making	• social activities • fun activities • activities that motivate them • peers more than teachers • music • topics/issues important to them as individuals or as a group	• all locomotor and nonlocomotor movement • all dance forms • games, team and individual sports	• perfecting steps, dance patterns, and combinations • participate in group activities • dance making in groups • choreography (teacher and student) • performing dances • dance class for fun, enjoyment, personal development, or enrichment • dance as a career • dance as education	• ballet • tap dance • modern dance • jazz dance • folk dance • square dance • social dance • contra dance • aerobic dance

(continued)

Table 7.4 (continued)

Learn by	Need to have	Relate to	Motor skills	Dance activities	Dance forms
				• interest in attending performances and learning about dance • dance appreciation	

students with special needs were sometimes a part of general education classrooms; this is known as *mainstreaming*. Since the 1990s, they have been fully included in classrooms, performing at different levels according to their abilities; this is called *inclusion*.

Teaching dance to physically, mentally, psychologically, and behaviorally challenged students is stimulating and fulfilling, but the teacher needs to be patient, kind, knowledgeable, creative, and sensitive to each person's needs. Students with special needs often are developmentally delayed. Individuals with special needs often have difficulty in generalizing a concept to other situations or experiences. Providing opportunities to apply these concepts helps the person find these connections. Conversely, the average person makes these corrections often without repeated opportunities.

For example, an individual learns the effort action, dab. A circle is predrawn on a sheet of paper. He is given a magic marker. He dabs with the marker on the inside, outside, and around the circle. Next in space, he dabs in front, back, to the sides, up, and down. He then dabs on various body parts to the rhythm of the music. Another experience is to say the word "dab" while dabbing a body part or naming the body parts while dabbing them. He performs a dab while moving in space to music and freezing in a shape. Then he dabs a body part in place and through space while performing the dab to music. Finally, he uses a prop, such as a yarn ball, and dabs it in space and on different body parts.

This progression is applicable to the other effort actions and with the manipulation of the other dance elements. Other props that are appropriate for the action or elements also can be used.

Special populations require structure, consistency, stability, and repetition in a dance class. You will need to overplan, make alternative plans, think on your feet, and be creative when preparing and implementing a dance lesson for people with special needs. The language and vocabulary must be clear, concise, and consistent. Too many new words often make instructions unclear and confusing. For more tips on constructing a dance class for special populations, see the following box.

Hints for Teaching Students With Special Needs

- Keep to your theme or concept.
- Make sure your activity relates to your theme or concept.
- Use clear, concise, and consistent language.
- Use signals or sign language.
- Have signals for stop and start.
- Create beginning and ending rituals.
- Create alternative and related activities if something does not work.
- Remember to overplan.
- Select appropriate music or accompaniment.
- Think creatively while you are teaching.
- Find ways to make the dance experience meaningful and fun for every person.
- Use props, chants, and songs when appropriate.
- Plan boundaries of physical space and behavior.
- Be consistent, firm, and caring.
- Be open to ideas, not manipulative.
- Keep conversation between specific people in the class to a minimum.
- Limit sharing and conversations until after class.

Children with special needs usually find dance activities fun, rewarding, and challenging. Dance also provides a physical, social, and mental outlet. Many times these students may be more attentive because opportunities in dance are often sparse or unavailable.

All of these considerations might seem overwhelming; but when you have the opportunity to teach children with special needs, you will find it a very rewarding and challenging experience. It is so exciting to see a student do something that he has never experienced. The look on his face makes the experience one you will never forget.

Cultural Diversity in Dance

We can gain insight, understanding, and an appreciation of others in our global community by learning about cultural diversity. We can learn the customs and mores of a specific society or group of people and the relationships among the arts of one or more cultures. Our world has expanded, so we must become aware of and able to accommodate cultural differences because students in our dance classes represent these differences.

Multiculturalism comprises ethnicity, gender, culture, and religion. Each of these factors must be taken into consideration within the educational setting. Fear and hatred often are spawned by prejudice, which is usually a result of lack of information. Knowing what is important within a culture helps in understanding it.

The arts bridge cultural gaps because they embody the customs and traditions of a culture. The arts give us an idea of what is important to a particular culture. Movement is universal, so everyone can learn the function and techniques of dance and participate in it. Through this participation, respect, enjoyment, and understanding are natural outcomes of the experience.

Effective dance teachers are aware of multicultural differences in the classroom and are respectful of students' cultural differences. For example, one of my dancers came from a Navajo reservation. A problem arose because she missed a dress rehearsal. When we talked about this situation, she did not look me in the eye. In my culture, if a person does not maintain eye contact during a conversation, it is a sign of disrespect. In the Native American culture, to look into the eyes of someone that is respected is a sign of disrespect. I was not aware of this when I talked with her. It would have helped me to understand her and communicate with her better had I been aware of the social etiquette of her culture. Table 7.5 identifies the unique characteristics of people in relation to their culture and its values.

Dance teachers who work in public schools must understand multiculturalism and support diversity. The school environment is a global community where you will teach; your students are your focus when you develop your class, teaching styles, and strategies.

Developing Psychosocial Behaviors in the Dance Class

Psychosocial development focuses on classroom behaviors and expectations to foster personal development and group development. *Psychosocial* means the interfacing of the psychological with the social attributes of a person. Each person is a product of heredity and environment; each dancer learns what is acceptable in her environment, the dance classroom.

The teacher establishes a classroom atmosphere by setting up the expectations for the class with ensuing positive student behaviors that are conducive to a learning environment. Dance is a disciplined art, and each dance form has specific classroom expectations. The teacher must be clear, consistent, and specific when creating her parameters of acceptable behavior within the classroom.

In the dance class, students begin showing good behavior by wearing proper attire, using appropriate etiquette, listening, and asking questions in the dance class. Movement is the goal in the dance class, so talking in class is unnecessary most of the time. Students are expected to concentrate so that they can learn dance and attain personal development.

Personal Development

The study of dance provides an outlet for personal development. A dancer's body image, self-esteem, and self-confidence are heightened through the study of dance. The abilities to attend class, follow instructions, remember the movement, and incorporate corrections are part of the

Table 7.5 Cultural Considerations

Cultural aspect	Anglo-American perspective	Culturally different perspectives
Family name	• Father's surname usually used	• Father's and mother's surnames are used • Family name may be written first, followed by the given name
Family	• Nuclear families • Marriage contract can be terminated • Smaller families • Partnership status • Child centered	• Extended families • Variety of family arrangements • Child subordinate to parents • Older children care for younger siblings • Authority delegated by maleness and age
Social distance	• Moderate distance for conversation • Value own space	• Close distance for conversation • Close physical contact welcomed
Age orientation	• Youth oriented • Young people think independently and make decisions	• Elders respected • Tradition important
Education	• Universal • Formal and technical • Social mobility and security • Pragmatic • Stress on verbal fluency and application to life • Teacher is an authority figure or surrogate parent • Emphasis on evaluation	• High aspiration • Ability to feel comfortable in mainstream society • Obstacle course to be surmounted • Learning and doing integrated • Stress affective and psychomotor skills
Individuality	• Individual shapes own destiny • Self-reliance important • Hero is a person of action • Self-disciplined	• Anonymity • Accepts group sanctions • Dependent on others—families and peers • Humility valued
Work achievement	• Material and spiritual acquisitions • Money is symbol for success, intelligence, and power	• Work to satisfy present need and physical survival • Follow ways of parents • Share group spirit of achievement • Cooperative • Acceptance of the status quo • Manual labor respected
Time	• Time consciousness • Governed by clock and calendar • Like routines • Future oriented • Value efficiency and speed	• Concerned with joys of the present • Little concept of wasting time • People control time • People are more important than time
Touching	• Acceptable in some situations	• May be a sign of acceptance in some groups; may be offensive for religious reasons or others
Smiling	• Shows pleasure and acceptance • Sign of disrespect if one smiles when being reprimanded	• Used to hide embarrassment, to show respect • Used to act as an interrupter in conversation
Eye contact	• Shows interest in what is being heard • Shows honesty and respect	• May be indirect in conversation • Indirect eye contact is a sign of respect

Cultural aspect	Anglo-American perspective	Culturally different perspectives
Work habits	• Independence preferable to dependence • Competitive	• Dependence sometimes acceptable • Cooperation preferred to competition • Hard work valued
Teacher's role	• Respected	• Highly respected • Honored
Teaching strategies	• Teacher-directed lessons and work are familiar	• Teacher-directed activities are familiar • Lecture method commonly used
Noise tolerance	• Silence preferred to noise	• Noise tolerance high • Noise shows enthusiasm • Noise preferable to silence
Waiting one's turn	• Not waiting for turn in line and in conversation is considered impolite	• May not form an orderly line • Getting service by getting the attention of the clerk may be acceptable • Interrupting in conversation may show enthusiasm and interest • Waiting may also show respect
Use of language	• Language used for direct communication • Concise and clear • Linear organization	• Language may be used to express feelings • Language may be used to show status within a group • Organization may be nonlinear, circular, or zigzag in nature
Listening style	• Listen to one person at a time	• Capable of listening to more than one person at a time even while talking
Discipline	• Consequences should fit the misconduct • Punishment is logical	• Punishment may be effective • Punishment may involve shaming • Punishment may cause "loss of face"

Chart compiled using information from a cultural chart by Yvonne Cadiz; a cultural chart by The Intercultural Development Research Association in Training Module III, "Recognizing Cultural Differences in the Classroom"; and a cultural chart by Louise Hart, Robin Matthes, and Verna Nelson in *Caring and Preparing to Meet the Needs of the Limited-English-Proficient Student* for Hillcrest Elementary School, Orange County Public Schools (John B. Martin, Principal).

student's development. Patience—with oneself and with others in the class—is another psychosocial aspect that serves the teaching and learning process well.

The teacher creates a learning environment that nurtures yet challenges students' personal development. Group and individual corrections are movement centered; a good teacher refrains from negative and unkind comments directed to the person. What the teacher says influences the students' development positively or negatively.

According to Taylor and Taylor in *Psychology of Dance* (1995), a dancer is able to change physically, technically, or mentally through the following three steps:

1. Awareness deals with a conscious recognition of what he is doing and a necessity to change. This is realistic self-assessment of strengths and weaknesses.
2. Control refers to actively taking steps to change through information and feedback about skills the dancer wants to change.
3. Repetition is necessary for change to take place. This requires a dancer's time andeffort. Consequently, through awareness, control, and repetition, positive change occurs.

Positive change is further reinforced by using the performance pyramid, devised by Taylor and Taylor (1995), which consists of four levels. The foundational level is motivation, and the second level is self-confidence. The third level deals with intensity level during performance, and the last, or top, level is the concentration or focus of the dancer. Performance profiling aligned with this concept is the next logical step.

Performance profiling (Butler 1989) is a graphic tool that identifies strengths and areas that need to be developed further. It gives a visual picture of how the person sees herself in relation to psychological, emotional, social, physical, and technical facts that affect her performance. These profiles give teachers and students insight into behavioral change. They can help evoke change, whether it be technically, physically, or mentally.

Crucial to the psychological, emotional, and social health of the dancer is attitude, which takes several forms. Attitude is a vital part of psychosocial development. An attitude is a person's state of mind when approaching a situation. Your attitude toward something affects what you say and do and how you feel about situations, and it can determine your success. The proper attitude determines your development as a dancer and as a dance educator.

An attitude of openness and self-evaluation is essential in this process of self-development. It is a constructive way to alter behavior (Butler 1989). In elementary school, children are taught to implement specific ways to socially interact; these work for other age groups too. An example is the stoplight symbol described in emotional intelligences. At first the stoplight is posted at the front of the classroom, then the student internalizes it as a mental image that he uses when assessing a situation and determining his reaction to it.

Some of the social graces of dance class are based on respect for the teacher, students, and the subject matter. If the teacher does something different, try to incorporate it into your movement, as long as it doesn't harm you. In this case, you may learn something even if you do not agree with the teacher. Politeness is a skill as a means of showing respect between teacher and student. The dance teacher is responsible for positively motivating and creating appropriate challenges to enhance students' psychosocial attributes as a member of the class.

Group Development

Group development in a dance class varies depending on the dance form. Some dance forms (such as creative dance and improvisation, social, folk, square, and contra dance) require more interpersonal activities than other forms. In these forms members of the group use the personal and group social skills of participation, cooperation, teamwork, and trust activities.

Group-centered dance forms require the teacher to guide the group in an organized and logical manner. Within those individual-centered dance forms, group development occurs in several ways. The individuals in the group often perform in unison or as an ensemble such as in a contra, folk, social, or square dance. Performing requires the subtle give-and-take to make it synchronized in movement, timing, and feeling. The corps de ballet moving as one person or the high energy of a kick line communicates the power of ensemble dancing to the audience.

Improvisation and contact improvisation in modern dance, creative movement, and choreography are common group-development tactics. The spontaneous movement requires each person to be in tune with the energy and timing of the other individuals in the group. The continual interplay among the dancers, who see an opportunity and explore it in movement within the parameters given to the group, is fascinating to be a part of and to watch. The group practices so that each dancer becomes sensitive to the other dancers' movement responses; use of energy, weight, timing; and approach to the solution to the movement problem. Viewing this collaborative effort among a group that has been together for a long time is viewing a work of art unfold before your eyes.

Behavior, personal development, and group development are integral to the learning environment. Each school environment is unique, though all share some characteristics. Dance is taught in a variety of settings with as many or more purposes. An important aspect of any setting is the dance teacher's professional identity.

Understanding Dance and the Dance Teacher in Public Education

Dance forms offer participation for learners from preschool through high school. Dance in public education is taught and performed in many settings: for example, the theatre, the dance studio, and the all-purpose room. The dance teacher is viewed as a professional educator within the school environment and the community.

The dance teacher preparing in the dance studio.

Dance performance in all-purpose room in elementary school.

Dance in Public Education

In preschool, learners focus on movement exploration, dramatic play, and creative movement experiences. Beginning in kindergarten and progressing through the primary grades, dance instruction centers on rhythms, creative movement and dance, and folk dance. In upper elementary school, creative dance expands to modern dance. Jazz dance, square dance, and social dance are other forms appropriate for upper elementary students.

In middle school, modern and jazz dance, social, square, and folk dances continue to be choices in dance. These same options form the basis for the high school dance offerings with the addition of ballet, tap dance, and aerobic dance. Usually the dance courses available reflect the training and experience of the dance teacher. Elementary, middle, and high schools that are arts magnet schools allocate faculty lines to instruction in the arts. These schools may be part of a network of schools that have similar missions. Dance in public schools is often part of a greater network of dance education in the community.

Dance Teachers As Education Professionals

In K-12 education settings, dance teachers come from a variety of backgrounds that include dance, physical education, other arts specialties, and classroom teaching. Dance artists and private studio teachers often augment dance education programs in public schools.

The dance teacher is a role model for students and creates an identity as a professional educator. The teacher selects and wears attire suitable to the dance form and setting. If the dance teacher chooses to wear clothing other than dance attire for teaching, then he should specify the dress requirements for students. Tights and a leotard are not applicable in all settings, such as the elementary school. Regardless of the dance form or setting, the teacher should wear clean, suitable clothing and shoes.

Professional dance educators dress in dance clothes for most dance classes. For classes that do not require demonstration, the dance educator wears street clothes. It is considered unprofessional to appear in tights, leotard, or other dance clothing in the halls or offices of schools. Keep cover-up clothing in your office if you have to appear outside the dance studio. Appropriate attire conveys a professional identity.

Proper conduct is another way to convey professionalism. As a professional educator, a dance teacher's behavior is evident in the classroom, student relations, choreography, research, and professional organizations. At the heart of the profession are your ethics as a dance teacher. In the teaching environment, education organization, community, and profession, you serve as a resource, a liaison with parents and students, a colleague with other faculty, a member of a school staff, a member of the community, and a member of your profession.

You must be prepared to step into various roles as a dance teacher. If you have psychological problems or biases that are unhealthy or unprofessional, you should examine them. Most of all, you cannot bring these problems into the classroom or into interactions with students and other professionals. This is a personal and professional journey that you must undertake to become a part of a school and community.

Characterizing the Community

Dance in various sectors of the community can foster relationships, each supporting the other and the community. Professional dance companies do residencies in the schools. Universities and colleges provide outreach programs and performances for public school students. Community and arts education organizations offer grant opportunities for the various sectors of dance in the community. All of these dance education entities contribute to making a dance community. Within the community various educational institutions may provide suitable facilities, outreach programming, continuing education opportunities, and other support systems for dance programs in the public schools. Community and college libraries provide resources for dance teachers in public schools. In the community, these educational institutions strive to activate bonds between one another to support dance and the arts in the settings of the community.

The type, amount, and intensity of dance instruction or programming directly relate to the organization, its administration, and support of the program. The organization in turn is part of the community in which it exists. When proposing or developing a dance instruction unit or program, one must define the demographics, ethnic diversity, educational institutions, and leisure features of the community. Dance in the public schools must connect with these features to be meaningful for the participants and supported by the organization and the community at large.

Demographics of the Community

Demographics of a community include the location of the community and its social, economic, and political systems. Demographic research provides important background information from which decisions can be made about a specific type of dance program that aims for success in a community.

Know your community, the surrounding area, and the region of the country. The United States has state and regional differences that are reflected through each community. Ascertain the major industries in the community and the area and the percentage of people that are employed in these industries. Beyond the facts about economic and financial aspects of the community, other information about the community often comes with working and living in the community.

When researching the community, consider how well it supports the arts, especially dance. How many dance organizations exist in the community? What is their focus—performance, education, physical fitness? Analyze and then create a profile of the community based on demographic information before embarking on the next step of developing a school-based dance program. The people of the community are your key factor in making decisions about the type of dance program that will be supported in the community.

Diversity of the Community

The ethnic, religious, social, and economic diversity of the community directly influence the type of arts programming available. Awareness of the ethnic and religious groups that make up the community will provide information about the importance of dance as a cultural or personal choice. The socioeconomic makeup of the community can determine the support and roles dance can have in the community. Nurturing all of these aspects can yield a rich foundation for dance to develop and enhance the community's values.

Identifying Values in the Community

Community has many meanings: a school community, a neighborhood community, a city or town, and the global community of which we are all a part. The ideas and values that the community supports, tolerates, and instills are the strands that form its culture. A community value system comprises values from different segments that make up the community. Community value systems are reflected in the following ways:

- They concentrate on history and traditions.
- They expand educational experiences that enhance the quality of life of the people in the community.
- They strive for excellence in the individual as well as the group to meet certain expectations set by society today.
- They emphasize the process, not the product.
- They take a holistic, global approach. The value system considers the body, mind, and spirit stemming from the individual and expands it to include the community, state, and country.

These boundaries of various value systems may not be clearly defined. You may see different value strands in the community, and you must decide the more salient features of the community. For example, a community may hold on to what they consider the best of their past while trying to implement innovations that will enhance the future of the community.

Gaining awareness of community values and its overall culture provides the basis for making decisions about dance. As dance educators we need to be aware of our community values to make dance a worthwhile and viable option for participation.

Traditions

If a community treasures its past, it fosters traditions while conservatively broadening its horizons. To accomplish or enhance this situation, dance educators must find opportunities to educate people about how the forefathers of the community and the nation valued dance as a social, physical, artistic, and recreational outlet. Annual events, traditions, and art forms are part of a community value system imbued with a history. If the community has had social dance events, recreational dance groups, a civic ballet, or modern dance performing group, these activities have gained community support. Participation and support of traditions continue the historical and cultural values of the community.

Educational Opportunities

If people in the community want their children to participate in arts education, then dance has a place as a recreational or educational outlet. People in the community may voice these desires as, "I never was able to take dance lessons" or "I always wanted to go see a ballet but never had the opportunity." These situations present opportunities for people to participate in dance.

To instill the importance of dance as an educational opportunity, develop community awareness of the value of dance in the development of the individual. These opportunities occur through education in the community. An emphasis on providing a variety of opportunities for the students to dance in educational and community settings is vital to this aspect of the value system.

Individual Accomplishment

The familiar saying of "Be all you can be" is another community value. This value centers on the individual and what he or she accomplishes. This type of community value provides opportunities for the person to strive for excellence. The arts are part of communication, ritual, community life, creativity, values, mores, and self-expression. Dance provides a physical, psychological, social, and creative outlet. Discipline, technique, social interaction, self-esteem, and self-image are lifelong skills that dancers use in any discipline. Dance also instills a sense of challenge, or competition, with the self and with others. The focus of educational and community programs for dance is on personal and professional excellence.

Process Versus Product Values

Communities that value the dance process rather than the dance product give students opportunities to expand their innate abilities. The process focuses on the development and creative aspects of a work or skills; the product in dance is a performance, which is only a small part of the entire process. The formulation of an idea; the discovery, selection, and creation of movements into a dance; and the teaching and rehearsing of the dance are a part of the process for creating a dance. The selection of space and technical aspects of the performance, the rehearsing, and the coaching of the dance are essential for the ultimate event, the performance.

In process value orientation, all the steps leading to the performance are important. This value orientation supports discipline and organization, selection of an idea and its development, creation of movement into a dance, skills to teach the movement to the dancer, and the ability to produce an artful presentation. These dance experiences feed the creative process and creative outlet.

This focus on process is further heightened through the cultivation of the creative process. Dance as an outlet for creativity gives students problem-solving experiences in finding alternative solutions and opportunities for success. This type of dance program emphasizes that both students and teachers make dances.

Global Values

The last value orientation of a community connects the entire living world or takes a holistic approach to life. It begins with the individual and connects the person with the community, state, country, and global world. In this value system everyone affects everyone else's body, mind, and spirit as well as every living thing on this planet. It recognizes living in the moment but also knowing that a chain reaction occurs with every living thing. In this value orientation, the individual is important but is also attuned to the world, making it a better place. In dance, the individual expresses and creates and gives himself a physical, psychological, and spiritual outlet for self-expression. Also, the interaction with teachers, other dancers, technicians, other artists, and audiences promotes an understanding of ideas. This value shares the process and product of a dance work with others and the ultimate art product itself with others.

In the global community value many movement and dance possibilities exist. These include classes in yoga, meditation, improvisation, somatic techniques (Bartinieff Fundamentals, Ideokinesis, Feldenkrais Method) and others, such as tai chi, aikido, and other martial arts. Performance in dance and other movement forms incorporates the creative process. Nurtured by the global value, the arts are deemed vital for survival of everyone and everything on our planet.

These value systems affect *whom* you teach and *where* you teach and have important relationships to *why* we teach dance, which in turn are linked to *what* we teach. These connections have become more apparent because of the development of arts education standards. The standards support *why* we teach dance and recognize dance as a viable discipline and content area identified for study with meaningful implications for learning.

Summary

To effectively teach in public school settings, you must know the general characteristics of learners from preschool through high school and students with special needs. To understand the psychosocial aspects within a dance class, become aware of classroom behaviors to develop appropriate and realistic expectations for students. In dance classes many opportunities for personal and group development exist.

Knowing about the public education environment and its connection to the community is essential for developing a dance program. Understand your professional identity as a dance teacher in the school and community. Be aware of the characteristics of the community; identify its cultural diversity and values to develop appropriate learning experiences and select dance forms appropriate for your students.

References

Butler, R.J. 1989. Psychological preparation of Olympic boxers. In *The psychology of sport: Theory and practice,* edited by J. Kremer and W. Crawford, 74-84. Leicester, England: British Psychological Society.

National Standards for Arts Education. Music Educators National Conference. Reston, VA, 1994.

Taylor, J., and C. Taylor. 1995. *Psychology of dance.* Champaign, IL: Human Kinetics.

It's Your Turn

1. Observe learners of two different ages in a dance class. Fill out the observation form (form 3.1 on page 41) and write a one-page comparison using examples to support your work.
2. Research both your community and school to identify important values and demographic data. Compile this research into a short report; assess whether the environment is supportive for dance.

CHAPTER

8

Categorizing Dance Forms and Their Artistic Demands

Chapter Objectives

By the end of this chapter, you should be able to do the following:

- Understand how people acquire dance content knowledge.
- Know the unique characteristics of four dance form categories.
- Understand how the movement principles relate to dancing.
- Relate the choreographic principles to dance making.
- Connect the aesthetic principles to dance appreciation.
- Understand the artistic impact of various styles, production, and performance attributes.

Dance in public schools encompasses a broad range of dance forms. This chapter will help you understand the four dance form categories and the characteristics of each form so that you can select appropriate dance forms for your teaching setting. Likewise, comprehending movement, choreographic, and aesthetic principles and how they relate to each dance form provides the foundation for dancing, dance making, and dance appreciation in the dance class. Acquiring content knowledge of dance forms gives you the means to increase and support your development as a dance teacher.

Subject matter, or dance content knowledge, is obtained through an expert system involving a question-and-answer format that gathers knowledge from books, videos, films, periodicals, and the Internet. Other ways of gaining information include interviews and surveys of expert dance teachers who teach different dance forms.

Gathering Content Information to Teach Dance

The process of gaining knowledge is known as the knowledge acquisition technique (Gaines 1987). In this technique, a person who is trained in knowledge acquisition (or you, the dance teacher) investigates experts' claims about a certain topic. This information is applied to a knowledge structure of dance categories. The knowledge is obtained through four methods: text analysis, structured interviews, stimulated recall, and analogical derivation. Knowledge integration and validation become the end products of these methods (Vickers 1990). The most common method is access of resources usually available in a library.

Studying Media Materials

Media materials such as books, manuals, films, videos, software, and Internet sites created by dance experts become the sources for text analysis. After analyzing these materials, the teacher uses them as references to support the dance content used in the classroom. Awareness of knowledge developed by dance experts is essential to the process of becoming a master teacher. The next method of acquiring knowledge involves interviews with expert teachers.

Interviewing the Teacher

New professionals in the field of dance find that structured interviews aid in the process of compiling and analyzing dance content. In this type of interview the dance expert or master teacher answers a series of prepared questions. The interviewer (a student or new teacher) makes an audiotape of the responses, which is analyzed and interpreted. After gathering this information from the interview, the teacher uses protocol analysis. This type of analysis classifies, sorts, and defines the underlying principles of dance content that enable dance experts to solve problems within the class. The teacher compiles and organizes this collected information in a way that benefits her teaching. Another method of information gathering involves viewing videotaped classes of expert teachers.

Videotaping the Expert Teacher

When a dance teacher reviews and analyzes a videotape he made of his teaching of a dance class, he uses the stimulated recall technique. The new or prospective dance teacher poses questions to the expert teacher that are similar to those used in the interview process. The video becomes the basis for discussion of the instructor's teaching behaviors in the class.

Often, a master teacher is unaware of his teaching methods because the methods are innate to the process and because he may not have been asked to articulate his methods. After viewing his teaching behaviors, the teacher becomes aware of behaviors that are part of his teaching process, and he becomes more insightful and articulate about what and how he teaches.

Self-analysis optimizes the teacher's consciousness during class and stimulates his ongoing teaching and learning process. Reflecting on teaching behavior choices, the expert teacher refines his teaching process that in turn may expand to development of new methodologies.

Videotapes of dance performances and technique classes taught by expert teachers are readily available. Watching and analyzing videotapes may inspire you to introduce new material, alternative techniques, or behaviors not previously considered. Videotaped performances provide access to the techniques and significant works of dance literature by choreographers and performers throughout the world. Broadening your knowledge of dance requires the study of different dance forms.

Survey of Different Dance Classes

A survey of different dance classes yields a model from which dance content is derived using analogy. This knowledge acquisition technique of analogical derivation selects a concept, such as flexibility, then creates appropriate exercises and combinations based on various sources. For example, a dance instructor teaches a stretch class. The emphasis is on flexibility, or acquiring a full range of movement (ROM), around a joint. The teacher focuses on the muscles and joints of the spine (cervical, thoracic, lumbar, sacrum), shoulders, elbows, hips, ankles, and wrists. Then she devises a class using various flexibility exercises that progress through the body from head to toe. The exercises use passive, static, ballistic, and proprioceptive neuromuscular facilitation (PNF) stretches to promote flexibility throughout the body. The instructor reminds the students to remember their inflexible areas so that they can work on these problem areas outside of class.

Using knowledge acquisition techniques, the new teacher develops awareness and increases dance content knowledge. Personal research leads to exploring other areas and cross-disciplines for related information that supports and expands the dance content. The teacher's ultimate goals for using the knowledge acquisition techniques are integrating and validating new knowledge. Implementing and practicing these techniques until they become second nature are the means by which a teacher advances to the expert level.

Becoming an Expert Teacher

It takes time to become an expert teacher. The veteran and the new teacher have different degrees of experience, proficiency, and personal development. Less-experienced teachers who can identify experts' teaching behaviors will have opportunities to nurture their skills so that they can become better teachers.

Expert dance teachers tend to chunk, or clump, knowledge or content; they synthesize knowledge from a variety of sources for easy access. They also are able to think and plan globally with respect to a prospective course and specific lessons yet focus on details, such as one student's problems, within one class.

The dance expert asks questions about the parameters that affect the teaching situation, such as facilities and equipment. The expert solicits information about students, class size, and technique levels. Using this information, she builds a movement profile of the learners and the class. The dance expert poses questions to students in the class as a way to transfer responsibility for learning to the student. Self-analysis is an important function that the dance educator uses to find new ways to explain a concept or a step to students. The dance expert continues an internal dialogue, which causes reflective assessment of the teaching process.

Dance experts create progressions of specific exercises that are natural, logical, efficient, and effective. They tend to have a hierarchical approach to teaching a certain exercise. All dance experts may not teach the same in terms of progression, approach, and content, but they have similar methods. Experts plan classes and courses well but also create alternative options for learners.

Expert teachers know how to teach to the level of the student (beginning, intermediate, and advanced). Their description and images are clear, diverse, and appropriate. Their teaching strategies are as individualized and varied as the learners in the class. They look at their class as a group of individual students, each with unique needs and abilities.

Overpreparation is a characteristic of expert dance instructors. They prepare well ahead of classes and foresee potential problems so that they are more flexible when problems arise. Before and after class, expert teachers analyze and keep records of what they have taught and how successful it was, and they keep track of alternative ways they have identified to approach a specific movement task.

Expert teachers use class time efficiently and effectively. They understand when the class as a whole is ready to move on to new material. Their teaching of dance content shifts forward and back to review and refine the work. If something is not working, they change and go on to something else during that class. The expert teacher provides individual challenges and options for students within the class to ensure success and progress. Sometimes, when asked a question about how she specifically teaches something or manages a situation, she must think before answering.

An expert teacher's management skills are often not apparent in the class unless it is necessary for them to surface. The effective instructor has insightful teaching skills that she often implements unconsciously and automatically that she must think about before she can articulate them. The expert teacher is confident and at ease with the dance content and its implementation so that she can focus on the students and observe them in the learning process.

New teachers are often overwhelmed by the entire teaching situation: the students, the content, and the management of the class. In contrast to expert teachers, new teachers underplan for a class. Often they overlook the necessity of prior thought and written planning. They often are shy and resistant to ask questions about facilities, equipment, students, and their level of study.

As a group, new teachers have few similarities among themselves when selecting and implementing content. New teachers have difficulty in selecting material that can be grouped together or developing a natural progression of steps appropriate for the level of the students' learning. Frequently they get lost in the dance content so that their presentation of content and progression are erratic. In the teaching process, the new teacher neglects to break down the content or cue it in a meaningful way for the students. After a class, they forget to analyze their teaching or record what worked and what did not work. They often neglect to engage in problem-solving approaches or develop alternatives for future classes.

New teachers find it difficult to be flexible or adapt dance content and are unable to foresee problems that may arise. They focus on the dance and less on observing whether the students understand the movement and can execute it successfully. If you asked several new teachers what they would teach in a beginning class, few would give the same answers. Likewise, new teachers have difficulty distinguishing between beginning, intermediate, and advanced content. New teachers who are prepared will be motivated and challenged to take the steps to become expert teachers and reap the inherent rewards.

One of the first steps in preparing to teach is to understand and select the dance forms appropriate for your students. To make these important choices, review the dance forms and their categories.

Identifying Characteristics of Dance Forms

Although dance has evolved into many forms, subforms, and hybrid forms, the dance forms selected for this book are those that are used in the public school environment from preschool through high school. These 10 dance forms are as follows:

1. Creative movement and creative dance
2. Folk dance
3. Square dance
4. Contra dance
5. Social dance
6. Ballet
7. Modern dance

8. Jazz dance
9. Tap dance
10. Aerobic dance (dance fitness)

Each of the dance forms contributes to dance as a performing art or recreational or fitness activity.

The 10 dance forms fit into 4 dance form categories:

1. Creative movement and creative dance
2. Recreational dance
3. Concert dance
4. Aerobic dance (dance fitness)

Each dance form category has distinct features (see table 8.1). Understanding these features will give you insight into their value and place within the curriculum.

By knowing the four dance form categories and their characteristics, the teacher can select dance forms appropriate for the learner and the environment. The next step is to study the format for a dance class for each category.

Table 8.1 The Four Dance Form Categories

Dance form category	Unique features	Dance forms
Creative movement and creative dance	• Uses basic and everyday movements, elements, and concepts in movement studies and dances. • Provides experience with the elements and choreographic structures of dance; permits learners to creatively discover, explore, compose, and refine their movement and dance works. • Is a support system for improvisation, other arts disciplines, and physical education. • Introduces learners to dance and becomes a natural means for studying the included dance forms.	• Modern dance • Jazz dance • Other dance forms
Recreational	• Provides leisure-time activities that are social in nature. • Contra and square dance have less intricate steps and footwork but use more intricate formations and figures. • Contra and squre dance use a caller to direct the dancers. • Contra and square dance originated in the British Isles, England, Scotland, and Ireland. When these forms were introduced to the United States, they evolved and were adapted to American culture. • Folk dance uses a variety of steps, more than contra and square dance. Folk dances incorporate many partner positions. The quality of the dance depends on steps, leading and following, and executing specific dances and dance styles. These dances and dance styles mirror specific cultures and eras.	• Folk dance • Contra dance • Square dance • Social dance
Concert	• The dance class format encases the exercises, steps, and combinations. • The focus is learning exercises that are the components of steps that in turn become part of combinations. The combinations are performed either adagio (slowly with continuous, fluid movement) or allegro (quickly either with small, sharp movements or with large movements that have long moments in the air). • Ballet, jazz, and tap dance forms are step driven. Jazz and tap dance focus on isolation of body parts. • Modern, jazz, and tap dance forms are indigenous to American culture. • Ballet has adapted to capture the 20th-century American spirit, becoming modern ballet, which has enabled it to convey personal choreographic statements.	• Ballet • Modern dance • Jazz • Tap dance

(continued)

Table 8.1 *(continued)*

Dance form category	Unique features	Dance forms
	• Modern dance began as creative expression through movement. It became codified as personal techniques developed; as a result it crystallized into a modern dance genre. • A response to codified modern dance was the postmodern era, a return to simplicity of movement that shed the traditional forms and techniques to find new and authentic ways to express contemporary themes by using improvisation and contact improvisation.	
Dance fitness	• Focuses on developing cardiovascular endurance, flexibility, and muscular strength. • An outgrowth of the aerobic fitness movement. • Often uses line dance steps that are simple, repetitive, and fun. • Point of aerobic dance is to participate in a lifelong activity. • Can be executed at a low, medium, or high impact level.	• Aerobic dance

Understanding the Format of the Dance Class

The components that make up the format of concert, creative, recreational, and aerobic dance classes are slightly different; but they do contain commonalities, such as the warm-up, exercises, activities and steps, combinations and dances, and cool-down (or closing).

The warm-up is the first part of the dance class. It prepares the dancer physiologically for movement. The warm-up may have different names, such as pre-barre, barre, strengthening, flexibility, and conditioning exercises. The warm-up prepares the muscles and joints to move, and it raises the core temperature of the muscles. Warming up the body to dance is important, but its role is a preface to the focus of the class.

The exercises, activities, combinations, and dances are the components of the dance class. Each of these components is specific to the dance form being taught. In general, exercises include skills, steps, and figures that the dancer learns and practices to gain technique, competency, and proficiency to execute the dance form. In some dance forms it is difficult to ascertain where the warm-up ends and the "body" of the class begins. Many exercises relate generally to dance as well as specifically to body parts and dance forms.

The cool-down, or closing, is the final segment of the class. The cool-down allows the dancer to slow down physiologically and return his breathing and heart rate to normal. Sometimes this does not happen in a dance class. The cool-down is recommended both as a physiologically and psychologically sound choice for the final part of a dance class. In academic situations, the student should also mentally return to a neutral place. Dancing is an exhilarating physical and mental activity, but students must shift gears from dance class to the next class. A cool-down facilitates this process. The generic format of a class reflects the characteristics, traditions, and teaching methods used in the dance form.

Creative Movement and Creative Dance Class Format

Creative movement and creative dance are distinguished by the purpose of the class, and often this is not a distinct difference. In creative movement, the general focus of the class is exploration and understanding of the elements of movement (space, time, and force). In creative dance, the children explore elements of movement that are structured with a beginning, middle, and end. This structure may then expand into a choreographic form thereby extending creative movement into creative dance.

Exercises and activities are repeated in creative movement and creative dance classes to reinforce the movement or serve as a ritual. These repetitive components are foundational skills and provide reassuring and recurring activities that children expect and enjoy. Children will remind you

Shapes in space in creative dance.

of these activities if you forget them! Dance activity rituals act as a stabilizing and centering force that assists in a teacher's control of the class. Traditional rituals include entering the class, forming a circle, taking turns executing the movement, and doing activities to end the class. You will discover and invent other rituals as you teach.

The creative dance class has a warm-up followed by activities. The individual activities often lead into a culminating activity, after which the class comes to a close (see table 8.2).

Recreational Dance Class Format

The format of recreational dance classes differs from that of concert and creative dance classes. The specific parts of social, square, folk, and contra dance classes are less defined (see table 8.3). Some recreational dances are often aerobic in nature. After each folk dance, the dancers pause to listen to the music or mark the steps of either the previous or the next dance. The dancers may take their pulses to determine whether they are working in their heart rate range and obtaining a training effect. In most recreational dance classes, the focus is on enjoying dancing.

Concert Dance Class Format

Concert dance forms have similar class formats that include the warm-up, exercises and

Table 8.2 Dance Class Format for Creative Movement and Dance

General features	Warm-up	Activities	Cool-down and closing	Characteristics
• General dance space can be defined by tape or poly spots • General space is the space through which the dancers move • Personal space • Personal space: carpet square, tape on floor, or laminated paper with child's name • Circle • Stand in lines	• Exercises to increase body awareness, flexibility, strength • Introduction of elements and concepts used in the class • Performed while lying on the floor, sitting in tailor position, kneeling, standing • Use of analogies to explore movement	• Exploration of elements (space, time, and force) • Teacher guides children through activity by cueing, posing questions, giving statements • Students create movement sequences with beginning, middle, and end • Student creates dances alone or in a small group • Students observe others dancing and discuss what is observed	• Free dance: time to explore movement or review key elements and concepts from the day's lesson • Relaxation exercises • Perform ritual or other closing activity to review elements and concepts of the lesson	• Explores and expands foundational movement vocabulary and concepts • Communicates feelings • Enhances creativity and decision making and promotes high-level thinking skills

Table 8.3 Dance Class Format for Recreational Dance Forms

Warm-up	Exercises, figures, combinations, and dances	Cool-down	Characteristics
• Gain flexibility of feet and legs • Execute steps that will be performed in the dances during the class • Review previously learned dances, simple to complex	• Learn steps, figures, partnering that constitute practice clusters • Connect practice clusters into larger blocks into a dance • Listen to music and mark the dance • Balance class with slow-, moderate-, fast-tempo dances	• Review mark, or walk through dances	• Folk, square, contra, and social dance are aerobic in nature; take pulse to obtain heart rate • Correct execution of steps, figures • Attention to style and quality of dance
Folk dance	• Footwork and steps • Formation and partner holds		• Dances from all over the world
Square dance	• Review figures and formations		• Figures • Calling
Contra dance	• Review figures, formations, and sets		• Longways formation • Hey (figure) • Sets: perfect and imperfect • Regional styles of music and performance
Social dance	• Footwork, steps • Partnering holds; leading and following		• Footwork • Partnering techniques • Styling • American dances • Latin dances

Taking the first steps in the swing.

Partner lifts in modern dance.

combinations, then the cool-down or closing of the class.

The warm-up is specific to the dance form. The teacher knows the exercises and steps, and she creates the combinations and dances. These combinations can be a series of steps linked together (four or more steps combined), which create a movement phrase. As dancers gain technical skills, the combinations contain more elements with increased difficulty, including partner lifts; more complex musicality; and development of artistry. Combinations become the basis of extended combinations and dances

The cool-down or closing is the final part of the concert dance class. After the cool-down or close, the students applaud the teacher and the accompanist for the class. If this is a master class given by a master teacher or guest artist, students wait until the applause is complete and then approach the teacher to thank him for the class.

The specific format for the concert dance class is identified in table 8.4.

Table 8.4 Dance Class Format for Concert Dance Forms

Dance form	Warm-up	Exercises, steps, and combinations	Cool-down and closing	Characteristics
Ballet	• Pre-barre warm-up • Barre exercises	• Barre exercises • Center steps and combinations relate to barre • Center structure: center barre, adagio, sautés, petit allegro, grand allegro	• Révérence (bow and curtsy) • Stretching at the barre or on the floor	• Turnout • Codified technique • Principles and rules
Modern and jazz dance	• Exercises lying on the floor, sitting, standing, and moving	• Flexible structure for exercises and technique interchangeable within the first part of the class • Steps, combinations, technique, and studies performed in the center or across the floor	• Roll-downs and stretches • Bring the body and breathing back to a neutral place	Modern dance • Parallel and turnout of legs and feet • Pointed and flexed feet • Contraction and alignment • Personal and codified techniques and styles Jazz • Body isolations • Polyrhythms • Adopted steps and styles from other dance forms and periods

(continued)

Table 8.4 (continued)

Dance form	Warm-up	Exercises, steps, and combinations	Cool-down and closing	Characteristics
Tap dance	• Flexibility exercises for feet, ankles, and legs • At the barre, in a chair, and in the center	• Steps and combinations performed in center • Locomotor steps move across the floor • Combinations become longer and more difficult with increased rhythmic complexity	• A final combination, extended combination, or dance • General stretching on the floor, at the barre, splits	• Clear tap sounds • Flexibility and ease of movement • Incorporation of styles

Aerobic Dance (Dance Fitness) Class Format

Aerobic dance focuses on developing cardiovascular and muscular endurance and flexibility. Participants monitor their heart rates during exercise to determine whether the exercise produces a training effect and whether they are working in their target heart rate range. Students monitor their heart rates at least three times throughout the class. The aerobic dance class format includes a warm-up and flexibility exercise, strengthening exercises, then aerobic dancing. The class ends with a cool-down (see table 8.5).

- **Warm-up and flexibility exercises:** The aerobic dance class begins with a head-to-toe warm-up. Often more than one body part is used at once during the exercises.
- **Strengthening exercises:** This portion of the class focuses on exercises for the upper body (push-ups), abdomen (modified crunches), back (pelvis lift from the floor), and legs (leg lifts, lunges).
- **Aerobic dancing:** These dance forms use simple, repeatable dance steps and combinations that later become line dances. This section of the class focuses on developing cardiovascular endurance.
- **Cool-down:** The movements slow down and segue from the dances to flexibility and strengthening exercises in this part of the class. These exercises stretch and strengthen the upper body, abdomen, arms, and legs. The heart rate slows during the cool-down. Where you teach the strength and flexibility exercises in the class depends upon how you were trained to teach.

In concert, recreational, aerobic, and creative dance forms, each part of the dance class supports the other parts to create a balanced class that will in turn develop a balanced dancer. In some of the dance forms, the components of the class are based on tradition. However, dance science interjected into the dance class reinforces dance as a viable outlet for training the body. Dance connects with other arts and disciplines, which give dance and its collaborating subject a new view and a new way for children to access learning.

Dance and Other Disciplines

Dance in arts education expands beyond its discipline to develop interrelationships with other arts that may contribute to the dance class. One of the most obvious collaborations for dance is music. The portrayal of emotion through dance movement merges with drama. In a performance, other visual arts media (costume design, lighting, and set design) interact with dance. In the dance itself, the spatial design of the dance manifests as an abstract moving design in the space.

Another feature of the dance class, more often seen in creative movement and dance, is integration with other disciplines in the curriculum. Although this educational technique has been associated with creative movement and creative dance, it can be implemented into other dance forms. Recreational dance forms offer many op-

Aerobic dance gives students an opportunity to gain flexibility.

Table 8.5 Dance Class Format for Aerobic Dance (Fitness)

Warm-up	Strengthening exercises	Aerobic dance section	Cool-down	Characteristics
• Warm and prepare the body to move using a head-to-toe warm-up • Use flexibility exercises for the back, legs, and other parts of the body	• Use strengthening exercises for the abdomen, upper-arms, legs, and back	• Learn dance steps and use them in a line dance • Maintain the heart rate range for 20 minutes	• Gradually slow down the speed of the movement • Lower the heart rate using flexibility and strengthening exercises for the arms, legs, abdomen, and back	• Monitor heart rate throughout the class • Work within the heart rate range • Move continuously throughout the class • Repeat steps that are simple and easy • Face different walls during the line dances

portunities for dancers to develop integrated and multicultural experiences. These forms easily relate with the disciplines of social studies and geography, foreign language, and language arts. Integrating dance with other subjects creates new ways of looking at the world outside of the dance class.

The class format gives the teacher an outline of areas of study to be included when developing a complete and balanced class. The ingredients for each section of the class come from personal experiences, knowledge acquisition, and dance cross-disciplinary categories. The teacher must know and apply principles that pertain to all dance forms.

Utilizing Principles of the Dance Form

The principles of a dance form encompass movement, choreography, and aesthetic aspects of dance. Collectively these principles provide important criteria that permeate the content of each dance form and interweave into all dance forms and categories. The principles together create a synergy of the concepts that support the dance form; individually, they emphasize an aspect of the content specific to a dance form. Although these principles work together, we discuss each separately. The first group of principles is movement principles.

Movement Principles

Movement principles are laws of physical movement that can be applied to every dance form. Certain principles may be more appropriate for some dance forms than for others. The movement principles are alignment (which anchors the principles), turnout, stance, distribution of weight, transfer of weight, counterpull, squareness, pull-up (lift), aplomb, counterbalance, and balance (which connects to each of the principles) (see figure 8.1).

- *Alignment* is the correct posture of the entire body. With the body in alignment, the dancer stands and moves efficiently and effectively.
- *Turnout* is the rotation of the legs from the hip joints. This principle is important in many theatrical dance forms; it is a primary feature of ballet.
- *Stance* refers to the dancer's position on one or both feet. In movement, stance means changing from one foot position to the other on the floor.
- *Distribution of weight* is vital to alignment. This relates to weight placement on the feet or foot in positions from full foot to full point. In full-foot position, the weight is distributed over the toes and the area from the first to fifth metatarsals to the heel, which form a triangle. In a balance on three-quarter relevé, the weight is distributed on the metatarsals. On the full point, the entire weight of the body balances on the tips of the toes.
- *Transfer of weight* is the shift of weight from two feet to one foot, or from one foot to two feet, or from one foot to the other foot. This includes shifting weight that is equally distributed between both feet to one foot.
- *Counterpull* is a movement principle in which the body resists the opposing forces of gravity. Gravity and weight pull the body downward when the dancer descends. Counterpull is a non-muscular sensing that the dancer uses to appear to pull upward or support the body weight against gravity. This principle, coupled with pull-up, keeps the weight off the legs so that the dancer can move more freely.
- *Squareness* is the principle that stipulates that the shoulders and hips be on the same plane. Squareness leads to proper placement.
- *Pull-up*, or lift, allows the dancer to resist the pull of gravity. The pull-up is three-dimensional as the legs, abdomen, and torso lift upward from the floor. Countering the pull-up, the shoulders remain open and down while the spine elongates downward toward the floor. The principle of pull-up helps center the dancer's vertical alignment, which in turn allows the dancer to appear to defy gravity.
- *Aplomb* (from the French for *perpendicular)* uses an imaginary vertical line that runs from the top of the head through the middle of the nose, chin, sternum, navel, and pubic bone and between the two feet (front view). An imaginary vertical line is also on the side of the body; it starts

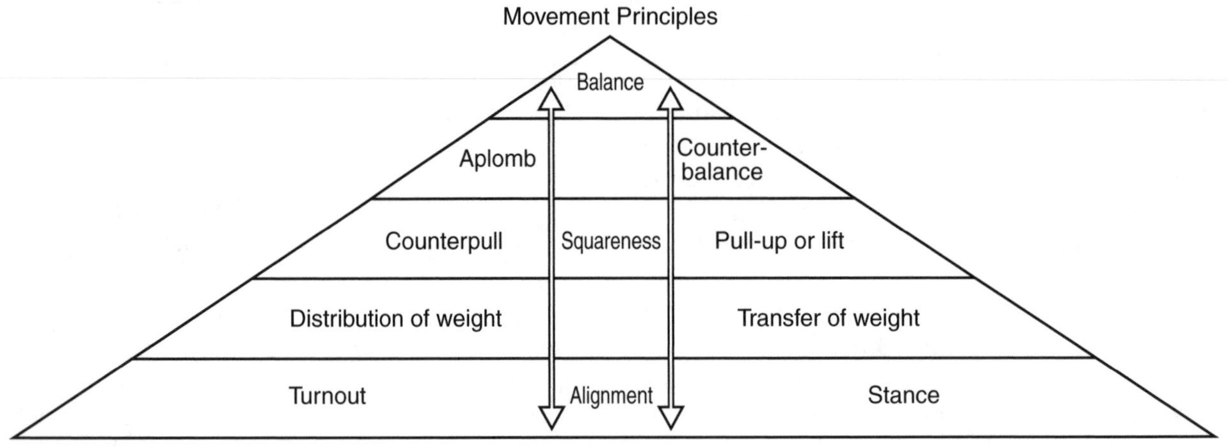

Figure 8.1 Movement principles underlie each dance form.

in the center of the head and travels through the middle of the ear, shoulder, hip, thigh, knee, calf, and in front of the ankle bone (side view). In moving, the dancer applies aplomb to move vertically upward and downward.

- *Counterbalance* is the tilt of the torso on a forward and upward diagonal to balance the body when the working leg is lifted behind.
- *Balance* is the point at which all three planes intersect: frontal plane (dividing the back and front of the body; this is also known as the longitudinal plane) sagittal plane (dividing the right and left sides of the body), and transverse plane (dividing the upper half and lower half of the body). Balance consists of subtle adjustments made by the different body parts to maintain equilibrium in a position or while moving.

The movement principles are the basis of dance technique, exercises, and steps. In the sample units in chapter 13, movement principles will be identified for each specific dance form using the movement principle icon (the applicable movement principles will be shaded; see figure 8.1). Movement principles permeate into choreographic principles. The audience sees the choreography; but internally, the movement principles are at work to ensure correct performance of technique in the dance form. So the next step is to comprehend choreographic principles.

Choreographic Principles

Choreography is the composition of exercises and combinations in class; it is also the art of creating, developing, and planning a dance for performance. The elements of dance—space, time, and force—become the materials for choreography that are put together with different emphasis according to the dance form. Choreography for each dance form has a specific internal structure (see figure 8.2). The following information is a summary of the components of the choreographic principles.

Traditional Dance Elements

The traditional dance elements are space, time, force (energy), and relationships; see figure 8.2 for the subcomponents of each of these elements.

Space. Space refers to the areas that the dancer occupies (during nonlocomotor and axial movement) and moves through (during locomotor movement). The dancer occupies a personal space and shares general space with other dancers. *Personal space* is the dancer's own area in which he moves. *General space* is designated dance space through which a dancer and dancers move. Visualize general space as the volume of the dance space. The following are components of space:

- Directions (up, down, right side, left side, front, back, forward and backward diagonals)
- Dimensions (small, medium, large)
- Levels (high, middle, low)
- Shapes (straight, curved, angular)
- Pathways (curved, circular, zigzag, serpentine) and focus (direct, indirect with various body parts)
- Focus (the direction in which the dancer projects the movement)

Time. *Time* involves duration and tempo of the movement. It is also influenced by the weight of the movement (the strong or light quality of a movement). *Duration* is the length of the movement (short, medium, long). *Tempo* refers to the speed of the movement (fast, medium, slow).

Accompaniment, which relates to time, can encompass music, self-accompaniment, percussion, text, vocal, and environmental sounds. A *pulse,* or beat, is the underlying rhythm, much like a heartbeat. An *accent* is an emphasis on a pulse that occurs regularly. A natural accent occurs on the first beat. Unnatural accents come on the second and fourth beats. *Rhythmic patterns* use accents that occur irregularly. An example of a rhythmic pattern that uses *mixed meter* is 1, 2; 1, 2, 3, 4; 1, 2, 3; 1, 2, 3, 4, 5. *Accumulative rhythm* increases the rhythm sequentially; an example of accumulative rhythm is 1, 2; 1, 2, 3; 1, 2, 3, 4.

A *musical phrase* has regularly occurring accents that form measures in 2/4, 4/4, 3/4, and 6/8 meter. In 2/4 meter, there are 2 beats to a measure and each quarter note receives 1 beat. In 4/4 meter, there are 4 beats to a measure and each quarter note receives 1 beat. In 3/4 meter, there are 3 beats to a measure and each quarter note receives 1 beat. The 6/8 meter indicates 6 beats to a measure and each eighth note gets 1 beat. *Meter* indicates the time signature: 2/4, 4/4, 3/4, 6/8, 5/8, and so on. A musical phrase is a short group of measures coming to a temporary or permanent finish.

Choreographic Principles

Choreographic elements	Choreographic structures	Choreographic designs	Choreographic devices	Choreographic relationships
Motif Phrase Theme and variation	Simple musical forms • AB (binary) • ABA (ternary) • Rondo • Theme and variation Contrapuntal forms • Canon (round) • Fugue Others • Narrative (story) • Open (free)	Dancer's body shape Dancer's pathway through space Visual design • Symmetrical • Asymmetrical Symbolism • Representational • Abstraction • Distortion Relationship • Unison • Sequential • Successional • Oppositional • Complementary	Repetition Reverse Alter • Addition or subtraction • Directional change • Facing or focus • Level • Dimension • Tempo • Rhythm • Quality or effort action • Positioning • Movement section	Solo Duet Trio Quartet Small and large groups

Traditional Dance Elements

Space	Time	Force	Relationships
Directions Dimensions Levels Shapes Pathways Focus	Duration Tempo	Movement qualities • Sustained • Percussive • Swinging • Suspended • Collapsing • Vibratory	Among body parts Among people Between people and props

Laban's Dance Elements

Space	Time	Weight	Flow
Direct or indirect	Sudden or slow	Light or strong	Bound or free

Effort actions (use space, time, and weight)

• Dab • Flick • Punch • Slash • Glide • Float • Press • Wring

Figure 8.2 Choreographic principles and dance elements.

Force. *Force,* also known as energy, reinforces, heightens, expands, and highlights parts of a movement theme or section of a work. Another word for energy is effort. *Effort,* put together with weight and time, works in varying proportions to produce an unlimited variety of movements from which the choreographer may select.

Movement qualities, a subcomponent of force, describe how a dancer moves. There are six movement qualities:

1. Sustained (slow, sustained)
2. Percussive (sharp with sound) and abrupt (fast and sharp without sound)
3. Swinging (pendular)
4. Suspended (defying gravity)
5. Collapsing (sinking)
6. Vibratory (shaking)

Relationships. Relationships of dance elements concern the dancers' bodies and body parts and how they move in relation to other body parts, with the floor, with other dancers, and with props.

These movement qualities constitute one view; another view is Laban's effort actions.

Laban's Dance Elements

Laban's eight effort actions use the elements of space, time, and weight in various combinations to create the actions. The effort actions range from everyday activities to movement education, sports, and dance. Rudolph von Laban was a movement analyst. He devised a system through which everyday movement can be observed, notated, and analyzed to describe a person's predisposition to certain types of movement. Since the 1940s, many dancers and dance instructors have adopted his system of Labanotation and Laban movement analysis. The eight effort actions comprise movement that uses space (direct or indirect), weight (light or strong), and time (sudden or slow movements):

1. Dab (sudden, light, and direct)
2. Flick (sudden, light, and indirect)
3. Punch (sudden, strong, and direct)
4. Slash (sudden, strong, and indirect)
5. Glide (slow, light, and direct)
6. Float (slow, light, and indirect)
7. Press (slow, strong, and direct)
8. Wring (slow, strong, and indirect)

Laban's eight efforts are another way of referring to dynamics. *Dynamics* combine energy (force), weight, time, and flow in the performance of a movement. *Flow* refers to an action dealing with the body's weight in time and space that is either free (difficult to stop, ongoing, unpredictable, meandering) or bound (easy to stop, controlled, restrained, still). *Tension* is the degree of energy intensity, which conveys various shades of emotions or qualities of movement.

The elements of space, time, and force combine in various ways with movement phrases. A series of movement phrases unite into a dance through the use of choreographic structures.

Choreographic Structures

Choreographic principles beyond the elements of dance expand to create various structures for dance that often mirror musical forms or other structures.

Simple Musical Forms. Musical forms that support choreography include the following:

- AB is a binary, or a two-part, form. It contains two different themes that relate to or contrast each other.
- ABA is a ternary, or three-part, form. It has two different movement themes ending with a repeat of the A, or first part.
- Rondo form (ABACADA and so on) has three or more sections. This form begins with a main theme followed by another theme or movement material, but the A theme returns after each new movement material, much like the chorus of a song.
- Theme and variation (A_1, A_2, A_3, A_4, A_5) uses a theme, and all subsequent themes build on the main theme (augmented, adjusted, altered, and distorted).

Contrapuntal Forms. These forms of music also lend themselves as underpinnings for choreography. *Canon,* or round, has a single theme that plays with and against itself. It begins as a single theme, then is restated and layered at successive intervals. An example of the round is the song "Row, Row, Row Your Boat." The round ends with the original single theme. A canon's original theme changes through manipulation; it becomes faster or slower, reversed (started at the end and goes to the beginning) or inverted (turned upside down), or augmented (performed two to three times slower than originally performed).

Fugue, like canon, is more complicated and considered the most difficult of the music forms to translate into choreography. The original theme repeatedly overlaps itself, developing and usually building to climax. In choreography of the fugue, the movement may be inverted (positioned upside down), reversed, augmented (slowed down), or diminished (movement performed two to three times faster than the original).

Other Choreographic Structures. Other choreographic structures include narrative and open frameworks for movement. *Narratives,* or story-based dramatic choreographic forms, tell a story through movement, gestures, and pantomime. Narrative choreography requires the dancer to assume a character's role. This dual role of acting and dancing must be performed seamlessly with facial expressions and body movement to convey the emotions of the character during the dramatic action of the dance.

In an *open,* or free, structure the movement or dance idea being expressed creates the structure for the dance. Most choreography uses a linear progression starting at the beginning and progressing to the end. Literary or dramatic devices in choreography use flashback or episodic mechanisms. Another aspect of the choreographic principles is visual design.

Design in Choreography

Choreography is a visual art that constantly changes its use of design elements to communicate the purpose of the dance. Design in choreography uses visual design elements in two specific ways: body shapes and movement.

- The dancer or dancers' body shape is curved, angular, straight, or twisted.
- The dancers' pathways move through space on a diagonal; in a straight line; in a curved, zigzag, spiral, or circular pattern.
- Visual designs are either symmetrical or asymmetrical. Symmetrical designs in shapes and formations are balanced so that each side mirrors the other. Asymmetrical designs in shapes and formations are unbalanced, unequal, or different on either side.

Symbolism in design, movement, and gestures takes three forms:

1. Representational movement and gestures present literal meanings.
2. Abstraction takes the essence of a literal interpretation of movement and gives it symbolic meanings.
3. Distortion alters the shape or movement, the intent, and meaning of the movement or gesture.

Dancer relationships add another dimension to choreography. Relationships that dancers create with one another and with theatrical props and sets contribute to visual design. How the group performs the movement is an equally important factor.

- Unison movement occurs when all of the dancers perform the same movement together. This type of performance is particularly powerful with many dancers whose movements are synchronized so that they all seem to move and breathe as one dancer.
- Sequential movement travels through a body or bodies in a logical sequence. For example, in modern dance a roll-down begins in the standing position with the head relaxed forward, followed by the neck, rolling through the spine one vertebra at a time, and continuing down until the upper body hangs from the hips.
- Successional movement is similar to sequential movement. One movement is performed after another in a domino effect. An example of this is a wavelike movement through a group of dancers.
- Oppositional and complementary relationships add variety to choreographic structures. *Oppositional movement* refers to shapes, movement, and dynamic and rhythmic elements that oppose each other. For example, one person moves slowly while another person runs around the other person quickly. Another example is one person at a low level while another person is at a high level. An example of *complementary movement* is a dancer performing the same movement as another dancer but on the opposite side.

Choreographic Relationships

Choreographic relationships of a dancer or dancers include the following:

- A solo is a dance for one dancer.
- A duet is a dance for two dancers.
- A trio is a dance for three dancers.
- A quartet is a dance for four dancers.
- A small group consists of more than two people.
- A large group has five or more people.

Choreographic Devices

Choreographic devices are ways to manipulate motifs, movements, and movement themes. Within choreographic structures is the subject matter of a movement theme or a dance. The simplest form is the recurring *motif* or smallest repeated element of movement that unites the parts of the dance together. *Movement themes* are similar to musical themes in their development and use of contrasting components. Movements and movement themes are linked by *transitions* that use movement logic, such as organic transitions that grow out of one movement into another or connect one movement theme to the next. Movement themes develop using musical, dramatic, or other structures. The result is a dance in which movement themes develop in relation to or in counterpoint to the music, with transitions that logically lead the audience from a beginning, through a middle, and to an end in the choreographic work. Movement themes can be manipulated in many ways within the structure of the dance. The following are selected choreographic devices for manipulating movement (adapted from Blom and Chaplin 1995):

- Repeat the movement in exactly the same manner.
- Reverse the movement sequence beginning with the last movement and ending with the first.
- Alter the movement by one or more of the following devices:
  - Add or subtract from the original movement in a variety of ways. Perform it in place or while moving through the space. (Adding is enhancing a movement by integrating a jump, leap, or turn into it; subtracting is simplifying movement by removing embellishments from the original movement sequence.)
  - Change direction of the movement sequence (up, down, right side, left side, front, back, forward and backward diagonals).
  - Have the dancers face different corners or walls while they perform the movement.
  - Adapt the level (high, middle, low) of the movement sequence.
  - Change dimension (small, medium, large) in the movement either while moving in place or while moving through the space.
  - Alter tempo (slow, medium, fast) of the movement for contrast.
  - Perform rhythm movement motifs or sequences with varying tempo and accents in relation to the music or other choreographic devices.
  - Use quality or effort actions that complement or contrast one another.
  - Position the dancer or group of dancers at different places on the stage.
  - Select movement sections from a movement theme and then perform them alone or blended with other movement sections.

When making a dance, select and use choreographic principles to provide an inner structure. In each of the sample units in chapter 13, a choreographic principles icon (see figure 8.2, page 118) will provide insight as to which principles are applicable (the shaded principles) to the dance form.

Choreographic principles blend with aesthetic principles. Sometimes it is difficult to discern one from the other because both groups of principles are important in designing choreography. Choreographic principles provide the structure of a dance; aesthetic principles provide ways for choreographers and dancers to communicate to the audience the meaning of the dance as a work of art.

Aesthetic Principles

Aesthetic principles govern the artistic parameters by which an artistic work is judged. Aesthetic principles provide an avenue for expression among the choreographer, the dancers, and the audience. The following principles are general aesthetic principles that apply to dance as an art form.

- *Unity* focuses on coherence, logic, wholeness, and clarity. When a movement theme threads continuously throughout an entire dance work, it gives the dance a unifying strand.
- *Balance* ensures a sense of proportion within a dance work. Balance supplies moments of rest, symmetrical designs in space, or dance shapes that provide a breathing place for the audience to digest the choreographic work as it unfolds. This principle gives the work a sense of equality among and between the parts of the dance.
- *Variety* refers to using different types of movement that expand through the dance. Variety in a movement theme manipulates direction of the movement, number of people performing the movement, energy used to perform the movement, the amount of space the movement uses, and variations of the speed of the movement. This aesthetic principle holds the dancer's and the audience's interest.
- *Repetition* in choreography promotes unity within the dance through the recurrence of themes using altered or augmented elements. The use of repetition makes the audience feel comfortable and familiar with the dance.
- *Contrast* adds interest and highlights to different sections of a dance. A dance can become monotonous if too many movements are the same. Contrast stimulates the eye of the audience, and it helps separate important features of the dance.

The choreographer considers each of the aesthetic principles separately and synergetically

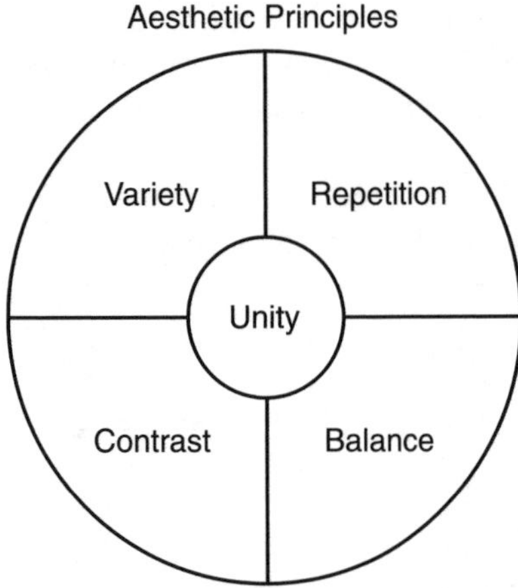

Figure 8.3 Aesthetic principles support dance and other art forms.

when creating a dance (see figure 8.3). In the sample units in chapter 13, the aesthetic principles apply to different dance form categories in different ways. An aesthetic principles icon (see figure 8.3) will visually present how the principles apply to each dance form by shading the applicable principles.

All the principles contribute to the development of the dancer as an artist. The dancer starts the process of becoming an artist in the beginning dance class; the student requires the teacher's constant attention to develop competently as a technical and expressive dancer.

Teaching Artistic Development

The dancer develops a sense of artistry in the process of learning dance and performing it as an art form. Teaching artistic development is based on two premises: First, understand and meet the artistic demands of the dance form, which entails knowing the specific methods, schools, or styles. Second, nurture artistic development in the learner, which hinges on guiding students through artistic style development by choreographing and providing performance opportunities for them to practice developing artistry.

Understanding the Artistic Demands of a Dance Form

Knowledge about artistic demands of a dance form includes understanding and being able to teach different styles associated with a dance form. This knowledge comes from training in the style; performance experiences; and research such as reading, viewing videotapes, seeing performances, and attending workshops. The teacher is responsible for knowing the breadth of artistic demands to effectively teach the form beyond its basic exercises, steps, positions, and figures.

Another artistic demand is knowing and teaching codified methods, schools, or styles of specific dance forms. Examples of this include the Russian school and the Cecchetti method in ballet; the Graham or Horton techniques in modern dance; and exhibition ballroom techniques or various regional styles of contra and square dancing. The dance teacher must have studied these specific dance forms and be actively engaged in knowledge acquisition to be qualified to teach these specific schools, methods, and styles. This type of knowledge allows the dance teacher to put it into the context of choreography.

The artistic demands of choreography include technical, musical, stylistic, and aesthetic considerations. These characteristics vary depending on the dance form and the purpose of the performance. The teacher not only implements the choreography, but she also meets the artistic and stylistic demands of the work. Choreography may reflect a period or style of a dance form. The teacher researches, analyzes, selects, then synthesizes to produce a unified choreographic work of art.

The teacher creates performance opportunities in informal or formal settings for her students. Learning how to perform begins in the classroom. From the beginning class on to the master class, the teacher must emphasize the artistic aspects of the dance form and require learners to acquire a performance attitude. If the techniques are practiced consistently, learners gain movement and become more confident when performing in the classroom. The teacher orchestrates these learning experiences so that they transfer to performance situations outside of the classroom and students gain experience in developing performance artistry.

Developing Dance Artistry

Dance artistry begins when the dancer learns to assume a performance attitude in the beginning dance class. Teaching artistry is a long-term commitment; the teacher disperses it in small amounts at appropriate times. The teacher stresses this concept consistently while executing the parts of the dance class, rehearsing, and leading performance situations. Effective teaching of artistry is embedded into the teaching and learning process. The dance teacher keeps proportion in teaching the components of technique and style within the artistic vision of the dance form. This vision guides the dancer from his status as a student performing in the classroom to a dancer performing on stage.

Extending Dance Through Production to Performance

Dance performances are integral to teaching dance. Dance production includes bringing together technical aspects that support dance performance. To produce a dance performance, the dance teacher organizes and knows what, when, where, how, and with whom to accomplish the many tasks of the dance production. These tasks are charted on a production calendar.

A production, or master, calendar is a time line for all the contributing parts of the dance performance. After establishing a performance date, the teacher works backward in the calendar, inserting deadlines for when components of the production should be accomplished. The teacher uses the master calendar to schedule and manage the following tasks involved in mounting a production:

- Devise schedules for rehearsals (space, equipment).
- Select personnel (artistic and technical) for the performance.
- Select costumes (order, design, and contract).
- Create lighting plots and set designs.
- Record the music at the appropriate speed for the dance.
- Create an audio tape or compact disc in the program order. Listen to the performance recording to ensure that the music, speed, and order are correct.
- Design and print posters, programs, and tickets for the performance.
- Provide publicity and other public relations to ensure people attend the performance.

Because performance is the goal of most dance forms, the teacher must be well acquainted with dance production elements and procedures to adapt them to all types of performances. These elements include using publicity; creating a program of dance works; budgeting effectively; developing posters, programs, and tickets; running the box office; getting the performance space and equipment; and retaining the production crews.

Publicity

In the production of a performance, good publicity ensures that an audience will attend. Although part of the audience will be dance students, parents, and other relatives, you must reach the entire school and the community. Publicity includes press releases in newspapers, feature articles and interviews by reporters, flyers and posters, and media publicity that uses radio and television public service announcements.

Program Balance

When building a dance program for public presentation, the teacher considers the audience as well as the dancers who are performing it. A program balances the artistic with the practical aspects of scenery and costume changes and lighting requirements.

Likewise, the teacher considers the artistic nature of the production and its impact on the audience. A dance performance begins with a dance that invites the audience to sit back and stay for the program. Dramatic and more serious dance works are balanced with lighter, comical, whimsical works during the concert. The dance selected to precede intermission should make an impression on the audience and bring them back to their seats. The dance after intermission rekindles their interest in the program. The final dance of the production should be a crowd pleaser that leaves the audience wanting more. The length of the program is an important consideration, especially from the audience's perspective. Equally important is the placement of the intermission and its length.

Budgeting for the Production

Budgeting for a performance is as important as keeping to the production schedule. Most dance education settings have strict budgets for performances, so learn to work within your budget.

Budget allocation most often does not meet artistic desires; but creativity, imagination, and in-kind services often fill in these gaps. Begin by estimating your costs realistically. Do your homework by researching the costs for each area of the production. This means getting on the telephone and perusing costume and lighting catalogs. Compare retail prices on proposed purchases before you buy the items. Fill out all requisitions and purchase orders early to avoid complications. Monitor expenses throughout the production process. Make a contingency plan in case of emergencies. Be prepared for unforeseen post-production expenses; always budget in a contingency factor.

Printed Materials for the Concert

Posters, programs, and tickets have separate deadlines for development and delivery. Each of these printed items requires a design, proofing of the copy, printing, and a second proofing of the final copy. Programs have to be folded, picked up, and delivered. Create these printed materials to allow enough time for ordering, printing, and delivering. Rush jobs cost more! Use the production master calendar and always factor in additional time between the delivery of the printing job and the concert. When you get the estimate, get it in writing. But make sure all of the requirements for the job are clearly specified, especially the date of delivery to the box office.

Box Office

Running the box office requires competent personnel to manage its operation of selling tickets. The box office should be equipped with a money box, adequate change for each performance, and a secure method of depositing the box office receipts after the performance.

Performance Space and Equipment

If you rent a performance space, lighting equipment, or dance floor, you will need to book these rentals well in advance. Order glow tape, flashlights, batteries, tape for the floor, and electrical tape. Ask questions: Does rental of the performance space require that you use their crew, lighting equipment, lamps, gels, and other items? What charges in addition to the rental of the space are incurred with a performance? What are the pick-up and return dates for equipment? Ask so that you have no surprise bills after the concert. Tightly estimate the number of hours you will need in the facility and the crew time if rented by the hour. If this is the case, prepare—overprepare—so that when you move into the space you are able to do it quickly, rehearse efficiently, and save money.

Managers and Production Crews

For the production, a stage manager; light, sound, running crews; house manager; and box office personnel are the bare necessities of the technical and house personnel. Students and parents may be solicited as dressers and ushers if they are allowed.

The house manager supervises the areas of the theater open to the public. He routinely performs maintenance checks throughout the auditorium and other public areas. He controls the front of the theater and auditorium for the safety and comfort of the audience. He seats latecomers between dances and prepares the lobby for intermission. At the end of intermission, he signals the audience to return to their seats.

Selecting a competent stage manager is most important for the dance production. She should know dance movements, music, and each dance in the performance; in addition, she should have excellent communication and theater production skills. She is in charge of running the show by calling the cues and directing the backstage crews. The stage manager is the person responsible for the quality of the production.

Frequent production meetings ensure that deadlines are met, budgets are adhered to, and the entire production process is moving toward its goal: the performance. A smooth, well-organized performance that you can be proud of speaks well of your professional abilities. Associated with every production is Murphy's Law ("If anything can go wrong, it will go wrong!").

To produce as professional a performance as possible within time and budget allocations is your goal as a dance educator. The audience easily reads the degree of professionalism inherent in the performance. Sometimes, you must be satisfied with the knowledge that things happen beyond your control. On the other hand, ensuring that dancers present themselves professionally in the performance environment is a skill that you develop in the classroom.

Promoting Performance Attributes

Performance attributes involve acquiring professional attitudes. Other attributes include technical proficiency, musicality, ease of movement within a style, versatility, projection, expression, and communication of the dance with artistry. All of these attributes begin with forming a professional attitude in the dance class.

Professional Attitude

A professional attitude entails meeting the demands of the profession as a dancer; if you are the teacher, it involves meeting the demands as a dance educator. You have many demands and often little time to accomplish all of them without sacrificing your time and your energy. So, prioritize them and select what must be done first. Give yourself enough time to accomplish the demands that help you accomplish your goals as a dancer or dance teacher.

As a dance teacher you are a professional role model as a dancer, an educator, a production manager, an administrator, and in other roles both in the educational setting and in the community. To demonstrate professionalism in all of these roles, be prepared. Allot time to prepare for rehearsals, meetings, and other events. Dress appropriately for the event; bring your public relations and leadership skills with you to support you. This is the persona you present to the public eye beyond the dance classroom. Equally important as a performance attribute is developing technical proficiency in your roles as dancer and dance educator.

Technical Proficiency

Technical proficiency in dance is the ability to move with efficiency using the technical and conceptual requirements of a specific dance form. As a dancer and dance educator, strive for achieving the technical excellence within each dance form you learn. You will have many responsibilities. Strive to be the best you can be within your situation.

As a dance educator, you must have technical proficiency in dance forms and their cross-disciplinary subjects within the body of dance knowledge and within the greater scope of their impact on students' learning and skill acquisition for lifetime endeavors. Look at these demands as a series of ever-widening circles of influence creating connections within the limits of the teaching situation.

Summary

Four ways of gathering information to teach the dance form content are text analysis, structured interviews, stimulated recall, and analog derivation. Dance has many forms; the 10 dance forms are divided into four categories: creative movement and creative dance, recreational (folk, square, social, and contra), concert (ballet, modern, jazz, and tap) and aerobic dance (dance fitness). These categories comprise similar dance forms that are related but have distinct characteristics. Dance forms from each category have similar class formats. Each of the dance forms connects to movement, choreographic, and aesthetic principles. The four dance form categories use these principles in similar ways. Movement, choreographic, and aesthetic principles have intellectual and physical relationships with the content and the choreographic and aesthetic aspects of the dance forms. Artistic development of the dancer involves understanding the demands of dance forms and dance artistry. Students gain artistry through the production and performance of dance concerts. Performance attributes are acquired through the use of professional attitudes and technical proficiency.

References

Blom, L.A., and L.T. Chaplin. 1995. *The intimate act of choreography.* Pittsburgh, PA: University of Pittsburgh Press.

Gaines, B.R. 1987. An overview of knowledge acquisition and transfer. In *Knowledge acquisition for knowledge based systems,* edited by B. Gaines and J. Boose. Toronto, ON: Academic Press.

Vickers, J. 1990. *Instructional design for teaching physical activities.* Champaign, IL: Human Kinetics.

It's Your Turn

1. Interview a teacher of a dance form that you know nothing about. Write a one-page paper on your interview.
2. Watch a video or performance of two dance forms of different dance categories or two dance forms within a category. Write a one-page paper that describes the movement, choreographic, and aesthetic principles as they apply to what you saw and remembered.

PART II

Implementing Dance Pedagogy: What You Need to Do to Create a Dance Curriculum

In part II, you will apply the pedagogical content knowledge of dance into creating parts of the dance curriculum. **Chapter 9, Developing the Lesson Plan,** provides an understanding of learning experiences and connects them to the three domains of learning. In this chapter, the parts of the objective are analyzed in their relation to their learning domains. **Chapter 10, Selecting the Appropriate Assessment Tools for Dance,** explores the types of assessment techniques available for the dance teacher. Evaluation techniques applied to dance include performance testing, process evaluations, and written examinations. **Chapter 11, Writing and Delivering the Lesson Plan,** takes you through the steps of creating a lesson plan, preparing to teach a lesson, presenting a lesson, and evaluating your teaching. In **chapter 12, Creating a Curriculum,** four dance curriculum models are examined. The teacher learns the components to design a dance unit or a series of units that become a one-year or multiyear dance program. Evaluating the dance program serves to determine whether the program meets school requirements and state or national standards. **Chapter 13, Sample Units for Dance Forms,** provides content for 10 dance forms that are taught in public education. **Chapter 14, Culminating Curriculum Portfolio,** synthesizes all of the pedagogical content knowledge for dance into a model plan that demonstrates your ability to create a dance curriculum. The epilogue is a culmination of the teaching and learning process model for dance.

The six chapters in part II guide you in implementing dance pedagogy in public education, from writing lesson plans to developing an entire dance program curriculum. Get ready to explore the world of dance education and develop your portfolio to prepare for you job interview and your career in the world of dance!

CHAPTER

9

Developing the Lesson Plan

Chapter Objectives

By the end of this chapter, you should be able to do the following:

- Understand the components of a learning experience.
- Comprehend the three domains of learning and how they apply to dance.
- Identify the four components of a behavioral objective.
- Match the appropriate assessment criterion to the behavioral objective.

After considering the learner, the environment, and the content, the dance teacher prepares to develop a lesson plan. This chapter will help you understand the dimensions of learning in the dance classroom. Learning experiences are the dance content components of the lesson plan. Behavioral objectives for a lesson plan determine what learners will achieve as a result of the lesson. These objectives meet physical, intellectual, social, and emotional goals for learning. Effective lesson plans are built on quality learning experiences.

Setting Up Effective Dance Learning Experiences

Learning experiences may be different depending on the dance form and also what the goal is for the experience. In the concert, recreational, and fitness dance categories, the learning experiences are a progression of skill development and combinations, figures, and dances of increasing difficulty. In creative movement and modern dance, learning experiences may focus on building technique, using the elements of the dance form, and choreographic and aesthetic principles to increase the learners' abilities. Regardless of the goal of the learning experiences, students must meet some overall requirements. The following requirements are adapted to dance from Rink (1998), who provides a model for developing learning experiences.

- Improving or striving to attain a technique or skill
- Providing practice time for all skill levels of students in the class
- Selecting content appropriate for the age and experience of the class
- Connecting psychomotor experiences to cognitive and affective aspects of the topic and dance content through the dance experience

These general criteria for learning experiences must connect with several other important components for effective teaching and learning in dance. These components are part of understanding how students learn movement. Reading part I of this book and your previous experience in dance and education prepare you to formulate a lesson plan for a dance class.

Describing the Lesson Plan

The lesson plan begins as an outline for the dance class (see form 9.1a). The teacher develops it into a detailed written document that describes the day's lesson. Form 9.1b includes notes to help explain different parts of the lesson plan. The lesson plan indicates the following:

- Who and what the teacher will teach: the population and the content
- What supporting materials and equipment are necessary to teach the class
- What are the exercises, combinations, and dances and when they are presented during the class
- What teaching and management strategies are identified for the class
- Why you are teaching this content or the objective of the class
- How the student learning will be assessed

A lesson plan gives structure to what will be taught during the class; it ensures that the teacher considers and notates all of the information to

FORM 9.1a

Dance Lesson Plan

Grade

Introduction **Development** **Review**

National Dance Standards

Concept/Focus/Theme

Objectives

Psychomotor:

Cognitive:

Affective:

Vocabulary

Equipment and Materials

Procedure and Description of Exercises, Combinations, Activities, and Dances

Write the exercises, combinations, activities, and dances for the class. Attach them to the lesson plan. Include in the lesson plan a brief explanation of how the following items will be implemented into the lesson.

Instructional Procedures

Teaching styles
Presentational methods
Skill, technique, or activity cues
Verbal clarity
Rhythmic correctness
Imagery
Review questions about key points

Class Management

Entering and exiting classroom
Group selection (if applicable)
Adaptability
Organization
Class control
Presentation
Use of time and pacing
Feedback

Assessment

Develop the rubric or performance testing scale.

Interrelated Arts or Integrated Course Variations

FORM 9.1b

Dance Lesson Plan

Grade → *Who are you teaching?*

Introduction **Development** **Review** → *What kind of content—new or previously presented?*

National Dance Standards → *list them or note standards*

Concept/Focus/Theme

do these support one another?

Objectives

Psychomotor:
Cognitive:
Affective:

relate to objectives of the class

Vocabulary → *taken from the content of the lesson*

Equipment and Materials → *music, sound equipment, and props*

What you will teach

Procedure and Description of Exercises, Combinations, Activities, and Dances

Write the exercises, combinations, activities, and dances for the class. Attach them to the lesson plan. Include in the lesson plan a brief explanation of how the following items will be implemented into the lesson.

Sequence of exercises, combinations, and dances presented during class.

Instructional Procedures

Teaching styles
Presentational methods
Skill, technique, or activity cues
Verbal clarity
Rhythmic correctness
Imagery
Review questions about key points

Class Management

Entering and exiting classroom
Group selection (if applicable)
Adaptability
Organization
Class control
Presentation
Use of time and pacing
Feedback

Teaching and managing strategies to implement the lesson

Assessment

Develop the rubric or performance testing scale. → *Connect to objectives and exercises, combinations, and dances.*

Interrelated Arts or Integrated Course Variations

What interrelationships are possible for the lesson?

From *Dance Teaching Methods and Curriculum Design* by Gayle Kassing and Danielle M. Jay, 2003, Champaign, IL: Human Kinetics.

implement into the day's lesson. A dance lesson plan is broken down into parts that build on one another.

Begin by identifying what you know about the dance class and the students that you will teach. In turn, this information determines the content and objectives of the dance class along with the teaching and management strategies used to present the content. You will specify these components; this leads to selecting the assessment appropriate for the dance class, followed by a final check of the lesson plan.

Identifying Preliminary Knowledge for Your Lesson

Before writing a lesson plan, identify the ages of the students, the dance form, and the equipment and materials necessary for conducting the lesson. These topics, covered in earlier chapters, become the foundation on which you build your lesson plan. The answers to these questions provide the rationale for the lesson plan.

- What grade or age group is the class?
- Is this lesson an introduction? Is it a development of a concept or theme? Or is the lesson a review of content for the students?
- What is the concept, focus, or theme of the lesson? Determine the topic of the lesson to select the dance form content for the lesson.

The content for the lesson is presented through learning experiences that use appropriate dance content.

Selecting the Content for Your Lesson Plan

The content of the lesson will be determined by two factors: 1) the dance form that is both age and developmentally appropriate and 2) dance steps or dances that are age, developmentally, and technique or skill appropriate for the students of the class.

First establish the dance form skills, techniques, concepts, or dances that you will teach during the class. This information determines the vocabulary that students will learn during the class, and you can define these terms. These preliminary tasks set the stage for planning the structure of the lesson.

Preparing to Write Your Lesson Plan

If this is your first experience writing a lesson plan, be prepared to set aside time to accomplish all of the parts of the lesson plan. The time spent in learning how to write a lesson plan will serve you well in your future as a dance educator.

Establish the structure of the class. The structure of the lesson connects to the type of dance form you will be teaching: creative, recreational, aerobic, or concert dance class. The sample unit plans found in chapter 13 will assist you in identifying the exercises, steps, combinations, and dances that will be part of the lesson.

Once you identify the dance skills and techniques, the next step is to determine the processes students participate in when learning a dance skill and their stage of learning. A clear understanding of the students' skill levels provides you with the information to write the objective for each day's lesson.

Relating Objectives to a Learning Taxonomy

An objective sets a goal and guides the students' learning. A lesson plan specifies the learning goal for the day's class. Objectives act as a teacher's guide to teaching and testing. For students, objectives specify what they will learn. A student's objective is a behavioral objective because it describes what a student will be able to do in dance:

- Perform or physically learn dance skills.
- Know or process factual and conceptual, theoretical, and aesthetic information about dance.
- Develop attitudes and values about dance, dancing, dance performance, and dance education.

Each of these types of learning relates to a specific province of learning, or a domain: physical, intellectual, or attitudinal. Within each domain exists a hierarchy of learning attributes that build on one another; this creates a model, or taxonomy. The three major domains of learning are psychomotor (physical), the cognitive (intellectual), and the affective (attitudes and values). Using established taxonomies from the three domains, the dance teacher selects the level of learning to write the objective for his class. Central to the dancer's physical training is the psychomotor domain.

Psychomotor Domain

The psychomotor domain focuses on physical learning. Two taxonomies in the psychomotor domain have been selected as applicable to dance forms. The first taxonomy focuses on skill acquisition and is parallel to the stages of motor learning. This taxonomy is appropriate for dance forms that require students to learn a vocabulary of increasingly difficult steps or figures (for example, in ballet and square dance).

Psychomotor Domain

1. Perception
   - Sensory stimulation
   - Cue selection
   - Translation (perception to action)
2. Set (readiness for action)
   - Mental set
   - Physical set
   - Emotional set
3. Guided response (instructor)
   - Initiation of other people
   - Trial and error
4. Mechanisms (learned response becomes habitual)
5. Complex overt response
   - Resolution of uncertainty
   - Automatic performance
6. Adaptation
7. Origination

(Simpson 1966)

A description of each level follows:

- **Level 1, perception,** uses the learner's sensory stimulation. He watches the movement and hears the teacher's verbal cues and the music that accompanies the movement. The teacher presents the movement and says the dance vocabulary as external prompts that the student translates into action through an attempt to execute the movement.

- **Level 2, set,** is the learner's readiness for action. The teacher motivates learners by promoting interest in the activity and explaining its purpose. At this level the learner mentally knows what the movement is, physically understands the sequence of actions that make up the exercise or step, and emotionally feels confident of his knowledge and ability to perform the movement. This knowledge comes from the motivation that the teacher provides to support the learner's risk and success in the class. The teacher accomplishes this by teaching steps that are within the capabilities of the learners in the class.

- **Level 3, guided response,** allows learners to learn movement by watching the instructor model the movement correctly or watching other learners execute the movement. The instructor uses teaching strategies to help learners acquire a visual and verbal description of the step.

  A second part of guided response is the trial and error that the learner goes through to learn the movement correctly. The teacher's pinpointing and feedback are important attributes in completing this task. As the learner becomes more accustomed to assimilating the movement into his repertoire, he begins to accept more of the responsibility of replicating the movement.

- **Level 4, mechanical reproduction,** takes place when the movement becomes a learned response. At this level the learner can duplicate the movement with the first two steps of motor learning in place. The learner is in charge of taking general or individual feedback as a basis for self-assessing his execution of the step to continually improve his performance.

- **Level 5, complex overt response,** encompasses performing complex movement sequences with the dancer in control of all technical and artistic aspects of the performance. He makes continuous decisions of subtle changes to convey meaning and personal style. This level of highly sophisticated movement is an automatic response. The dancer monitors his performance beyond the steps but at a level where he can oversee the constant flow of musicality, artistic performance, and relationships with other dancers and groups in the dance.

- **Level 6, adaptation,** is taking skills and abilities and putting them into a new context or dance.

• **Level 7, origination,** is creating new or original movement, such as in creative and modern dance.

To better understand the physical performance domain, picture a beginning dancer learning a basic ballet step, such as a chassé. At the first level, the dancer follows the teacher's instructions in the sequence of movements that make up the step. As the student moves up the taxonomy, he recognizes chassé as a step and is able to execute it after seeing or hearing the word. Then he learns that the step can be performed either quickly or slowly within combinations. Later he is able to perform the step without thought; but he focuses on its relationship to other steps in the combinations, its style, its emphasis, and other attributes. The final stages include adapting the chassé into new combinations and then inventing a new step based on the original.

A second psychomotor taxonomy presents a hierarchy for gaining movement skills and concepts that lead to divergent thinking. This hierarchy is pertinent for creative and modern dance improvisation, creative studies, and choreography.

Psychomotor Domain

1. Generic movement
   - Perceiving (identify, discover)
   - Imitating (replicate, pantomime)
   - Patterning (arrange into successive harmonious acts)
2. Ordinate movement
   - Adapting (adjust, apply)
   - Refining (control, regulate, improve)
3. Creative movement
   - Varying (alter, revise)
   - Improvising (interpret, extemporize)
   - Composing (design, symbolize)

(Jewett and Bain 1985)

The levels of this taxonomy include the following:

• **Level 1, generic movement,** includes authentic movement or everyday movement such as walking, skipping, galloping, leaping, and other locomotor and nonlocomotor movements and gestures. At this level of the learning, the student perceives the movement through identification or discovery, imitates the movement by replicating it, then creates patterns with the movement that create a combination.

• **Level 2, ordinate movement,** refines the basic movement in various situations by adapting it.

• **Level 3, creative movement,** occurs after the learner has command of the movement vocabulary or creates personal movements that he manipulates. The learner varies the movement by altering it, changing it, or revising it. The learner uses the movement to improvise or solve problems. The movement may be interpreted in a variety of consciously directed ways, or the movement may be a spontaneous kinesthetic response. The final phase of this level is composing movement into dances that have structural designs and communicate meanings through abstraction and symbolic movement.

Both taxonomies are applicable to dance teaching and interconnect in dancing and choreography. The models form the basis for learning in the dance classroom. They link to knowledge about dance and the feelings and values attached to dance.

The movement–language connection in dance is a powerful conduit for learning and for becoming articulate in and about the dance form. This cognitive understanding is the intellectual basis for knowing dance and about dance as a means to communicate it to others. Dance is a nonverbal art that we express in words that dance students and people unacquainted with dance can understand. This is an important characteristic for the educated dance student to gain. Talking about dance and using the dance vocabulary are second nature for the dance educator, so the cognitive domain is easily engaged.

Cognitive Domain

The cognitive domain emphasizes the intellectual capacities of the learner. Bloom's taxonomy (Bloom 1956) of the cognitive domain begins with identification and ends with evaluation. The higher-level thinking skills range from analysis to application, synthesis, and evaluation. These intellectual skills, coupled with the psychomotor skills in the class, empower the learner with the language of

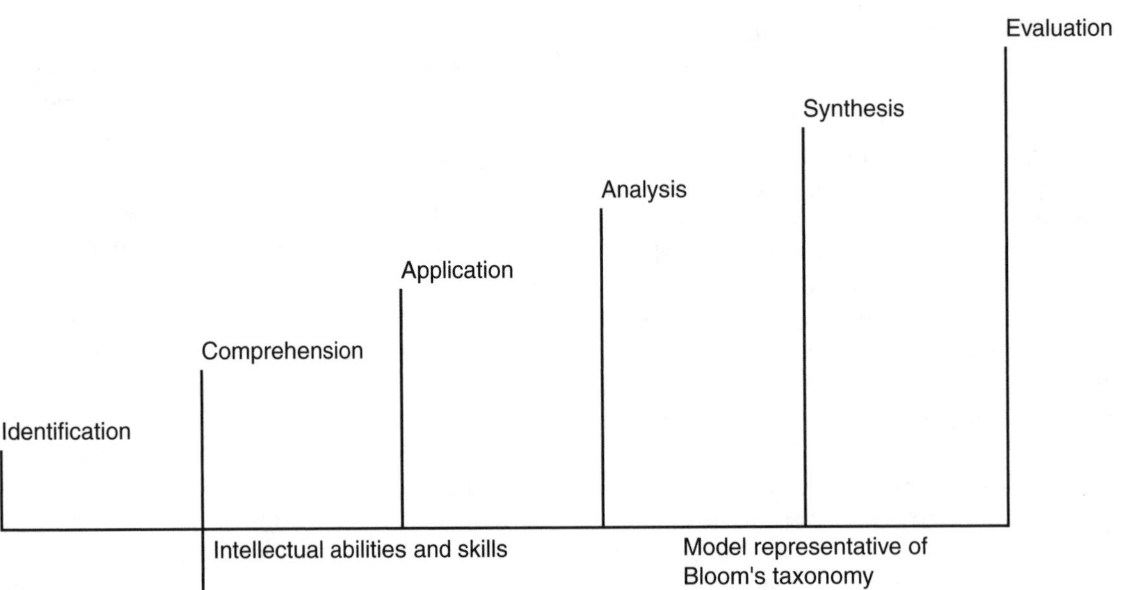

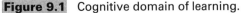

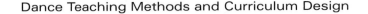

Figure 9.1 Cognitive domain of learning.

dance, physically and intellectually. This allows the learner to become literate in the art and through practice in translation between the psychomotor and cognitive taxonomies. Using the cognitive domain, the dancer becomes intellectually involved with the study of the art (see figure 9.1).

The cognitive domain includes both levels of knowledge and intellectual abilities. Each succeeding level builds on the preceding one.

- **Level 1, identification,** is knowing specifics such as facts and terminology. The second part of this first level is knowledge of methods and procedures. The third part of this level of knowledge is theories and principles. These levels of knowledge span from concrete to abstract levels of knowledge.
- **Level 2, comprehension,** is the ability to interpret facts, methods, and theories; give examples; or translate information from one language to another. This second level of the taxonomy is the first level of intellectual abilities and skills.
- **Level 3, application of knowledge,** is the ability to conceptualize situations and apply knowledge into new paradigms.
- **Level 4, analysis,** requires the ability to break down a problem or situation into its component parts.
- **Level 5, synthesis,** is the level in which the student builds new models based on arrangement of the components in another way specific to solving the problem.
- **Level 6, evaluation,** uses students' assessment of established models or newly synthesized models by analyzing how the models can be used in various situations.

Higher-level thinking skills range from level 3 of the domain (application) through level 6 of the domain (evaluation). In dance education these higher-level thinking skills are most often used in choreography, dance theory classes, and research projects.

The nature of dance is difficult to capture. Often it is apparent in the attitudes and values that the dancer and the dance educator demonstrate in the classroom. Many of these ways of doing things in the class are a continuance of traditions that contribute to the development of the dancer's persona. Most apparent as outcomes of children's dance education is the expression of these attitudes and values through the affective domain.

Affective Domain

The affective domain examines behavior related to feelings and attitudes, values, appreciations, and social attributes that lead the dancer to gain values about a subject. In dance learning, the affective domain mirrors the professional attitude expected in class, the traditions and values that the dance teacher imparts, and the oral traditions that dancers have passed down from generation to generation.

A dancer's training focuses on the physical, requires the intellectual, but is communicated through the affective domain. The affective domain is often demonstrated in the dance class through attendance, response, cooperation, and practice of professional attitudes and behaviors. Because dance is a nonverbal art, the development of this domain is an important part of self-perception and self-esteem. The taxonomy for the affective domain outlines these attributes (see figure 9.2).

The five levels of the affective domain begin with the following:

- **Level 1, receiving,** is the awareness and willingness to receive information with controlled, or selective, attention. Students must attend visually, auditorily, and kinesthetically in the dance class. Attending requires the learner to be quiet and to open the senses to learn.
- **Level 2, responding,** includes the acquiescence, the willingness, and the satisfaction found in responding.
- **Level 3, valuing,** encompasses the acceptance, understanding, and commitment to the values that are inherent in the subject matter or tradition.
- **Level 4, organization,** requires that the learner conceptualize his values and organize them into a value system.
- **Level 5, characterization of complex values,** requires that the dancer accept general values and have an in-depth understanding of the roles and features of specific values and how they reside within a personally developed value system.

Spanning several of these levels are cross-themes that include the following:

- **Interest** begins in receiving information and continues to perception of values.
- **Appreciation** begins with selective attention and continues to perception of values.
- **Attitudes and values** start with gaining satisfaction from responses and extend to conceptualization of a value.

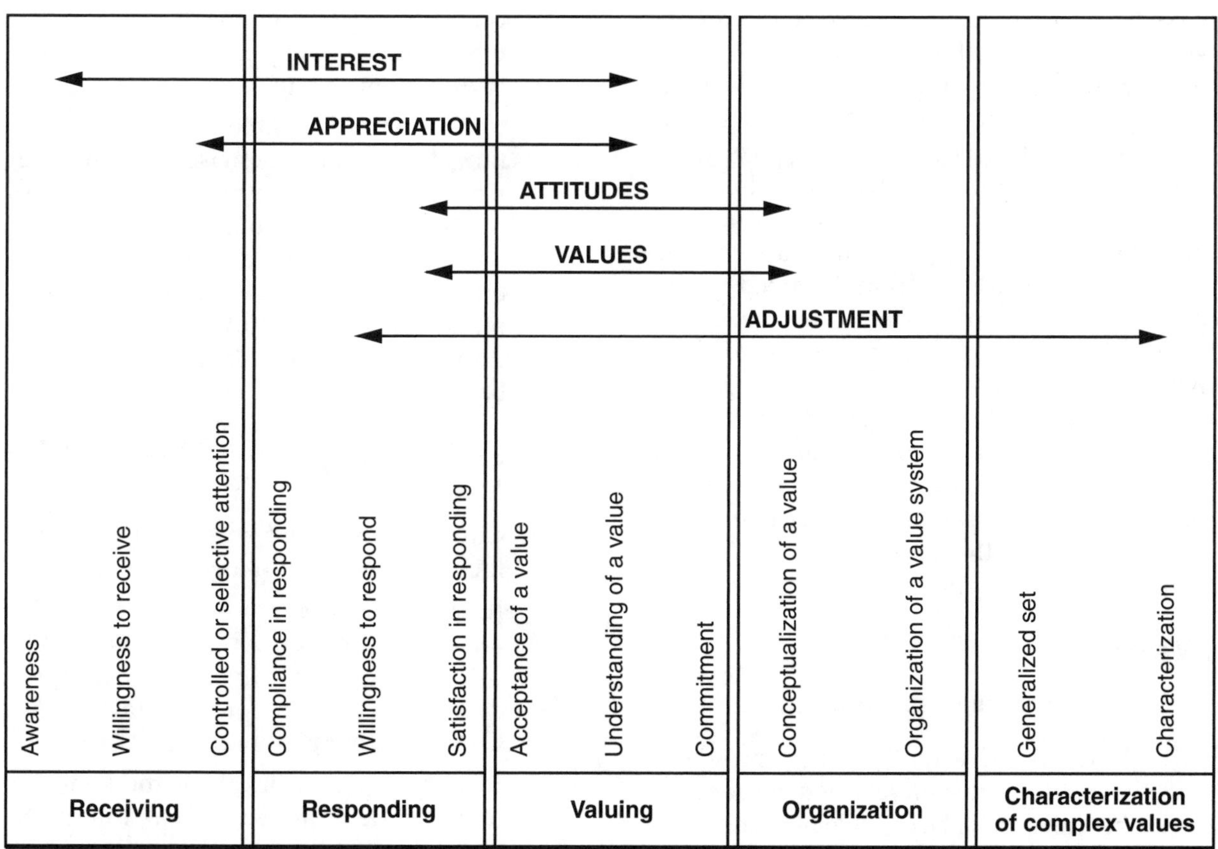

Figure 9.2 The affective domain.

- **Adjustment** initiates from willingness to respond and ends in characterization of values (Krathwohl, Bloom, and Masia 1964).

Each of these levels and cross-themes contributes to the social development and maturity of the learner in the dance class as he practices the etiquette to acquire a professional attitude. In the classroom, these affective attributes manifest as self-confidence, cooperation, social skills, self-respect, and respect for the members of the class and the teacher. The affective domain is integrated throughout the parts of the dance class, adding substantially to the physical and intellectual learning in the class.

Gaining an understanding of the three domains provides a broad view from which we extract the objectives for each lesson. The next step is to recognize the parts of an objective so that we join them into a cohesive unit.

Discerning the Parts of the Objective

A learning objective is the goal you are trying to attain by teaching the learning experiences that make up the class. Learning objectives describe what the student will be able to physically perform, know, feel, or value after participating in these learning experiences. Objectives specify what types of learning will take place in the psychomotor, cognitive, and affective domains.

For an objective to be applicable, it must be observable, measurable, and attainable. Objectives must be clearly and simply stated so that others can read and understand them and assessment is defensible. With this overview of objectives, the next step is to understand the parts of the objective and how the parts fit together to make the objectives appropriate and attainable for the student, and observable and measurable for the teacher. The parts of the objective are the stem, the behavior, the conditions, and the performance standard criteria.

Stem

Two ways to state the stem are as follows:

1. A traditional way: "The student will be able to . . ." The stem sets the stage for what the learner will be capable of doing at the end of the lesson in the psychomotor, cognitive, or affective domains.
2. Another way is "At the end of the lesson, the student will be able to . . ." or "after viewing a jazz dance performance, the student will be able to . . ."

The stem sets the stage for the next part of the objective, which describes the learner's behavior.

Behavior

The behavior is what the student has to *do* to show he has learned what you want him to learn. The behavior uses an action verb that is observable. Some action verbs describe relatively simple, everyday kinds of behavior, such as *draw, catch,* and *list.* Sometimes the verbs used for dance are generic, such as *demonstrate, execute, perform, create,* and *choreograph.* To make the verbs correspond to the level of difficulty indicated in the taxonomy, do one of the following two things:

1. Select from the descriptive terms for each level of the taxonomy.
2. In the psychomotor domain, if you use terms such as *beginning, intermediate,* and *advanced level,* list specific skills, concepts, or dances from the dance form that match the level of performance. The following is an example:

   The student will be able to execute a beginning ballet barre exercise (demi-plié in first, second, and fifth positions; battement tendu, battement tendu relevé, battement dégagés, rond de jambe à terre en dehors and en dedans, battement frappé, petit battement sur le cou-de-pied, battement développé, grand battement).

Keeping these two ideas in mind, write the behavior part of the objective:

1. Choose a verb that specifies the precise level of moving, thinking, or feeling.
2. Review the taxonomies and the descriptors used for each level. In most cases, these descriptors or their synonyms changed into verbs provide the concise levels of moving, thinking, and feeling.
3. Identify a precise level for the behavior that correlates to your goal for teaching and later for testing. Related to determining the student's behavior are the

conditions under which the behavior occurs.

Conditions

The conditions part of the objective includes where and when the student performs the behavior, such as in the classroom or another setting. The final part of the objective identifies how to determine whether the student has successfully achieved the behavioral objective.

Criteria for Performance

The criterion for performance states the expectations for student performance. The performance standard is the criterion for measuring the effectiveness of performance, which can be stated in a variety of ways.

First, determine the minimum acceptable accomplishment. This can be expressed either as a percentage or as a ratio. For example, "The student will be able to write the names of 20 American folk dances with 90 percent accuracy." Sometimes percentages are not a reliable way to measure the accomplishment of the student.

Another way to indicate the criterion is using a ratio. For example, the student will be able to execute triplets across the floor in a direct path three out of four times correctly. This type of performance standard specifies a definite number of times as the measure and the total amount of trials of the performance.

Specifying the assessment of the objective makes what is observed measurable. The performance criteria connect the method of assessment to the behavior and the conditions of the learning objective.

Relating Objectives to Assessment

Assessment of the dance class or specific items in the class are recorded in the lesson plan to expand on what was stated in the objective. The assessment items are listed with the rating scale or rubric included.

When developing the assessment strategies for the dance class, the dance educator determines the goal for the class. The dance teacher chooses the evaluation tool depending on the type of dance class she will evaluate. In dance technique classes, the singular goal is to increase the dancer's skill or technical abilities. The obvious choice for the majority of these classes is using performance testing methods. The teacher selects the individual exercises, steps, combinations, activities, or dances that she will teach and assess in the class. This selection must support the needs of all students as well as represent the dance content of the level of the class.

Putting It Together

You have done all of the parts of writing a behavioral objective; now it is time to put it together. The next step is to read your objective and determine whether it is observable, reasonable to accomplish in the class time allotted, and appropriate for the students in your teaching environment (see figure 9.3).

To get comfortable with writing objectives follow these steps. Write the stem (the who) and fill in the blanks for the remaining parts of the objective (the what, the when and where, and how or how much). After practice in writing a psychomotor objective, determine the parts of the cognitive and affective objectives. Figure 9.3 walks you through two ways to write a psychomotor objective. Figure 9.4 contains examples of cognitive and affective objectives.

Developing the objectives for the dance lesson plan requires that you write objectives in each of the three domains. You write objectives to establish the goals of your lesson plan and guide you through writing the lesson plan.

Summary

In developing the lesson plan, the dance educator considers the types of learning experiences that are appropriate for the dance form, learner, and environment. The lesson plan is an outline of what will happen in the class: the who, the what, the when, the where, and the how. When developing a lesson plan, the teacher focuses the objectives on what will be accomplished through doing (psychomotor), thinking (cognitive), and feelings and values (affective). The teacher must understand each of these three domains to write the lesson plan. These domains help the dance educator develop the three types of objectives for the dance class. The objective has four parts: the stem, the behavior, the condition, and the criterion for performance. The objective is the foundation for writing the lesson plan.

Stem: *"The student will be able to . . . "* If you have to write this a number of times, the anagram "TSWBAT" is often used for this phrase.	**OR**
	The who: *"The student."* [will be able to]
Behavior: *"Execute a beginning level ballet barre."* Indicate all specific exercises.	**The what (behavior/specific exercises):** "Will execute a beginning level ballet barre."
	The when and where (conditions): "By the last three weeks of the semester in class performance."
Conditions: The when—*"by the last three weeks of the semester"*—or some specific amount of time and the where—*"in classroom performance."*	**The how (performance criterion):** "Correctly" (100%–no range; between 80 to 90% accuracy–specifying the range; or competently–at least 70% correct).
Performance standard criterion: Correctly.	**OR**
How much or many times to meet the standard: *"At least six out of eight times."*	**The how much (performance standard):** For example, three out of four times or six out of eight times.

Figure 9.3 Two examples of psychomotor objectives.

Cognitive domain	Affective domain
The student will be able to (TSWBAT) name 10 European folk dances with at least 90% accuracy.	TSWBAT participate in social dancing during the class at least 80% of the time.
TSWBAT arrange the square and contra dances learned during the semester in their order of difficulty beginning with the easiest and ending with the most complex with at least 80% accuracy.	TSWBAT formulate the values of viewing a live dance performance versus a videotaped performance with at least 90% accuracy after participating in these two experiences.
	TSWBAT practice a performance attitude while performing beginning level jazz combinations by the end of the term, four out of six times.

Figure 9.4 Examples of cognitive and affective objectives.

References

Bloom, B.A., editor. 1956. *Taxonomy of education objectives: The classification of educational goals. Handbook I: Cognitive domain.* New York: David McKay.

Jewett, A.E., and L.L. Bain. 1985. *The curriculum process in physical education.* Dubuque, IA: Brown.

Krathwohl, D.R., B.S. Bloom, and B.B. Masia. 1964. *Taxonomy of educational objective domain.* New York: David McKay.

Rink, J.E. 1998. *Teaching physical education,* 3rd ed. Boston: WCB McGraw-Hill.

Simpson, E.J. 1966. *The classification of educational objectives: Psychomotor domain.* Vocational & technical education grant contract NOOE 85-104. Washington, DC: U.S. Department of Education.

It's Your Turn

1. Write several learning activities that relate to each of the three domains. Think of them as psychomotor (doing), cognitive (thinking), and affective (feeling).
2. Practice writing objectives in small groups. Begin by writing an objective in the psychomotor domain. One person from each group can share the group's work with the entire class to provide a variety of examples for each of the domains.
3. Using the charts and the examples, write your psychomotor objective. Select from the chart to compose the psychomotor objective. Then write another objective in the same domain. Underline and label each part of the objective (stem, behavior, conditions, and performance criteria). Discern the difference between action verbs chosen for an objective in the psychomotor *(do),* cognitive *(think),* and affective *(attitude and values)* domains. Check the action verb in relation to the domain; each objective should represent a single domain of learning.
4. Practice writing objectives by repeating these exercises for the cognitive and affective domains.

CHAPTER

10

Selecting the Appropriate Assessment Tools for Dance

Chapter Objectives

By the end of this chapter, you should be able to do the following:

- Understand the variety of possible assessment tools for dance.
- Select the most appropriate assessment tools for the learner, the lesson, and the environment.
- Create original performance scales, rubrics, and written tests.

Assessment as part of the teaching and learning process determines whether learning has occurred in the dance class. This chapter will help you understand types of assessment tools the dance teacher selects to test learners in the dance class. Assessment tools include performance examinations and written tests. Each of these tools serves different purposes in the dance class and provides a variety of feedback to the teacher and students. Learning how to assess dance is as important as learning how to write and deliver a lesson plan.

Using Assessment Techniques in the Dance Class

Assessment is a global term for types of evaluation tools that the teacher selects from when measuring students' performance and progress. Some general principles of classroom evaluation apply to all types of tests—performance, process, or written. The teacher uses the following steps to select an appropriate assessment tool:

1. Determine what is to be evaluated and its priority.
2. Select evaluation tools compatible to the testing situation.
3. Apply a variety of testing tools.
4. Understand the strengths and limitations of the testing tool.
5. Evaluate and test by using the principles of learning appropriate for the age and level of the learner (readiness); reflect needs and interests of the learners (motivation); remember what was learned (retention); and apply to various situations (transfer).

In dance technique classes, the goal is to increase the skill and technical abilities of the dancer. The obvious choice for the majority of dance classes is using performance testing methods. Later in creating a dance curriculum, you will encounter the following types of assessment tools:

- **Product,** such as performance testing, rating scales, and written testing
- **Process and product,** such as rubrics and contracts
- **Process,** such as process folios (e.g., journaling, reflections), portfolios (e.g., photographs, programs, dance roles performed), and group projects

Some types of assignments can be viewed as either product or process and product, depending on the teacher's point of view. These include written assignments such as dance concert or video reports, research papers, and oral presentations. When evaluating dance as both process and product, the teacher uses formative and summative evaluation, performance and authentic assessment, and objective testing modalities for grading students' work.

Formative and Summative Evaluation

Formative evaluation is ongoing. Each time an instructor teaches a class, he most likely does an informal evaluation; after the class he writes down what the students need to practice at the next class. The instructor also gives general and individual feedback to the dancers during each class.

Summative evaluations are usually done at certain points during and at the end of the unit or term to determine whether the dancers learned the new material and improved their skills. Evaluation tools specific to dance include performance tests administered throughout the unit or term. The results of these performance tests and other evaluation tools, such as written tests, oral reports, short research papers, and projects, determine whether dancers advance to the next level or stay at the same level.

Performance Evaluations

When the teacher creates performance tests, she identifies the content to be tested and the rating scale to be used. Performance evaluations use criterion-referenced evaluation tools, which focus on the student's performance in relation to defined criteria for an exercise, step, or combination. The teacher and the student may generate the criteria for performance either individually or together.

Performance testing takes place during the dance class. A videotape of a performance test allows the teacher and the dancer to rate the dancer's performance, and it provides the student with a permanent record of his performance. This recording can become part of a dancer's developing portfolio. Sometimes students do not understand how they executed a combination or how to correct their technique until they see it on videotape. With videotaped evaluation, teachers have a place to begin dialogue with students regarding their training in that setting.

Performance testing tools include checklists, rating scales, and Likert scales (see form 10.1). In these forms of performance evaluation, a student's performance is judged against established criteria. The teacher prepares the students for performance testing by explaining and using cues that are the criteria for performance. Cues are used as the criteria for performance because they contain the essential technical information about how an exercise or step is executed correctly. Each student's performance is judged against the established criteria appropriate for a specific performance level. The students rehearse and perfect the material for the dance performance test, and the teacher provides feedback to enhance each student's performance.

Checklist

The teacher or both the students and teacher develop a checklist of the attributes of correct performance of an exercise. In performance testing, the student either does it correctly or not.

Rating Scale

The teacher selects a rating scale: 1 to 5, 1 to 4, 1 to 3, or some other range—usually no more than a 10-point range. He designates the highest and the lowest number on the scale and develops a criterion for correct performance of each exercise. The teacher rates each student's performance against the established criterion.

Teacher and students viewing a video of their dance performance test.

Teacher videotaping a performance test.

Likert Scale

A Likert scale, named after the man who developed the system, uses either a 5- or 4-point rating scale for judging performance. The problem with using a 5-point scale is that a rating of 3 is often selected for mediocre performance. Using a 4-point scale, the evaluator must discriminate between what constitutes a 3 and a 2 on the rating scale. A 3-point scale is suitable for determining basic movement skills, as is the checklist.

The Likert scale is similar to a rubric. The highest number and lowest number on the scale are identified. Each number on the scale has an indicator that qualifies it within the range. For example, a 4-point scale could use the following descriptive terms:

- 4 = distinguished
- 3 = proficient
- 2 = apprentice
- 1 = beginner

All rating scales give numerical values to judgments about students' performance. In evaluating exercises and steps that have observable criteria, this type of measurement is very sound; the bottom line is that you can see what is performed and how well it is executed.

Designing a rating scale is simple. Draw lines down a sheet of paper to create a grid. List the skills across the top of the paper. On the lines down the side, list the names of the students. As the students execute the skills in small groups, write the numerical rating in the column under each skill and in the row with the student's name.

A rating scale is a quick method of performance testing, but it requires you to determine and communicate the criteria to students throughout the teaching and learning process. Before testing, students should rehearse the performance test in class. Students in the class can also provide feedback using reciprocal teaching to enhance the performance. You must have a clear understanding of the criteria for each item on the test and determine what constitutes each level of the rating scale. Furthermore, write short notes in the boxes provided as reminders about the numerical score. After the performance test, allow students to review their scores. Be prepared to answer their questions about their scores. If a student does ask you why he received a certain score, ask him to perform the exercise or combination again; more often than not, he will be able to tell you the reason for the score. Beginning students may experience performance testing anxiety. Try to alleviate this by keeping the rehearsal and testing process as similar as possible. Give beginning students the benefit of the doubt when you score their first attempts in a performance test.

If you use a rating scale to evaluate combinations and dances, you will find that you must define the attributes of a successful performance. From there you define what constitutes the highest level of performance, the level below average, and so on down to what you consider an unacceptable performance. These specific descriptions

FORM 10.1

Performance Testing Examples

Sequential Body Rolls

Beginning in a standing position, start the roll from the top of the head down, and then up, sequentially through the body.

Stand in parallel second position. Begin the roll from the top of the head to the chin touching the chest, then return to beginning position, 2 times. Roll from the head through the back to the waist, then return to beginning position, 2 times. Roll from the head through the back and pelvis to the knee, then return to beginning position, 2 times. Roll from the head through the body (back and pelvis) so that the hands touch the floor, then return to beginning position, 2 times.

Checklist

Observe the student executing the sequential body roll. If the student performs the movement correctly, make a check by the item on the list. If the student performs the movement incorrectly, make a minus by the item on the list.

Assessment of Sequential Body Rolls

1. Stand in parallel second position. _____
2. Roll from the top of the head to the chin touching the chest and return. _____
3. Roll from the head to the waist; return. _____
4. Roll from the head through to the knee; return. _____
5. Roll from the head through the body so that the hands touch the floor; return. _____

Rating Scale

Observe the student executing the sequential body rolls 4 times. Using a 3-point scale, write a 3 by the item on the list if the student performs the movement correctly all of the times. If the student performs the movement correctly 2 or 3 of the times, write a 2 by the item on the list. If the student performs the movement 1 or 0 time correctly, write a 1 by the item on the list.

Assessment of Sequential Body Rolls

1. Stand in parallel second position. _____
2. Roll from the top of the head to the chin touching the chest and return. _____
3. Roll from the head to the waist; return. _____
4. Roll from the head through to the knee; return. _____
5. Roll from the head through the body so that the hands touch the floor; return. _____

(continued)

(continued)

Likert (4-point) Scale

Observe the student performing the sequential body roll 4 times. Use the criteria defined below to evaluate the student's performance.

Rating Scale: 4 = highest; 0 = lowest

Knowledge: Sequence of the specific movement and transition (does the student know the combination?)

Timing: Using correct counts and proper phrasing (is the student moving on the correct beat?)

Execution: Performing the movement correctly with appropriate technique (does the student perform the individual movements of the exercise or step correctly?)

Placement: Using correct body alignment throughout the movement (does the student use proper placement?)

Energy: Utilizing the correct energy during the movement sequence (does the student possess appropriate movement quality?)

Musicality: The dancer's ability to transcend the counts and dance (does student dance to the music using breath and phrasing?)

Name of class ______________________________

Rating 0-4

Name of students	**Knowledge**	**Timing**	**Execution**	**Placement**	**Energy**	**Musicality**
Apple, May						
Doe, John						
Coe, Susan						

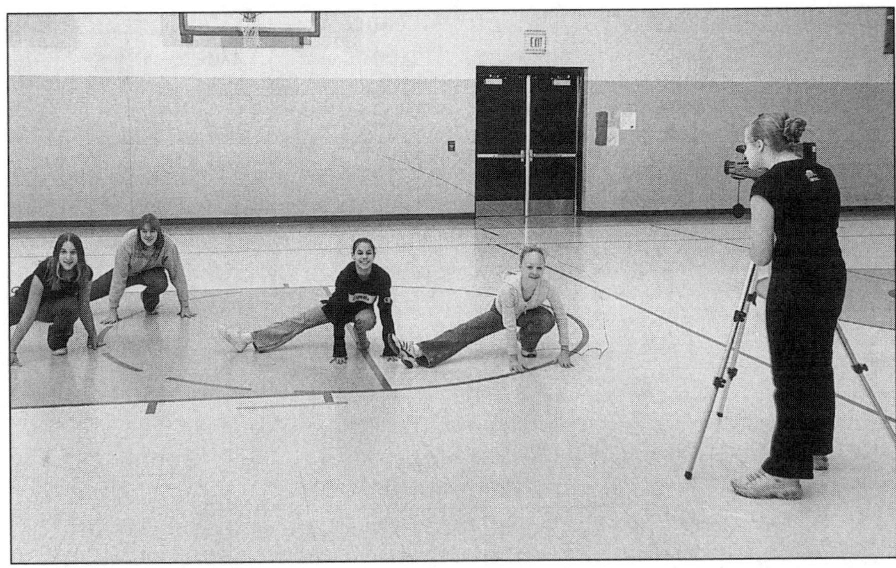

Student operates video camera while other students perform.

lead you to write rubrics for performance testing as a part of authentic assessment.

Authentic Assessment

Assessment that takes place as close as possible to a real-life situation is authentic assessment. Wiggins (1999) defines *authentic assessment* as assessment in which a student must perform exemplary tasks that are typically required when one has mastered a particular discipline. The following are some factors to consider when developing authentic assessments (Lazear 1999):

- Use learning, thinking, critical-thinking, and problem-solving skills.
- Execute tasks that lead to a quality performance or product such as a dance.
- Integrate research that produces knowledge rather than reproduces facts.
- Identify meaningful tasks at which students should excel.
- Create challenges that require analysis and evaluation of knowledge.
- Mentor the student to enhance performance.
- Involve students in the learning and assessment processes to demystify the processes.

Authentic assessment in performance entails selecting exercises, steps, combinations, and dances for evaluation appropriate for the skill and motor learning level, cognitive level, and age of the students. The teacher makes the performance testing setting as similar as possible to the students' real world, as in a performance situation. The dancers perform the prescribed exercises, combinations, or dances without input (or with minimal input if they are beginners) from the teacher. The teacher and students develop criterion-referenced evaluation tools, or rubrics, to define the expected outcomes for the performance or choreography.

The rubric is a versatile evaluation tool for dance assessment, but other valid authentic evaluation tools also exist. Some authentic process and product assessments include group projects, oral reports, dance concert or video reports, process and progress folios, portfolios (print, electronic, and video), projects, reflective journals and logs, and contracts.

Rubrics

The rubric is an authentic assessment tool. All rubrics contain the following features (Pickett and Dodge 2001):

- Focus on measuring a stated objective of performance, behavior, or quality
- Establish a range to rate the performance
- Contain specific performance characteristics arranged in levels indicating the degree to which a standard has been met

The following are the advantages of using a rubric in authentic assessment (Pickett and Dodge 2001):

- The assessment is objective and consistent.
- The teacher clarifies criteria in specific terms.
- It shows how students' work will be evaluated.
- It promotes students' awareness and focus on the criteria selected.
- It provides a method for feedback regarding students' performance and instruction effectiveness.
- It establishes benchmarks by which to measure student progress.

Teachers and students can develop rubrics. Teachers can empower students' learning by guiding students to assess other students' performance or to design a rubric based on the established criteria. Rubrics ensure students' accountability for the material. Students can develop and use them to understand their expectations for every level of performance.

Rubric development for the lesson plan begins with reflection and analysis on how well the objective and the dance lesson correlate. These are the steps for developing a rubric (Pickett and Dodge 2001):

1. Determine the learning outcomes or criteria. Sometimes there are categories of criteria, such as in a group project that entails written work, oral reports, performance, and group process.

2. Within a category, each rubric item should focus on a different skill. Evaluate only measurable criteria.

3. Choose a ranking system with a range of three or four levels of performance.

4. Select indicators for each level of performance in an ascending order of competence. Use neutral words as indicators to avoid the implication of good versus bad words. Each indicator includes a numerical ranking. Here are some examples of indicators:

Needs improvement (1)	Satisfactory (2)
Good (3)	Exemplary (4)
Beginning (1)	Developing (2)
Accomplished (3)	Needs work (1)
Good (2)	Excellent (3)

5. Write the descriptor for the highest level of performance on the rating scale.

After you complete the five initial steps of writing the rubric, circle the concept words that can vary in a descriptor. These words will be the ones that you change as you write the category below the highest level. The concept word conveys the levels of performance from *all* to *none, complete* to *incomplete, always* to *generally, sometimes* to *rarely.*

If the descriptor is a series of aspects of the performance, underline the word or words and define its components, such as in the following example:

Students assess peers' performances.

- *Technique:* skill in executing dance movements that meet the demands of the dance form.
- *Timing:* execution of movement using correct rhythm and counts to the music.
- *Principles:* movement laws and rules for executing dance skills (list principles appropriate for the dance form).

Then, each category of performance levels is described:

- Exemplary: performance using precise technique and timing and complete integration of principles.
- Accomplished: performance with accurate technique and timing with frequent application of principles.
- Developing: performance with unclear technique and timing with some application of principles.
- Beginning: performance with minimal technique and timing with rare application of principles.

In developing a rubric, indicate the importance of each item in relation to the entire lesson or project. Keep the rubric short and simple, use brief statements and phrases, and select 4 to 15 items to evaluate—ideally, the entire rubric should fit on one sheet of paper (see form 10.2). See forms A.1 through A.3 on pages 405-412 in the appendix for more detailed rubrics for evaluating the psychomotor, affective, and cognitive objectives found in the dance units in chapter 13.

When students participate in developing the rubric, engage them in the process of determining the criterion for evaluation. Reevaluate the rubric after using it in the class. (Did it work? Was it sufficiently detailed? Do you need to revise it?)

Group Projects

Group projects are an important part of student-centered learning. When devising group projects, the teacher must have in mind a goal for the outcome of the project. He should have a sense of each class member's personality and how the students interact with one another. The teacher often selects the members of the group to ensure a positive group dynamic for a successful project.

The scope of group projects depends on the topic, the expectations of the project, and the time available in or outside of class to develop it. Group projects can involve performing a combination and creating choreography. Other types of projects may involve researching dance topics, related arts, and interdisciplinary work.

Oral Reports

Talking and dancing are two very different methods of expression. Oral reports are generally not a dancer's strength, and they can be stressful for dance students to present to the class. Begin with short reports to ease students into longer presentations.

Dance Concert and Video Reports

Viewing and reporting on a dance or video performance help students develop an appreciation of dance and a sense of the teaching and learning process involved. Learners develop observation skills by identifying the elements and principles of dance in a structured performance. Students analyze a performance and communicate their impressions about it through reports and critiques. A typical dance concert or video report includes information about the dancers' execution and artistry, the choreography, and the production aspects of the performance.

Process Folios

Process folios include initial drafts, notes, and journal entries about the steps the student took from searching for an idea to producing a completed product. In this model learners analyze what they know, evaluate their thinking, and select strategies to solve problems. The process folio involves six steps:

1. Acquire the basic facts.
2. Understand how you feel about the project.
3. Determine what you know about the subject.
4. Grasp the dynamics and variables that are part of the problem.
5. Create an inner dialogue as you sift through and refine ideas about the problem.
6. Synthesize knowledge learned and transfer it into everyday application for future use.

FORM 10.2

Types of Rubrics

Observe the student performing four sequential body rolls and

- apply the performance criteria generically stated in the following three performance rubrics, or
- the teacher determines, selects, and lists the psychomotor, cognitive, or affective factors of the performance that will be evaluated (see forms A.1 through A.3 in the appendix for a more detailed rubric using the domains).

Using a Rubric With a Four-Point Scale

The observer views the student executing the body roll, applies the performance criteria (listed in the left column of the rubric form) and then determines the student's performance by indicating one of the four categories (low [1] to high [4]):

- Beginning (1): The student executes the body rolls *rarely* applying performance criteria reflecting a basic level of performance.
- Developing (2): The student executes the body rolls *sometimes* applying performance criteria reflecting development and movement toward mastery of performance.
- Accomplished (3): The student executes the body rolls *most of the time* applying the performance criteria reflecting mastery of performance.
- Exemplary (4): The student executes the body rolls *always* applying the performance criteria reflecting the highest level of performance.

Selected criteria	Beginning (1)	Developing (2)	Accomplished (3)	Exemplary (4)
Rolls down through vertebrae.				
Returns through vertebrae.				
Connects to counts for exercise.				
Applies technique.				
Applies principles of element.				
Uses breathing.				

FORM 10.2

Using a Rubric With a Three-Point Scale

The observer views the student executing the body roll, applies the performance criteria (listed in the left column of the rubric form) and then determines the student's performance by indicating one of the three categories:

- Needs improvement (1): The student executes the body roll *seldom or ineffectively* applying the performance criteria reflecting a superficial level of performance.
- Satisfactory (2): The student executes the body rolls *usually* applying the performance criteria reflecting a development toward mastery of performance.
- Excellent (3): The student executes the body roll *accurately* applying the performance criteria reflecting a *commendable* level of performance.

Selected criteria	Needs improvement (1)	Satisfactory (2)	Excellent (3)
Rolls down through vertebrae.			
Returns through vertebrae.			
Connects to counts for exercise.			
Applies technique.			
Applies principles of element.			
Uses breathing.			

(continued)

(continued)

Write name of exercise, step, combination, or dance here

Selected criteria	Possible points	Self-evaluation	Peer evaluation	Teacher evaluation
Application of technique	10			
Sequence of combination or dance	10			
Application of principles	10			
Correct timing, rhythm	10			
Use of qualities or efforts	10			
Total possible points	**50**			

Rate each category of criteria according to the following scale: 9–10 = excellent, 7–8 = very good, 5–6 = good, 3–4 = satisfactory, 1–2 = needs improvement, and 0 = unsatisfactory.

Multiple Performance Evaluations Rubric

The teacher selects the criteria. If the criteria are general, such as application of technique, then the teacher must have a written list of the specific criteria, and its point structure should equal the total possible points to be consistent in evaluation for all students' performances.

The total possible points can be changed to a rating scale of 5 or 4 or 3. The criteria must be adjusted to reflect this change. This form of rubric allows the student to conduct a self-evaluation as well as to participate in reciprocal teaching if this is a method that the teacher selects in addition to teacher evaluation. In some models, the student can use the self-evaluation and peer evaluation to achieve the next to the highest rating for his performance, but to be evaluated for the highest level of performance, the student's performance must be evaluated by the teacher.

In the learner's journal, the learner initiates the writing assignments or the teacher prompts the assignments. The teacher can gain an understanding of the student and his learning style and comfort level through assignment of expository writing exercises. The following are some general journaling prompts:

- Daily self-assessment of effort and identification of areas of future work or accurate records of dance activities
- Personal analysis of attitudes toward dance and dance class or personal strengths and weaknesses
- Specific assignments that analyze a performance
- Preparation and updates of personal plan to improve one component of dance
- Analysis of personal performance (dancing or teaching)
- Descriptions of choreographic motivation, concepts, or aesthetics

Journal entries often include reflection and problem solving. These processes are the same as those we do in our workplaces and our personal lives. Authentic assessment tools provide practice in developing everyday skills. Journal entries often become part of process folios of work.

Progress Folios

A progress folio is a student's record of his development over time as a performer, a choreographer, or a teacher. This type of folio is a collection of different kinds of evidence of a student's progress toward becoming a professional. The following are types of evidence that might be included: different kinds of process folios, written assignments, observation reports, research papers, dance concert reports, written evaluations, video evaluations, pictures, programs, and newspaper reviews of performances. This repository becomes the basis from which the student selects items to include in his portfolio.

Portfolios

Portfolios include samples of students' work and assessments of the work. A portfolio demonstrates progress, skill development, and achievements as well as personal developments that give a broad view of the student's abilities. A portfolio includes samples of work in various forms:

- Journal entries about choreographic ideas, performances, and progress in technique classes
- Performance rating scales and written tests
- Drawings of choreographic ideas, costumes, and other design elements
- Written reports, papers, projects, and notes for oral reports
- Analysis of choreography, one's personal performance, others' performances, and media reviews
- Videotapes or photos of a student's performance

Information in the portfolio is organized in chronological order and by categories for the work samples or by area of the curriculum. Once organized, the portfolio presents a sequential view of the learner's progress toward meeting standards that are consistent with the curriculum goals.

Video Performances

Video performances of dance students have a place within process folios and portfolios. A video performance, which includes recordings of stage performances and technique examinations, is the systematic recording of the dancer's development in one or more dance forms over time.

Projects

Projects are exhibits, performances, and displays central to a specific discipline. According to Howard Gardner (1993), in this model students produce, perceive and reflect, and self-assess their work. Repetition refines the process so that it becomes automatic to the student. The dance educator is responsible for setting up the process so that it meets the artistic and professional standards demanded of the art. That way, students can use the process successfully rather than reconstruct it with new and more specific requirements at a later time.

Reflective Journals and Logs

Students use writing and drawing in reflective journals and logs to record their observations, thoughts, feelings, ideas, and questions. One type of log is a thinking log, which students use to identify a problem and areas of discovery, understanding, and confusion; they also use the log to explore the problem's application to real life. In another type of log the student addresses feelings, thoughts, and images associated with the problem before and after so that he can view both perspectives (Lazear 1999).

Contracting

A performance contract is an individualized learning and assessment strategy that allows students to determine specific learning goals for the semester. An effective contract states performance goals that are measurable and attainable (Kassing 1992). The following scenario illustrates a student's use of a contract to attain goals.

Myra is a high school student enrolled in an advanced-beginning jazz class. She is highly motivated to achieve technical proficiency to move to the next level of study. She wants to become more responsible for improving her technique, so she uses a contract to focus on attaining goals. The following might be two such goals for Myra:

1. I want to increase the number of turns I can perform.
2. I want to improve my transitions between movements.

Usually, students focus on no more than three identified goals at one time, which may range from technical to aesthetic. When writing the contract, the student lists her goals on a sheet of paper. Using a rating scale, the student specifies the number she considers as her current level of performance and her performance goal for the end of the contract period. Again, the ranking scale can be either a 4- or 5-point scale. Using a 5-point scale, Myra analyzes her current performance as a 3 for the first goal and a 2 for the second goal. She proposes her ranking for the end of the contracting period as a 5 for the first goal and a 4 for the second goal. She gives her contract sheet to her teacher. In their short conference, the teacher may clarify goals or discuss possible beginning or ending rankings. The teacher ensures that the student has selected appropriate and achievable goals.

At the middle of the contract period, the teacher and Myra meet to review her progress on meeting the goals. At this time, the ranking goal for the end of the semester can be adjusted. Myra believes she will be able to meet her second goal successfully. She is still encountering problems with her pirouettes, so she and the teacher agree to change her rating for goal 1 from a 5 to a 4. At the end of the semester, Myra gives her contract sheet to the teacher for review. They discuss Myra's performance of her contracted goals. Myra then identifies her new goals for the next contract.

A contract can be an evaluative tool that is part of the student's grade, or it can be a voluntary, independent project. This tool helps students take responsibility for the process of learning and focus on identified items throughout their daily work. Students create their own priorities and develop personal responsibility for their progress.

Although these evaluation tools are subjective in nature, they provide many ways for the student and the teacher to assess progress over time. To determine the structure and requirements for projects, think through the project before presenting it to students. Share your criteria with the students when introducing the project so that students creatively develop the project in their own way. Analyze the criteria after the initial time students have completed the project; then you can streamline it for the next time you use it with a class.

Table 10.1 presents an overview of product, process and product, and process assessment tools and their uses in the dance class.

Although authentic assessment gains continued recognition and support in academic situations, traditional evaluation methods continue to be part of the total evaluation picture for students' progress.

Written Tests

As a dance educator, you must choose the right evaluation tools to adequately represent each student's performance skills, knowledge, and intellectual abilities. You must also understand the basics of developing written tests and their application to dance.

Developing Written Tests

Written tests for dance are as necessary as performance tests in most educational environments. Developing written tests requires an understanding of testing terminology:

Table 10.1 Types of Evaluation Tools

Product	Process and product	Process
Performance tests • Criterion-referenced evaluation. • The criteria are the cues for the exercise, step, or combination. **Checklists** • Teacher or students and the teacher develop a checklist. • The teacher checks the student's performance. **Rating scales** • Teacher selects a rating scale (1-5, 1-4, 1-3, or another range), usually up to a 10-point range. • Designate the high and low of the scale. • Dévelop criteria (cues) for correct performance of each exercise, step, or test. • Specify performance expectations for each number value on the scale. • Teacher rates each student's performance against the established criterion, or • A student rates another student's performance. Then if the student performs the skills for the teacher, he may increase his rating.	**Rubrics** The rubric is a rating chart that is adaptable to performance, projects, and written work. A rubric contains the following features. • A chart designed to measure a stated objective (performance, behavior, or quality) • establishes a range to rate the performance • contains specific performance characteristics arranged in levels indicating the degree to which a standard has been met. Rubrics can be developed by the teacher and by students. **Contracts** Students involved in contracting gain ownership in the process and responsibility in deciding what they consider important in their learning. • At the beginning of the term, the student (1) identifies what he will do to increase his performance skills or to earn credit for a project or course, or (2) selects no more than three aspects of his performance that he wants to focus on in the dance class. • These range from the concrete to the abstract. For example, a concrete skill is to improve his demi-plié in all combinations. An abstract skill is to increase the use of breath phrasing while doing combinations. • After the items have been identified, using a Likert scale the student assigns a value to his present performance level. • The student determines the personal performance goal that will be reached by the end of the term. For example, his demi-plié is a 2 at the beginning of the term and he sets his goal that his performance of the demi-plié at the end of the term will be a 4. • The teacher reviews the student's performance contract for elements chosen, beginning ratings, and the goal. Sometimes the teacher redefines these performance goals to become manageable and attainable. • The teacher and student review and sign the contract. • Midway through the term, the teacher and student meet to discuss the progress being made for each of the elements. At this time the contract can be negotiated as to modify the end-of-term goal. The goal may stay the same or go up or down on the rating scale. • At the end of the semester, the student determines if he has reached his contracted goals for the term. • He conferences with the teacher, discussing his self-analysis and the teacher's analysis of his performance goals. • After the conference and while his performance is fresh in his mind, he notes three possible aspects of performance that he will focus upon during the next term.	**Process folios** A process folio is a student's record of his impressions and learning from undergoing a process. • The student's point of view can be performer, choreographer, or teacher. For example, if a guest artist or faculty member sets a dance on a group of students, they may be asked to keep a record of the process. • The process folio includes personal perceptions and observations that are often in the form of journal entries. • The process folio includes the following aspects: *production* (utilizing the craft—technique and principles, revising work—by viewing it from various points of view, solves the problem creatively, and expresses an idea or feeling in the work) *reflection* (self-evaluation of work, has a sense of standards, application of critical comments and suggestions, evaluate others' work and articulate goals about a particular work and art works in general) *perception* (from journal and discussion, the dimension of the understanding, the

(continued)

Table 10.1 *(continued)*

Product	Process and product	Process
Likert scales A Likert scale uses either a 5- or 4-point rating scale. • Choosing a 4-point scale, the evaluator must discriminate between what constitutes a 3 and a 2 on the rating scale. • See instructions for rating scales.	**Oral reports or presentations** Talking and dancing are two very different ways of expressing yourself. Oral reports are generally not a dancer's strength, and it can be extremely stressful for dance students to present oral reports to the class. • Begin with mini-reports to ease the student into longer presentations. Specify length. • Preparing for oral reports requires research and writing to create the report. Writing for an oral presentation uses a different structure than writing a paper. • Allowing students to use note cards for the oral report gives them additional support. • Stress presentational skills such as stance, speaking slowly, and making eye contact with the audience. • Both oral and written assignments should include written feedback from the teacher on the evaluation sheet. **Written assignments** Written assignments should be given periodically to enhance the student's ability to describe and explain his art; like learning to dance, writing is a skill that must be practiced. Writing about the art of dance develops a more literate and knowledgeable person. • Written assignments should relate to the dance form and course content. • Types of writing assignments include: essays, philosophical statements, biographies of dancers, historical research papers, self-analysis during a process, journal entries, tests, and other assignments. **Dance concert and video reports** Viewing a performance and then writing about what was observed hones students' observation, critical thinking skills, and writing skills. The dance concert or video report form provides ways of examining dance performance. These reports are viable assignments for dance technique courses, composition, and history courses. • The dance concert report may describe what the student saw during the performance. • The report may include a critical examination of the performance or the dance work. • It may be supported by research that includes what dance critics wrote about the dance or aesthetic, historical, and/or cultural information about the performance of the dance work. • The form itself is somewhat generic so it can serve most concert and other dance form performances. **Journals** Expressing personal points of view in writing helps students engage in increasing their perceptions and astuteness about the dance process and their personal journey.	ability to discriminate, awareness as to properties, qualities of the work within its environment) *approach to work* (the teacher observing the student's engagement in the work, ability to work independently or collaboratively, and utilization of resources—books, videos, music, and people) **Portfolios** A portfolio is a record of a student's process of learning over a certain amount of time. This could be a semester, a year, or a four-year program. • The portfolio is a collection of evidence that traces how the student learns, what was learned, and documents his progress during the specified time period. • The material in the portfolio is organized by chronological order and categories with all entries dated. • The portfolio contains various records: written works, videos, photographs, journals, and so forth. In addition it includes student and teacher evaluations of performance that include rating scales and rubrics, personal development contracts, and other graded

Product	Process and product	Process
	The teacher can gain an understanding of the student and his learning style and comfort level through expository writing. Journals have many uses in the dance classroom. They can be personal or shared with the instructor. They can be the work of one individual or part of a community journal. • Writing assignments are either initiated by the student or prompted by the teacher. Some generic suggested journaling prompts include: • daily self-assessment of effort and identification of areas of future work • accurate records of dance activities • analysis of personal attitudes toward dance and dance class • awareness of areas of personal strengths and weakness • specific assignments such as analysis of a dance video • preparation and updating of personal plan to improve in dance • analysis of personal performance (dancing or teaching) • descriptions of choreographic motivation, processes, ideas, concepts, or aesthetic evaluation Journals, written assignments, and videotaped examples of performances and the student's choreography are often collected in a process folio or portfolio. **Group projects** Group projects are an important aspect of student-centered learning. Devising group projects requires the teacher have • a goal in mind for the outcome of the project; and • a sense of the personalities of each of the class members and how they interact with one another. The teacher often determines the members of the group to ensure a positive group dynamic for a successful end result or product. The scope of group projects depends upon the topic, the expectations of the project, and the time available in or outside of class to develop it. Examples of group projects can be performing a combination or creating choreography. Other types of projects may involve related arts or interdisciplinary work. Students and/or teacher develops the rubric for the parts of the project: written work, oral presentation, performance, individual participation, and group collaboration.	assignments such as lesson plans, lighting designs, choreographic charts, written analysis, historical research papers, and dance concert or video reports. The portfolio documents a student's progress, but is not a vehicle for comparison of one student's work with another. Many believe that the portfolio allows students to reflect and self-assess their work that will in turn stimulate better work in the future and greater involvement in deciding how to proceed in their learning.

- **Validity** is how well the evaluation tool serves the use for which it was intended.
- **Reliability** is the consistency or accuracy of the test scores from one group to the next.
- **Usability** is the practicality of administering the test and reporting the test results.

These testing basics are applicable to both performance and written tests even though each approach comes from a different perspective. Performance tests use criterion-referenced evaluation (the results of a person's performance compared to an established criterion). In written tests, norm-referenced evaluation (a student's score compared with other students' scores) is used.

Types of Test Questions

Written test questions are either objective or subjective. Objective written test items include the following:

- Short answer and completion, in which the learner supplies information
- True or false, matching, and multiple choice, in which the learner selects an answer

Subjective test items leave room for interpretation:

- Extended response or essay questions
- Restricted response (for example, when the learner is asked to state two advantages or disadvantages of using static stretches versus using PNF stretches)

The attributes of each type of written test are compiled in table 10.2.

Developing Written Test Items

To a dance instructor, writing examinations is very far from dancing. Academic institutions rely on written documentation to verify students' learning, and written tests are still the predominant mode of evaluation. There are several strategies that can make the process easier.

Writing test items takes time. You will find it easier to write the test items as you progress through the unit or term rather than come up with all the questions at the end of the term. Write a few test items after each class session to reinforce the important points made, especially in dance theory classes. The following are suggestions for writing test items:

- Write the test items on note cards.
- Avoid trick questions and too much humor.
- Consider the number of items and the time allotted for the test.
- Keep each item isolated rather than dependent on the correct answer from the previous question.
- Group all of the same types of questions together.
- Arrange the items in order of difficulty, beginning with the easiest questions and moving to more difficult questions.
- Balance the types of questions (multiple choice, true and false, matching, essay, and short answer) that the test contains. This will ensure fairness for students who excel in one area over another.

Scoring subjective items such as essay tests requires preparation before you administer the test. After you have written the question, write out the acceptable responses and the key points you expect. When you begin to grade the exam, score one of the essay questions on all papers, then shuffle the papers. Write comments on the essay, indicating strengths as well as suggestions on making the essay stronger.

After the students have taken the written examination, run a test item analysis. On a copy of the test, list the number of students who answered each of the questions correctly and incorrectly. This type of feedback will provide information about each question. Keep your note cards with you as you write the test item analysis on the back. These questions can be used in a different order in future tests. Put test questions into separate computer files organized by dance content and types of questions. This way, you begin a test bank from which you can draw for future tests.

Grading Students' Work

Oral, written, and group projects in dance require an instructor's objectivity and consistency of standards adapted to the level and to each student.

Table 10.2 Types of Written Tests

Type of test	Advantages and disadvantages	Suggestions for construction
Short answer or completion *Instructions:* Fill in the blank to make the statement correct. Complete the statement to make it correct.	*Advantages* • Easy to construct • Reduces guessing • Requires knowledge of answer *Disadvantages* • Unsuitable for complex learning • Requires careful wording to get the correct answer	• Create a statement so that the required answer is definite and brief. • Do not take statements from textbooks as the basis for short-answer questions. • Use a direct question instead of an incomplete statement. • If the answer is numerical, indicate the type of answer required. • Blanks for answers should be to the right of the question and of equal length. • In a completion statement, limit the number of blank.
True-false or alternative-response items *Instructions:* Read each of the following statements. If the statement is true, circle the "T." If the statement is false, circle the "F."	*Advantage* • Easy to construct *Disadvantages* • Usually obvious or ambiguous • Requires material stated without qualification or exception • Suitable for basic knowledge testing • High guessing odds (50% correct) • Reliability is low because of guessing factor • Diagnostic value of test is low • Validity of response is questionable	• Avoid general statements that are judged either true or false. • Avoid trivial statements. • Avoid negative statements and using double negatives. • Avoid long, complex sentences. • Avoid including two ideas in a statement unless the focus is cause and effect of a relationship. • If opinion is stated, designate the source, unless the ability to identify opinion is the point. • Both true and false statements should be approximately the same length. • The number of true and false statements should be approximately equal.
Matching *Instructions:* On the line to the left of each statement in column A, write the letter of the appropriate answer from column B. The answers in column B may be used once, or you may specify that items in column B may be used more than once. Only one response per question.	*Advantages* • Ability to identify relationships between two items • Compact form covers a large amount of material • Easy to construct *Disadvantages* • It is as easy to write a poor matching statement as any other • Material in column B must be homogeneous	• Use only homogeneous material in the matching section. • Include unequal number of responses and statements (premises). • Tell the student whether the responses are used once or more than once. • Keep the list of items brief; if one or two words, place at the right of the statements. • Place all parts of the matching test section on the same page. • Keep all extraneous materials out of column B. • Statements are numbered; responses are lettered sequentially.

(continued)

Table 10.2 *(continued)*

Type of test	Advantages and disadvantages	Suggestions for construction
Multiple-choice items *Stem:* The direct question or incomplete statement *Alternatives:* The list of suggested solutions *Distractors:* Incorrect or remaining alternatives *Best answer response:* Used for HOW and WHY questions *Correct answer response:* One absolutely correct answer Select either 3 or 4 alternatives for the entire bank of multiple-choice questions. *Directions:* Write the letter of the correct answer to the question in the space provided at the left. Circle the letter of the correct answer to the question.	*Advantages* • Most widely used testing item format • Can measure complex learning outcomes • Flexible • Avoids ambiguity and vagueness • Greater reliability • Best answer reduces qualification problems that lead to generalizations • Homogeneous alternatives are not necessary • Plausible but incorrect alternatives indicate students' thinking or other problems *Disadvantages* • Limited to verbal responses • Not well adapted to problem solving or mathematical skills • Not well adapted to measuring organization ability and presentation of ideas • Sometimes difficult to create with plausible alternatives	• The stem of the item should (1) be meaningful in itself, (2) present a definite problem, and (3) include as much of the information as possible without irrelevant materials. • Use negatively stated items only when significant learning requires it. • Alternatives should be grammatically consistent with the stem of the item. • An item should have only one correct or clearly the best answer. • Items that measure understanding may contain some humor or novelty (for applied situations to demonstrate a principle). • All distractors should be plausible. • Verbal associations or repetition between the stem and answer should be avoided. • Alternatives should be the same length. • The correct answer should appear in all of the alternative positions but in random order. • Use "none of the above" or "all of the above" sparingly. • Use multiple-choice items only when other types of items are inappropriate.
Essay items (example) *Instructions:* In narrative form, indicate differences between ___ and ___. **Extended response questions (example)** *Instructions:* Compare ___ and ___ in terms of significant developments. Cite specific examples.	*Advantages* • Provides a way to measure complex learning • Emphasis is on integration, application, and problem solving • Develops writing skills • Easy to construct *Disadvantages* • Unreliability of scoring • Increased time for scoring the answers • Limited sampling of material	• Restrict the use of essay questions to learning outcomes that are best met using this type of item. • Formulate questions that elicit the behavior specified by learning outcomes. • Phrase the questions so that the student clearly understands the task. • Indicate an appropriate time limit for writing the answer to the question. • Avoid using optional questions.

Suggestions for scoring an essay or extended response question

- Prepare an outline of the expected answers in advance.
- Use an appropriate scoring method such as points or rubric.
- Decide on how to handle extraneous or irrelevant content.
- Evaluate all answers to the question before going on to the next question.
- Evaluate answers without being aware of the student's name.
- If this is an outcome test, get two independent ratings of the work.

Develop different levels of expectations and criteria for learners in relation to their age, level of study, and the unit or course.

Select a logical grading system to reflect appropriate emphasis on the work involved in the project. The grading system should be easy to handle and efficient to maintain. You can use a spreadsheet to create a grading system or invest in a grading program. The system should be numerical and can be based on either a point system, a percentage system, or a pass/fail system. A numerical system is more accurate than a letter grade system because it uses a number grade that gives you a more specific score within a range of numbers.

Point System

A point system sets up a number of points within a range that equates with an assignment or project. The sum of the points equals all of the evaluation methods used during the course. Accompanying this system is a grading scale that assigns the numerical range for each of the letter grades. To determine the numerical ranges, calculate 90 percent of the total points, 80 percent, 70 percent, and so on.

Percentage System

A percentage system is based on 100 percent. All the evaluation methods used during the course are assigned a percentage, which together add up to 100 percent. Accompanying this system is a grading scale that assigns the percentage ranges to letter grades.

Pass/Fail System

Pass/fail is a system that determines whether students meet at least the minimum requirements for passing the course. This evaluation method is often used in general education and can be elected by the student. A teacher may not be aware that a student has chosen this option until she completes the final grade sheet.

Grading Scales

Grading scales designate the range of the letter grades. A standard grading scale is as follows:

- 100–90 = A
- 89–80 = B
- 79–70 = C
- 69–? = D
- ?–? = F

The teacher makes several decisions about the grading scale. These include what constitutes an F (or failing grade) and where the numerical cutoff point is between a D and an F. Effective teachers grade students consistently in relation to standards that are reasonable, fair, and attainable. Dance is a subjective discipline, and too often instructors in academic settings have relied on subjective methods in grading. Subjectivity in dance will always be an inherent factor, but we can strive to implement reliable testing and grading methods that have validity in the academic community.

Regardless of the type of testing used, feedback is an important attribute. Personalized notes can include positive feedback about a student's performance as well as suggestions for those areas that need further work. This furthers the teaching and learning process, fosters communications between the teacher and learner, and offers a means to begin a dialogue to address the work in the future.

Summary

As educators, we are accountable to the school, to the district, and to state and federal agencies that support us. Our accountability demonstrates that dance is a worthwhile and viable academic subject. The use of a variety of assessment techniques also supports dance as a valuable academic subject. Dance assessment tools include videotaped evaluations, checklists, rating scales, and rubrics. Authentic assessment takes place in conditions that reflect real-life situations. This type of assessment encompasses group projects, oral reports, progress and process folios, portfolios, and contracts.

Teachers use written examinations composed of different types of test questions to evaluate students' work throughout the unit or semester; they also grade students' progress from one class meeting to another. The teacher selects a grading system that helps synthesize all the information acquired during the unit. The data show the students' progress and whether the unit is a worthwhile learning experience.

References

Gardner, H. 1993. *Frames of mind: The theory of multiple intelligences.* New York: Basic Books.

Kassing, G. 1992. Performance contracting and goal setting in the dance class. *Journal of Health, Physical Education, Recreation and Dance* 75: 54-55.

Lazear, D. 1999. *Multiple intelligence approaches to assessment: Solving the assessment conundrum.* Tucson, AZ: Zephyr Press.

Pickett, N., and B. Dodge. 2001. Rubrics for Web Lessons. Available on-line at http://webquest.sdsu.edu/rubrics/weblessons.htm. Accessed July 31, 2002.

Wiggins, G. 1999. Foreword. In *Multiple intelligence approaches to assessment: Solving the assessment conundrum,* edited by D. Lazear. Tucson, AZ: Zephyr Press.

It's Your Turn

1. Select an appropriate assessment tool for a particular learning experience in dance. Write a rationale for using this assessment tool.
2. Select three different dance forms and develop these three assessment tools for each form: a performance scale, a rubric, and a written examination. Select the content to be tested that is appropriate for the learner. Develop the assessment tool. Use it in a mock testing situation with at least five or six classmates. Review students' tests and their feedback about the examination.
3. Select a grading scale that would be appropriate for the assessment tools and the learners.

CHAPTER

11

Writing and Delivering the Lesson Plan

Chapter Objectives

By the end of this chapter, you should be able to do the following:

- Formulate lesson plans appropriate for the learner and the environment.
- Teach and assess your lesson plan.

You have accomplished all of the background work; now it is time for you to put principles into action. In this chapter you will learn to write the dance lesson plan, prepare to teach it, and then assess your performance. This is one of many experiences in teaching dance that requires you to just *do* it to learn what to do and whether you could have done it better. Through repeating this process, you will become more proficient and gain confidence in planning, writing, teaching, and assessing in the dance class.

Writing the Lesson Plan

The lesson plan organizes the subject matter that you will present during the lesson and is a practical blueprint for accomplishing the psychomotor, cognitive, and affective behavioral objectives.

Approach the written lesson plan in three steps:

1. Determine basic information.
2. Determine content, objectives, and state or national dance standards.
3. Select and develop an assessment tool.

Begin with a blank lesson plan form (see form 11.1).

Type the topics of the lesson plan in a word-processing document, and save it as a template. This is helpful for when you write a series of lesson plans for various students and situations. Here are five examples:

- For beginning, intermediate, and advanced levels with one dance form
- For different age groups
- For different dance forms
- For different activities associated with the dance form (dancing, seeing a performance, creating a dance, writing a report)
- For building a sequence of lessons into a unit

The lesson plan format is generic so that it can be adapted to a variety of dance forms. You must ascertain the lesson format used by your school. The first step is to record the basic information about the class you will teach.

Basic Information

The basic information for the lesson plan format is derived from specific details about the class and the specific assignment that you give to the class. The following is the basic information for constructing your lesson plan:

- Grade or level of class
- Type of lesson (introduction, development, or review)
- Concept, focus, or theme. These items are delineated before the content is chosen.
- National or state standards. The national or state standard is the larger goal to which the lesson plan connects. In public education, you must include one or more dance standards (either national or state) in the lesson plan.
- Vocabulary. Identify vocabulary that you will introduce or review during the lesson. You will check and add to this section of the lesson plan after writing the content.
- Equipment. Describe the equipment and materials necessary for conducting the lesson. This section of the lesson plan may be a standard list of required equipment, but it should include anything that is unique to the lesson. For example, scarves for creative dance, a handkerchief for folk dance, or props such as hats and canes for tap dance. Include in the list the records, tapes, and compact discs used for the class. List the recorded music selections for each exercise at the beginning of its description.

Dance Lesson Plan

Grade

Introduction **Development** **Review**

National Dance Standards

Concept/Focus/Theme

Objectives

Psychomotor:

Cognitive:

Affective:

Vocabulary

Equipment and Materials

Procedure and Description of Exercises, Combinations, Activities, and Dances

Write the exercises, combinations, activities, and dances for the class. Attach them to the lesson plan. Include in the lesson plan a brief explanation of how the following items will be implemented into the lesson.

Instructional Procedures

Teaching styles

Presentational methods

Skill, technique, or activity cues

Verbal clarity

Rhythmic correctness

Imagery

Review questions about key points

Class Management

Entering and exiting classroom

Group selection (if applicable)

Adaptability

Organization

Class control

Presentation

Use of time and pacing

Feedback

Assessment

Develop the rubric or performance testing scale.

Interrelated Arts or Integrated Course Variations

Relationship of Lesson Objectives to Content

Begin the second step of writing the lesson plan by reviewing the content that you will teach in that lesson. Then you will write behavioral objectives for each of the three domains. After you complete this, write the exercises, combinations, activities, and dances in the order in which you will teach them.

Behavioral Objectives

In the dance lesson plan, write the behavioral objectives for the psychomotor domain, followed by the cognitive domain, and then the affective domain. The first example (the psychomotor domain learning objective) in the following box lists the specific exercises and steps that each student will learn.

Examples of Learning Objectives

Learning Objective for the Psychomotor Domain

The student will be able to execute a beginning ballet barre exercise (list specific exercises: demi-plié in first, second, and fifth positions; battement tendu; battement tendu relevé; battement dégagé; rond de jambe à terre en dehors and en dedans; battement frappé; petit battement sur le cou-de-pied; battement développé; grand battement) during the class at least four out of six times correctly during the last 3 weeks of the 10-week term.

Learning Objective for the Cognitive Domain

The student will be able to compose a 16-count movement phrase using three different locomotor movements (list them) and execute the phrase correctly three out of four times by the end of the unit.

Learning Objective for the Affective Domain

The student will be able to follow the teacher's directions during the class at least 80 percent of the time.

Table 11.1 provides items that you can select for each part of the objective. This will enable you to frame a basic behavioral objective to develop further with specific information to make it applicable to your situation.

The following lists include additional examples of learning objectives for the psychomotor, cognitive, and affective domains.

Psychomotor Domain

- By the end of the term, the student will be able to perform all of the steps (list them)

Table 11.1 Parts of a Behavioral Objective

Stem	Behavior	Condition (the *when* and the *where*)	Performance criteria standard
The student will be able to (TSWBAT)	• Execute • Demonstrate • Perform • Create • Choreograph • Compose • March, skip, gallop, leap (specific locomotor terms), or • Bend, stretch, twist, rotate, elevate, and fall; shape; levels; symmetrical and asymmetrical designs (specific nonlocomotor terms)	• At the end of the class • At the end of the fourth (or another) week • At the end of the unit or semester • In the studio classroom • As classroom performance • In a performance testing situation	• Decide how often you would view the skill to accurately assess it. • Using either a percentage (for example, 90%) or a ratio (such as 4 out of 5 times), select the level of performance to demonstrate competency or mastery. • Use a performance rating scale. • Use a rubric.

learned in the aerobic dance class with at least 80 percent accuracy.

- By the end of the term, the student, with a partner, will be able to create a 64-count foxtrot combination that includes at least three different variations; the student will execute the exercise to the music with 80 percent accuracy.

Cognitive Domain

- The student will be able to compare and contrast the geographic and climatic aspects related to five selected folk dances from around the world with at least 80 percent competency.
- The student will be able to define then tap steps selected by the teacher with at least 80 percent accuracy.

Affective Domain

- The student will be able to demonstrate cooperation in the creative dance class 8 out of 10 times.
- The student will be able to demonstrate commitment to performing the contra dances with the group 90 percent of the time.
- The student will be able to demonstrate self-confidence at least 80 percent of the time when executing a square dance in the class.

Now we are ready to put the objectives and the content of the lesson plan together.

Dance Content

Write the content and descriptions of the exercises, combinations, activities, and dances in sequential order according to the structure of the dance class. In dance forms with a formal vocabulary, such as ballet, tap dance, or folk dance, this is a straightforward task. In other dance forms, such as modern dance and creative dance, the assignment is sometimes more challenging. At the beginning of each of the exercises, combinations, and dances, write the music selection. Beside each of the exercises, combinations, and dances are the counts for each step or figure. After writing an exercise and combination, do the following:

1. Dance what you have written to music.
2. Check the counts of the movement with the music.
3. Make sure the exercises or combinations equal musical phrases and work with the music selected.

When selecting recreational dances for a lesson, read different descriptions and instructions on the dances and move through them without and with the music. Determine whether you can understand the vocabulary of movements and each writer's expression of the dance and whether it works with the music. If the dance is not understandable to you, the teacher, how can you communicate it to students who do not know the dance? After reading several versions of the dance, from different authors, you may wish to interpret the dance using these resources as a basis. If you restage a dance from a written or oral source or if you interpret the dance from your readings, your goal is to be accurate and authentic to the spirit of the dance.

Write down the exercises, combinations, and activities for the class and attach them to the lesson plan. For an example of written exercises and combinations, see form 11.2. Why do you have to write the exercises, combinations, and dances in such detail for the lesson plan? There are several reasons:

- It gives you practice in writing dance movements.
- You apply and learn vocabulary.
- You gain proficiency in using the dance vocabulary.
- You strengthen the movement–language connection that you use when teaching the content in the class.
- You present the vocabulary that students will learn during the class. Highlighting new vocabulary is a part of the basic information of the lesson plan.
- Writing helps you remember the material you will present to the class.

Learning to write exercises with counts, arm movements, and other important information may seem like a foreign process. Dance education is a part of the world of dance, but with requirements beyond learning and performing dance. The key word here is *education*. If dance education is to become accepted as an important aspect of a student's education, then writing objectives and lesson plans similar to those for any other

FORM 11.2

Writing the Dance Class Lesson Plan

This guide is for writing exercises, combinations, and dances for lesson plans.

I. Title of the exercise or combination (include the music, artist, and cut)

II. Identify the beginning position of the dancers and location in the classroom or stage space. Indicate whether the exercise is at the barre,* a center exercise, or a combination:

_________, _________ foot front, _________, (_________).
position right/left direction arms

*If the exercise is performed at the barre, then indicate whether it's different than the standard, which is with one hand on the barre.

A. The following terms describe stage directions
   1. Upstage—away from the audience
   2. Downstage—toward the audience
   3. Stage right—to the dancer's right
   4. Stage left—to the dancer's left
   5. Center stage
   6. Combination of directions (e.g., downstage right, upstage left)
   7. Ballet stage directions used before and during an exercise or combination
      Facing corner or direction (can be abbreviated as C or D). Indicate whether you are using the Cecchetti or Russian stage directions.

B. Dancer's position
   1. On the floor
   2. Kneeling
   3. Standing
   4. Relevé

C. Directions in which the dancer performs leg gestures or executes steps (ballet terms in parentheses)
   1. Front (devant [forward], en avant)
   2. Side (à la seconde or de côte)
   3. Back (derrière [backward], en arrière)
   4. Diagonal (en diagonale)
   5. In place (c. sur place)
   6. Turning in a circle (en manège) [clockwise/counterclockwise], or in place
   7. Turns, promenades, and steps using ballet terms
      a. (En dehors/en dedans)—rond de jambe à terre and en l'air, pirouettes and promenades
      b. (Dessous/dessus)—turns and steps
   8. Moving a step
      a. (Volé)
      b. (Porté)

D. Arm positions
   1. Arm positions (see modern dance or jazz dance sample units)
   2. Choreographed arm positions

3. Ballet arm positions
    a. Port de bras before an exercise and in which arm position it ends.
    b. Arm positions (full or demi) are part of performing a step.
    c. Oblique arms should be specified. Classic positions are assumed.
    d. Poses
        (1.) Arabesques—identify by school or method; indicate number or arm positions.
        (2.) Attitudes
            (a.) Devant or derrière (standard arms are assumed; if different, then indicate).
            (b.) Effacé or croisé.

E. Step beginnings and endings, embellishments
1. Piqué
2. Relevé
3. Abaissé (lowering without demi-plié)
4. Flexed foot
5. Fondu
6. Pointe tendu (including <u>position</u> [crossed or open] and <u>direction</u> [front or back])
7. In the air (en l'air)
8. On the floor (à terre)
9. Closed (fermé)
10. Open (ouverté)
11. Position of the working leg (parallel or turned out)

F. Body shape
1. Aligned
2. Stretched
3. Contracted
4. Twisted
5. Axial (in place) or locomotor (moving through space)

III. Format and examples of writing combinations

Format for Writing Modern Dance, Jazz Dance, and Tap Dance Combination
Beginning position: Counts, steps (arms explained in parentheses)

Example
Beginning position: Standing downstage left with left foot front, right foot pointed back; facing the downstage left corner (right and left arms extended overhead, palms out).

Counts
5-8* Introduction (*this is an example; can be different number of counts for introduction)
1-2
3-4
5-6
7-8

(continued)

FORM 11.2 *(continued)*

Format for Writing Ballet Combination

Beginning position and stage direction:

Counts Steps (arms)

Preparation:

Ballet Example

Beginning position and stage direction: fifth position, right foot front, facing en face (direction 5).

Counts

Preparation:

5-8 First port de bras, ending en bas or au repos

&-1 Glissade sans changé (arms demi-seconde) to direction 6

&-2 Jeté en avant (fourth position en bas)

&-3 Jeté en avant (fourth position en bas)

&-4 Assemblé dessus (left arm opens à la seconde, obliqué; right arm opens demi-seconde)

Format for Writing Creative Movement and Creative Dance Combination

Equipment and materials:

Activity description (in narrative or in steps):

Assessment criteria:

Example

Fast and slow

Materials: none

Activity

1. Children move through the dance space quickly, then more and more slowly.
2. Contrast fast movement sequences with slow movement sequences.
3. Explore different ways to move (pounce, run, collapse) with slow (creep, sneak, crawl). Use images for slow (such as a turtle, a snail) and quickly (such as a racecar, a jet plane)
4. Build a movement sequence using fast and slow movement: A lion stalking his prey (sneaking) and then quickly pouncing on it.

Activity Assessment

Did the learner

perform movement quickly? slowly?

perform movement to other fast or slow words?

perform contrasting movements related to fast or slow?

transfer imagery into fast or slow movements?

academic subject is the means to making dance an accepted and a viable subject of study.

After writing the objectives and content of the lesson plan, determine the teaching strategies, management strategies, relationships to other arts, and integration with other disciplines.

Teaching Strategies

Some teaching styles are inherent to the dance form (for example, ballet, square, and contra dance use the command style). If a specific teaching style is used, indicate it; if not, select the teaching style and review how you would present the exercise in that style.

Think about other teaching strategies, such as cues and imagery, that you will use in the presentation. Practice describing movement precisely to attain verbal clarity. Count the music while doing the movement to ensure rhythmic correctness. Make sure you know what movement happens on what count so that you can communicate this clearly to your students.

Frame guiding questions and statements to lead students through the activity. Formulate review questions that check students' understanding after they participate in the process. Parallel to these teaching strategies are class management strategies that allow the class to flow easily from start to finish.

Class Management Strategies

Although some class management is inherent in the dance form and the structure of the class, much is either teacher-directed or student-initiated. Ultimately, the teacher is responsible for developing a plan that moves the class through each part of the lesson. This begins with procedures for entering and exiting the classroom, positioning at the barre or in the center, forming groups and couples, sharing the space effectively, moving in a space and across the floor, and moving in small groups or all at once.

Other classroom management strategies stem from teaching strategies in the class. Often these management strategies are invisible on the lesson plan and only become apparent in the teaching process. That is why determining your strategies and visualizing and practicing them before performing them in the teaching situation are crucial to your success in teaching the class. These strategies include the following:

- ❑ Analyze the presentation methods in terms of classroom management strategies.
- ❑ Arrange for partners and groups when appropriate.
- ❑ Give groups and individual students a variety of feedback.
- ❑ Display organization, good time management, and pacing during the class.
- ❑ Prepare to adapt to unforeseen situations.
- ❑ Keep the class under control and hold your students accountable for their attitudes and behaviors.

Prepare your classroom management strategies to ensure that the class moves smoothly from beginning to end. Other arts and disciplines are either a natural part of dance or can be incorporated into dance forms in various ways.

Interrelating Arts and Integrating Course Variations

Interrelated arts or integrated course variation extends specific dance forms such as folk dance, creative movement, and creative dance into other academic disciplines. Imagery, analogies, examples, and supportive activities expand the dance experience, giving new insights to students and providing connections to other disciplines.

For an interrelated arts variation, you determine which arts are involved in the lesson. Generally, music is a given; however, sometimes the dance lesson topic involves a story line, theme, costuming, or props. These items incorporate drama and visual arts into the dance activity. If the dance lesson plan connects to other subjects in the school curriculum, determine the integrations. For example, a creative movement lesson could connect with science through a dance activity that explores magnets; a jazz dance can reflect a certain historical period of musical theatre history, such as the 1940s; or a modern dance can use a literary theme from a well-known poem as an impetus for choreography. For more information on interrelated arts and integrated course variations, see chapter 2, pages 29-30. The final part of the lesson plan involves discerning how to assess the day's lesson.

Selecting the Assessment Tool

Assessment is a part of the objective for a day's lesson plan. Selecting, developing, and aligning the assessment tool makes the behavioral objective and the lesson plan complete. You will not assess every lesson plan in a formal manner. But, every day, you will assess the students to ascertain what they learned or did not learn.

The information presented so far becomes the basis for developing or adjusting the next or another day's lesson plan. After you write the lesson plan, it is time to get ready to teach it.

Teaching the Lesson

Preparing to teach the lesson requires that you rehearse presenting the lesson with all of its components, just as if you were preparing to perform a dance. Teaching is a different type of performance and requires a different type of preparation than dancing requires. Before teaching the class, complete the following steps:

- Review the lesson plan.
- Practice the lesson plan in "real time."
- Pace the class.
- Implement all instructional and class management strategies.
- Evaluate your lesson plan.

Review the Lesson Plan

Check your lesson plan for detail and clarity so that another dance teacher could read your lesson plan and deliver it to the class if you were unable to teach your class. This is the ultimate test of effective lesson plans.

Overprepare the number of exercises, combinations, activities, and dances. Sometimes the work in class goes faster than you expect. This depends on the number of people in class and the difficulty of the work. Also, beginning teachers are often nervous when presenting a class, which makes the presentation rushed without full exploration. Finally, be flexible in the class and have alternative exercises, combinations, activities, and dances that you can implement if necessary. Prepare alternative work for a variety of situations (if something just does not work, if the material is too difficult or too easy for the students, if the students are not committed to the work, or if you need additional material).

Check that all of the components of the lesson plan relate and the progressions are logical and appropriate. Prepare the written lesson plan assignment in advance to allow at least one or two days before reading it again. Review it and be prepared to make modifications, and then practice presenting the lesson. This procedure ensures a positive and successful presentation. Review the teaching evaluation form (form 11.3) thoroughly before teaching the class; it provides the criteria for the teaching presentation.

The form helps you prepare to teach the class and later serves as the evaluation for your teaching. The next step is to prepare to teach the class.

Practice the Lesson Plan in "Real Time"

Know it, do it, say it, and do it with music and without note cards. Memorize the lesson that you will present! Transfer a copy of each exercise, combination, activity, and dance from your lesson plan to an index card. Include musical information (name of music, selection number, time signature, counts) and cues that will guide the students through the movement. Although you memorize the class, take the cards to the class to serve as a security blanket if you become nervous. Only refer to the cards if you need to refresh your memory.

Rehearse the class presentation several times and listen to what you plan to say and how you will tell students the information so that they understand and perform the movement.

Pace the Class

Time each section of the class structure as you practice it; then time the entire class. What parts are too long? How long did the warm-up take? The class should flow from one exercise to the next, from one combination or activity or dance to the next. Although you should spend minimal time preparing to present the next part of the class, you should make sure to plan breathing spots, or mental and physical relaxation times, for you and the students.

FORM 11.3

Teaching Performance Evaluation

Rating Scale: 5 = excellent, 4 = good, 3 = fair, 2 = below average, 1 = poor, 0 = unacceptable

Professional Conduct

- ❑ Prompt
- ❑ Planned or rehearsed presentation
- ❑ Enthusiastic
- ❑ Professional appearance and appropriate attire

Rapport/Delivery

- ❑ Established a positive, warm attitude with the class
- ❑ Exhibits self-confidence

Management

- ❑ Preparation of the area
- ❑ Safety (people/area)
- ❑ Active supervision (circulates in class and offers suggestions)
- ❑ Patience
- ❑ Perseverance
- ❑ Displays knowledge and skill of the activity
- ❑ Foresightedness (in movement cues: adaptive, creative [thinking ahead]

Instruction

- ❑ Introduction (stimulates interest, explains why activity is important)
- ❑ Explanation of the activity
    - ❑ Cues
    - ❑ Teaching style (uses logical, sequential cues)
    - ❑ Uses imagery
    - ❑ Checks for understanding (asks questions, looks for raised hands, uses student demonstration)

(continued)

FORM 11.3 *(continued)*

Demonstration

- ❑ Modeling
  - ❑ Whole sequence with counts (say and do)
  - ❑ Repeat
  - ❑ Parts
  - ❑ View
- ❑ Exhibits movement confidence
- ❑ Exhibits rhythmic literacy
- ❑ Exhibits verbal clarity

Practice

- ❑ Activity (appropriate, ample, vigorous, timely)
- ❑ Progressive (task, sequence, part to whole, alone or in group)

Feedback

- ❑ Specific cues (original, positive, prescriptive, other; verbal, manipulative, individual, group)
- ❑ Appropriate feedback (correction of errors, reinforcement cues)
- ❑ Pinpointing actions and skills (desirable or undesirable, correct biomechanical or applied kinesiology explanation)

Implement All Instructional and Class Management Strategies

The teacher places students at the barre; students spread out across the dance space. Later the teacher groups students to move across the floor. She calls people back together into a circle or the center. She determines if students face or do not face the mirror. After practicing the lesson plan, run through your teaching checklist:

- ❑ Dress in appropriate attire.
- ❑ Arrive early so that you become acclimated to the studio.
- ❑ Determine whether the studio is clean and safe for the dancers. Look at the thermostat to see if it will be comfortable for dancing.
- ❑ Check audio and other equipment to ensure it works.
- ❑ Rehearse any potentially troublesome transitions between exercises, combinations, and dances.
- ❑ Teach the class!

After the class, it is time to reflect on what you taught and how you taught it. Gaining confidence in teaching endows you with new sensitivities that later become intuitive. These intuitive responses alert you to problems so that you can dissipate them before they occur. Intuition prompts you to find ways to enhance students' learning. You will need time and patience to acquire intuitiveness; it is a welcome reward for your preparation and diligence in practicing your teaching skills. After the lesson, take time to evaluate what you have done in the classroom.

Evaluate Your Lesson Plan

After teaching the class, reflect on your teaching and evaluate your strengths and challenges in teaching. If content and class management problems occurred, diagnose why they happened. Try to determine solutions that you could implement in the future. Next, look at the lesson plan to determine what changes you would make if you were to teach it again. Identify the specific areas and write notes on a copy of the lesson plan so that you can revise it for future use.

Next, write a self-analysis of your teaching experience. Use the lesson plan for your prompts. This part of the process may be reflective or may be a response to a videotaped recording of yourself teaching the lesson.

Using a videotaped recording of your teaching allows you stand outside yourself to see your teaching, your interaction with the students, and how the students received the presentation. Videotapes allow an objective view of the teaching and learning situation. After watching and analyzing a videotape of your teaching, write a self-analysis. You can write a personal essay or use the teaching evaluation form as the basis.

Exploring Other Options

Learning to teach involves more than writing lesson plans. Other options are necessary for acquiring knowledge and content in developing as a teacher. Some of the following activities will add to your knowledge base and adaptability in the classroom.

- **Select a written folk dance and record a cassette tape of the music.** Interpret the instructions and teach the dance to a group. Inform the students that they may take license with the instructions if necessary to make the dance successful for the class. The folk dance assignment is applicable for other dance forms as well. This assignment prepares you for reading dance combinations in printed sources. As a subsequent assignment, you can learn a dance from a videotaped source and then teach it to the class.

- **Determine the level of instruction you are most comfortable with.** Write the first lesson plan at this level; then write subsequent lesson plans adapting the dance content to other levels. For example, if you are most comfortable teaching at the advanced level in jazz dance, this is the first lesson plan you write. Next, write the intermediate, then the beginning level. Use that format and create lesson plans for other age groups, levels of instruction, and dance forms.

FORM 11.4

Card File Format and Evaluation

Title card:

Name: ____

Number of cards: _____ List categories: ______________________________

Date: ______________ Course: ______________________________

Overall list for each exercise, combination, or activity (this is your personal checklist for the card file):

Title of exercise, combination, or activity: _______ Props or visuals included: _______

Subsequent cards, titled and stapled together: _______ Source designated: _______

Each exercise, combination, or activity card includes ______________________________

Age level: _____

Technical requirements for performance (list steps or concepts): _________

Music/record/accompaniment and specific artist or cut: _________

Time signature of music (if applicable to dance form): _________

Procedure/description of activity

Concept/focus/theme: _________

Description of activity in a sequence of steps: _________

Cues: _________

Key points: _________

Assessment: _________

Interrelated arts or integrated course variations: _________

Comments (put this section on the back of the cards to complete after teaching):

• **Write lesson plans** that focus on integrating arts education and education theories such as multiple intelligences or other theories.

• **Create a card file** that includes a variety of activities, dances, or extended combinations for each age group in several dance forms (see form 11.4). For this assignment, develop a series of file cards that identify the age and level of instruction. Each card presents the steps for teaching a dance, activity, or combination. Highlight vocabulary and underline cues. Include a basic assessment tool. Cite the source for the dance or activity. Leave space for comments on each card. After presenting the activity, analyze its success and make comments or changes to improve it for the next time you present it.

Attach the card to a cassette with the music chosen for the dance activity. If the activity requires visual aids or props or other materials specific to the lesson, include these items in a bag with the cassette and card.

A card file of age-appropriate and level-appropriate dances, dance activities, and combinations provides students with a variety of ready-made learning experiences and activities. This requires that you research and become familiar with a variety of dance sources that will broaden your dance education. Music is an important component of this project, so students will become familiar with and expand their knowledge of various types of music. The requirements of the form become the evaluation of the project.

Planning, organizing, and practicing the lesson are essential to the success of your lesson. Be prepared to teach the lesson, present it, and then analyze it to gain insight on devising your next lesson plan.

Summary

This chapter focuses on developing the lesson plan. Before writing the lesson plan, identify preliminary knowledge necessary to write a lesson plan, select the content for the lesson, and prepare to write your lesson plan. An important part of learning to write the lesson plan includes understanding learning taxonomies and domains and their relationship to an objective. Next, discern the parts of an objective (stem, behavior, conditions, and criterion for performance) and how they will be assessed (performance testing, rubrics, contracting, oral reports, written assignments, process folios, portfolios, group projects, and written tests). These assessment strategies translate into methods of grading students' work. Write the lesson plan by inputting the information, objectives, and content; determining teaching and class management strategies; and selecting the assessment tool. The final step is to prepare to teach the lesson plan. After presenting the lesson, evaluate your lesson plan and teaching. You can also explore future options to enhance your teaching.

It's Your Turn

1. Create a 30-second infomercial to introduce the dance lesson. This is the "hook" that will get students' attention and give them information about the historical, cultural, or societal aspects of the dance or specific style that is the topic for the day. Creating a short infomercial is a way to develop connections to disciplines beyond the dance class.
2. After teaching your lesson plan, write a one-page self-evaluation of your lesson plan and your teaching.

CHAPTER

12

Creating a Curriculum

Chapter Objectives

By the end of this chapter, you should be able to do the following:

- Understand the four curriculum models for dance and how they affect curriculum development.
- Identify and develop strategies for organizing dance content.
- Understand the four components of curriculum development and how they relate to one another.

Dance curriculum development involves understanding curriculum models and selecting the one most appropriate for the learner and the teaching environment. The dance teacher implements strategies for organizing the content. This chapter will help you learn how to develop dance curriculum and design a dance program.

Designing the Dance Program Curriculum

Although no widely accepted definition exists for the term *curriculum,* it is often defined by its approach to education in relation to society and the specific objectives designated for a course of study. Therefore, a dance curriculum consists of the subject matter of a specific dance form. A dance curriculum can be a single dance unit, a series of dance units, or courses that cover an entire year of study or a four-year progressive plan.

A dance curriculum must satisfy several goals beyond being an outgrowth of your background, training, and experiences as a dancer and a teacher. First, the dance curriculum is the conduit for the dance education of the students in your school over a designated period. Likewise, a viable dance curriculum reflects the underlying values of the community; these values are emphasized in the courses offered by the school district. A curriculum acknowledges the needs of both the learner and society and seeks to find a position that will merge them.

Learning how to write dance curriculum is an important skill for the new dance teacher. It is often what determines whether you get the job. The process requires knowledge of the dance form, the students, the setting, and all the other items presented in previous chapters as a prerequisite for planning a logical, sequential curriculum and dance program.

Creating curriculum begins with writing a lesson plan, the basic module that covers a day's learning in dance class. A series of lesson plans that provide progressive learning experiences are the basis for a dance unit. A series of units or courses may constitute the curriculum for a program of study that ranges from a part of the school year to a one-year or a four-year program. Now you

- determine what the dance curriculum is;
- select a curriculum model;
- review its aspects;
- determine the strategies of the curriculum; and
- develop the scope and sequence of the curriculum that will relate to you as the teacher and to your students, your school, community, and established standards.

Differences in curriculums are largely a choice of design and components and their relation to the assumptions made about the learner, society, teaching environment, and delivery of the content. Together, these components specific to dance actuate several curriculum models.

Surveying Four Options for Dance Curriculum Models

Four curriculum models have been selected to demonstrate the range of curriculum design appropriate for dance. The choice of models depends on the teacher's experience and training, the school, and the community. The four models are process, product, combined (Smith-Autard 1994), and discipline-based dance education.

Defining the Process Model of Curriculum

A process model in dance stresses the way a person learns, which encourages the growth of creativity, imagination, and individuality. This model emphasizes the subjectivity of an experience and the dancer's feelings. The process is the path a person follows and experiences. Elements and principles are a source of the content and problem solving in the teaching approach. The teacher guides and the dancer learns in his own way by developing his solution to the problem. The process model is appropriate for creative dance students in preschool through fifth grade. At the high school level, this model is used in improvisation and choreography classes.

In the extreme view, the process becomes paramount and the product is not important. But in the current educational atmosphere, the acquisition of skill and knowledge of subject matter mandates the teacher's emphasis on evaluation, assessment, and accountability for the student's learning. Teachers who use this model must be able to assess the quality of the process. They achieve this by looking at the skills and determining their quality in relation to an established standard. The learner's personal maturity and artistry are constantly stimulated and encouraged.

The importance of creativity cannot be underestimated in the process model. As artists, dancers and choreographers value creativity as an attribute of 21st-century society. The skills of creativity are measurable, as demonstrated by Torrance (1981) in his movement test, Thinking Creatively in Action and Movement. These skills include the following:

- Fluency (the number of ways something is performed)
- Frequency (the number of times something is executed)
- Originality (how inventive or unique the movements are as well as how adequate, relevant, and appropriate they are)
- Imagination (how movement is expanded, revised, or altered)

Through peer review and artistic reputation, dance works are evaluated in relation to the choreographer's previous dance. The process skills of the performance model are artistry, technique, focus, expression, and projection. These skills are assessed by criteria from experts in the field of dance. In definite contrast to the process model is the product model of curriculum.

Defining the Product Model of Curriculum

A product model focuses on the end result and is also known as the performance model. In this curriculum, technical training is paramount in the concert dance forms. The students strive to achieve the level of proficiency associated with professional dancers. This becomes the expected outcome of the training; the dance technique is the content, and the teacher, who directs the teaching, is considered the expert model for the dance form. The product model may lack the essential process steps of learning the content if the teacher is inexperienced in determining the age and level appropriateness of the dance form and the progressions to teach.

The performance curriculum model emphasizes acquiring high-level technical skill and the ability to emulate styles of the dance form. This model concentrates on a single technique, such as the Horton or Graham technique in modern dance; it excludes other techniques or dance forms. The cultivation of imagination and use of creativity are not as important in this model. The product curriculum focus limits the dancer's training and exposure to other techniques and theories of movement. The next curriculum model lies between the process and product models.

Defining the Combination Model of Curriculum

The combination model is a composite of both the process and product (performance) curriculum models. It combines the best of both models. The downside of this model lies in its implementation, which requires resources, facilities, faculty, and community support. The combination model emphasizes the ideas of dancing, dance making, and dance appreciation expressed in the National Standards in Dance and several state standards.

Within each of the models are three foci. Each focus is combined with the other two in varying proportions to create a complementary synergy of the artistic, aesthetic, and cultural aspects within a dance curriculum.

Artistic Aspect

The artistic aspect centers on the technical and performance factors involved in learning dance forms as professional training. This aspect is performance and product based in that it uses learning activities and assessment strategies. For example, in concert dance classes, the students learn vocabulary, steps, and combinations. They practice and perfect the work. Then the instructor evaluates their work using performance testing methods (checklists, Likert scales, or rubrics). In some performance classes, dancers keep a journal. It contains such items as a written account of exercises, steps, and combinations learned in the class; what the dancer has accomplished after each day's class; and self-assessments of performance in class.

In magnet and performing arts schools that use a performance curriculum, the dance student creates a portfolio that consists of a vita specifying training, dance roles, performances, and experiences. The portfolio includes process folios with indicators of the dancer's progress from one term to the next and one year to the next. Progress indicators comprise performance or written tests, written assignments, journals, and teachers' evaluations. A video folio, part of the process folio, documents the dancer's performance of different roles, dance forms, and choreographic works.

Aesthetic Aspect

The aesthetic aspect focuses on what the audience observes in a performance of the dance forms. It emphasizes experience, perception, feeling, observation, and evaluation of dance. This aspect is process based with some product aspects. In the modern dance technique, composition, or history class, the aesthetic aspect is easily implemented through the following steps:

1. The students view a modern dance performance.
2. They observe, reflect, write, and discuss the performed work. In their writings, they support their analysis by what they saw in the performance.
3. The students may view more than one dance performance video and compare different works by the same choreographer, or they may compare and contrast two choreographers' works on the same subject.

At the end of this process, the products can be in the form of an oral report, a written critique, a group discussion, or a debate.

Other student-centered processes involve research of written sources (such as analyses, critiques, and historical background of the work) that illuminate a choreographer's point of view. Using the choreographer's stylistic elements and additional research, the dancer creates a work for other dancers in the spirit of the choreographer's original work. During the process, the student develops a process folio of the project. She writes about the research, analysis, and choreographic process, including reflections, insights, and interactions between the student and the dancers who perform the work.

Cultural Aspect

The cultural aspect examines the social, political, religious, and psychological climates in which the dance form is performed. This aspect cultivates an appreciation of dance associated with specific cultures. The cultural aspect is both product and process oriented. The following example presents the learning activities and assessment strategies for dancers who are learning and performing dances from different cultures. The students take the following steps:

1. Research the dances.
2. Explore the geography, climate, music, customs, and mores of the culture.
3. Select a dance as an example of the culture and analyze the dance for its meaning, place in traditions, and significance to the culture.
4. Perform the dance, which is evaluated by a performance rubric that either the students or the teacher develops.
5. Take a written test on the significance of the dance, its characteristics, how the dance is viewed in the culture, and its impact on tradition.

Or, the dancer selects a world dance form or specific dance to study. The student conducts research to prepare an oral report or a paper. During this process, the dancer views videos of the specific world dance. She identifies the elements of the dance, characteristics of the dance, and her reflections on the dance form. The student collects this information in a process folio and includes a summary about the dance form, what she learned about the dance, and how it relates to her understanding of the culture.

The dancer can also write in a journal after viewing a video performance of a specific world dance. The journal entries are reflections on the dance and a record of its characteristics, qualities, and essence. Using these impressions, the student choreographs a dance based on her impressions and research of the experience. At the end of the project, the dancer writes about the choreographic process: the problems posed, solutions that evolved during the project, and concerns and insights gained from choreographing in this manner. These aspects form the basic goals of the student's artistic, aesthetic, and cultural education. Another curricular view of achieving these goals is through discipline-based dance education.

Discipline-Based Dance Education Model of Curriculum

Discipline-based dance education is an outgrowth of the discipline-based arts education movement associated with the Getty Center for Education in the Arts in Los Angeles. This curriculum model integrates content and skills into four components: dance history, dance criticism, dance aesthetics, and dance production (or performance of a dance form). This model focuses on dancing and creating; critical observation, analysis, critical response, and writing; and aesthetic perception and value of dance. In this model, grades kindergarten through 5 use creative movement, then modern educational dance as the basis for dancing and creating dance. Grades 6 through 8 add history and critical observation to their studies. For grades 9 through 12, all components are integrated into the curriculum (Barber, Clemente, Crawford, Friedlander, Hilsendager, and Vandarakis 1989). The discipline-based dance education model has been assimilated in numerous ways into dance education curricula. After selection of a curriculum model, the next step is to understand the components that make up the curriculum.

Developing the Components of a Dance Curriculum

The four components of a dance curriculum are interlocking—one component builds on the next. The basis for curriculum development is the dance *lesson plan;* a series of these lessons constitutes a dance *unit.* Several dance units, which constitute a *course,* may be taught during a term or semester. Two or more courses make up a yearly plan or *program* that may be part of longer programs of up to four years, such as those found in public schools or college settings.

The foundation of a curriculum is its instructional design, which refers to the methods and processes that are used in planning, delivering, and evaluating lessons and units. The design contains the management strategies for the classroom situation. Implementing the instructional design process begins by setting lesson plan objectives and assessment measures that extend to the unit and larger curriculum components.

Selecting Objectives

Unit and course objectives direct the teaching and testing. Writing a student behavioral learning objective and developing a lesson plan become the foundation for extending lesson plans into sequential lessons, or a unit. Unit and course objectives indicate the expectations for students to learn certain material, exercise intellectual abilities, acquire certain values, and master specific skills. The underlying assumption is that students retain content as they continue through the curriculum. As the material becomes more complex, students interpret content through new situations to augment and compound their knowledge.

A number of units or courses and their objectives in turn become the components of the program. Objectives for lessons, units, and courses build successively on one another to create program objectives. Concurrent to building the objectives is selecting the types of assessment that will make the objectives measurable.

Integrating Assessment Modes

Specific assessment methods are outlined for the lesson plan. For the unit, course, or program, the context of assessment becomes broader. Using assessment methods becomes the foundation of formative and summative forms of evaluation that apply to unit, course, and program evaluation.

Formative Assessment

Formative assessment is the continual assessment that takes place from day to day throughout a unit or course. This type of assessment focuses on what students have learned about the dance content presented in the unit. Often formative assessment is informal and guides the teacher in her teaching and development of curriculum.

Formative evaluation is applicable in most dance settings. In class, the teacher assesses students as they perform; then she writes notes immediately after class about what content was learned, what she will review at the next class meeting, and whether students are ready for new content. She includes notes on specific students' progress or problems. This assessment may be for the students in the class, or the teacher may keep her self-assessment in another notebook. Regardless, the teacher then incorporates these notes into subsequent lesson plans in the unit. During the unit, formal assessment must occur as a measurement of students' progress.

Summative Assessment

Summative assessment takes place at designated points during or at the end of the unit or course. This formal assessment may be in the form of performance tests, written assignments, oral presentations, group projects, and performances. Summative assessment is the collection of evaluative data from a series of assessments during a period or throughout an entire semester. The data are synthesized into a singular numerical or equivalent letter grade that reflects the student's work and effort during the unit or course.

To implement summative assessment plans when you write your dance curriculum, begin by looking at the unit plan you have developed and the calendar for the unit or course. Spread out the summative assessment testing and assignments throughout the unit or course. It is neither fair to students nor prudent to do all assessment at the end of the unit or term. When designating class time for testing, allocate time for personal feedback and student conferences. Both formative and summative assessment strategies work in tandem throughout the lessons of the unit to present a complete picture of students' learning. Keeping in mind the importance of selecting appropriate objectives and assessment tools for the unit, you are ready to begin the process of developing curriculum.

Writing a Dance Curriculum

After you select the dance curriculum model, objectives, and assessment tools, the next process is to define the dance content to present during the unit. You also must define the scope and sequence of the content and select the strategy for presenting the dance form, lesson, or project.

Developing a Scope and Sequence

A scope and sequence is a planning technique that enables the dance teacher to choose what and when and how the subject matter is introduced, taught, practiced, performed, and evaluated. When planning a unit or course, the teacher develops a diagram that displays the scope and sequence for the unit (see sample dance units in chapter 13).

Before formulating the scope and sequence, the dance teacher identifies this information:

- The level
- The age
- Each person's actual experience in dance
- The dance content that is appropriate for the physical, mental, and social ability of the students
- The organization that supports the dance unit or course
- The goals of the educational or recreational setting

Keep this information in mind because it determines the context in which you will present the dance unit. The scope of a course deals with what is taught during a unit, term, or semester. To determine the scope of a unit, first identify the dance form or forms, list the dance content of the form or forms that you plan to teach, and then proceed to formulating their sequence. The sequence indicates when the specific exercises, steps, elements, or activities will be introduced during the unit or course. Each element, exercise, or step is enumerated in the order that it will be taught during the unit. Consider these two issues when developing the scope and sequence of your unit plan:

1. Establish the length of the unit so that you can formulate the unit plan. The length of the unit plan depends on the setting in which it is taught. In some settings, the unit can be as short as three weeks or as long as nine weeks or an entire semester. Ascertain the number of weeks in the unit, the number of class meetings, and the length of the class meetings.

2. The number of objectives for a unit plan should coincide with the time period specified for the unit; that is, they should match the number of class periods in the unit, course, or program. The objectives build on prior objectives to become increasingly more complex and difficult. Then identify the dance form and specific exercises, steps, elements, or activities to teach during the unit or course. Correlate your work to your information about the learner and the environment before going on to the next step.

The scope and sequence for a unit or course is usually presented in a graphic organizer (see form 12.1). This visual representation summarizes the unit and shows the progression of learning for students.

After creating the scope and sequence for a dance unit, determine strategies for presenting the dance content to the students.

Strategies for Presenting Dance Content

Two basic strategies exist for presenting dance content. One is called *bottom–up;* the other is *top–down.*

Bottom–Up Strategy

The bottom–up strategy, used whenever order and safety are important, is the most traditional way of teaching dance. It uses the command and practice teaching styles. The strategy has the following features:

- The content progressively builds from simple to complex exercises, steps, elements, and activities.
- It uses the part–whole or the add-on method.

The bottom–up strategy is used in ballet, tap dance, and recreational dance forms. The folk dance "Seven Steps" illustrates this strategy:

1. The dance instructor teaches the schottische step (step, together, step–hop). The students practice the step forward and backward and sideward.
2. Then the instructor teaches the step–hop, which alternates feet: step–hop, right; step–hop, left; repeat right and left.
3. The teacher instructs the dancers to form two concentric circles with men (or leaders) in the inside circle and women (or followers) in the outside circle. All dancers face counterclockwise, joining inside hands.
4. The dancers start on the right foot, or the outside foot.
5. The first section of the dance consists of running forward for 7 counts and holding on count 8; then the dancers run backward for 7 counts and hold on count 8 again. The dancers practice this until they master it.
6. Then the dancers perform a schottische step to the side (step, together, step–hop, step, together, step–hop). The dancers start on different feet, and they move in opposite directions.
7. They dance the first section (run) forward and backward; then they add the second part, the schottische.
8. The dancers then perform four step–hops in a circle with both hands joined and facing one another. The leaders end by facing their partners and with their backs to the inside of the two concentric circles. They practice the step–hop in the circles, then they repeat and practice the dance from the beginning.
9. For the next section, the dancers face each other and perform a sideward schottische twice. The men (leaders) perform four step–hops forward to the next woman (follower), while the followers perform them in their own small circle.
10. Dancers practice the entire dance, first without the music and then with the music.

The bottom–up method is a traditional way of teaching that progresses from the beginning and

FORM 12.1

Scope and Sequence

New = N   Review = R   Create dance = CD   Perform dance = PD   Review for test = RT   Performance test = PT   Informal test = IT
Listening test = LT   Quiz = Q   Call dance = CLD   Hand in = HI

	1	2	3	4	5	6	7	8	9	10	11	12	13	14	15

builds into an entire dance. The second strategy is top–down; it requires more preparation, time, and thought to develop a layered and interwoven strategy using many disciplines.

Top–Down Strategy

The top–down strategy is more complex to conceptualize, implement, and evaluate than the bottom–up strategy. This strategy uses guided discovery and problem solving. The top–down method provides advantages for both the teacher and the students. The teacher presents the content using the whole–part–whole method. This strategy is more applicable for intermediate and advanced dancers; it lends easily to creative, modern, and jazz dance. It is a viable model for short units in an educational, studio, or workshop setting. The top–down model gives a teacher a variety of ways to approach a topic. The focus is on the concept first and then the use of problem solving to create a new product using its essences—the qualities, the types of arm movements, the body shapes and gestures, and steps.

For example, after viewing a dance work of a famous choreographer, students begin the unit by observing and building on the original dance. They take stylistic elements from it, such as steps and gestures, and build a dance work from the extracted components. This process leads the students to learn about the historical, societal, and cultural context of the original dance. In turn, this experience stimulates students' use of critical-thinking skills. The experience enriches the learners' dancing and dance experience. The top–down strategy allows students to gain access to dance heritage through the experience of performing, conceptualizing, and evaluating a dance as a work of art. This type of experience facilitates in-depth learning by supporting the dance work through the historical, societal, and cultural aspects of the time in which it was created.

Another example for a beginning modern dance class is learning about symmetry and asymmetrical design. Students develop a short modern dance study that shows three asymmetrical and two symmetrical designs on different levels. In the study, the learner chooses to enter and exit the dance space or begins and ends in a certain shape in the dance space. Within the study, the student uses locomotor and nonlocomotor movements and levels as transition elements between the designs. Evaluating the study, the audience identifies the elements in the composition. The student includes evaluation criteria in the composition, and the audience identifies the following:

- Three asymmetrical designs
- Two symmetrical designs
- Entrance, exit, or shape held at the beginning or end
- Use of different transitions between each design
- Use of levels for the designs
- Overall unity of the composition
- Application of technique in the composition

To score the composition, use a checklist or Likert scale, or create a rubric.

No one of these strategies is better than the other. You choose the one you feel the most comfortable with. The top–down model requires students to engage in student-centered learning, but you as the teacher must do your homework on the process within the project to guide and mentor the students to achieve success in their projects. With these two strategies in mind, you will next chart the block time plan form for the unit.

Charting the Block Time Plan Form

After writing the scope and sequence for the dance unit as discussed earlier, now transfer this information into a block time plan form. This form functions as a calendar for the number of classes in the unit. For each class, write the exercises, steps, activities, and dances that constitute the lesson for that day. Looking at the block plan allows you to check for technique or skill progression; a variety of dancing, dance making, and dance appreciation experiences; and adequate time and places throughout the unit for assessing performance and projects. See the sample units in chapter 13 for examples of block time plans. Form 12.2 is a blank block time plan form.

After creating the scope and sequence and block time plan, develop a series of lesson plans that match the block time plan for the unit. These components will become part of the unit plan. The final step is to prepare and write the unit plan.

FORM 12.2

Block Time Plan

Class 1	Class 2	Class 3	Class 4	Class 5
Class 6	**Class 7**	**Class 8**	**Class 9**	**Class 10**
Class 11	**Class 12**	**Class 13**	**Class 14**	**Class 15**

Writing the Unit Plan

A unit plan is a document that outlines students' accomplishments in relation to the public education setting. Before writing a unit plan, research appropriate documents for your particular teaching setting to write the unit to meet the requirements of the school or school district. Equally important is acquiring a copy of a unit plan that has been accepted by the school; this will provide you with a model for your plan. The unit plan outline we have chosen is a generic outline form. The information required may be the same or somewhat different in various schools. A unit plan has two parts that may be thought of as the *external* and the *internal.*

The external part of a unit plan addresses the learner and the environment. It begins with an introduction followed by a description of the learner, the school, and how the dance unit plan relates to them. The internal part of the unit applies to the teaching and learning process experiences of the unit. The internal part of the unit plan focuses on the instruction that takes place during the unit; this is supported by assignments, tests, rating scales, rubrics, and other information pertinent to the delivery of the content. Both the internal and external parts must align and interlock to build a solid case for the unit to be included in the curriculum of the school.

To begin the process of developing a unit plan, read form 12.3 to gain an understanding of what each part contains and how each part supports the other. In parentheses are items usually addressed under that topic. When writing your unit plan, select one or more items listed that are most appropriate; write short descriptions characterizing your specific students and teaching situation as they relate to the dance unit. Form 12.3 contains specific instructions to help you in writing your unit plan.

Using the unit plan outline, draft a plan in a dance form you are familiar with. Exchange your unit plan with another student and give each other feedback as to how well each of the parts of the outline are addressed. If you have not taught dance classes, then exchange your work with someone who has had experience either in the dance form or with the age group you have selected for the unit plan. Discuss with others some of the problems you encountered and possible solutions related to specific dance categories and forms. Take notes on the information you have learned from others who have had experience teaching the dance form. This may help you in future planning and implementation, especially if you are unfamiliar with the dance form. Although this exercise is theoretical now, it provides you with a blueprint of what you would implement in the classroom.

Developing the One-Year Curriculum

When developing a one-year dance program, you have additional considerations to address beyond one unit or one course. The course content and continuity are important if you plan to create a synergetic learning experience for the students. Otherwise the dance experiences may be an elective smorgasbord of courses in a variety of dance forms. If the primary goal is to create a one-year foundational dance program, then you should keep all this information in mind if the possibility to expand the program presents itself.

When creating one-year dance programs, consider the following factors:

- Length of grading terms in your school: semester or term, quarterly, nine-week period, or three- to four-week sequence of courses
- Space requirements and availability
- Facilities: floor problems (gym floors, theater floors) noise control, mirrors, barres, equipment availability
- Department, school, and community calendars
- Teachers' assignments: areas of expertise, number of preparations, preparation time (how many classes are scheduled back to back?)
- Other student assignments: either curricular or extracurricular assignments, such as pom-poms, drill teams, school musicals, orchestra, dance team, dance company, and extra performances
- Rationale: why is the course being taught, what courses will you offer, when will you offer it, who will teach it, where will they teach it? Will it meet the established goals and standards of the department, school, and state?

FORM 12.3

Unit Plan Format

Write the unit plan in narrative form using complete sentences.

Title Page

Include a separate title page with the unit plan title, your name, the school's name, and the date.

I. Part I

Part I is the external information about the school and the learner and how the dance unit will relate to them.

Introduction

Address each of the items listed below under the description of the setting.

A. Description of setting
   1. School name, department in which dance is located, type of programs in the department, dance unit(s) currently taught or proposed
   2. Description of population (grade level, gender ratio, background of students in relation to federal grants)
   3. Program scope (specify time frame for each class period, number of class periods per week, length of unit)
   4. Types of instruction and teaching styles used in the unit (directed activity, guided discovery, reciprocal teaching, lecture, contract learning, student-centered learning strategies)

B. Focus (mission of program, department, or school)

C. Rationale for dance unit (related to mission of program, department, or school; include state or National Standards)

   Each numbered item contains suggested items that may describe your unit. Write a brief description of how the items characterize your unit or program.
   1. Purpose of the unit: Creative, rhythmic, participation in an art form, physical fitness, coordination, cardiorespiratory strength, body alignment (posture), carriage, social skills, others
   2. Type of unit (choose one): Dance as a performing art; dance appreciation and dance related to other art forms; discipline-based dance education
   3. Relating the unit to goals of dance education, the department, the school, and standards: arts education, interdisciplinary learning, dance and use of technology, education theories (multiple intelligences, emotional intelligences, brain or mind principles, and others)

D. Instructional environment
   1. Dance facilities: Describe the dance studio(s) or space(s).
   2. Equipment: List available equipment.
   3. Instructional media: Indicate media resources that support the unit.

E. Activities included in the unit

   Write an overview of the specifics in the unit. Explain how each item will be used in the unit.
   1. Identify the dance form for the unit.
   2. Specify activities:Technique classes; student, teacher, or guest artist performed in class or gave public performance.

FORM
12.3

3. Learn dance vocabulary and history of the dance form.
4. Describe individual and small-group projects in choreography, viewing, reporting, and evaluation of dance performance activities.

Write student expectations and instructions and include rubrics and other performance evaluation tools.

5. Indicate self-assessment, peer assessment, and teacher assessment tools for performance and projects, performance tests, and written tests.

   Identify expectations, procedures, and performance evaluation tools in a summary.
6. Specify supporting skills that students will acquire during the unit: accompaniment, production, related arts, leadership, administration.

II. Unit Plan

Part II includes the internal information about how the dance unit will be delivered and the student outcomes will be achieved.

A. Goals and objectives for the unit

   Identify the domain of each objective for the unit.
   1. Cognitive objectives
   2. Affective objectives
   3. Psychomotor objectives
   4. State or National Learning Standards

      List state or National Standards met by the unit.

B. Content outline
   1. Skills taught in the unit
      a. Warm-up, techniques, skills, activity, cool-down
      b. Movement, choreographic, and aesthetic principles that support the unit
   2. Vocabulary

      List and define dance form terminology.
   3. History of the dance form

      Brief overview; include important personalities.

C. Scope and sequence of the unit
   1. Identify each skill taught.
   2. Identify the progression of skills taught in the unit.

D. Block time plan
   1. Include a diagram indicating dance content for each class meeting in the unit.
   2. Include daily lesson plans.
   3. Indicate a breakdown of instructional time for each class meeting.

      How much time is spent on each activity?

E. Class organization
   1. Structure of class time

      Indicate time allotted for each activity; give a rationale.
      a. Dressing
      b. Roll taking

(continued)

FORM 12.3 *(continued)*

c. Types of teaching modes
d. Types of student participation
e. Practice

2. Classroom etiquette and dress requirements
3. Safety precautions

F. Method(s) of instruction

1. Teacher's roles

   Indicate teaching styles and strategies and student-centered learning strategies used.
2. Types of feedback

G. Motivational techniques for the unit

1. Challenges

   List specifics in relation to students and the unit.
2. Personal goal setting
3. Performance viewing (field trips to performances or video performances)
4. Guest teacher
5. Student projects

H. Assessment and evaluation

1. Types of evaluation

   List types of performance, written, authentic.
2. Formative evaluations
3. Summative evaluations
4. Explanation of evaluation procedures (rating forms, rubrics)
5. Example of written test and performance examination

I. Support materials

1. Terminology handouts
2. History handouts
3. Other handouts

J. List state or National Standards in dance as they relate to the unit.

K. Indicate how the unit interfaces with related arts and integrates with or supports other subjects in the school curriculum.

L. Connect dance and technology.

M. Specify how multiple intelligences, emotional intelligences, brain or mind principles, and other education theories are addressed during the dance unit.

III. Summary

Summarize the important features and benefits to make a case for the dance unit to become part of the school curriculum.

Creating a Four-Year Plan

In the high school setting, some dance programs span four years. These programs require additional considerations beyond planning for the one-year program. Programs must meet the needs of a variety of students to provide appropriate experiences.

The major components of designing a four-year dance program include the audition or placement class, technique level discrimination, choice of courses, schedule of courses, course rotation, and plan of study.

Audition or Placement Class

Auditions are held for students before they enter the program. Students can participate in a placement class before entering the program; these mechanisms determine their level of dance technique. A placement class can also be a regular technique class for existing students, and potential students join that class for the day to determine whether they belong there or in a higher or lower class. In some settings the audition establishes whether students have sufficient technique to be admitted to the dance program.

The placement class can also be an audition for the program. Placement classes are scheduled before the term begins or on the first day so that students can make adjustments to their schedules if necessary.

In the high school setting, prospective dance students often attend a two- or three-day workshop before entering the program. This workshop includes students participating in various dance forms for the teacher to evaluate if the students are admitted into the program and at which class level.

Technique Level Discrimination

The four-year dance program must include courses in one or more dance forms for students at the beginning, intermediate, and perhaps the advanced level. The amount of skill level discrimination in the classes depends on the scope of the dance program, the number of courses, and the length of time allocated to study.

Designing the scope of the dance program depends on the support and mission of the department and school. Sometimes students want to continue their dance experiences to higher levels; schools may add higher-level courses as a result of this demand.

Choice of Courses

Course selection depends on faculty expertise and departmental support. The courses selected for the curriculum should provide a balance in technique, dance forms, composition, and dance theory such as history and production.

Schedule of Courses

The scheduling of courses demands both an internal and external view. The internal view includes having the appropriate number of faculty for the number of students and determining whether musicians for dance are available for dance classes.

Table 12.1 includes a few of the internal questions related to scheduling. External questions also exist. The categories they address include facility use (or shared facility use) and equipment and classroom availability. Other concerns include scheduling a class at the same time students are required to take another course. If there are multiple sections of the other courses, this is generally not a problem. However, scheduling against a course with only one course section, taught on a rotational basis every two years in another department, requires adjustment. Some of these intricacies of scheduling do not become apparent until you confront them. When scheduling dance courses on a rotational basis, try to find out what course requirement conflicts students might encounter if you scheduled a dance production course on Monday, Wednesday, and Friday beginning at 10:00 A.M. You won't win all the time, but course scheduling will be less stressful if you keep track of other required courses and make adjustments. An intricate part of scheduling is selection of courses offered on a rotational basis.

Course Rotation

Course rotation involves offering a course once a year or once every two years. Offering courses that rotate is both cost and time effective. Scheduling rotational courses requires advance planning and communication. You must make students and other faculty aware that a course will or will not be offered during a specific term. Students must also plan to include the rotational

Table 12.1 Considerations for Scheduling Dance Courses

Student schedule	Faculty schedule	Musician for dance schedule
• How many courses does the student (for each year of study) take on Monday, Wednesday, and Friday; Tuesday and Thursday; or Monday through Friday?	• How many preparations does the faculty member have to make for the term?	• How many classes does the musician for dance play each day?
• How many classes are back to back?	• How many preparations does the faculty member have a day?	• How many classes are back to back on the schedule?
• Does the student have a chance to eat lunch?	• Does the faculty member come early and stay late?	• Does the musician for dance play for different classes or only the same dance form? (This may relate to her strengths and interests.)
• What is the distribution of the load from day to day and during the day, and the balance of technique and theory courses?	• How much time is there between classes?	• Does the musician for dance have allocated time for recording the music for productions (if this task is within her job description)?
	• How many classes are taught back to back?	
	• Does the faculty member have time to prepare for extracurricular activities?	

courses in their plan of study so that they can complete their course of study on time. Examples of rotational courses include the following:

- Courses that students take in sequence, such as Composition I and Composition II, can be offered in the fall term (Composition I), then the spring term (Composition II).
- Courses that students in either the upper or lower division can take can be offered once a year or every other year. (There are many ways to implement division rotational courses; these are only a few.)
- Specialized courses that fulfill electives, such as special topics courses in which faculty members decide on the topic, can be offered on a rotational basis.

Plan of Study

When outlining the four-year dance program, the dance administrator creates a plan of study for the students. This organizes the courses that students are required to take in a sequential plan for each of the four years of study.

The plan of study indicates for each term the number and name of the courses and the total number of credit hours. The number of hours should be similar for each semester. Rotational courses and courses that require prerequisites are highlighted with additional information.

Developing and Evaluating Dance Curriculums and Programs

A curriculum is a changing set of documents. It is subject to trends in education and changes in philosophies of departments and schools, and it may depend on mandates from boards of higher education and state and national boards. The focus is twofold in developing a curriculum as a one-year program to a four-year program: What will students learn, and what are the objectives of the program? Students' work is evaluated in a variety of ways during and after each unit or course and at the end of the program. Curriculums and programs undergo evaluations at various times as well.

Curriculum Process

The curriculum process can be initiated as either bottom–up or top–down. The process can begin with a teacher or committee in the school; or it can come from the school district, state, regional, or national directives. Either way, it requires the development of a curriculum proposal. The curriculum proposal can encompass one course, several courses, or an entire curriculum. Once the proposal is complete, it is submitted to the appropriate people for review. This takes place on one or more levels, depending on the structure of the organization. At any of these levels, the curriculum proposal may be passed, revised, or stopped. After the curriculum proposal has passed internal review, it is sent to outside bodies for approval. After a course has become part of the curriculum, it is tracked along with other course offerings as part of curriculum evaluation. Curriculum is evaluated in several ways to ascertain its effectiveness in meeting the established goals and mirroring the philosophy of the institutions that house it.

Evaluating Curriculum

In curriculum evaluation, the goals for the units, courses, and program must match those of students and faculty to create a viable curriculum. Evaluation tools that address these variables are used to conduct continuous or periodic monitoring of the curriculum, including evaluation of

- **students:** Testing takes place during the course or at the end of the course of study. Student outcomes are often specified by state and national standards. Important data are obtained through the tracking of students who enter and stay in programs. For the high school program, this data may include the number of students accepted by a college, entering a career, or receiving a scholarship from a professional company.
- **teachers:** Formal evaluation of teachers by supervisors and committees form the basis for increase of salary and rank.
- **facilities:** Evaluate the capacity and use of the facility to support students and its viability to conduct appropriate teaching and other activities. In dance this often includes the performing spaces available and their usability.
- **program:** Evaluate the ability of the curriculum to adequately prepare graduates in relation to the school's or department's mission. Analyze the systems used for recruiting students, advising students, placing students in appropriate classes, and awarding scholarships; the number of performances both on campus and off campus; activities that students, teachers, and the program participates in; and field trips.
- **graduates:** Establish a follow-up survey of graduates from the program to ascertain their career development and employment record in the field. Often these types of evaluations include responses about the program's effectiveness in preparing them for a career in their field.

All of these evaluations form the basis for the development of reports. These reports evaluate the effectiveness of the program.

Types of Reports

Curriculums and programs are evaluated by the school, the district, the state department of education, or a national accreditation agency. These agencies require periodic reports.

Programs are reviewed in respect to meeting the goals of these organizations and producing graduates. Regional and national accreditation reports usually take place every few years. These reports require extensive self-study, planning, and writing to satisfy the intense scrutiny of every aspect of the program.

Summary

Understanding the dance curriculum models (process, product, combination, and discipline-based dance education) enables the teacher to better address the viewpoints, needs, and desires of the school district and the community. Dance curriculum models reflect what is taught and how it is taught. The selection of a dance model has an effect on the type of unit plan, the choice of the dance form, its content, and order (scope and sequence and block time plan). The curriculum model guides the implementation of these dance forms through bottom–up or top–down strategies and assessment through formative and summative evaluation.

Developing one or more unit plans to create a logical progression of studies constitutes a program. Long-term planning is essential to the success of one-year or four-year dance programs. Within dance programs, administrative processes can include auditions for placement in classes, offering choices of courses, and scheduling faculty and facilities. Program evaluations provide information necessary for reports for the school and state, regional, and national accrediting agencies.

References

Barber, D.W., K. Clemente, J. Crawford, J.L. Friedlander, S. Hilsendager, and C. Vandarakis. 1989. Discipline-based arts education: Attaining its goals without forfeiting the essence of dance as a meaningful participation experience. AAHPERD Convention, Boston, MA.

Smith-Autard, J.M. 1994. *The art of dance in education.* London: A.C. Black.

Torrance, P.E. 1981. *Think creatively in administration, scoring, and norms manual action and movement.* Bensenville, IL: Scholastic Testing Service.

It's Your Turn

1. Select two dance curriculum models and write a one-page scenario that uses each of the models. Justify your rationale for the selection of each curriculum model in terms of your students, setting, and community. Compare rationale with other students in the class.
2. Devise a scope and sequence and block time plan for a three-week unit in two different dance forms from two different dance form categories.
3. Write a one-page paper in which you describe a school setting and identify the learners. What dance units would you teach, and what is the order in which you would teach them? Develop a rationale for your units.

CHAPTER

13

Sample Units for Dance Forms

This chapter provides beginning-level sample units of the 10 dance forms commonly taught in public schools. The units provide teaching and content information for 4 dance form categories and the 10 dance forms in these categories.

Overview of Dance Forms

The dance forms selected are those that can be implemented in public schools. Dance in public schools originates from 4 dance form categories, and the dance form categories encompass 10 different dance forms.

- Creative movement and creative dance make up one category.
- The dance forms in the recreational dance category are folk, square, contra, and social dance.
- The dance forms in the concert category are ballet, modern dance, jazz, and tap dance.
- Aerobic (dance fitness) constitutes one category.

As you can see, each of the 4 dance form categories has distinct characteristics; each of the 10 forms has distinct characteristics within the categories as well. Understanding the individual forms through the sample unit plans gives you insight into their value and position within the curriculum. Beginning in kindergarten and continuing through high school, the learner may experience dance forms in the order presented in figure 13.1. However, this depends on the expertise of the faculty and the support of the school system.

The sample units will be presented in the same order as they are generally taught. Each dance form sample unit guide contains two parts: a teaching overview and a content overview.

Teaching Overview

The teaching overview includes the following elements:

- **Objectives and evaluation** specify goals and assessment of students' psychomotor, cognitive, and affective learning. The items listed can become the general criteria for evaluation of an activity, combination, or dance. You can determine the criteria for performance as either a ratio or a percentage.
- **Scope and sequence** for the dance unit outlines what and when exercises, steps, combinations, figures, and activities will be taught.
- **Block time plan** organizes the scope and sequence into a calendar format.
- **Teaching approaches** introduce various ways to present the dance unit.
- **Specific teaching methods** are listed for each dance form.
- **Musical accompaniment** information provides insights into music selections for the dance form.
- **Specific dance class format** addresses the sequence of the class.

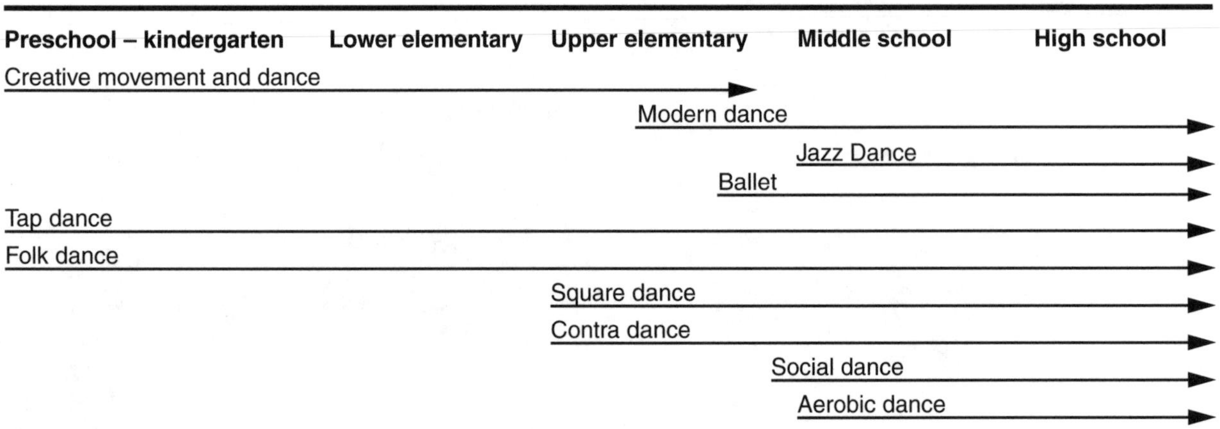

Preschool – kindergarten | **Lower elementary** | **Upper elementary** | **Middle school** | **High school**

Creative movement and dance →
Modern dance →
Jazz Dance →
Ballet →
Tap dance →
Folk dance →
Square dance →
Contra dance →
Social dance →
Aerobic dance →

Figure 13.1 Sample curriculum overview of dance in K-12 education.

- **Classroom considerations** review such items as safety, attire, and etiquette.
- **Beyond technique assignments** give dance making and dance appreciation activities for the unit.

Content Overview

The content overview presents a foundation for teaching a beginning-level unit in 10 dance forms. The following information is included:

- **Definition of the dance form and a brief historical survey,** which include the people significant to the development of the dance form.
- **Special features or benefits** for the beginning level of the dance form that identifies its uniqueness.
- **Movement, choreographic, and aesthetic principles** as they apply to the dance form are shown as icons, with the applicable principles shaded.
- **Dance vocabulary** for each exercise, step, and skill appropriate for the beginning unit is described. Where applicable, short combinations or dances for the beginning level are included.
- **Selected resources** include texts, music, and videos that are helpful in teaching the dance form. These should be used in conjunction with books and video sources for that particular dance form.

Each of the sample units is designed for 15 classes; the content presented can be adapted to fit individual needs. For example, you may need to select just part of the content for a short unit. Or, you can extend the content to accommodate an entire semester if students meet twice a week for short classes. The scope and sequence and block time plans have been developed for different populations and settings, but they are easily adaptable for most settings and age groups:

- **Creative movement and creative dance** has two different plans. One is for lower elementary students. The second plan is for preschool children with special needs.
- **Folk dance** is for upper elementary, middle school, or high school students.
- **Square dance** is for upper elementary, middle school, or high school students.
- **Contra dance** is for upper elementary, middle school, or high school students.
- **Social dance** is for upper elementary, middle school, or high school students.
- **Ballet** is for middle or high school students.
- **Modern dance** is for middle or high school students.
- **Jazz dance** is for middle or high school students.
- **Tap dance** is for middle or high school students.
- **Aerobic dance** is for middle or high school students.

The sample units for dance forms are models for study in dance pedagogy and the art and science of dance. They will guide you in your discoveries and learning journeys in teaching dance.

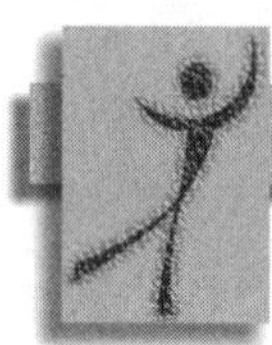

Creative Movement and Creative Dance Unit

Teaching Overview

Psychomotor Objectives

- Execute basic creative dance elements and vocabulary.
- Demonstrate the dance form's relationships to music (tempo, rhythm, counts).
- Perform concepts as they apply to creative dance (e.g., personal and general space).
- Create dances with a beginning, middle, and end to meet the objective of the activity.

Psychomotor Evaluation

- Test performance of selected creative movement activities (execute movement, to music, with other dancers; understand and apply concepts; create a dance to meet appropriate criteria of the activity).

Cognitive Objectives

- Recognize creative dance vocabulary.
- Translate (listen and follow) the teacher's instructions.
- Conduct a self-evaluation or a peer evaluation of a beginning creative movement or dance performance.

Cognitive Evaluation

- Complete written test of knowledge of dance skills, terminology, definitions; translate teacher's instructions into movement with the music; conduct self-assessment of performance.

Affective Objectives

- Know and demonstrate etiquette for the creative dance class.
- Demonstrate movement confidence.
- Interact successfully with other persons in the class.

Affective Evaluation

- Demonstrate etiquette, movement confidence, cooperation, contribution, and leadership within the group and class.

Teaching Approaches

Your background as a teacher determines how you will teach creative movement and creative dance. Your preparation may range from physical education to dance to education. Because of this range, the delivery and content may vary considerably. The dance classes may consist of activities based on a dance element or theme; rhythmic games; or folk, square, contra, and popular dances. The activities may also involve problem-solving strategies for creating dances or dance that relate to other arts or integrate other academic subjects.

You should be comfortable with teaching movement and dance. Related to and often embodied in this creative, elemental movement dance form are several other applications:

- Movement education focuses on learning movement with and without manipulatives (balls, sticks, and other props). This approach is the basis for physical education in the elementary school.

FORM 13.1

Scope and Sequence for Creative Movement and Creative Dance

New = N Review = R Create dance = CD Perform dance = PD Performance test = PT

	1	2	3	4	5	6	7	8	9	10	11	12	13	14	15
Rules and etiquette parameters	N														
Circle personal and general space	N														
Warm-up, identification of body parts	N	R	R	R	R	R	R	R	R	R	R	R	R	R	
Sitting bend and stretch; point and flex feet	N	R	R	R	R	R	R	R	R	R	R	R	R	R	
Standing demi-plié	N	R	R	R	R	R	R	R	R	R	R	R	R	R	
Battement tendu	N	R	R	R	R	R	R	R	R	R	R	R	R	R	
Move and freeze in personal and general space	N														
In circle, review concepts	N														
Levels (high, middle, and low)		N		R	R	R									
Move and freeze high and low		N													
In circle, review levels		N													
Walk levels, slow			N	R											
Directions: forward, side, backward			N	R	R	R									
Runs			N	R											
Gallops			N	R											
Review free dance and use concepts			R-N												
Jumps, hops				N											
Create movement sentence				N											
Body shapes					N										
Move quickly and slowly					N										
Nonlocomotor bending stretches (curving, rotating)					N										
Explore positive and negative spaces with partners					N										
Shape: move and freeze					N										
Favorite shape					N										

(continued)

FORM 13.1 *(continued)*

New = N   Review = R   Create dance = CD   Perform dance = PD   Performance test = PT

	1	2	3	4	5	6	7	8	9	10	11	12	13	14	15
Line up and move across room in group						N									
Combine prior locomotor movement						N									
Chassé side, front, in a circle						N									
Movement sentence: three locomotor movements						N									
Shape favorite locomotor movement						N									
Movement sentences with locomotor and nonlocomotor movement							N								
Skips							N								
Shape and touching							N								
Group sculpture							R								
Free dance							R								
Locomotor movement pathways								N							
Spinning movement								N							
Run and leap								N							
Dimension, large and small								N							
Writing your name									N						
Run and lead dance									R						
Qualities of effort action (collapse, swing, percussive, sustained, vibratory, suspended)									N						
Line across and rotate									N						
Select contrast qualities									N						
Movement quality sentence									N						
Free dance with different types of movement									N						
Read story and explore characters and plot										N					
Emotion and qualities										N					

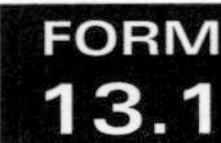

New = N Review = R Create dance = CD Perform dance = PD Performance test = PT

	1	2	3	4	5	6	7	8	9	10	11	12	13	14	15
Use qualities to communicate										N					
Observe each other										N					
Movement sentence: A B form											N				
Groups of 1, 2, 3, 4, create dance											N				
Perform for each other											R				
Relaxation story											N				
Subject study in another class												N			
Small group dance explore, select, and create												CD			
Create rubric with class												N			
Observe dance and provide feedback													N		
Perform dance													N		
Revise dance													N	R	
Add-scenario costume elements														N	
Perform															PD
Evaluate and analyze dance															PT
Goodbye dance															N

FORM 13.2

Creative Dance for Lower Elementary Students Block Time Plan

Class 1	Class 2	Class 3	Class 4	Class 5
• Circle: personal and general space • Warm-up using identification of body parts (use chants and music) while sitting (bending and stretching body; pointing and flexing feet); standing (demi-pliés and battement tendus in parallel position) • Move and freeze (personal and general space) • Circle: review of key concepts	• Warm-up: identify and move body parts (use chants and music) sitting; standing (demi-pliés and battement tendus in parallel position) • Introduce levels (high, middle, and low) • Review move and freeze game; add-on (freeze at a different level, then move at a different level) • Closing dance and review of key concepts	• Warm-up: move various body parts and make sounds to accompany the movements or sing chants • Introduce walks (pedestrian then dance walk); add levels (middle, low, high); walking fast and walking slowly • Introduce walking forward, backward, and to the side • Run (short distance and freeze); add levels to freeze • Gallops: practice with both right and left foot in front • Introduce free dance (teacher cued): while the students move through the space, cue them with names of steps or concepts learned that day and alternate to free dance in which they can explore the space • Teacher observation and informal assessment	• Warm-up: identify and move body parts while sitting, standing • In the general space, learn jumps and hops • Review walks, runs, gallops • Add directions (forward, backward, and side) to movement separately; walk, run, hops, jumps • Create a movement sentence: begin in a frozen shape, then perform three locomotor movements across the floor and end in another frozen shape at a level different from the one at the beginning. Half the class performs their movement sentences; other half of class sits and observes. Then reverse. • Free dance (teacher cued to work in class)	• Warm-up: move body parts while sitting, standing • Explore body shapes (straight, bent, and curved); add levels • Explore nonlocomotor movement and add shapes • Create a personal shape dance • With a partner explore positive and negative space; one person takes a shape; the other person moves creating body designs while moving through the negative spaces. Reverse roles. Half the class watches the sculptures created by the other half of the class; then reverse roles. • Move and freeze in a bent shape, a straight shape, a curved shape, shape at a high level, different shape, at a low level, at the middle level • Closing: sit in a circle and each person takes a turn to show three favorite shapes; other children identify the shapes

FORM 13.2

Class 6	Class 7	Class 8	Class 9	Class 10
• Warm-up: sitting, standing, kneeling (straight back, curved back) • Learn protocols for going across the floor[1] • Execute across the floor: walk, run and freeze, gallop, hops and jumps, combined steps • Introduce chassés (side, front, then in a circle) • Create a movement sentence: Begin in a shape, choose three locomotor movements. End by freezing in a different shape and level. Repeat movement sentence and add a change in direction. Repeat movement and add a level change. Repeat and add a freeze and nonlocomotor movements; then complete the sentence[2] • Closing: Sitting in a circle, choose a locomotor movement and execute it going from your place around the circle and returning to your place.	• Warm-up: sitting, kneeling, and standing • Review of movement sentences: One line creates the sentence; the next line observes and describes the sentence (bent shape high; three hops and one jump; freeze while bending; chassé sideways and freeze curved shape low). This is achieved through the teacher's guided questions. • Learn skipping (hands on the hips) • Review shapes and talk about touching gently • Group sculpture[3]: Children have to learn how and where to touch someone else gently for this activity. • Closing: free dancing with move, freeze, shapes; nonlocomotor movement (teacher cues locomotor movements only if necessary)	• Warm-up: sitting, kneeling, and standing • Practice locomotor movements across the floor exploring pathways (straight, curved, angles) • Give movement sentences that include spinning • Explore running and leaping through the space • Explore dimensions of movements (big and small) • Write your name with your arm or leg in space. Moving through the space write your name with different body parts (elbow, nose, shoulder); write a word small as if on a card, large as if on a billboard. Half the class writes and the other half observes; reverse. • Closing: teacher-directed dance (big/small movements, running/freeze, leaps, shapes, pathways through the space in groups)	• Warm-up: repeat • Learn qualities or effort actions while sitting; practice them standing and moving through space • Learn how to move across the floor with two other people in a line • Select contrasting qualities or effort actions and create movement sentences that explore them. The two qualities can be linked with a nonlocomotor movement as a transition from one to the other. • Create a second movement quality sentence. Link the two sentences together. Practice and perform the two sentences in small groups. Each person's sentence will be different. Focus on pictorial relationships. • Free dance: Choose a collage or select different kinds of music and ask students while they dance to demonstrate qualities of movement that mirror the music.	• Warm-up: repeat • Read an action story and ask the children to explore each of the characters and the plot through movement. Have half the class or small group perform the story while the other group watches. Then other group(s) perform. How do the characters show the emotions in the story? What are the qualities of their movement? • Closing: teacher-directed dance recalling the characters and plot of the story

[1]Learn to line up (look and remember who is in front and who is behind you); take your turn and move from one side of the room to the other; then the first person goes to the back of the line and the second person becomes the new leader.

[2]The complexity of the movement sentence depends on the age of the children in the class and their ability to understand and add new movement.

[3]Half the class participates; the other half observes. One person volunteers to take a low (comfortable) shape. Another person takes a shape on another level and connects to the first; the next person takes a shape on another level and connects to either of the dancers; and so on. The group holds their sculpture and the watchers walk around the sculpture. The teacher acts as the guide asking the watchers for adjectives to describe the sculpture (a title for the sculpture). Then the two groups reverse roles and the activity is repeated.

(continued)

FORM 13.2 *(continued)*

Class 11	Class 12	Class 13	Class 14	Class 15
• Warm-up • Ask each child to create a movement sentence (A) and a second sentence (B) that contrasts the first one. In groups of three or four, the "1" performs two movement sentences (AB). The "2" person performs two movement sentences (BA). The "3" person performs two sentences (AA). The "4" person performs two sentences (BB). Children enter and exit using locomotor movements or begin and end in a shape. Repeat with different variables or focus on one or more variables. • Each group performs their movement sentence for the rest of the class. Suggestions are given for possible revisions. Each group revises their work and performs it again. • Closing: relaxation story read by the teacher	• Warm-up • Ask each child to bring to class a list of things they are studying in other classes (the space, the sea, transportation). List these on the board. • Place children in small groups (second grade on up). Ask the group to choose a topic and create an adventure. They explore movement, and select and create a dance. • Class and teacher develop a rubric for evaluating the dances and the group cooperation that created the dance.	• Warm-up • Look at each dance and give feedback • Perform draft of the dance for the group • Revise it	• Warm-up • Practice the dance • Add scenic or costume elements	• Perform the dance • Evaluate the dance • Analyze the dance within the group • Celebrate with a goodbye dance

FORM 13.3

Scope and Sequence for Creative Movement and Creative Dance for Special Needs

New = N Review = R Performance test = PT Create dance = CD Perform dance = PD Informal test = IT

	1	2	3	4	5	6	7	8	9	10	11	12	13	14	15
Rules and parameters of personal and general space	N														
Warm-up, identification of body parts	N														
Standing and sitting dance	N														
Closing and review	N														
Identify and move body parts		R	R		R					R					
Review chants and songs		R			R										
Create movement sentence with three or four body parts		N													
Practice and observe		N		R	R		R								
Perform dance closing ritual		R													
Sound made with body parts			N	R	R										
Make own sentence and pass it on			N												
Body facing front, back, side				N											
Move from one body part and facing to another				N	R	R									
Walks						N		R	R						
Walk on different body part						N	N			R					
Move and freeze dance with drum and on music						N									
Create a dance of walks						N									
Various animal walks							N								
Levels, direction, pathways through space									N						
Machine walks								N							
Run, freeze, and walk dance									N						
Identify level, parts, directions of locomotor movement								N		N					
Informal assessment										IT					

(continued)

FORM 13.3 *(continued)*

New = N Review = R Performance test = PT Create dance = CD Perform dance = PD Informal test = IT

	1	2	3	4	5	6	7	8	9	10	11	12	13	14	15
Shape of body											N				
Letters of names											N		R		
Numbers												N	R		
Create number dance												N			
Leaps														N	
Partner dance letters and numbers dance													N		
Create dance shape, leap, run														N	
Perform dance and evaluate															PD

FORM 13.4

Creative Dance for Pre-K Children With Special Needs Block Time Plan

Class 1	Class 2	Class 3	Class 4	Class 5
• Rules and parameters: personal and general space • Warm-up by identification of body parts (use chants and music) while sitting and standing • Closing dance	• Identify and move body parts • Review and learn chants and songs • Create movement sentence with three or four body parts • Practice, observe, and perform • Closing dance	• Review, identify, and move body parts (song, chants, and music) • Sounds made with various body parts • Make own movement sentence and pass it on	• Review sounds of various body parts • Explore body facings (front, back, and side) • Explore and move to different body part • Create, observe, and perform dances	• Review chant and song • Use body parts and sound • Explore balancing on different body parts • Create, perform, and observe dances
Class 6	**Class 7**	**Class 8**	**Class 9**	**Class 10**
• Review balance on body part • Teach various walks using different body parts (high, medium, low levels) • Move and freeze with drum or music • Create a dance of walks	• Review walks; lead the walks with different body parts • Show pictures of animals and explore various animal walks • Create, practice, and perform an animal dance that emphasizes walks and gesture of animal	• Review walks • Explore levels, directions, pathways through space • Walk movements of various machines • Show pictures and select a machine; explore their movement parts • Create movement phrase using the movement of the machine	• Review walks • Teach runs (direction, levels, pathways) • Run, freeze, and walk; dance with drum or music • Create a dance with walks, runs, and freezes	• Verbal review of various concepts, elements • Identify parts of body; directions, levels, glances, walks, and runs • Informal assessment
Class 11	**Class 12**	**Class 13**	**Class 14**	**Class 15**
• Review walks and runs • Explore shape of body (curved, linear, zigzag, wavy) • Make a dance with letters of names	• Review body shapes • Explore numbers using body • Create a dance using numbers	• Review letters and shapes • Explore leaps • Assign partner; explore and create a letter and number dance with your partner	• Review leaps, runs, walks • Create a dance with your partner that uses shapes, leaps, and runs	Assessment day • Practice with partner, show dance. Evaluate the partner dance using the criteria.

- Keep vocabulary consistent.
- Don't use too many words that have the same meaning (e.g., shake or flick).
- Use pictures or visual representations.
- Use sign language when appropriate.
- Often children with special needs are not able to generalize concepts, so they may need to have different experiences to reinforce a concept.

- Movement exploration, similar to movement education, is basic to developing movement skills for physical education and dance activities in preschool through the primary grades.
- Creative or dramatic movement includes pantomime and dramatization (being a machine, force of nature, or animal). This form uses creative dance concepts of space, time, and force and may be stimulated by music and supported by imagery or literature (Doll and Nelson 1965).
- Rhythmic form develops rhythm and movement through the study of elements of rhythm through movement. The use of games, folk dance, creative movement, and musical instruments develop students' awareness of basic time patterns and movement concepts. The content depends on your teaching philosophy (Doll and Nelson 1965).
- Play dancing combines movement with pantomime in social play situations. Developed by Diane Lynch Fraser (1991), it explores fantasy, realism, emotions, and elementary movement concepts through activities in social play situations from early childhood to kindergarten.

The following are suggested ideas for creative dance:

- Preschool children can use stories and tales, bright colors, familiar objects, occupations, animals, machines, songs, chants, fantasy and pretending, and props (ribbons, scarves, yarn balls).
- Students in grades 1 through 4 can use animal movements, modes of transportation, environments (zoo, farm, forest, jungle), music, specific dance steps, dance vocabulary to explore movement, and props. Students at this level can also integrate dance into other school subjects.

Specific Teaching Methods

Teaching styles and content vary depending on your background and intent for the class. You may use command and other teacher-centered teaching styles that take the form of structured dances. Or you may use student-centered teaching styles of problem solving and guided discovery as the basis for the class.

Through creative movement and creative dance, children perform stories and poems, explore dance elements and choreographic principles, or use movement to demonstrate a concept from another academic subject. To meet these varied needs, you will adjust your teaching strategies of cueing and imagery through guided discovery so that students can thoroughly investigate the possibilities of the topic through movement and dance.

Musical Accompaniment

Musical accompaniment for creative movement and creative dance is varied. The purpose is to introduce children to a wide variety of music and musical styles. Accompaniment may be either recorded or teacher-generated. If you are the accompanist, you will play a hand drum or another percussive musical instrument (a block, tambourine, or sticks) as you move through the class. You must become proficient at integrating your accompaniment into the lesson without overshadowing the major focus, which is teaching the class.

Augmenting your own accompaniment are CDs and cassettes. A wide variety of music (instrumental pieces or songs from classical, New Age, country, folk, or world) provides children different stimuli for movement. You must screen all music before class to ensure that any lyrics, or religious or holiday themes in the music, are appropriate for the public school setting and the children. Most creative movement and creative dance teachers collect a wide assortment of music for various activities and projects.

Dance Class Format

The dance class format of the creative movement or creative dance class varies. The following list is one of two examples of a warm-up for creative dance:

1. A set warm-up, which includes exercises from modern dance and ballet, can include demi-pliés, battement tendus, battement dégagés, battement tendu piqué, foot exercises, roll-downs, leg swings, and leg lifts. Students can perform exercises while lying, sitting, kneeling, and standing.
2. Use questioning to guide how various body parts move.
3. Select locomotor and nonlocomotor movements that the students explore during the warm-up.
4. Choose elements and concepts introduced to the students that are part of the activities that will be explored later in the lesson.
5. Create a culminating activity using the elements and concepts of the lesson.
6. Begin a class with a ritual to draw the students into class activities.

The second kind of class format includes an introduction, development, and review of the theme of the lesson.

1. Give the students the problem, idea, or theme that will be explored. Students can explore the theme in small parts, which lead to a culminating experience or dance; or they can explore the entire concept at once. Use elements of the theme as the warm-up for the class.
2. Students explore the activity individually, in small groups, and with the entire class during the period or over several class periods.The activity expands and develops into a form, or you can mold the activity into a culminating experience for the students.
3. Students may review previous activities, studies, or dances and refine them.

Both types of classes contain activities and culminating experiences:

1. The students present the day's movement activity or dance. The entire class performs the dance together. Small groups perform for the remainder of the class; the other students observe, discuss, and evaluate the activity or dance.
2. If the movement activity or dance is incomplete by the end of the class, the dancers perform parts of the activity or what they have created so far. Often a spokesperson for the group explains his solution to the problem or describes his approach to expressing the idea in movement.

The following are some ideas for closing the class:

1. Free dance allows the children to select and execute movement to express themselves through dance.
2. During free dance, you may guide the children through a review of the movements and concepts that the students studied in the day's lesson.
3. The dancers participate in an ending ritual that brings them together and closes the class.

4. Relaxation experiences neutralize the high energy level from a culminating activity or dance and center students to return to academic classes.

Classroom Considerations

In the creative movement and creative dance classroom, you develop rules for safety and management of the class. If the children change clothing or shoes, appropriate places must be available for storage. Explain the rules for the dance class and post them as a reminder for students. These rules should be brief. In the first class, specify how children enter and exit the dance classroom and ask questions; also review general considerations for each person sharing the space. Establish cues so that children know how to behave during the class. For example, you may tap the drum or turn the music off or on to get students' attention.

Safety

For safety, the dance space should be marked off with gymnastics tape. This device safely controls the area in which children move. Another safety strategy is to provide a specific place that gives each child adequate space to sit and move in the circle or on lines. Taped spots, carpet squares, or other commercial products such as poly spots can serve as markers for students.

Attire

Children should wear comfortable clothes (pants and T-shirts or dance attire) in which they can move. Children in public school settings either dance in their shoes or in bare feet (the latter depends on the surface of the floor). Footwear can be athletic shoes or dance slippers with elastic straps.

Classroom Etiquette

You must establish classroom etiquette for creative movement and creative dance classes. This sets the tone and expectations for behavior in the class. Create rituals that reinforce the expected behaviors in the class. For example, when children enter the dance space, they march around the dance space before forming a circle. Children learn how to line up and take turns going across the floor, or each child creates and stays in his personal space as others move through the general space without bumping into others. Other rituals are established for participating in discussion and for ending the class. At the end of class, other rituals include a good-bye dance. Each child can also dance a key idea from the day's lesson as he leaves the dance space.

Beyond Technique Assignments

Beyond technique assignments incorporate dance making and dance appreciation activities into the unit to support and enhance the primary study of learning dance skills. The following are some beyond technique assignments for students in dance making and dance appreciation:

- Create a movement sentence. (A movement sentence has a beginning movement, a middle or second movement, and an ending movement.) Create a movement study using the elements of space. (A movement study is an extended exploration of a topic. The study can contain several movement sentences or be a long series of movements that cohesively address movement concepts or a movement element, solve a problem, or explore a specific topic. A movement study could be as short as 32 counts or as long as a minute or two, de the complexity of the study. Like a dance, the movement study has a middle, end, and transitions, but it is shorter and less structured th Create a dance based on a topic from another discipline, such as lang (poetry), science (nature).

- View other students' dances in the class; the observing students state whether they believed the dancers solved the movement problem posed by the teacher. Students keep a journal during the class, during a guest artist residency, or through the process of learning and preparing a dance for performance.
- Have students develop a process folio for the dance unit of journal entries, reflections during the dance-making or dance-learning process, photos and drawings of choreography, and how they and the other dancers work as a group during the creation of the piece. Then add a videotape of the performance to the process folio with a written analysis of how to refine the piece.

Content Overview

Content overview for creative movement and creative dance comes from a vast array of cross-disciplinary categories that support it in its many forms. Content overview also serves as a method for integration and interdisciplinary studies.

Definition and History

Creative movement focuses on exploring the elements of time, space, and energy (force) and creating shapes through everyday and dance-specific locomotor and nonlocomotor movements to gain movement competency. The aim of this dance form is to preserve the child's spontaneity of movement while enhancing movement vocabulary and repertoire. Creative movement and creative dance often are merged, each taking on characteristics that make them appropriate for different teaching situations. As an abstract dance form, creative movement focuses on using the basic principles and concepts of dance to form simple choreographic structures. The dance form is age appropriate for preschool through elementary children.

Creative movement and creative dance are an outgrowth of the aesthetic dance movement at the end of the 19th century. Originally, aesthetic dance and other names it was given were for college-aged women. Many early 20th-century American dance educators, such as Colby, Larsen, and H'Doubler, sought a dance form that would be relevant to graduates who taught in physical education departments of public schools. Dance educators, physical educators, arts educators, and other educators in the United States and abroad have created many views of creative movement and creative dance resources. Creative movement and creative dance, regardless of what titles they are given, provide age-appropriate movement and dance experiences that support learning in other dance forms, other art forms, and in physical education.

Rudolf von Laban (creator of Labanotation) was a driving force in the development of creative dance because of his movement analysis. His paradigm became a foundation for teaching and creating dance. Many dancers and dance educators adopted von Laban's ideas. This paradigm or theory provided a standard vocabulary for dance movement, which in turn facilitated teaching, creating, and appreciating dance.

In the 1990s, with arts education becoming an important partner in the educational reform movement, creative dance became the foundation on which access to dance was grounded. Creative movement and creative dance have gained further support from educational theories such as multiple intelligences, integration, and brain research.

Special Features

Creative movement and creative dance have the following features:

- They provide learners with experiences that use everyday movements to explore dance elements and choreographic structures and creatively discover, explore, compose, and refine their movement into a study or dance.
- They encourage participation in dancing, dance making, and dance appreciation through observation, discussion, and evaluation of dance works.
- These forms, often regarded as only for young children, are a powerful presence in movement therapy modalities and enhancement of senior citizens' body awareness, self-image, and movement confidence.
- Creative movement and creative dance have become support systems for physical education and other arts disciplines and the vehicle for integrated and interdisciplinary learning.
- They introduce learners to dance and become a natural conduit to the study of modern dance, jazz dance, and other dance forms.

Principles

Movement, choreographic, and aesthetic principles that specifically apply to creative movement and creative dance are shaded in the icons on pages 217-218.

Vocabulary

The vocabulary for creative movement and creative dance includes dance skills, movements, elements of dance, choreographic structures (choreographic

Children moving in wide and narrow and big and small shapes.

Movement Principles of Creative Movement and Creative Dance

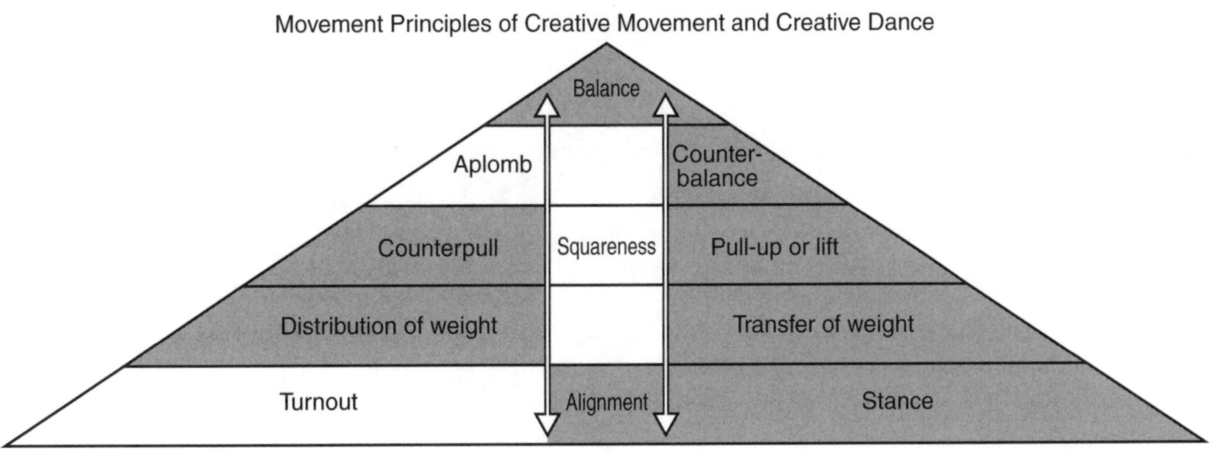

Choreographic Principles of Creative Movement and Creative Dance

Choreographic elements	Choreographic structures	Choreographic designs	Choreographic devices	Choreographic relationships
Motif Phrase Theme and variation	Simple musical forms • AB (binary) • ABA (ternary) • Rondo • Theme and variation Contrapuntal forms • Canon (round) • Fugue Others • Narrative (story) • Open (free)	Dancer's body shape Dancer's pathway through space Visual design • Symmetrical • Asymmetrical Symbolism • Representational • Abstraction • Distortion Relationship • Unison • Sequential • Successional • Oppositional • Complementary	Repetition Reverse Alter • Addition or subtraction • Directional change • Facing or focus • Level • Dimension • Tempo • Rhythm • Quality or effort action • Positioning • Movement section	Solo Duet Trio Quartet Small and large groups

Traditional Dance Elements

Space	Time	Force	Relationships
Directions Dimensions Levels Shapes Pathways Focus	Duration Tempo	Movement qualities • Sustained • Percussive • Swinging • Suspended • Collapsing • Vibratory	Among body parts Among people Between people and props

Laban's Dance Elements

Space	Time	Weight	Flow
Direct or indirect	Sudden or slow	Light or strong	Bound or free
Effort actions (use space, time, and weight) • Dab • Flick • Punch • Slash • Glide • Float • Press • Wring			

Aesthetic Principles of Creative Movement and Creative Dance

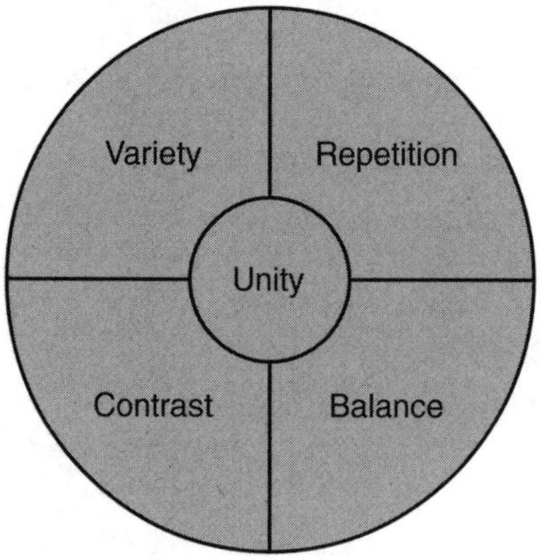

elements, choreographic devices, choreographic connections, choreographic relationships, dancer relationships, number of dancers), musical forms, and other choreographic forms.

Dance Skills

Body awareness is the awareness of body parts, their locations, the types of movements they perform, and the relation of each body part to others and the entire body moving through space. For example, "Touch your nose, shoulders, knees, and toes."

Personal space is the space that your body takes up while still or moving; it is also known as *positive space.* For example, "Stretch your arms up, out, and down to define your own space," or "Imagine you are moving through the dance space in a bubble."

General space is the common dance space shared with the group; it is the space around the body, or *negative space.* For example, "Stay in your bubble as you move through the space. Be sure your bubble doesn't touch anyone else's bubble in the dancing space."

Movements

Nonlocomotor movement involves body parts that move around a stationary base by bending (flexing), stretching (extending), or twisting (turning) on an axis. This is also referred to as *axial movement* (see modern dance unit, page 329).

Locomotor movement involves movement that travels from one place to another; these include both even and uneven rhythm steps (see modern dance unit, page 342).

Even rhythm steps are walk, run, hop, leap, and jump.

Uneven rhythm steps are slide, gallop, and skip.

Combined movements are two or more movements performed together, such as step–hop.

Elements of Dance

Space is the area through which the dancers move.This includes **personal space** and **common space.** In the space the dancer encounters direction, level, pathways, formations, dimension, and design elements.

Directions are forward, backward, sideways, on a diagonal, in an arc, in a circle, and up and down.

Children showing various directions.

Children moving at different levels.

Levels are high (from standing to in the air), middle (from standing through demi-plié and lunging movements), and low (from kneeling to lying on the floor).
Pathways are floor patterns and movement through the space in angular, curved, straight, or twisted routes, which encompass both direct and indirect pathways.
Body shapes involve creating shapes that are curved, stretched, twisted, angular, or straight while executing either nonlocomotor or locomotor movements.
Dimension is how big or small the movement is performed in the space or as a floor pattern.
Time is the length or duration of a movement study or dance, which is determined by the dancer and the music, the sound collage, or other accompaniment. In creative movement and creative dance, time refers to using musical components such as beat, measure, tempo, accent, and phrasing.
Beat is the underlying pulse.
Tempo is the rate of speed of the movement: fast (presto) to slow (adagio).
Measure is a grouping of beats separated into intervals by a primary accent.
Accent is the emphasis on a beat or equal groups of beats.
Rhythmic patterns are beat patterns. Mixed meter is 1, 2; 1, 2, 3, 4; 1, 2, 3; 1, 2, 3, 4, 5.

Accumulative rhythm is 1, 2; 1, 2, 3; 1, 2, 3, 4.
Musical phrase is a short group of measures coming to a temporary or permanent finish.
Force is the amount of intensity in movement (also referred to as *energy*).
Movement qualities are the amount of energy used and the manner in which it is released that give the movement a distinctive character.

- **Pendular movement** is a light, free, swinging movement.
- **Collapse** is a quick release of all energy.
- **Suspension** is a floating, effortless movement that seems to defy gravity.
- **Sustained** is steady, continuous movement.
- **Vibratory** is repetitive, rapid movements usually involving smaller body parts.
- **Percussive** is strong sharp movement with the force checked suddenly. This is often accompanied by a sound. Without sound it is referred to as *abrupt.*

Effort actions relate to everyday movement as well as sport or any other movement activity. Laban developed a system for categorizing movement. His system identified individual movement preferences and classified them as effort actions:

- Dab (sudden, light, and direct)
- Flick (sudden, light, and indirect)
- Punch (sudden, strong, and direct)
- Slash (sudden, strong, and indirect)
- Glide (slow, light, and direct)
- Float (slow, light, and indirect)
- Press (slow, strong, and direct)
- Wring (slow, strong, and indirect)

How the dancer moves from one effort and through another is called **flow.** The amount of flow used relates to space, time, and energy changes.

Choreographic Structures (Dance Making)

Choreography is developing a series of movements and phrases that create cohesive and thematic unity, which in turn produce a dance with a beginning, a middle, and an end.

Choreographic Elements

Motif is the smallest repeated element or movement.
Phrase is a short series of movements that connect.
Theme is a series of movements or phrases that the dance is based on.
Choreographic design is the body shape and line in space and in relation to other persons and objects in the space. The design is either symmetrical (balanced on each side) or asymmetrical (unbalanced).
Visual design is the overall pictures created through the use of choreographic elements that include dancers' body shapes and pathways and group formations.
Group formations are a square, a triangle, two parallel lines, a straight line, a circle or part of a circle, a V, or inverted V.

Choreographic Devices

Representational movements are the literal movements or gestures of the body.
Abstraction involves taking the essence of an idea from a literal reproduction; the movement extraction may be symbolic.
Distortion is to alter a form or shape.

Children connecting to each other.

Choreographic Connections

Tension is the degree of energy intensity, which construes various shades of emotions or qualities of movement.
Transition is the way in which a movement phrase connects to the next. Organic transitions involve a growing out of one movement into the next.

Choreographic Relationships

Unison involves all dancers in the group executing the same movements at the same time.
Sequential movement is a wavelike pattern in which all dancers do the same movements in a successive order rather than all at the same time.
Opposition is movement that opposes or contrasts the original movement or the movement of another dancer (under/over, together/away, mirrored/moving toward or through, up/down, forward/backward).
Complementary movement is another person performing the same movement with the opposite side of the body as the other person.

Dancer Relationships (Adapted From Purcell 1994, p. 26)

Copy is two or more dancers performing the same movement or movements.
Mirror is two dancers facing each other to execute the same movement using opposite sides, as in a mirror.
Repeat (or **echo**) movements involve one dancer executing a movement that other dancers execute, after the first has completed it.
Successive movement occurs while one dancer executes a movement phrase and a second dancer begins the same phrase; a third dancer begins the phrase while the second dancer executes the phrase, and so on.
Contrasting movements involve one or more students using opposite body shapes, directions, qualities or efforts, and timing in relation to the group.
Tracing (shadowing) involves one dancer in front of another and both do the same movement.
In **question and answer,** two dancers perform; one dancer makes a movement statement, then the other responds either by agreeing by repeating the same movements or responding with another movement statement.
Connections are two or more students attached to each other by a body part to make a shape or move together.

Supporting involves two or more dancers supporting some or all of the body weight of one or more of the dancers.
In **find and leave,** two or more dancers move toward one another and then away from one another.

Number of Dancers

Solo is a dance for one person.
Duet is a dance for two people.
Trio is a dance for three people.
Quartet is a dance for four people.

Musical Forms

AB is dance theme A followed by a contrasting but related theme of B.
ABA is dance theme A followed by a contrasting theme B and ending with a restatement of theme A, which may be an exact A or, more commonly, a variation of A.
Theme and variation is a thematic statement that is modified through style, qualities, tempo, dynamics, or other ways. It is notated as A1, A2, A3, and so on.
Rondo is a main theme alternating with contrasting themes: ABACADA, and so on.
Canon, or **round,** is a single theme that plays within and against itself. It begins as a single theme, then is restated and layered at successive intervals. A round is what occurs in the song "Row, Row, Row Your Boat." The round ends with the original single theme. A canon's original theme is manipulated by being played faster or slower, reversed (starts at the end and goes to the beginning), or inverted (turned upside down) and augmented (performed two to three times slower than originally performed).
Fugue is like a canon but is more complicated and considered the most difficult of the music forms to translate into choreography. The original theme overlaps itself, usually building to climax. In choreography of the fugue, the movement, like the music, may be inverted (positioned upside down), reversed, augmented (slowed down), or diminished (movement performed two to three times faster than the original).

Other Choreographic Forms

Narrative, or **story-based,** dramatic action tells a story through movement alone or through pantomime and movement. Narrative choreography requires the dancer to perform a character's role. This dual role of acting and dancing must be seamless to convey emotions through facial expression and body movement during the dramatic action of the dance. In an open, or free, structure, the movement or dance idea being expressed creates the structure for the dance. Most choreography uses a **linear progression** starting at the beginning and progressing to the end. Other literary or dramatic devices include the use of **flashback** or **episodic** mechanisms.

References

Doll, E., and M.J. Nelson. 1965. *Rhythms today.* Parsippany, NJ: Silver Burdette.

Fraser, D.L. 1991. *Playdancing: Discovering and developing creativity in young children.* Pennington, NJ: Princeton.

Purcell, T. 1994. *Teaching children dance: Becoming a master teacher.* Champaign, IL: Human Kinetics.

Selected Resources

Selected resources include creative movement and creative dance texts, music, and videos.

Texts

Barlin, A.P. 1971. *The art of learning through movement.* Claremont, CA: Bowman/Noble.

Boorman, J. 1969. *Dance in the first three grades.* Don Mills, ON: Academic Press.

Boorman, J. 1971. *Creative dance in grades four to six.* Don Mills, ON: Longman.

Boorman, J. 1973. *Dance and language experiences with children.* Don Mills, ON: Longman.

D'Amboise, J. 1983. *Teaching the magic of dance.* New York: Simon and Schuster.

Diamondstein, G. 1971. *Children dance in the classroom.* New York: MacMillan.

Doll, E., and M.J. Nelson. 1965. *Rhythms today.* Parsippany, NJ: Silver Burdette.

Fleming, G. 1976. *Creative rhythmic movement: Boys and girls dancing.* Englewood Cliffs, NJ: Prentice Hall.

Fraser, D.L. 1991. *Playdancing: Discovering and developing creativity in young children.* Pennington, NJ: Princeton.

Gilbert, A.G. 1977. *Teaching the three Rs through movement experience.* Minneapolis: Burgess.

Gilbert, A.G. 1992. *Creative dance for all ages.* Reston, VA: National Dance Association, American Alliance for Health, Physical Education, Recreation and Dance.

Humphrey, J. 1987. *Child development and learning through dance.* New York: AMS.

Joyce, M. 1973. *First steps in teaching creative dance.* Palo Alto, CA: Mayfield.

Joyce, M. 1984. *Dance technique for children.* Palo Alto, CA: Mayfield.

Logsdon, B.J., L.M. Alleman, S.A. Straits, B.E. Belka, and D. Clark. 1994. *Physical education unit plans for grades 3-4: Learning experience in games, gymnastics and dance.* 2nd ed. Champaign, IL: Human Kinetics.

Logsdon, B.J., L.M. Alleman, S.A. Straits, B.E. Belka, and D. Clark. 1997. *Physical education unit plans for preschool children.* Champaign, IL: Human Kinetics.

Logsdon, B.J., L.M. Alleman, S.A. Straits, B.E. Belka, and D. Clark. 1997. *Physical education unit plans for grades 1-2.* Champaign, IL: Human Kinetics.

Logsdon, B.J., L.M. Alleman, S.A. Straits, B.E. Belka, and D. Clark. 1997. *Physical education units for grades 5-6.* Champaign, IL: Human Kinetics.

Lowden, M. 1989. *Dancing to learn as a strategy in the primary school curriculum.* London: Palmer Press.

McGreevy-Nichols, S., and H. Scheff. 1995. *Building dances: A guide to putting movements together.* Champaign, IL: Human Kinetics.

McGreevy-Nichols, S., H. Scheff, and M. Sprague. 2001. *Building more dances: Blueprints for putting movements together.* Champaign, IL: Human Kinetics.

Minton, S. 1997. *Choreography: A basic approach using improvisation.* 2nd ed. Champaign, IL: Human Kinetics.

Murray, R.L. 1975. *Dance in elementary education.* 4th ed. New York: Harper Row.

Pica, R. 1991. *Early elementary children: Movement and learning.* Champaign, IL: Human Kinetics.

Pomer, J. 2002. *Perpetual motion: Creative movement exercises for dance and dramatic arts.* Champaign, IL: Human Kinetics.

Purcell, T. 1994. *Teaching children dance: Becoming a master teacher.* Champaign, IL: Human Kinetics.

Rowen, B. 1994. *Dance and grow: Developmental dance activities for three- through eight-year olds.* Pennington, NJ: Princeton, Dance Horizons.

Russell, J. 1965. *Creative dance in primary school.* London: Macdonald and Evans.

Slater, W. 1987. *Teaching modern educational dance.* 2nd ed. London: Northcote House.

Stinson, S. 1988. *Dance for young children: Finding the magic in movement.* Reston, VA: AAHPERD, National Dance Association.

Weikart, P.S. 1987. *Round the circle: Key experiences in movement for children.* Ypsilanti, MI: High Scope.

Weikart, P.S. 1988. *Movement plus music: Activities for children ages 3 to 7.* Ypsilanti, MI: High Scope.

Weikart, P.S. 1988. *Movement plus rhymes, song and singing games.* Ypsilanti, MI: High Scope.

Weikart, P.S. 1990. *Movement in steady beat: Activities for children ages 3 to 7.* Ypsilanti, MI: High Scope.

Zukowski, G., and A. Dickson. 1990. *On the move.* Carbondale, IL: Southern Illinois University Press.

Music

Anderson, L. 1992. *Leroy Anderson greatest hits.* New York: BMG (RCA Victor) Music 09026-1237. CD.

Buck, D. 1993. *Everybody dance.* Long Branch, NJ: Kimbo Educational. CD.

Buck, D. 1991. *All-time favorite dance.* Long Branch, NJ: Kimbo Educational. CD.

Chappelle, E. 1993. *Music for creative dance: Contrast & continuum.* Vol. I. Seattle: Ravenna Ventures RVCD 9301. CD.

Chappelle, E. 1994. *Music for creative dance: Contrast & continuum.* Vol. II. Seattle: Ravenna Ventures RVCD 9401. CD.

Chappelle, E. 1998. *Music for creative dance: Contrast & continuum.* Vol. III. Seattle: Ravenna Ventures RVCD 9801. CD.

Chappelle, E. 2000. *Music for creative dance: Contrast & continuum.* Vol. IV. Seattle: Ravenna Ventures RVCD 9901. CD.

Children's film favorites. 3 vols. 1999. St. Laurent, PQ: Madacy Entertainment Group. CD.

Lane, C. 1997. *Christy Lane's complete party dance music.* Palm Springs: Let's Do It.

Music for children. 3 vols. (Children Nursery Rhymes, Peter and the Wolf, Carnival of Animals, and Classical Music for Children). 2000. Valley Cottage, NY: Eclipse Music Group (5 36-2). CD.

Pica, R. 1991. *Early elementary children: Moving & learning.* Champaign, IL: Human Kinetics.

Pica, R., and R. Gardzence. 1990. *More music for moving & learning.* Champaign, IL: Human Kinetics.

Stewart, G. 1989. *Rock 'n' roll fitness fun.* Long Branch, NJ: Kimbo Educational.

Videos

Dancing thread. 1994. New York: Insight Media.

Lewis, J. 1996. *Moving freely: A creative dance class for ages 3 to 10.* Hightstown, NJ: Princeton.

Lowe, M. 1993. *Creative movement. A step towards intelligence.* Hightstown, NJ: Princeton.

Rowen, B. 1994. *Dance and grow: Development activities for three- through eight-year-olds.* Hightstown, NJ: Princeton.

Folk Dance Unit

Teaching Overview

Psychomotor Objectives

- Perform basic folk dances (steps, partner positions, formations, and figures) to music.
- Demonstrate the relationship of movement and music (count, rhythm, tempo, time signature).
- Demonstrate application of movement principles to folk dance.

Psychomotor Evaluation

- Performance test of selected folk dances (execution of steps, partner positions, formations, figures in relation to music and with application of movement principles).

Cognitive Objectives

- Recognize beginning folk dance terminology.
- Translate a beginning folk dance into movement from oral or written instructions.
- Conduct a self-evaluation or a peer evaluation of a beginning folk dance performance.

Cognitive Evaluation

- Complete written test of beginning folk dance knowledge (dances, dance skills, definitions of terminology, history and culture, self-assessment of personal performance).
- Translate written and oral instructions for a folk dance into movement with the music.

Affective Objectives

- Practice dance etiquette in the folk dance class.
- Demonstrate personal movement confidence and performance attitude.
- Work with the group to refine the performance.

Affective Evaluation

- Demonstrate etiquette, movement confidence, performance attitude, cooperation, contribution, and leadership within the group and class.

Teaching Approaches

Introduce the folk dance by giving a short explanation about the dance and its purpose, qualities, and country of origin. This information enables students to relate to the culture and the quality of the folk dance. With this brief summary, students are likely to remember the dance.

In the dance, notice how the body and the body parts move and the relationships of partners. This may give insight into gender roles, customs, and mores of the culture. Folk dance often provides students awareness of their cultural heritage and identity, which in turn establish a sense of pride.

Another approach to teaching folk dance is to first teach it using its traditional music. Then practice and perform it to contemporary music from that country or perhaps current popular music. These interpretations sometimes bridge the gap in the relationship between traditional folk dance and contemporary society.

FORM 13.5

Scope and Sequence for Folk Dance

New = N   Review = R   Listening test = LT   Performance test = PT

	1	2	3	4	5	6	7	8	9	10	11	12	13	14	15
Definition and history of folk dance	N														
Attire and etiquette	N														
Troika (Russia)	N	R	R	R	R		R	R			LT		R	R	PT
Runs, patterns, arches in a circle	N														
Misirlou (Greece)		N	R	R	R		R	R			LT		R	R	PT
Grapevine, two-step pivot		N													
Mayim, Mayim (Israel)		N	R	R	R			R			LT		R	R	PT
Grapevine, runs, hop, touch		N													
Schottische			N												
Seven Steps (Germany)			N	R	R		R				LT		R	R	PT
Two–step				N											
Nebesko Kolo (former Yugoslavia)				N	R		R				LT	R	R	R	PT
Polka						N	R								
Doudlebska polka (former Czechoslovakia)						N				R	LT	R	R	R	PT
Jessie polka (United States)						N	R	R			LT	R	R	R	PT
Two–step or Schottische						N	R			R					
Waltz								N							
Mexican waltz (Mexico)								N		R	LT	R	R	R	PT
Mazurka									N						
Journeyman's Blacksmith (Germany)									N	R	LT	R	R	R	PT
Varsouvienne (Sweden)									N	N	LT	R	R	R	PT
Heel and toe, slide and claps															

FORM 13.6

Folk Dance Block Time Plan

Class 1	Class 2	Class 3	Class 4	Class 5

• Definition and history of folk dance
• Attire and etiquette
• Warm-up: walks, changing directions
• **Troika** (Russia) *run, dance done in a trio*
	• Warm-up
	• **Misirlou** (Greece) *grapevine, step, step, step, hop; pivot, step; touch*
	• **Mayim, Mayim** (Israel) *grapevine runs, hop touch, runs*
	• Review
	  • Troika
		• Warm-up
		• Schottische
		• **Seven Steps** (Germany) *step, step, step–hop, step–hop*
		• Review
		  • Troika
		  • Misirlou
		  • Mayim, Mayim
			• Warm-up
			• Two–step
			• **Nebesko Kolo** (former Yugoslavia) *two–step, pas de bas*
			• Review
			  • Seven Steps
			  • Mayim, Mayim
				• Review
				  • Troika
				  • Misirlou
				  • Seven Steps
				  • Nebesko Kolo

Class 6	**Class 7**	**Class 8**	**Class 9**	**Class 10**

• Warm-up
• Polka
• Doudlebska polka (former Czechoslovakia) (closed dance position): *walks (tra-la-la), claps*
• **Jessie polka** (United States) *two–step, heel, toe*
	• Warm-up
	• Review
	  • Troika
	  • Misirlou
	  • Doudlebska polka
	  • Jessie polka
		• Warm-up
		• Waltz
		• **Mexican waltz** (Mexico) *balance, swing, waltz*
			• Warm-up
			• Review
			  • Doudlebska polka
			  • Jessie polka
			  • Mexican waltz
			  • Mazurka
			• **Journeyman's Blacksmith** (Germany) *claps, step–hop, skips, waltz*
				• Warm-up
				• **Varsouvienne** (Sweden) *step, cross, point*

Class 11	**Class 12**	**Class 13**	**Class 14**	**Class 15**

• Listening test	• Review
	  • Varsouvienne
	  • Mexican waltz
	  • Journeyman's Blacksmith
	  • Doudlebska polka
	  • Nebesko Kolo
		• Review all dances	• Review all dances	• Performance test over selected dances

Note: Dances are **boldfaced** on the day they are introduced.

Specific Teaching Methods

Progressively teach the steps of the dance using the add-on method. After the students master the steps of the dance, they listen to the music and mark the dance while either sitting or standing by using different body parts, such as arms or legs. Then the group practices the dance to the music and performs it.

Folk dance music is very predictable with musical phrasing that relates to the steps and sections of the dance. If you introduce the music too soon when teaching a folk dance, sometimes people get caught up in the music and are unable to do the steps. In this situation, they become discouraged, lose confidence, and don't want to participate.

If you are new to teaching folk dance, select a dance that you can teach. Practice the dance to the music. Know the steps, partner holds, and figures of the dance so that you can clearly demonstrate them with or without the music. If you have trouble reading and interpreting a dance as it is written, then take a chance and use your own interpretation as long as it fits the music. There are no folk dance police! Try it, have fun, and make it fun for your students.

Musical Accompaniment

Musical accompaniment for folk dance includes

- records, audio tapes, or compact discs;
- live music; and
- singing a cappella or with the music.

Dance Class Format

The class format for folk dance is as follows:

1. Warm-up
2. Review of previously learned steps, figures, and dances
3. Introduction of new steps and figures
4. New dances that incorporate steps and figures from the students' repertoire

Classroom Considerations

The space for a folk dance class should be uncluttered and well ventilated. If dancers wear street clothes, the clothing should allow them to move freely. Students should demonstrate politeness, manners, and cooperation. Make the class fun, and the class will be successful.

Safety

The biggest safety issue for the folk dance class is the size of the room; it must be large enough to accommodate the number of dancers. The area should be well lit, and the floor should be clean. A good floor for folk dance is neither slippery nor sticky.

Attire

Males wear street clothes: shirts and trousers. They can wear flexible oxfords or tennis shoes. Females wear skirts and blouses, shirts and pants, or leotards and tights with a skirt. They can wear flat-soled shoes, tennis shoes, ballet shoes, or character shoes. Shoes should either lace up or have a strap.

Classroom Etiquette

Ensure that everyone in the class has a partner or is a member of a group. S are quiet, courteous, and aware of themselves and others when moving through the space. Talking should be kept to a minimum. Hands should be clean.

Beyond Technique Assignments

The following are some suggestions for beyond technique assignments in folk dance:

- Perform a folk dance you know to a contemporary song.
- Create your own folk dance reflective of a certain culture or a concept (such as a rain dance).
- After performing a folk dance, create a dance on the same topic or contrast it with the original dance.
- Attend a folk dance festival and view the different dances. If possible, compare them to some of the dances you know.
- Research the history, culture, costumes, and customs of a dance you perform.

Content Overview

The content overview provides the necessary information for teaching the folk dance unit.

Definition and History

Folk dance is a recreational dance form that has its roots in the rituals, customs, culture, and mores of a particular country. Geography, climate, and other factors affect the makeup of the dances. Folk dance music is indigenous to the country or culture. The music and instruments reinforce the character and essence of the dance. Costumes mirror the lifestyles and occupations and reinforce cultural and national pride, which in turn enhance the spirit of dance. This dance form is appropriate for students in elementary school through high school.

Folk dance became popular in the 20th century. People were concerned about preserving the folkways, customs, tunes, songs, and dances that were threatened by the effect of the industrial revolution on society. These people formed dance societies, which helped preserve the folk dances, such as Cecil Sharp who formed the English Folk Dance Society in 1911.

During the 1920s physical educators understood the value of folk dance as a physical activity. Elizabeth Burchenal (1942) and C. Ward researched and compiled European folk dances that were then taught in secondary schools, colleges, and recreational programs. Burchenal was the first president of American Folk Dance Society. Mary Wood Hinnman was a physical educator who knew the value of the culture and the heritage of Americans. Her efforts brought about the establishment of folk festivals.

People formed international folk dance groups that encompassed square, contra, and round dances. Teachers and leaders held classes and formed clubs that were used as physical outlets and a celebration of culture. Jane Farwell also formed folk dance camps in the 1940s and 1950s. Often these camps brought together professional teachers that taught dances of specific ethnic groups.

Because of technology, sharing culture enables us to understand people in different countries. Sharing traditions specific to a culture gives us the opportunity to celebrate our diversity and acknowledge our similarities. Dance and movement are our universal language.

Special Features

The following are specific features of folk dances:

- Dances use simple steps, formations, and partner positions.
- Music indigenous to the culture accompanies the dance.
- Folk dances parallel the qualities and styles of the music.
- Some dances incorporate typical dance steps of a particular region or country.
- Dances reflect the traditions, occupations, and mores of a specific culture.

Principles

Movement, choreographic, and aesthetic principles that specifically apply to folk dance are shown in the shaded regions of the following icons (below and on page 231).

Folk Dances

The following are appropriate folk dances for beginning students:Troika; Misirlou; Mayim, Mayim; Seven Steps; Nebesko Kolo; Doudlebska polka; Jessie polka; Mexican waltz; Journeyman's Blacksmith; and Varsouvienne.

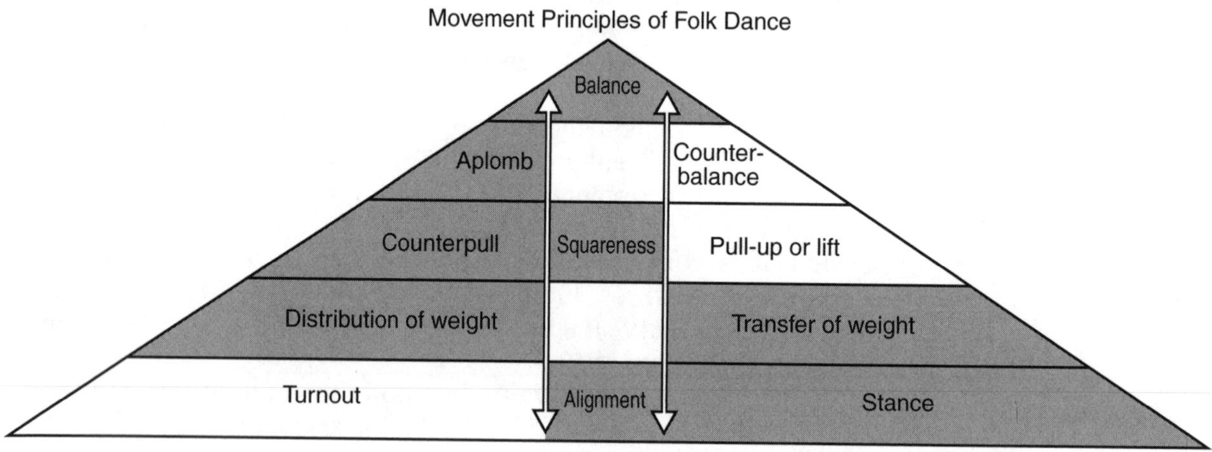

Choreographic Principles of Folk Dance

Choreographic elements	Choreographic structures	Choreographic designs	Choreographic devices	Choreographic relationships
Motif Phrase Theme and variation	Simple musical forms • AB (binary) • ABA (ternary) • Rondo • Theme and variation Contrapuntal forms • Canon (round) • Fugue Others • Narrative (story) • Open (free)	Dancer's body shape Dancer's pathway through space Visual design • Symmetrical • Asymmetrical Symbolism • Representational • Abstraction • Distortion Relationship • Unison • Sequential • Successional • Oppositional • Complementary	Repetition Reverse Alter • Addition or subtraction • Directional change • Facing or focus • Level • Dimension • Tempo • Rhythm • Quality or effort action • Positioning • Movement section	Solo Duet Trio Quartet Small and large groups

Traditional Dance Elements

Space	Time	Force	Relationships
Directions Dimensions Levels Shapes Pathways Focus	Duration Tempo	Movement qualities • Sustained • Percussive • Swinging • Suspended • Collapsing • Vibratory	Among body parts Among people Between people and props

Laban's Dance Elements

Space	Time	Weight	Flow
Direct or indirect	Sudden or slow	Light or strong	Bound or free

Effort actions (use space, time, and weight)

• Dab • Flick • Punch • Slash • Glide • Float • Press • Wring

Aesthetic Principles of Folk Dance

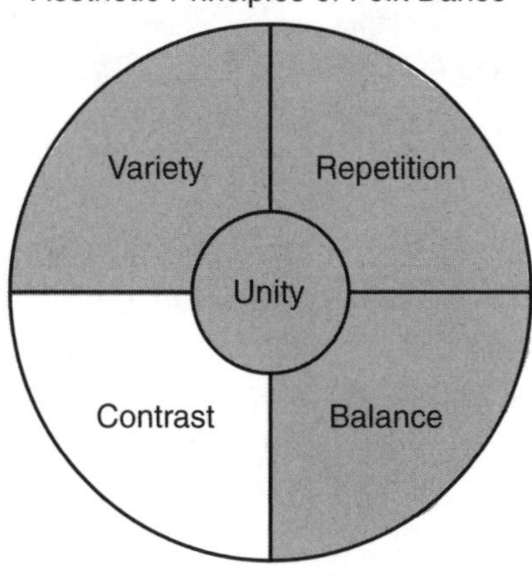

Troika (Three Horses)

This dance uses groups of three people. Generally, the middle person of the group is a man and the outside people are women. Standing in a line, the person in the middle holds hands with the person on either side. The people on the outside place their outside hand on the hip.

1. Run forward 4 times to right diagonal. Run forward 4 times to left diagonal. Run forward 8 times, bringing inside arms up to form two arcs. (Total of 16 counts in this part.)
2. The person on the right goes under the left arm of the person in the center while doing 8 running steps. The person in the middle will also turn under. Both come back to beginning position. Repeat the same action with the person on the left but go under the right arm of the person in the center and return to your place. (Total of 16 counts.)
3. Form a circle. Run to the right with 12 running steps and a stamp, stamp, stamp, hold. Reverse direction of the circle. Repeat the action to the left on the stamp, stamp, stamp, hold; come back to the beginning formation. (Total of 32 counts.)

Misirlou

Dancers form a single line, upper arms parallel to the floor, holding little fingers. In this formation, the dancers will move in a serpentine or snake-like pathway through the space.

Line formation with dancers connected by little fingers.

1. Step to the side with right foot, hold; point left foot front, hold; bring left foot behind right foot, step left; step side right, step left in front, hop on left, and pivot one-quarter turn left.
2. Step forward right, step forward left, step forward right, and hop on right; step back left, step back right, step back left, and hop on left.
3. Repeat entire dance.

Mayim, Mayim

Dancers form a circle and everyone holds hands.

Circle formation.

1. Start with the grapevine step: step side left, cross right foot over left; step left, step right behind left. Repeat the grapevine step 3 more times, continuing to the left for 16 counts.
2. Walk forward right, left, right, left. Arms come up slowly, then dancers say "Mayim, Mayim" and clap once. Walk backward right, left, right, left. Repeat entire walking sequence. (Do for 16 counts.)
3. Turn left and walk right, left, right, left.
4. Facing center, hop on right and extend left leg to dancer's front; hop on right and extend left to side. Repeat this action two more times. On last step, hop on the right leg and extend left leg front. Hop again on the right leg in place, ending with feet together. (16 counts total.)

Seven Steps

Dancers form a double circle. Men, or leaders, form the inner circle; women, or followers, are in the outside circle.

1. Start on the outside foot and run 7 counts forward and hold on count 8. Run 7 counts backward and hold on count 8. (Total of 16 counts.)
2. Perform the schottische: step together, step–hop moving to the side away from your partner; step together, step–hop moving back toward your partner; facing each other, clasp partner's hands and cross right hand over left; execute step–hop, step–hop, step–hop, step–hop, changing place by moving half a turn clockwise. (Total 16 counts.)
3. Each leader stands with back to the inside of the circle; each follower stands facing leaders. Schottische step together, step–hop, step together, step–hop. (Total of 8 counts.)

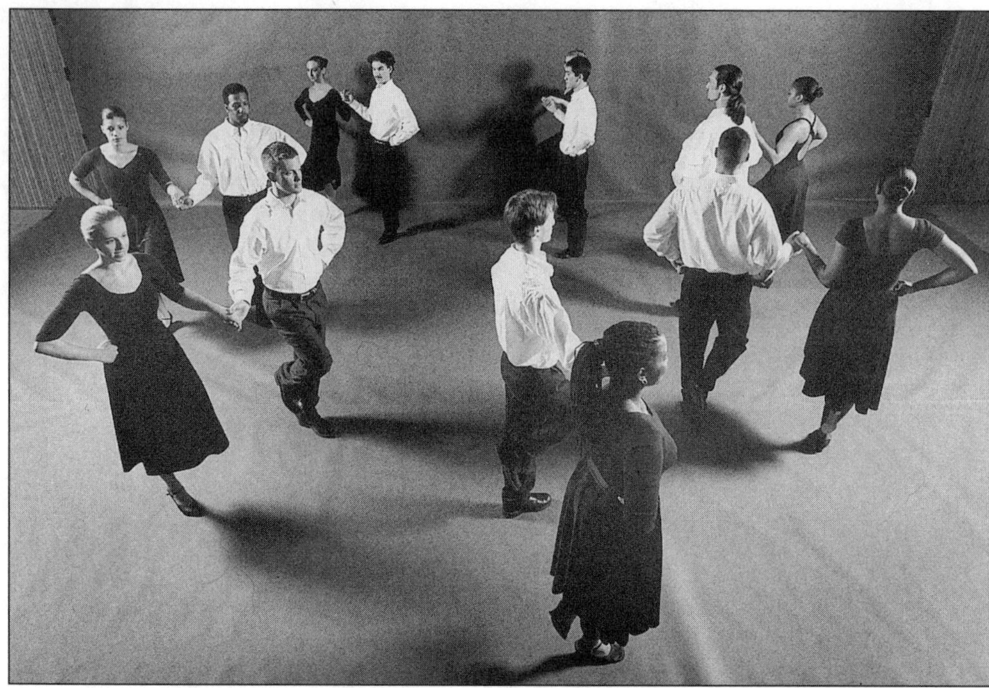

The double circle.

4. Leaders go forward, the inside circle moving counterclockwise while doing 4 step–hops for 8 counts, advancing to take a new partner when the dance begins again.
5. Followers go around in their own circle clockwise and begin the entire dance again for 8 counts.

Nebesko Kolo

Dancers form a circle.

1. Moving clockwise, step with right foot forward, step together (close) with left foot. Step right foot forward, hold (weight on right foot, left foot up), step left forward, close right. Step left, hold, and pivot to left. Repeat the same action and the same footwork to the left. Pivot on hold and face center. (Total of 16 counts.)
2. Bring right foot forward and step in place with left. Step right foot back and step left in place. Step right foot forward, step in place with left, and step right back and step left in place. This is like a rocking step. (Total of 8 counts.)
3. Leap onto the right, cross over with the ball of the left foot, and step in place with the right. Leap onto the left foot, cross over with the ball of the right foot, and step in place. Reverse to the right and left again. (Total of 16 counts.)
4. Stamp with right foot without putting your weight on it.

Doudlebska Polka

Couples form a circle in closed dance position. The men's, or leaders', backs are to the center of the circle.

Each leader connects to the inside shoulder of the leader in front of him.

1. Couples move away from the circle doing 8 polka steps (hop, step, step, step). Then they move back into one circle doing 8 polka steps. Leaders begin left foot and followers begin right foot.
2. Leaders and followers turn counterclockwise into the line of direction. The leader places his left hand on the left shoulder of the leader in front of him and holds the left hand of the follower. They take 32 steps walking in the circle, and sing "tra la-la."
3. Leaders drop hands and stand with their backs to the inside of the circle. Each leader claps his hands twice and claps once with both leader neighbors while followers do 16 polka steps around the circle. This should give each person a different partner. At the end of the 16 polka steps, the follower moves to a new partner, usually the next leader up from her original partner.
4. Repeat from the beginning.

Jessie Polka

Dancers start in varsouvienne position. The leader stands slightly behind the follower. The follower stands on the right side of the leader.

1. Begin by bringing left heel to the front; step on left foot with feet together. Touch right toe behind you and put right foot in place next to the left foot, or together. Right heel is placed forward and then together with the left foot. Place the left heel forward and then cross left toe in front of right foot (16 counts).
2. Step forward on left foot and bring the right foot together with the left. Step forward with left foot and hold. Step on the right foot, bring the left foot together with the right, and step on the right and hold. Repeat twice more. (16 counts total.)

Mexican Waltz

In a double circle, leaders are on the inside and followers are on the outside. Everyone faces counterclockwise with their inside hands joined.

1. Step on the outside foot and swing the inside leg slightly across the outside leg. Step on the inside foot and swing the outside leg slightly across the inside leg. Step and clap the hands twice. From the beginning, face the opposite direction and repeat three more times (start with inside foot, outside foot, and then inside foot).
2. Then the partners turn and face each other with both hands joined in front of them. Both step backward with the arms extended in front, pulling away from each other. Then they step forward and toward each other with the arms extended sideward, still keeping their hands joined. Then step back and clap hands twice. Step forward, coming toward partner with arms extended sideward, keeping hands joined. Then step backward with the arms extended in front and hands joined, pulling away from partner. Step front and clap hands twice. Repeat from the beginning two more times. On the last section (a total of four times: step forward, forward, backward, forward), reach behind your partner, clap hands twice.
3. Perform 16 waltzes in closed dance position, turning clockwise with partner. By the end of the 16 waltzes, partners stand side to side with the inside hands joined. Repeat from the beginning. See the "Steps" section of the vocabulary in this unit for a description of the waltz, page 242.

Journeyman's Blacksmith

Formation is two couples forming a square. Slap thigh, slap waist, clap right hand of partner, clap left hand of partner, clap both crossed. (Do 8 sets.)

1. Walk 8 steps clockwise in a circle. Walk 8 steps counterclockwise in a circle. During the chorus, the couples clap with the opposite partners.
2. Do 4 step–hops in a clockwise circle for 8 counts. Do 4 step–hops in a counterclockwise circle for 8 counts. Do chorus.
3. Skip for 8 counts in a clockwise circle. Skip for 8 counts in a counterclockwise circle. Do chorus.
4. Couples do 16 waltzes in closed dance position. Turn either clockwise or counterclockwise during the waltz.

Varsouvienne

Couples begin in varsouvienne position, the leader on the left and the follower on the right. During the first four combinations, they change place each time.

1. The leader steps with his left foot and crosses behind his right foot, and he steps to the side with his right foot. He then crosses his left foot over his right foot and places his right heel on the floor with the toes up and on a slight diagonal forward (back, side, cross, heel, step). Simultaneously, the follower steps with her left foot to the side, crosses over her left foot with her right foot, steps to the side with her left foot, and places her right heel on the floor with

the toe up on a slight diagonal forward (side, cross front, side, heel). Reverse and repeat two more times.

2. Step forward on left foot, step right foot to left foot, hop on the right, and cross the left with bent knee placed by the right ankle. Repeat the step again on the same side. (This is the mazurka step; see a detailed description of this in the "Steps" section of the vocabulary in this unit, p. 242.)Then cross the left foot over the right foot, step to the side with the right foot, cross left over right, step and place the right on a slight diagonal forward (cross step, cross heel) and reverse and repeat, starting with the right foot.
3. The couple turns, facing each other in closed dance position, and performs 8 waltzes. By the end of the 8th waltz, they are in varsouvienne position. Repeat the entire dance from the beginning.

Vocabulary

Folk dance shares vocabulary with other dance forms.

Partner Positions

In the **closed dance position,** the couple faces each other with their shoulders and hips square (see figure 13.2a). The leader places his right arm around the follower's back to give security and support.The leader's right hand is placed in the center of the follower's back below the shoulder blades.The follower's left hand rests gently on the leader's upper arm.When the leader's right hand adds pressure to the follower's back, she arches her back and moves where he directs. The follower's left hand is to the side slightly above shoulder level; the leader holds the follower's right hand in his left hand.

The **semi-open position** is similar to the closed dance position. Partners are slightly open forward, or to the direction of movement (see figure 13.2b).

Open position has the follower and leader standing side by side (see figure 13.2c).

Side position has the dancers facing in opposite directions; one faces forward, the other backward. Variations include **banjo,** in which the partners stand with right sides together (see figure 13.2d), and **sidecar,** in which partners stand with left sides together (see figure 13.2e).

Promenade has the dancers facing front and joining right hand to right hand and left hand to left hand (see figure 13.2f).

In the **shoulder–waist position,** the leader faces the follower and holds her waist. She places her hands on his shoulders (see figure 13.2g).

Inside hands joined position has the leader and follower facing the same direction and grasping inside hands (see figure 13.2h).

In **varsouvienne position,** the leader is slightly behind and to the left side of the follower. Both dancers' left arms are shoulder level; they hold their right hands slightly higher than shoulder level.The leader clasps the follower's right hand in his right; her left hand in his left (see figure 13.2i).

A **partner hold** is a general term for how a couple holds each other during a dance. Several variations exist: The couple can hold one hand or hold both hands, shoulders, or waist. Or the hand can be behind the back of the body.When partners do not use partner holds, the arms hang loosely at the sides of the body or are bent with the hands placed on the hips.

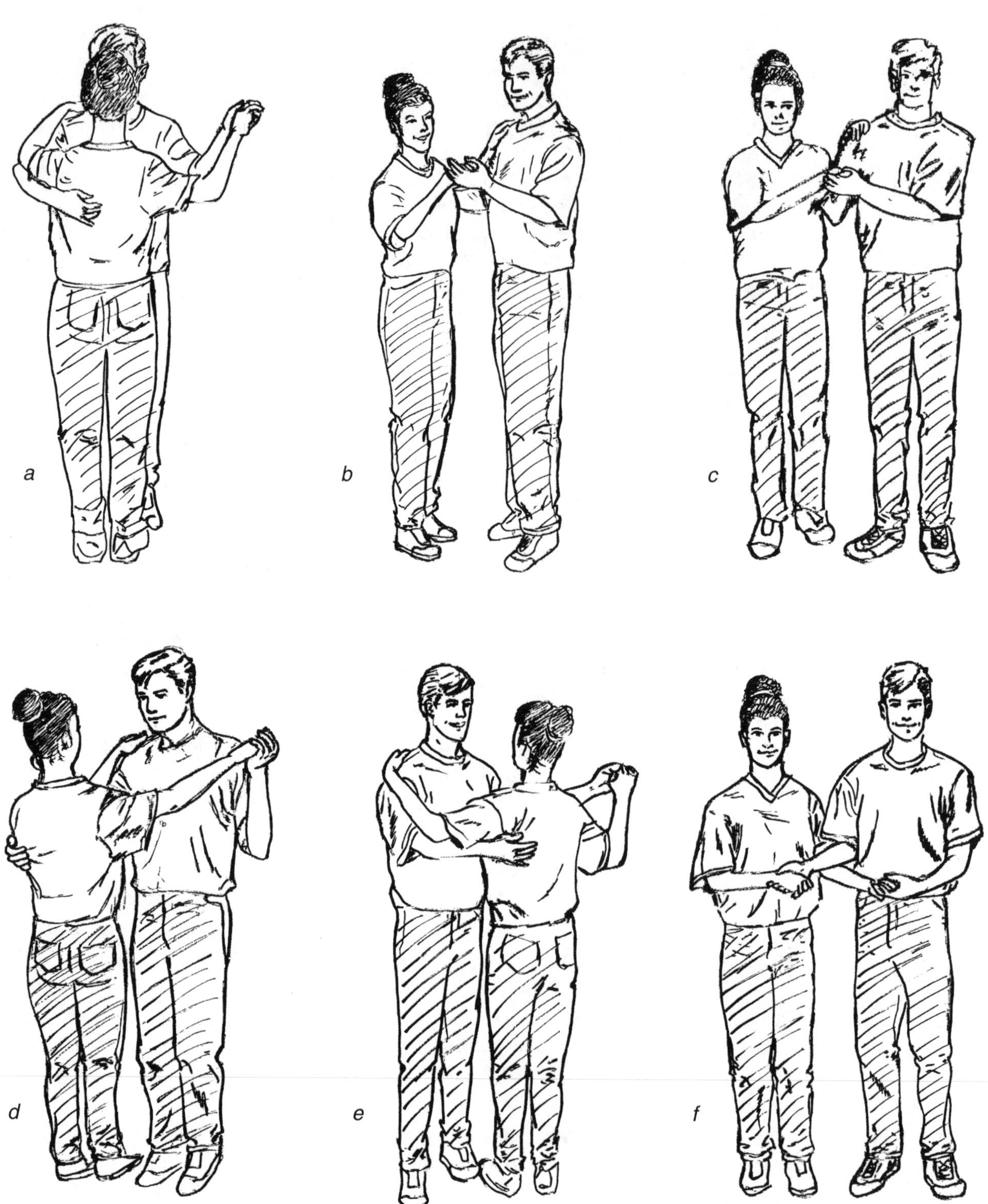

Figure 13.2 Partner positions for folk dances: *(a)* closed dance position, *(b)* semi-open position, *(c)* open position, *(d)* banjo position, *(e)* sidecar position, *(f)* promenade position, *(g)* shoulder–waist position, *(h)* inside hands joined position, and *(i)* varsouvienne position.

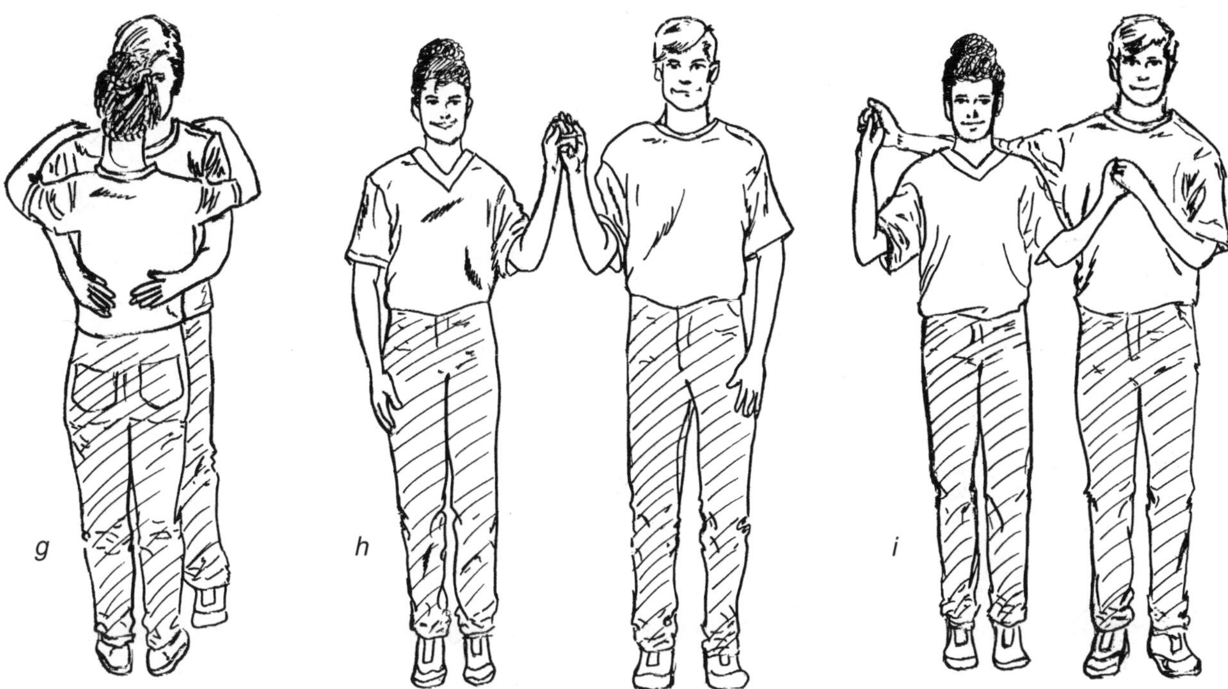

Figure 13.2 *(continued)*

Folk Dance Formations

Single circle has several variations. One is a group of dancers facing the center of the circle (see figure 13.3a).

Another is when partners face each other in a circle (see figure 13.3b).

Double circle involves couples facing counterclockwise (follower on the right side of leader) (see figure13.3c).

Another variation is partners facing each other: Leaders stand with back to center of the circle; followers face the leaders (see figure 13.3d).

A third variation is two sets of partners facing each other in a double circle (see figure 13.3e).

Set of three involves three dancers standing side by side in a line (see figure 13.3f) or three couples facing each other in a line (see figure 13.3g).

Longways, or **contra, formation** is a dance performed in two parallel lines with the dancers facing each other. It is said to be a dance of opposition. Longways dance is also known as a *country dance.* This type of dance consists of sequences of steps or figures that repeat many times. Some folk dances use these formations.

Square formation refers to a dance performed in the formation of a square with four couples. One couple stands on each side of the square.

Steps

The folk dancer uses simple, repetitive steps performed in various formations with or without partners. The steps are derived from the various locomotor movements (walk, run, leap, jump, hop, skip, slide, gallop).

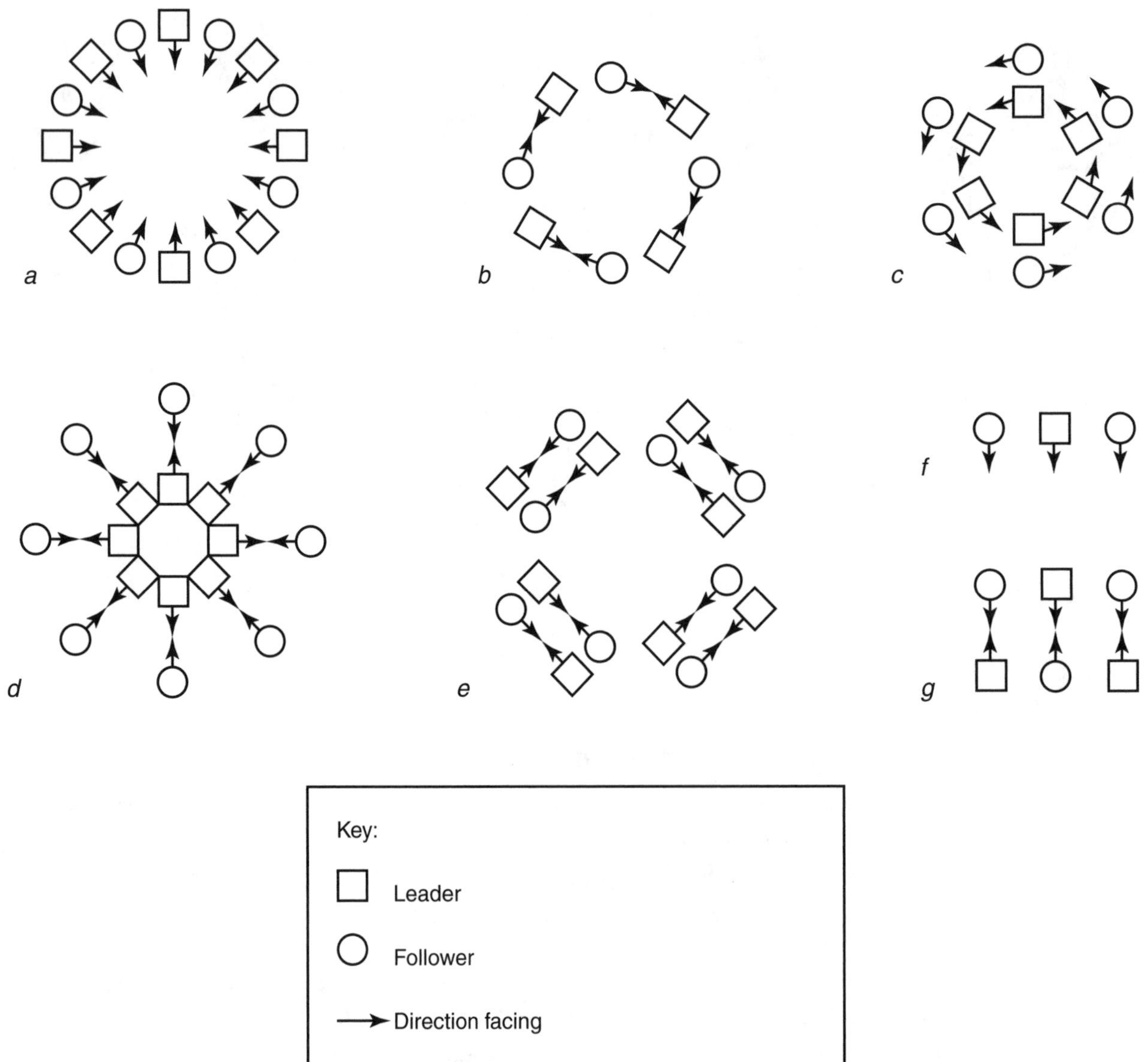

Figure 13.3 Folk dance formations. *(a)* Single circle, dancers facing center of circle; *(b)* single circle, couples facing each other; *(c)* double circle, couples facing counterclockwise; *(d)* double circle, couples facing, leader's back to center; *(e)* partners face each other in a double circle; *(f)* three dancers stand side by side; *(g)* three couples facing each other in a line.

Two–step alternates feet and is performed forward, backward, and to the side. In 4/4 meter

Count	Footwork	Cue
1	Step (left foot)	Step
2	Together (right foot)	Close
3	Step (left foot)	Step
4	Hold	Hold

When the dancer holds the weight on one foot, the other foot slightly touches the floor. This enables the dancer to step forward so that the step alternates. In 2/4 meter

Count	Footwork	Cue
1	Step (left foot)	Step
2	Together (right foot)	Close
1	Step (left foot)	Step
2	Hold (weight remains on left foot)	Hold

Schottische is three steps and a hop. The step alternates from side to side and travels front, side, or back. The meter of this dance is either 4/4 or 2/4. In 4/4 meter

Count	Footwork	Cue
1	Step (left foot)	Step
2	Close (right foot to left)	Close
3	Step (left foot)	Step
4	Hop (left foot)	Hop

In 2/4 meter

Count	Footwork	Cue
1	Step (left foot)	Step
2	Close (right foot to left)	Close
1	Step (left foot)	Step
2	Hop (left foot)	Hop

Step–hop has two movements: step and hop. This step alternates feet and may be combined with the schottische step. The meter of the step hop is either 4/4 or 2/4. In 2/4 meter

Count	Footwork	Cue
1	Step (left foot)	Step
2	Hop (left foot)	Hop

In 4/4 meter

Count	Footwork	Cue
1	Step (left foot)	Step
2	Hop (left foot)	Hop
3	Step (right foot)	Step
4	Hop (right foot)	Hop

Polka step consists of four movements that alternate feet; this is similar to a two–step. In 2/4 meter

Count	Footwork	Cue
&	Hop (left foot)	Hop
1	Step (right foot)	Step
&	Step (left foot)	Step
2	Step (right foot)	Step

Grapevine consists of four movements that cross in front and back. In 4/4 meter

Count	Footwork	Cue
1	Cross the right foot over left foot and step on the right foot	Cross front
2	Side step with the left foot	Side
3	Cross the right foot behind the left foot and step on the right foot	Cross back
4	Side step with the left foot	Side

Waltz has three steps that alternate feet and travel forward, backward, side to side, in a circle, and in a box (see the social dance unit for variations, p. 285). In 3/4 meter

Count	Footwork	Cue
1	Step full foot (left foot)	Step
2	Step on the ball of the foot (right foot)	Lift
3	Close on the ball of the foot (left foot)	Lift

The **mazurka** consists of three movements, but it does not alternate feet. In 3/4 meter

Count	Footwork	Cue
1	Step forward (left foot)	Step
2	Close (right foot to left)	Close
3	Hop (right foot), lift the left foot in front or back of right foot	Hop–cut

Chug step contains two actions: a falling step and a scoot. In various meters

Count	Footwork	Cue
1	Step (right foot)	Step
&	Chug forward (right foot) and scoot forward (right foot)	Scoot (chug)

A **buzz step** is performed in a circle around yourself. On the count, the left foot takes the full weight with the knee slightly bent, while the ball of the right foot pushes off the floor on the "and" count. In various meters

Count	Footwork	Cue
1	Step (left foot)	Step (or step, and)
&	Push (with ball of the right foot)	Ball

The buzz step is usually performed during turns.

Bleking step consists of a hop while the opposite leg extends forward with the heel touching the floor. This is all performed in one count. This step alternates feet. Word cues are hop, heel.

Step–draw is a slow, sliding step with a second step closing. This step is usually performed to the side. In various meters

Count	Footwork	Cue
1	Step (left foot)	Slide
&	Draw right foot to left, with the right taking the weight	Together

Stomp is a step that strikes the floor heavily and takes the weight.

Stamp is step that strikes the floor heavily but does not take the weight.

Step swing consists of two movements: step on one foot while other foot swings in any direction. A hop may be added to the step so that it becomes step, swing–hop.

Pas de bas is composed of three steps: a leap, step front, step back. This step alternates and generally is performed side to side in place. In various meters

Count	Footwork	Cue
1	Leap to left foot	Leap
&	Cross (right foot) over left, taking the weight on the ball of the right foot	Cross
2	Step on left foot behind the right	Step

Balance step has two different meanings: (1) In balance and swing, the couple steps away from each other and bows or curtsies, then each person steps forward and swings the leg; or (2) step on the right foot and hop; at the same time, the left foot swings front and across the right foot. Then repeat to the opposite side.

Reference

Burchenal, E. 1942. *Dances of the people. A second volume of folk dance and singing games.* New York: Schirmer.

Selected Resources

Selected resources include folk dance texts, music, and videos.

Texts

Burchenal, E. 1942. *Dances of the people. A second volume of folk dance and singing games.* New York: Schirmer.

Harris, J.A., A.M. Pittman, and M.S. Waller. 1999. *Dance a while: Handbook of folk, square, contra, and social dance.* 7th ed. Minneapolis: Burgess.

Highwater, J. 1992. *Dance rituals of experiences.* 3rd ed. New York: MacMillan.

Lane, C., and S. Langhout. 1998. *Multicultural folk dance treasure chest.* Champaign, IL: Human Kinetics.

Morton, V. 1966. *The teaching of popular dance.* New York: J. Lowell Pratt.

Weikart, P.S. 1982. *Teaching movement and dance.* 2nd ed. Ypsilanti, MI: High Scope.

Weikart, P.S. 1982. *Teaching movement and dance: Intermediate folk dance.* Ypsilanti, MI: High Scope.

Music

Buzz, H. 1998. *Circle and line dance vol. II (grades 4-9).* Freeport, NY: Activity Records CD 33.

Ellipsis Arts Sampler. Roslyn, NY: Ellipsis Arts. Web site: www.ellipsisarts.com.

Lane, C., and S. Langhout. 1998. *Multicultural folk dance treasure chest.* Champaign, IL: Human Kinetics.

Stewart, G. 1984. *Folk dance fun.* Long Branch, NJ: Kimbo Educational KIM 7037.

Stewart, G. 1991. *Children of the world: Multicultural rhythmic activities.* Long Branch, NJ: Kimbo Educational KIM 9123 CD.

Weikart, P.S. 1985. *Rhythmically moving.* Vol. 1-9. Ypsilanti, MI: High Scope.

Weikart, P.S. 1987. *Changing directions: Music for intermediate folk dance.* Vol. 1-6. Ypsilanti, MI: High Scope.

Videos

Ballet Folklorico of Mexico. 1990. New York: Insight Media.

Dances of Bali. 1973. New York: Insight Media.

Dunham, K. 1960. *The dance.* New York: Insight Media.

Flamenco dance. 1964. New York: Insight Media.

Into the circle: An introduction to Native American powwows. 1992. New York: Insight Media.

Jonas, G. 1995. *Dancing: Volumes I through VIII.* New York: Insight Media.

Karlin, E. 1976. *Country corners.* New York: Insight Media.

Kumu hula keepers of a culture. 1998. New York: Insight Media.

Lane, C. 1997. *Multicultural dance.* Champaign, IL: Human Kinetics.

On the move: The Central Ballet of China. 1987. New York: Insight Media.

Talking feet. 1988. New York: Insight Media.

Torres, E., and A. Bailar. *The journey: A Latin dance company.* New York: Insight Media.

Video anthology of music & dance of Africa. 1996. New York: Insight Media.

Weikart, P.S. 2000. *Rhythmically moving volumes 1 through 9.* Ypsilanti, MI: High Scope.

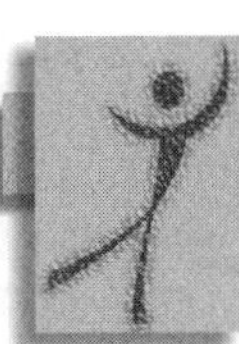

Square Dance Unit

Teaching Overview

Psychomotor Objectives

- Execute basic square dances (steps, partner positions, calls, formations, and figures) to music.
- Demonstrate the relationship of movement to music (count, rhythm, tempo, time signature).
- Demonstrate application of movement principles to square dance.
- Perform basic square dance steps with appropriate quality in the style of the dance.

Psychomotor Evaluation

- Performance test of selected square dances: execution of steps, partner positions, formations, figures in relation to calls and music (count, rhythm, tempo, time signature) with application of movement principles.

Cognitive Objectives

- Recognize beginning square dance terminology.
- Learn basic calls and respond to them.
- Translate a beginning square dance into movement from oral or written instructions.
- Conduct a self-evaluation or a peer evaluation of a beginning square dance performance.

Cognitive Evaluation

- Complete written test of beginning square dance knowledge (dances and dance skills, terminology, definitions, history, self-assessment of performance).
- Translate oral or written instructions for a square dance into movement with the music.

Affective Objectives

- Practice etiquette for the square dance class.
- Demonstrate movement confidence and performance attitude.
- Work with the group to refine the performance.

Affective Evaluation

- Demonstrate etiquette, movement confidence, performance attitude, cooperation, contribution, and leadership within the group and class.

Teaching Approaches

When teaching and participating in a recreational dance form such as square dance, make the class fun and success oriented. To reach these goals, be flexible, organized, and enthusiastic; also use your sense of humor. If dancing is not fun, the students will not want to do it!

At first make the figures easy to follow, and then gradually make them more intricate. Give the students adequate time to learn and perform each section of the dance. In an adult class, students expect to contribute to their learning by suggesting what square dances they want to perform.

FORM 13.7

Scope and Sequence for Square Dance

New = N Review = R Performance test = PT Create dance = CD Call dance = CLD Quiz = Q

	1	2	3	4	5	6	7	8	9	10	11	12	13	14	15
Definition and history of square dance	N														
Attire and etiquette	N														
Formation, position and figures, calls	N									Q					
Sicilian circle (progressive circle)	N			R		R		R		R	R	R			
Right- and left-hand star, basket	N														
Back to back, like do-si-do	N														
Portland Fancy (walk, ladies chain right and left through)	N		R	R		R		R		R	R	R			
Two lines, couples face each other	N														
Circle, right and left through, courtesy turn	N														
New partner	N														
Cumberland Square (slide, skip, step draw)		N	R	R	R	R	R			R	R	R			
Closed dance position, men back to back, ladies back to back		N													
Right- and left-hand star		N													
Circle promenade		N													
Puttjenter (walk, skip, stamp)			N	R	R	R	R			R	R	R			
Ladies weave in circle		N													
Gentlemen weave		N													
Right- and left-hand star		N													
Man in the Hay (walks, skip, slide)[1]					N	R		R	R	R	R				
Closed dance position slides					N										
Circle head and side basket					N										
Golden Slipper (changing partners dance)[2]															
Split the Ring							N		R	R	R				
Elbow swing in a circle							N								

New = N Review = R Performance test = PT Create dance = CD Call dance = CLD Quiz = Q

	1	2	3	4	5	6	7	8	9	10	11	12	13	14	15
Promenade allemande left							N								
Grand right and left							N								
Bad Bad Leroy Brown[3]								N	R	R	R				
Four ladies chain								N							
Allemande left, weave the ring do-si-do								N							
If they could see me now[3]									N	R	R				
Swing									N			PT			
Allemande left, grand right and left									N						
Do-si-do, promenade									N						
Forearm turn, courtesy turn									N						
Make and call your own dance with four in a group													CD	R	CLD
Devise rubric													R		

[1]More information can be found in Kraus (1962).
[2]More information can be found in Green (1984).
[3]More information can be found in Harris, Pittman, and Waller (1999).

FORM 13.8

Square Dance Block Time Plan

Class 1	Class 2	Class 3	Class 4	Class 5
• Define square dance • Relate brief history of square dance • Talk about attire and etiquette • Acquaint with formation, positions, figures, calls • **Sicilian Circle**[1,2] (progressive circles) *Couples facing each other, right- and left-hand star, back to back with opposite person and then partner, basket, forward and back, promenade* • **Portland Fancy**[3] (progressive circle) *walk, ladies chain, right left through, courtesy turn, lines two face each other*	• Warm-up • Walk through formations of prior dances • **Cumberland Square Eight**[2,3] (closed dance position) *slide back to back, right- and left-hand star; skip in a circle, step draw, promenade* • Review • Sicilian Circle • Portland Fancy	• Warm-up • Walk through formation of prior dances • **Puttjenter**[3] *walk, skip, stamp circle, weave, right- and left-hand star*	• Review • Sicilian Circle • Portland Fancy • Cumberland Square Eight • Puttjenter	• Warm-up • Walk through prior formation • **Man in the Hay**[3] *walk, skip, slide closed dance positions, slides; circle head and side basket* • Review • Cumberland Square Eight • Puttjenter

Class 6	Class 7	Class 8	Class 9	Class 10
• Review • Sicilian Circle • Portland Fancy • Cumberland Square Eight • Puttjenter • Man in the Hay	• **Golden Slipper**[4] *Changing partner dance elbow swing, promenade, allemande left, grand right and left*	• **Bad, Bad Leroy Brown**[5] *Four ladies chain, allemande left, weave the ring, do-si-do* • Review • Man in the Hay • Golden Slipper • Sicilian Circle • Portland Fancy	• **If You Could See Me Now**[5] *Swing, allemande left, grand right and left, do-si-do, promenade, forearm turn, courtesy turn*	• Quiz *formations, positions, and calls* • Review all dances

From *Dance Teaching Methods and Curriculum Design* by Gayle Kassing and Danielle M. Jay, 2003, Champaign, IL: Human Kinetics.

Class 11	Class 12	Class 13	Class 14	Class 15
• Review all dances	• Performance test over all dances	• Create your own square dance with eight other people; each person will call a part of the square dance • Create rubric for your square dance • Review parts of square dance: opener, main figure, break, ending	• Review and practice your square dance	• Call dance with group performing and calling at the same time • Teacher evaluates

Note: Dances are **boldfaced** on the day they are introduced.

[1]More information can be found in Gunzenhausar (1996).

[2]More information can be found in Riley (1988).

[3]More information can be found in Kraus (1962).

[4]More information can be found in Greene (1984).

[5]More information can be found in Harrison, Pittman, and Waller (1999).

Specific Teaching Methods

You can use choreographed square dances as an easy way to begin teaching. These prerecorded dances include calls. These recorded calls may be too fast for the dancers at the beginning of the class. If you do the calling, it is easier to control the group's progress and success. The goal of the class is for the dancers to perform and call the dances.

In teaching square dance, take the dancers through each step and figure slowly without the music. Practice short figures with the calls and then with the music. Most calls take eight counts, so create a series of calls that link these figures into short dances. Expand the short dances into square dances.

A square dance has four parts as a standard order. The four-part standard order of a square dance consists of the opener, the main figure, the break with the main figure and repeat of the break, then the ending. The standard order often extends to include a repeat of the main figure and the break before ending. In the main figure sections, partners change places. On the breaks, the caller either compresses or elongates the calls. The breaks are selected so that they differ but blend to give fluid transitions with the main figures. Breaks give the dancers time to return to their beginning, or home, positions (Harris, Pittman, and Waller 1999).

The following is an example of a square dance in its standard order with calls:

1. Opener: "Honor your partner, then your corner. All join hands and circle to the left. Get back home and give that partner a swing right and to the left."
2. Main figure: "One and three, go forward and back. Two and four, go forward and back. One and three, pass through and courtesy turn. One and three, go back, pass through and go home, then courtesy turn. Two and four, pass through, and courtesy turn. Two and four, go back, pass through and go home, then courtesy turn. Give your corner a swing and then give your partner a swing too. Weave the ring until you're home. Then give your partner a swing."
3. Break: "Gents, form a star to the left, then to the right, and go back home. Ladies, form a star to the left, then to the right, and go back home. Then all promenade the ring until you get home and swing that partner."
4. Ending: "Allemande left with your gal, pass her, and weave the ring. Get back home and promenade once around the ring. Give that gal a swing and bow to your corner and then to your partner."

Main figures and break can be repeated before the ending.

Two types of calls accompany square dancing: patter calls and singing calls. Patter calls use nonsense words and sounds; timing is important in the use of these calls. Singing calls sometimes use the lyrics of the song in the calls. Singing calls follow the movement sequence to the music.

The caller uses specific techniques. Calls of movement commands use short words spoken quickly so that the cues precede the movement phrases. This helps to keep the action of the dance continuing. At the beginning of the dance, the first call uses eight counts; then the calls continue to stay ahead of the next movement phrase. The calls cue the dancers to the next steps or figures. The same calls are often used in the opener, break, and ending.

Calls must be rhythmic and clear and projected with confidence, strength, and enthusiasm. The caller must think ahead and know what figures go together. The teacher usually acts as the leader and caller. A successful caller is both an experienced dancer and a knowledgeable teacher. If you do not know how to call a square dance, you can study from called records, CDs, or tapes or attend square dance classes or conventions to learn to call.

When the students have learned these dances, let them create their own dances. In the beginning, don't worry about the order of the square dance. Let them create and practice these short dances and calls to the music. Often the dancers learn the calls so that they are not completely dependent on the caller. Then they can create a square dance using the standard order for the parts of the dance.

Musical Accompaniment

Musical accompaniment for square dance includes the following:

- Recorded music with the calls
- Live music with a caller
- Recorded music with a live caller

Dance Class Format

The class format for square dance is as follows:

1. Warm-up
2. Review of previously learned steps, figures, and dances
3. Introduction of new steps and figures
4. New dances that incorporate steps and figures from the students' repertoire

Classroom Considerations

Students must be aware of the factors that affect their dancing, such as safety, attire, and etiquette. Dancing is enjoyable when everyone knows the rules.

Safety

Make sure the room is large enough to accommodate the number of squares that dancers will form. The area should also be well lit and well ventilated. The floor should be clean and neither slippery nor sticky.

Attire

Males wear street clothes: shirts and trousers. They can wear flexible oxfords, tennis shoes, or clean-soled shoes. Females wear skirts and blouses, shirts and pants, or leotards and tights with a skirt. They can wear flat-soled shoes, tennis shoes, ballet shoes, or character shoes. Shoes should either lace up or have a strap.

Classroom Etiquette

Ensure that everyone in the class has a partner or is a member of a group. Students are quiet, courteous, and aware of themselves and others when moving through the space. Talking should be kept to a minimum. Hands should be clean.

Beyond Technique Assignments

The following are some suggestions for beyond technique assignments in square dance:

- Find a square dance from a particular part of the country. Teach it to a small group and perform it.

- Create a square dance and select the music. Teach it to a small group and perform it.
- Attend a square dance in the community. Write a one-page description of your experience.

Content Overview

The content overview provides the necessary information for teaching the square dance unit.

Definition and History

Square dance refers to a dance performed with four couples in a square. Primarily, square dance includes dances executed in other formations, which are folk dances from the United States. The couples perform a series of figures directed by a caller. There are two styles of square dance: modern western style (club style) and traditional style. Modern western style square dancing is complex; it requires repetitive instruction and practice for performance. Traditional style square dancing has existed for generations; it has simple patterns and is easy to learn. This dance form is appropriate for students in upper elementary through high school.

American square dance has its roots in the country dances of England and France's *contredanse.* Circle quadrilles and longways dances were typical English dances. Later the French adopted the circle, or round, dances into a cotillion, a dance for two or four couples in a square formation like the quadrille (which were forerunners of the modern square dance).

The quadrille included five-figure dances for four couples in a square formation. In French quadrilles, the number of couple varied from two or more couples; four couples were the standard for the English quadrille. England used vibrant and lively music, whereas France used semiclassical music by noteworthy composers. Later couple dances such as the waltz, polka, and mazurka influenced the quadrille and became part of the dance. The quadrille highlighted the risqué dance positions of the couple dances. Quadrilles were brought to the United States from different countries in the 19th century.

In 19th-century United States, dance was a social event and a form of amusement, and it was used to celebrate occasions such as barn raising and threshing bees. The quadrilles were simple and known as singing quadrilles. Often these five-part quadrilles were titled to commemorate a historical event such as the laying of the transatlantic cable. In New England, the ministers or the teachers were the dancing masters. In the southern United States, the dances from the Appalachian Mountains and Kentucky that originally came from Northern Ireland and Scotland remained geographically isolated from other influences. These dances, which became known as *running sets,* were well-preserved dances from John Playford's dance book, *The Dancing Master* (1651). Characteristics of this form were the bouncy run and loose-limbed movement, also movements associated with clogging.

Special Features

The following are specific features of square dances:

- The dance is performed in a square formation with four couples.
- The caller leads the dance by talking the dancers through the parts of the dance. The caller is a link between the music and the dancers. He cues the

Square dance formation.

dancers to the next steps and challenges them by calling unexpected figures to provide variety to the dance.

- The parts of the dance are the opener, main figure, break, and ending.
- Big set dancing (also known as big circle or southern mountain style dances) originated in Appalachia. Part of the dance is performed in a circle; other parts involve couples pairing off to dance in figures of four people.

Principles

Movement, choreographic, and aesthetic principles that specifically apply to square dance are shown in the shaded areas of the following icons.

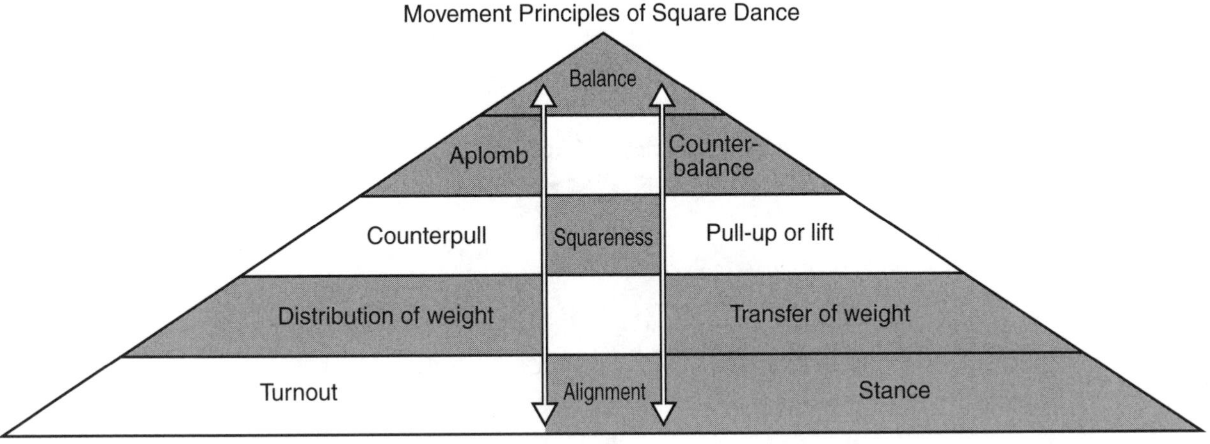

Choreographic Principles of Square Dance

Choreographic elements	Choreographic structures	Choreographic designs	Choreographic devices	Choreographic relationships
Motif Phrase Theme and variation	Simple musical forms • AB (binary) • ABA (ternary) • Rondo • Theme and variation Contrapuntal forms • Canon (round) • Fugue Others • Narrative (story) • Open (free)	Dancer's body shape Dancer's pathway through space Visual design • Symmetrical • Asymmetrical Symbolism • Representational • Abstraction • Distortion Relationship • Unison • Sequential • Successional • Oppositional • Complementary	Repetition Reverse Alter • Addition or subtraction • Directional change • Facing or focus • Level • Dimension • Tempo • Rhythm • Quality or effort action • Positioning • Movement section	Solo Duet Trio Quartet Small and large groups

Traditional Dance Elements

Space	Time	Force	Relationships
Directions Dimensions Levels Shapes Pathways Focus	Duration Tempo	Movement qualities • Sustained • Percussive • Swinging • Suspended • Collapsing • Vibratory	Among body parts Among people Between people and props

Laban's Dance Elements

Space	Time	Weight	Flow
Direct or indirect	Sudden or slow	Light or strong	Bound or free

Effort actions (use space, time, and weight)

• Dab • Flick • Punch • Slash • Glide • Float • Press • Wring

Aesthetic Principles of Square Dance

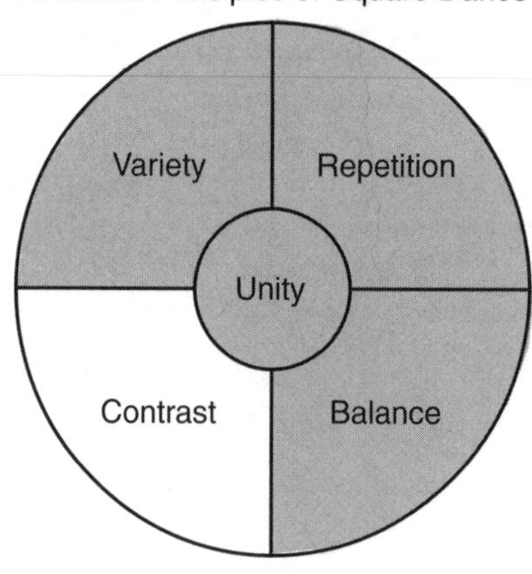

Vocabulary

The square dancer's feet and body move as a unit. The upper body is relaxed and leans into various movements to anticipate the next movement. The vocabulary for square dance is shared by other recreational dance forms.

Partner Positions

Partner positions vary in square dance. Couples can stand side by side with inside hands joined, left parallel (sidecar), right parallel (banjo), semi-open position, open position, promenade, two hands joined while couple faces each other, shoulder–waist, and varsouvienne. (See the folk dance unit, page 237, for descriptions of these positions.)

Partner Holds

The couple can put the little fingers and palms of one hand together, hold one hand, hold both hands, shoulders, or waist. Or the hand can be behind the back of the body. When partners do not use partner holds, the arms hang loosely at the side of the body or the hands are placed on the hips.

Active partners are the people who are moving: either couples 1 and 3 or couples 2 and 4. The head couple (couple 1) stands near and with their back to the music (see figure 13.4).

Steps and Figures

To **honor** is to face your partner. Man (or leader) bows from the waist with feet together; woman (or follower) curtsies. Honor first to your partner, then to your corner (person to the opposite side).

To **circle,** all dancers join hands and circle counterclockwise for 8 steps. Then circle clockwise ending at the starting positions.

Do-si-do starts with two dancers facing each other. They walk forward, passing right shoulders, step to the side so that they're back to back, and then return by moving backward and passing left shoulders. This process can also be reversed—passing left, then right shoulders. Arms are folded across the chest or hang free at the sides.

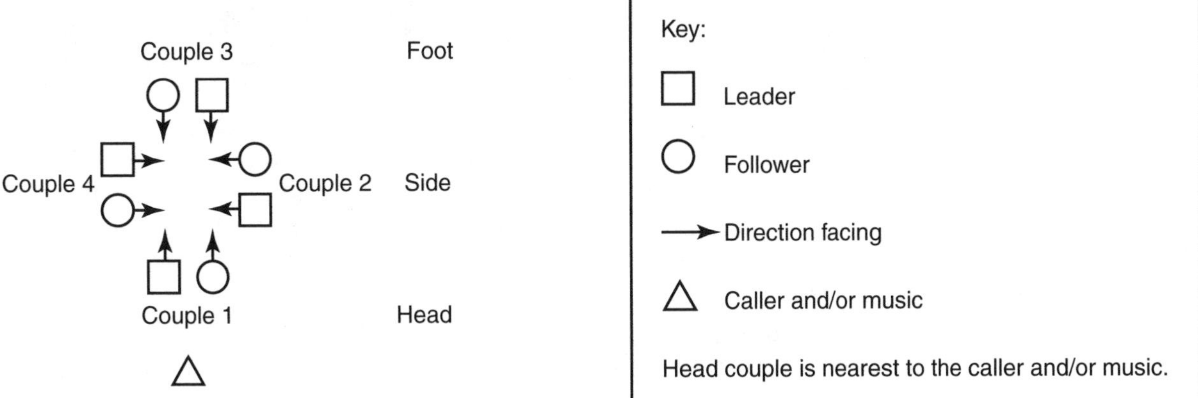

Figure 13.4 Square dance formation for a set of four couples.

Head couple moves to the center of the square.

Promenade in a circle.

In **promenade,** couples face line of direction in promenade position and walk counterclockwise until they return to their place. The leader holds the follower's right hand in his right hand and her left in his left. The promenade figure can also be performed in varsouvienne position (see the folk dance unit, page 237, for a description of this dancing position).

Swing has partners either hook right elbows or join both hands and skip in a circle counterclockwise. The swing can be done in banjo, sidecar, and closed dance positions (see descriptions in the folk dance unit, page 237).

In **grand right and left,** partners face each other. They clasp right hands and pass right shoulders to move past each other. Then they extend the left hand to the next person and pass left shoulders. The dancers continue to grasp hands while passing right and left shoulders until they return to their partner.

In **sashay,** the dancer slides to the right or left, leading with same foot, almost like a sideward gallop.

In **allemande left,** each dancer turns to face his or her corner. They connect left hands and perform a complete circle back to the beginning place. They disengage hands and face their partner. The allemande left is usually performed before the grand right and left.

Twirl has the partners standing face to face. The leader and follower take right hands, and the leader turns the follower clockwise under his right arm. After one or more turns, the couples go back to promenade position.

In **single-file promenade,** the couples move counterclockwise in a shuffle walk to form a single circle with one person behind the other. A shuffle walk is a casual walk to the beat of the music.

Waist swing involves partners in the sidecar or banjo position (left side or right side, respectively) performing a gliding walk for 4 or 8 counts. Later a buzz step can be used (see a description of the buzz step in the folk dance unit, page 242).

In **ladies chain,** couples face each other and the ladies (or followers) advance forward, connect right hands, and proceed to pass each other (chain). Then they join left hands with the opposing men. The man turns the lady with his right arm around her waist. The lady advances forward while the man backs up into place. The ladies chain their way back to the opposite side by extending the right hands to the other lady and passing. Then she joins left hands with her original partner and proceeds to execute the same turn.

In the **pass-through,** the two couples face each other, then pass the right shoulder of the opposite dancer.

In **split the ring,** the first, or lead, couple advances forward between the lady and man of opposite couple.

Dancers performing an elbow turn.

Side couples perform a star.

In **separate go around one,** an active couple moves forward, then separates. The leader moves to the left and the follower goes to the right, circling the nearest inactive dancer to end facing their partner in the middle of the square.

Forearm turn, or **elbow turn,** is a turn performed in place and uses a forearm grasp. Often it is referred to as a single-arm swing.

Texas star has many variations and is often used in the main figure. Either leaders or followers go into the center and touch fingertips with palms down and move around the circle either clockwise or counterclockwise.

In **box star,** all dancers walk in a forward direction as part of the star. The leader or follower grasps right or left hand on the wrist of a dancer who is in front of him or her. If moving to the right, grasp the right hand; if moving left, grasp the left hand. Sometimes only the leaders or followers perform the star.

In a **courtesy turn,** couples face in the same direction. The leader holds the follower's left hand in his left hand and rests his right arm around her waist. The leader backs up as the follower moves forward. They act as a unit. This turn often is linked to the ladies chain.

In **circle to a line,** either couples 1 and 3 or 2 and 4 move leading to the right, circling two-thirds around with hands joined. The leader who initiates the movement is the active leader; he releases his left hand and pulls the people into a straight line.

Bend the line begins in a line with an even number of people. The line separates in the middle. The center people retreat and the end people advance until the two sides of the line face each other.

Right and left through, or **right and left four,** is similar to ladies chain, but the active couples move. The dancer passes the person across from her on the right without touching hands. The couple may grasp hands on the courtesy turn that follows. If two men and two ladies pass through on the right, they may perform the courtesy turn side by side or place the nearest arm around the lady's waist.

Weave the ring is like a grand right and left, but instead of grasping right hands and left hands, they pass right shoulders and left shoulders.

References

Green, G. 1984. *Square and folk dancing: A complete guide for students, teachers, and callers.* New York: Harper & Row.

Gunzenhauser, M. 1996. *The square dance & contra handbook.* Jefferson, NC: McFarland.

Harris, J.A., A.M. Pittman, and M.S. Waller. 1999. *Dance a while: Handbook of folk, square, contra, and social dance.* 7th ed. Minneapolis: Burgess.

Kraus, R. 1962. *Folk dancing: A guide for schools, colleges, and recreation groups.* New York: MacMillan.

Playford, J. 1651. *The dancing master.* London: Author.

Riley, M. 1988. *English country dances for children.* Vol. 1 (cassette and booklet). Delphi, IN: Riverside.

Selected Resources

Selected resources include square dance texts, music, and videos. For other sources look in the folk dance sample unit. Quite often books, music, and videos for recreational dance forms pertain to several of the dance forms.

Texts

Damon, F. 1957. *The history of square dancing.* Barre, MA: Barre Gazette.

Gunzenhauser, M. 1996. *The square dance & contra handbook.* Jefferson, NC: McFarland.

Harris, J.A., A.M. Pittman, and M.S. Waller. 1999. *Dance a while: Handbook of folk, square, contra, and social dance.* 7th ed. Minneapolis: Burgess.

Harris, J.A., A.M. Pittman, and M.S. Waller. 1999. *Dance a while: Handbook of folk, square, contra, and social dance.* 7th ed. Minneapolis: Burgess.

Holden, R. 1956. *The contra dance book.* Newark, NJ: American Square.

Kraus, R. 1950. *Square dances of today, and how to teach them.* New York: A.A. Barnes.

Music

Capon, J., and R. Hallum. 1977. *Get to square dance.* Freeport, NY: Educational Activities.

Franklin, R. 1977. *Circle dances for today.* Long Branch, NJ: Kimbo Records KEA 1146.

Franklin, R. 1997. *Square dance fun for everyone.* Long Branch, NJ: Educational Activities.

Leger, R., and P. Phillips. 1981. *Square dancing: The American way.* Long Branch, NJ: Kimbo Records KIM 4061.

Ruff, B., and J. Murtha. 1969. *The fundamentals of square dancing.* Instruction Series Level 1, Level 2, Level 3 (each are separate records). Los Angeles: OFFICIAL Magazine of Square Dancing.

Videos

Jonas, G. 1995. *Dancing: Volumes I through VIII.* New York: Insight Media.

Karlin, E. 1976. *Country corners.* New York: Insight Media.

New England dances: Square, quadrilles and step dance. 1995. Chicago: Facets Video S30165.

Video of music and dance of the Americans. 1990. New York: Insight Media.

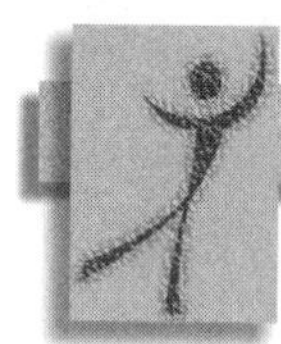

Contra Dance Unit

Teaching Overview

Psychomotor Objectives

- Execute basic contra dances (footwork, steps, partner positions, formations, figures, combinations of three to four steps and dances) to music.
- Demonstrate relationship of movement to music (count, rhythm, tempo, time signature).
- Demonstrate application of principles to contra dance.
- Perform basic movements with appropriate quality in the style of the dance.

Psychomotor Evaluation

- Performance test of selected contra dances (execution of footwork, figures, steps, partner positions, formations, figures, combinations of three to four steps and dances) in relation to music (count, rhythm, tempo, time signature) with application of principles.

Cognitive Objectives

- Recognize beginning contra dance terminology.
- Learn basic calls and respond to them.
- Translate a beginning contra dance into movement from oral or written instructions.
- Conduct a self-evaluation or a peer evaluation of a beginning contra dance performance.

Cognitive Evaluation

- Complete written test of beginning contra dance knowledge (dances, dance skills, definitions of terminology, history and culture, self-assessment of personal performance).
- Translate written and oral instructions for a contra dance into movement with the music.

Affective Objectives

- Practice dance etiquette in the contra dance class.
- Demonstrate personal movement confidence and performance attitude.
- Work with the group to refine the performance.

Affective Evaluation

- Demonstrate etiquette, movement confidence, performance attitude, cooperation, contribution, and leadership within the group and class.

Teaching Approaches

One way to teach contra dance is to present the first sequence of the dance and then execute it with the music. This process continues until students learn the entire dance. To get students involved, divide the students into small groups. Ask one student in the group to explain how to execute a figure in the dance. Another approach is to give each group a written description of the dance and have them translate it into movement.

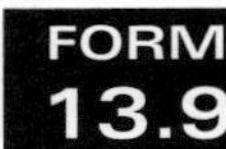

Scope and Sequence for Contra Dance

New = N Review = R Quiz = Q Review for test = RT Performance test = PT

	1	2	3	4	5	6	7	8	9	10	11	12	13	14	15
Definition and history of contra dance	N														
Attire and etiquette	N														
Formation: head, foot couples	N											Q			
Active and inactive couple	N														
Virginia Reel (walk and slide)	N	R	R		R					R		R	RT		
Arm around	N	R													
Reel, sashay, cast off	N	R													
Jefferson's Reel (walk)[1]		N	R	R	R				R	R		R	RT		
Circle, right and left star, single file		N	R												
Set of four in a line, couple arch		N	R												
Pop Goes the Weasel (walk, active, inactive)[1,2]			N	R	R	R			R			R	RT		
Circle, down outside, up inside			N												
Arch (inactive), pop through (active)			N												
Lady of the Lake (1, 3, 5 active, cross over)[1,3]				N	R	R			R			R	RT		
Balance and swing down center and back				N											
Cast off, ladies chain				N											
Glover's Reel (1, 3, 5 active)[2,3]						N	R		R			R	RT	PT	PT
Do-si-do, allemande right and left						N									
Swing down center two by two						N									
Right- and left-hand star						N									
Flower of Edinburgh (1st couple active; 2, 4, 6)[2,4]							N		R	R		R	RT	RT	PT
Head and foot forward and backward							N								
Head inside, down inside, up outside							N								
Chain, start right and left, cross over							N								

(continued)

FORM 13.9 *(continued)*

New = N   Review = R   Quiz = Q   Review for test = RT   Performance test = PT

	1	2	3	4	5	6	7	8	9	10	11	12	13	14	15
Black Nag (slide, walk, skip)[3]								N	R	R		R	RT	RT	PT
Slide down and up, siding								N							
Exchange first man last lady . . .								N							
Men's hey, ladies hey								N							
Hull's Victory (1, 3, 5 active)[2,3]										N		R	RT	RT	PT
Balance, four in a line										N					
Turn left and right hand, center two by two										N					
Cast off, right and left through										N					
Nottingham Swing (1, 3, 5 active)[4]											N	R	RT	RT	PT
Step–hop, swing											N				
Cast around											N				
Swing											N				

[1]More information can be found in Harris, Pittman, and Waller (1999).

[2]More information can be found in Holden (1956).

[3]More information can be found in Kraus (1962).

[4]More information can be found in Riley (1988).

FORM 13.10

Contra Dance Block Time Plan

Class 1	Class 2	Class 3	Class 4	Class 5
• Define contra dance • Give brief history • Talk about attire and etiquette • Teach formation and characteristics (active, inactive) • Head and foot couples • Arm and hand holds *Dance* **Virginia Reel**[1,2] *Walk, bows, arm around, two arms around, reel, sashay*	• Review • Warm-up • Walk forward, back, side, in a circle, go through pattern in dance • Virginia Reel • Introduce **Jefferson's Reel**[3] *Walks, circle, right- and left-hand star, set of four in a line, couple arch* **Pop Goes the Weasel**[1,3] *Active, inactive circle down, outside, arch (inactive), actives pop through*	• Warm-up with new dance music change directions by using new formation • Review • Virginia Reel • Jefferson Reel • Pop Goes the Weasel	• Warm-up with formation of new dance **Lady of the Lake** *(1, 3, 5 actives); cross over*[2,3] • Balance and swing down the center and back, cast off, ladies chain	• Warm-up • Walk-up up, back, side, ship, slide, and gallops • Review • Virginia Reel • Jefferson Reel • Pop Goes the Weasel • Lady of the Lake

Class 6	Class 7	Class 8	Class 9	Class 10
• Warm-up • Skip, gallop, slide, new formations and holds **Glover's Reel**[1,2] *(1, 3, 5 active), do-si-do, allemande right and left, swing down the center two by two, right- and left-hand star* • Review • Pop Goes the Weasel • Lady of the Lake	• Warm-up • **Flowers of Edinburgh**[1,4] *(1st couple active; 2, 4, 6) Head and foot couple move forward and backward; head inside and down inside, chain, star right and left; cross over* • Review • Glover's Reel	• Warm-up • **Black Nag**[2] *Slide down and up the set; siding, exchange first man and last lady . . .; sides change; once around; men's hey; ladies hey*	• Warm-up • Review • Jefferson's Reel • Pop Goes the Weasel • Lady of the Lake • Glover's Reel • Flowers of Edinburgh • Black Nag	• Warm-up • **Hull's Victory**[1,2] *(1, 3, 5 active) balance four in a line; turn left and right hand, center two by two; cast off, right and left through* • Review all dances

(continued)

(continued)

Class 11	Class 12	Class 13	Class 14	Class 15
• Warm-up • Review for quiz • **Nottingham Swing**[4] *(1, 3, 5 active)* *Step–hop, cast, swing elbow swing, 1st boy and 2nd girl link elbow swing; 2nd and 1st girl boy do the same; 1, 3, 5 join hand down center with step–hop, face up up the set and do the same; 1, 3, 5 cast around the couple next to them, 2, 4, 6 move up swing with step–hop*	• Quiz formations active and inactive couples • Review all dances • Draw for partners and sets	• Review for performance test	• Review for performance test	• Performance test

Note: Dances are **boldfaced** on the day they are introduced.

[1]More information can be found in Holden (1956).

[2]More information can be found in Kraus (1962).

[3]More information can be found in Harris, Pittman, and Waller (1999).

[4]More information can be found in Riley (1988).

Specific Teaching Methods

In contra dance, the dancer must know all the steps and figures in the dance to perform it. Walk through each figure using the add-on method to make sure each couple knows what they are doing, where they are going, whether they are active or inactive, and whether they move up or down the set. One way of distinguishing between actives and inactives is to have the dancers wear color-coded scarves around their necks or bands around their forearms. This device is helpful for elementary, middle, and high school dancers and beginners.

If the dancers have a problem or are confused, go back slowly over the steps and figure; mark the dance without the music, listen to the music, then perform the dance to the music. Cue the dancers until they know the dance. In contra dance, dancers repeat the sequence many times until the music is finished. After the dancers learn the order of the dance, they do not need to be cued. To add a closing to the dance, cue the last repeat of the dance.

In contra dance, the caller is the prompter who intermittently calls, or cues, the steps during the dance and attempts to rhyme the calls. Calls are often set, but the caller has the freedom to use his creativity in giving the cues. As in square dance, calls come before the movement, making timing an important factor. Periodic calls keep the dancers continually moving.

Musical Accompaniment

The contra dance is accompanied by live or recorded music and a caller. Some recordings include calls for one dancer; others do not and require the teacher to call the dance.

A contra dance has 64 counts, then the dance repeats. The musical form is AABB. All figures are followed with proper counts and sequence. If there is a problem, dancers halt and quickly move to the proper position. When the dancers know the pattern of the dance, the caller stops cueing. To add continuity, the caller cues the last two repetitions of the dance to the end.

Dance Class Format

The class format for contra dance is as follows:

1. Warm-up
2. Review of previously learned steps, figures, and dances
3. Introduction of new steps and figures
4. New dances that incorporate steps and figures from the students' repertoire

Classroom Considerations

Because the dancers perform the dance with other dancers, certain rules apply.

Safety

The biggest safety issue for the contra dance class is the size of the room; it must be large enough to accommodate the number of dancers. The area should be well lit, and the floor should be clean. A good floor for contra dance is neither slippery nor sticky.

Attire

Males wear street clothes: shirts and trousers. They can wear flexible oxfords or tennis shoes. Females wear skirts and blouses, shirts and pants, or leotards and tights with a skirt. They can wear flat-soled shoes, tennis shoes, ballet shoes, or character shoes. Shoes should either lace up or have a strap.

Classroom Etiquette

Ensure that everyone in the class has a partner or is a member of a group. Students are quiet, courteous, and aware of themselves and others when moving through the space. Talking should be kept to a minimum. Hands should be clean.

Beyond Technique Assignments

The following are some suggestions for beyond technique assignments in contra dance:

- Find the historical background of a dance from John Playford's *The Dancing Master* (1651). Read, reconstruct, and teach the dance to the other students in the class.
- Contra dances were performed by our forefathers. Find a contra dance done during George Washington's time. Read about, reconstruct, and teach the dance to the class.
- Research the origins of selected contra figures that stem from the Renaissance. Either write a paper on their origins or present an oral report to the class.
- Using the Internet, research contra dance in today's society by regions and groups. Compare and contrast the dances of various regions and bring examples of contemporary contra dances to class.

Content Overview

The content overview provides the necessary information for teaching the contra dance unit.

Definition and History

Contra, or longways, dance is performed in two parallel lines with the dancers facing each other. It is said to be a dance of opposition. Contra dance is also referred to as a country dance. This type of dance consists of a sequence of steps or figures that repeat many times. Contra dances are relatively simple, using various figures and steps that promote interaction between couples within a set. After the first repetition some of the dancers progress toward the end of the set or line; in the meantime, others move toward the beginning of the set.

The roots of the contra dance stem from England, Ireland, and Scotland. Contra dances originated in 17th-century England and were performed by both nobility and country folk. Many of these dances were collected by John Playford. Ireland influenced the contra dance with its bagpipe and harp music and jig dances. Scotland contributed country and highland reel dance forms for four to six people. Settlers from the British Isles and Europe brought the contra dance to New England. The dances were performed in ballrooms, dance halls, barns, and outdoors. Originally fiddlers played the dances; later two violins, a clarinet, a cornet, and a piano accompanied the dances.

Contra dance has thrived in the New England area of the United States since before the American Revolution. In the last several decades contra dance has become more popular throughout the United States. Various country dance organizations keep the tradition alive. Contra dance is a part of western European cultural heritage, social behavior, and etiquette.

Special Features

The following are specific features of contra dance:

- The dance is performed in two parallel lines.
- The dance is generally executed with six to eight couples (12 to 16 dancers).
- Couples are either active or inactive during the dance.
- Dances consist of simple footwork, intricate figures, and steps.
- The dance is called by either a dancer or a caller.
- The contra dance has specific terminology that the dancer must know to perform the dance form.

Contra formation.

An arch.

Principles

Movement, choreographic, and aesthetic principles that specifically apply to contra dance are shown in the shaded areas of the icons on pages 268-269.

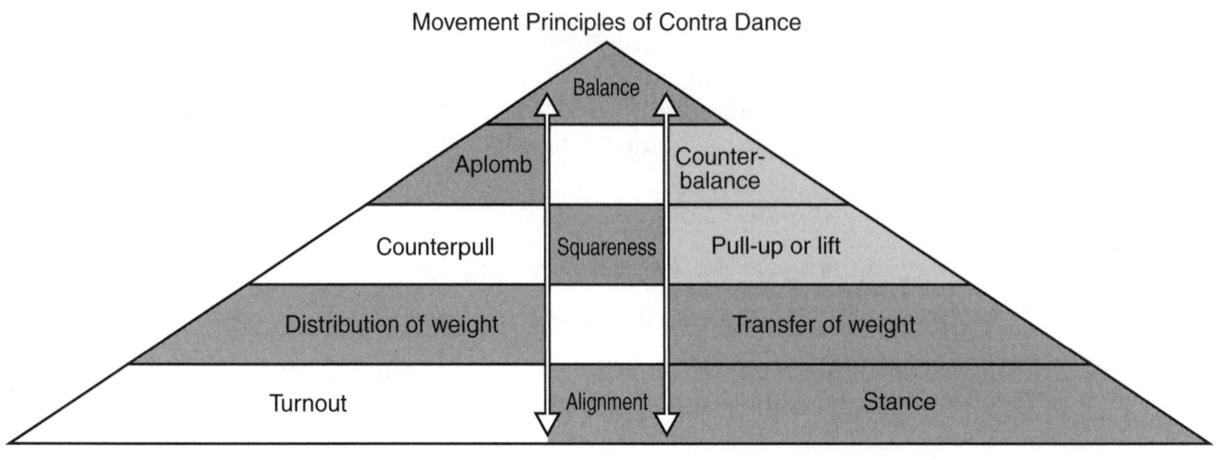

Choreographic Principles of Contra Dance

Choreographic elements	Choreographic structures	Choreographic designs	Choreographic devices	Choreographic relationships
Motif Phrase Theme and variation	Simple musical forms • AB (binary) • ABA (ternary) • Rondo • Theme and variation Contrapuntal forms • Canon (round) • Fugue Others • Narrative (story) • Open (free)	Dancer's body shape Dancer's pathway through space Visual design • Symmetrical • Asymmetrical Symbolism • Representational • Abstraction • Distortion Relationship • Unison • Sequential • Successional • Oppositional • Complementary	Repetition Reverse Alter • Addition or subtraction • Directional change • Facing or focus • Level • Dimension • Tempo • Rhythm • Quality or effort action • Positioning • Movement section	Solo Duet Trio Quartet Small and large groups

Traditional Dance Elements

Space	Time	Force	Relationships
Directions Dimensions Levels Shapes Pathways Focus	Duration Tempo	Movement qualities • Sustained • Percussive • Swinging • Suspended • Collapsing • Vibratory	Among body parts Among people Between people and props

Laban's Dance Elements

Space	Time	Weight	Flow
Direct or indirect	Sudden or slow	Light or strong	Bound or free

Effort actions (use space, time, and weight)

• Dab • Flick • Punch • Slash • Glide • Float • Press • Wring

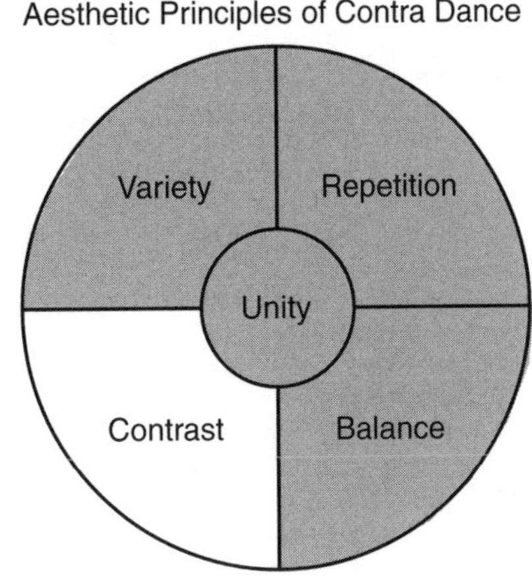

Vocabulary

The vocabulary for contra dance is shared by other recreational dance forms.

Partners

Partners in contra dance have different roles. If the dance instructions indicate **improper,** the couples cross over to the opposite side of the set. When the dance instructions show **proper,** this means that the couples do not cross over. Another pair of terms important to contra dance is **up** and **down. Up, above, top,** and **head** indicate the couple who is closest to the music and caller. **Down, below, bottom,** and **foot** indicate the couple who is the farthest from the music and caller (see figure 13.5, a–c).

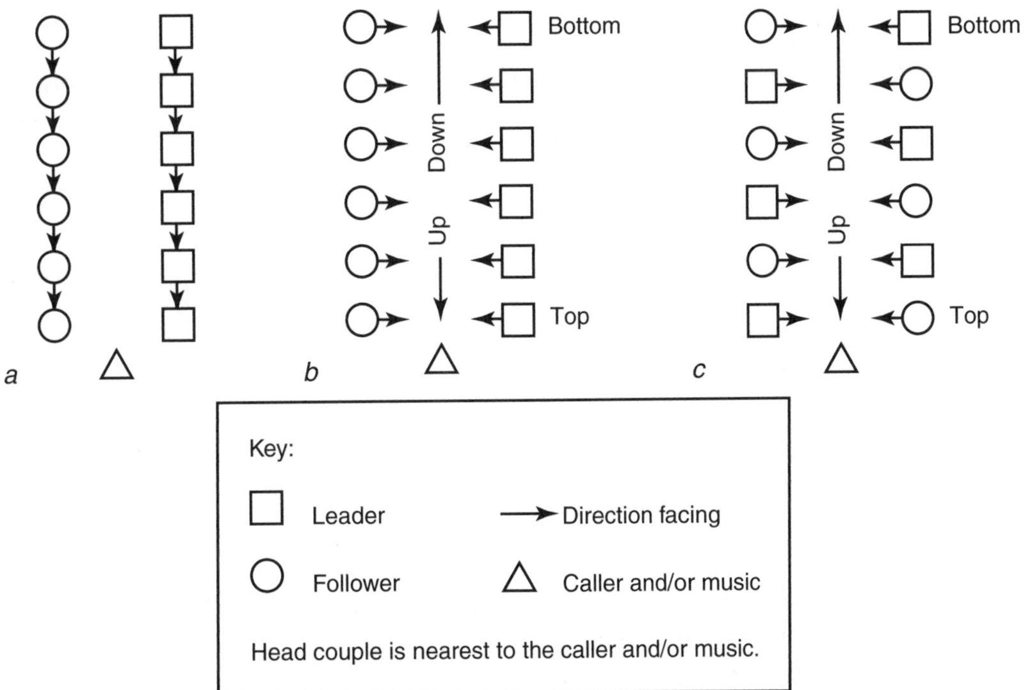

Figure 13.5 Contra dance formations. *(a)* Couples in a double file: longways or contra set, couples facing head (caller or music source); *(b)* couples in a line: longways or contra set, partners facing; *(c)* couples in a line: longways or contra set, couples 1, 3, and 5 cross over.

Sashay down the middle.

The number of couples and the progression of movement are of utmost importance in contra dance. Contra dances are performed in a duple minor, start from the top couple, and divide into 1, 2, 1, 2. The 1s are often called the **active couples** and the 2s are referred to as **inactive couples.** If each group of two couples joins, this is a minor set. When a triple minor is performed, the couples separate into 1, 2, 3, 1, 2, 3; this is a more complicated configuration and is not covered at the beginning level.

After each dance sequence or during the dance, the 1s move down the set by one place, gradually moving away from the music; the 2s move up the set by one place after each repetition of the dance.

Partner Positions

Partners use closed dance position, sidecar, banjo, and open position holding both hands facing each other. (See the folk dance unit, page 237.)

Partner Holds

Partner holds include little finger and palms together, hold one hand or both hands, hold shoulder and waist, or hold back and hand. Sometimes partner holds relate to partner positions.

Steps and Figures

In **walking step,** keep the feet close to the floor and walk with a glide or shuffle rather than a bounce.

Polka step is hop, step–together, step.

There are four variations of the balance step.

1. **Balance, or step-swing, to the side.**

Count	Footwork	Cue
1	Step to right on your right	Step
2	Swing the left foot in front of the right, bouncing slightly on the right foot	Swing
3	Step to the left on your left foot	Step
4	Swing the right foot in front of the left, bouncing slightly on the left foot	Swing

2. **Balance walking** is two steps forward and two steps back, starting with the right foot (cues: walk forward, forward, backward, backward).

3. **Balance to side** is step to right on right foot, bring left foot up to right without taking the weight; repeat to other side (cues: step, touch, step, touch).

4. **Balance forward and back** is more widely used and more vigorous; it's similar to a pas de bas (cues: step forward together, step backward together).

Count	Footwork	Cue
1	Step toward each other on the right foot; transfer weight to the left foot, and close to the right foot	Right forward, left together
2	Transfer weight back to the right foot, stepping in place with left	Right, in place left
3	Step away from each other on the left foot; transfer weight to the right and close to the left foot	Left backward, together
4	Step toward each other on the right foot, transfer the weight to the left, and close to right foot	Right forward, left

Buzz step: See the folk dance unit, page 242.

In **forward and back** (advancing and retreating or forward a double walk and backward a double walk), begin with the right foot. Walk 4 steps forward, then 4 steps backward, beginning with the right foot that returns to place. This step can also use 3 steps forward and hold, 3 steps back and hold. (Cues: Walk forward, forward, forward, forward. Walk backward, backward, backward, backward, or backward step, step, step, hold.)

Pas de bas: See the folk dance unit, page 243.

Pigeon wing is a step on the right foot, swing the left foot across the right, and shake the lower leg from the knee.

Two-step alternates feet and is performed forward, backward, and to the side. (See the folk dance unit, page 240, for further descriptions.)

Sashay, chassé, or **slip step** is a sideways movement or a syncopated sideways gallop step or sliding step. Step sideways to the right on right foot on the first note of the triplet, close the left foot to the right momentarily transferring the weight on the third note (cues: step together [close, going in one direction]).

Waltz: See the folk dance unit, page 242.

In **castoff,** each dancer in the active couple travels behind the person below them so that the active couple ends one place below where they started, facing each other. During the castoff, the man (leader) moves counterclockwise while the lady (follower) moves clockwise. The active couple casts off when they are in the middle of inactive couples of their minor set or in the "line of four figure" as the active couple returns to their beginning position. The following progressions are variations of the castoff.

- In **walk around,** active couples part and walk around to below the inactive couple and end facing each other. The inactive couple remains stationary.
- In **arm around,** active couples separate while inactive couples proceed up the set. The active and inactive couples place their closest arm around the next person's waist (man or lady). The inactives move backward or pivot as the actives go forward. They turn side by side. The active couple finishes one place below, and everyone ends facing their partner.
- **Unassisted, two dancers** is similar to the *arm around* because they move with shoulders and sides close together. The dancers turn as if they are a unit. The active partners end one place below and everyone ends facing their partner.
- In **hand castoff,** active couples move away from each other and clasp the closest inactive's hand. They join hands at shoulder height with the elbows down. Hands may be connected already with an inactive person because they may be moving forward in a line of four. An inactive is the pivotal person. Actives change places to one below, and everyone ends facing their partner.
- In **two couple,** an active couple progresses up the set as an inactive couple follows. The active couple divides and moves in a small circle to the place below the inactives. Inactives move away from each other and do a turn in place, moving backward into a line above the active couple.
- In **separately,** one person casts off during a star figure, and another person casts off in the following figure.

Right and left through (right and left four): See the square dance unit, page 258.

Contra corners turn in 16 counts uses turns in different directions. Contra dance corners are diagonally across the set for each dancer. If the dancer is diagonally right, this is the first contra corner. If a dancer is diagonally left, this is the second contra corner. When the caller says, "Turn contra corners," the active partner crosses the set and gives the right hand to his partner and does a half turn. Then the active person grasps the left hand of first contra corner, completes a turn, grasps the right hand of the active partner, and turns three quarters around, ending in the middle of the set. Then, grasp the left hand of second contra corner, do a full turn, and come back to the center of the set. Actives use the right hand then their left hand; the corners always the left hand. Each turn is done in four counts.

Hey for four (16 counts) has four dancers in a line with the center two dancers facing each other. They weave much like a grand right and left without hands touching; their shoulders pass right and left alternately. The dancers move in a

Contra corners: first change.

Contra corners: second change.

figure eight with an extra loop in the middle. The hey starts with two followers facing each other; a leader is behind each follower, passing right shoulders and moving toward the end of the line or opposite side. Next, the leader passes left shoulders, then passes the follower on the right, continuing to pass left to face center; then pass another leader's left and should be back to his beginning place. The leaders perform a little loop to the left, while followers begin traveling in the path the follower makes in front of them; pass left shoulder of another follower, right shoulder with a leader at the midpoint, left with his partner and loop left to face center. Leaders come back by passing on the follower's left, leader passes right at the midpoint then the follower's left, loops to the left and back to original position. The pathway is the same as a ladies chain. The leader does the same pattern as the follower.

Ones move down the set as twos move up the set.

Ones and twos have switched places.

References

Harris, J.A., A.M. Pittman, and M.S. Waller. 1999. *Dance a while: Handbook of folk, square, contra, and social dance.* 7th ed. Minneapolis: Burgess.

Holden, R. 1956. *The contra dance book.* Newark, NJ: American Square.

Kraus, R. 1962. *Folk dancing: A guide for schools, colleges, and recreation groups.* New York: MacMillan.

Playford, J. 1651. *The dancing master.* London: Author.

Riley, M.C. 1988. *English country dances for children.* Vol. 2. Delphi, IN: Riverside.

Selected Resources

Selected resources include contra dance texts, music, and videos.

Texts

Gunzenhauser, M. 1996. *The square dance & contra handbook.* Jefferson, NC: McFarland.

Harris, J.A., A.M. Pittman, and M.S. Waller. 1999. *Dance a while: Handbook of folk, square, contra, and social dance.* 7th ed. Minneapolis: Burgess.

Hendrickson, C.C. 1961. *Colonial social dancing for children: Social dancing of Washington's time arranged for today's young people.* Sandy Hook, CT: Hendrickson Group.

Holden, R. 1956. *The contra dance book.* Newark, NJ: American Square.

Music

Hendrickson, C.C. 1961. *Colonial social dancing for children: Social dancing of Washington's time arranged for today's young people.* Sandy Hook, CT: Hendrickson Group.

Riley, M.C. 1988. *English and country dance.* Vol. 1. Delphi, IN: Riverside.

Riley, M.C. 1988. *English and country dance.* Vol. 2. Delphi, IN: Riverside.

Videos

Jonas, G. 1995. *Dancing: Volumes I through VIII.* New York: Insight Media.

Karlin, E. 1976. *Country corners.* New York: Insight Media.

New England dances: Square, quadrilles and step dance. 1995. Chicago: Facets Video S30165.

Video of music and dance for the Americans. 1990. New York, NY: Insight Media.

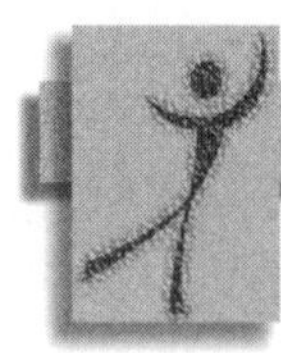

Social Dance Unit

Teaching Overview

Psychomotor Objectives

- Execute basic social dances (footwork and steps, practice clusters or combinations of three to four steps, partner positions, leading and following techniques, body and spatial awareness, standing and moving across the floor) to music (counts, rhythm, tempo, time signature).
- Demonstrate the relationship of movement to music (count, rhythm, tempo, time signature).
- Demonstrate application of movement principles to social dance.

Psychomotor Evaluation

- Performance test of selected social dances (execution of footwork, steps, practice clusters or combinations of three to four steps, partner positions, leading and following techniques, body and spatial awareness, standing and moving across the floor) in relation to music (counts, rhythm, tempo, time signature), with application of movement principles.

Cognitive Objectives

- Recognize beginning social dance terminology.
- Translate a beginning social dance into movement from oral or written instructions.
- Conduct a self-evaluation or a peer evaluation of a beginning social dance performance.

Cognitive Evaluation

- Complete written test of beginning social dance knowledge (dances and dance skills, terminology, definitions, history and culture, self-assessment of performance).
- Translate a written social dance into movement with the music.

Affective Objectives

- Practice the etiquette for dancers in the social dance class.
- Demonstrate personal movement confidence and performance attitude.
- Work with your partner to refine the performance.

Affective Evaluation

- Demonstrate etiquette, movement confidence, performance attitude and cooperation, contribution, and leadership with your partner and the class.

Teaching Approaches

Social dance is a recreational dance form that is part of social events, balls, and dances. Social dance is a fun way to interact with and meet people in ballrooms and clubs and should be an integral part of a person's social manners and lifestyle.

Social dance should be taught so that people can use it throughout life. Dancers need to know the basic steps and how to lead and follow. Dancers need to feel comfortable with the dance. Practice and encouragement are essential for success.

FORM 13.11

Scope and Sequence for Social Dance

New = N Review = R Review for test = RT Performance test = PT

	1	2	3	4	5	6	7	8	9	10	11	12	13	14	15
Definition and history of social dance	N														
Attire and etiquette	N														
Leading and following positions	N	R	R												
Rules	N	R													
Foxtrot (4/4)	N	R	R			R		R						RT	PT
Progressive, one step	N	R	R												
Turn, box step		N	R												
Combination		N	R												
Swing (4/4)				N	R	R		R						RT	PT
Single and double lindy				N	R	R									
Triple lindy				N	R	R									
Turns				N	N	R									
Waltz (3/4)							N	R							
Waltz, step, progressive							N	R						RT	
Box step, turn								N							
Hesitation								N							
Merengue (4/4)									N					RT	PT
Open and closed position merengue step									N		R		R		
Box										N	R		R		
Turn										N	R		R		
Cross										N	R		R		
Cha–cha												N	R	RT	PT
Closed position, face to face												N	R	RT	
Basic forward and backward												N	R	RT	
Crossover												N	R	RT	

FORM 13.12

Social Dance Block Time Plan

Class 1	Class 2	Class 3	Class 4	Class 5

• Define social dance
• History of social dance
• Attire and etiquette
• Rules (following and leading)
• **Foxtrot**
  • Foxtrot history
  • Progressive
  • Forward
  • Backward
  • One step
	• Review
	  • Leading and following
	  • Foxtrot
	  turn, box, combination
	  • Progressive
	  • One step
		• Review foxtrot
		  • Progressive
		  • One step
		  turn, box, combination
			• **Swing**
			  • Swing history
			  • Single
			  • Double lindy
			  • Triple lindy
			  • Turns
				• Review swing
				  • Single
				  • Double and triple lindy
				  • Turns

Class 6	**Class 7**	**Class 8**	**Class 9**	**Class 10**

• Review swing	• **Waltz**
	  • Waltz history
	  • Waltz step
	  • Progressive
		• Review waltz
		  • Box
		  • Turn
		  • Hesitation
		  • Waltz step
		  • Progressive
			• **Merengue**
			  • Merengue history
			  • Open and closed position
			  • Merengue step
				• Review merengue step, open and closed positions
				  • Box
				  • Turn
				  • Cross

Class 11	**Class 12**	**Class 13**	**Class 14**	**Class 15**

• Review merengue	• **Cha–cha**
	  • Cha–cha history
	  • Closed position
	  • Face to face position
	  • Basic forward and backward
	  • Crossover
		• Review
		  • Cha–cha
		  • Merengue
		  • Share
		  • Criteria for each dance
			• Review
			  • Foxtrot
			  • Swing
			  • Waltz
			  • Merengue
			  • Cha–cha
				• Select a dance that you will then execute for the performance test.
				• Evaluate the partner dance using the criteria.

Specific Teaching Methods

When teaching social dance, give the basic steps and practice and rehearse them until the dancers are comfortable. Provide them with a set routine to practice, then let them create their own routines or dance sequences. This way it becomes part of the dancers' movement repertory.

Adults usually have their own partners and want to have additional time to practice with their partners. Briefly review the dance patterns and let them dance their own routines. Often they may know the step but want to have the opportunity to dance with their partner.

Musical Accompaniment

Music is an important aspect of social dance. Keep your student population in mind. Your class can have traditional music or music appropriate to the age level. They need to be able to relate to the music that you choose. Know the musical trends and new dances. The following are two basic types of musical accompaniment:

- Prerecorded compact discs, cassettes, and records
- Live accompaniment of bands or orchestras

Dance Class Format

The class format for social dance is as follows:

1. Warm-up
2. Review of previously learned steps, figures, and dances
3. Introduction of new steps and figures
4. New dances that incorporate steps and figures from the students' repertoire

Classroom Considerations

Being socially adept is part of being an educated person. Knowing when, where, and how to dance makes you more comfortable in a social situation. Students become aware of safety, attire, and etiquette through the social dance class.

Safety

The room should be free of obstacles and well ventilated. The floor should be clean and neither slippery nor sticky.

Attire

Street attire is appropriate for social dance class. Male students wear a shirt, slacks, and dress shoes or tennis shoes. Female students wear blouses, skirts or dresses, flat shoes or heels, or shirts, pants, and tennis shoes. Clothes should be comfortable for movement.

Classroom Etiquette

The man asks the woman politely to dance. He escorts her to the floor to dance. He leads her through the dance using the appropriate hand signals. After the dance, he escorts her back to her seat and thanks her for dancing with him.

Beyond Technique Assignments

The following are some suggestions for beyond technique assignments in social dance:

- Research the foxtrot or another social dance and give an oral report on the historical development of this dance.
- Research the dance and fashions of a specific era (e.g., 1920s or 1930s). Also relate the dances to the social and political milieu of the times. This can be a formal research project with a paper and presentation of the dances.
- Keep a journal that contains reflections on how you feel about the dances you have learned in class and how you feel about dancing in general. Include a summary of what you got out of the class and whether you will continue social dancing.
- Practice social dancing at an event or in a social situation.
- Choreograph two different dances; perform them and then compare and contrast the dances for the class.

Content Overview

The content overview provides the necessary information for teaching the social dance unit.

Definition and History

Social dance is a recreational dance form that mirrors the music, movement, attitude of people, and the times. This dance form is usually performed with a partner. It often reflects social events, comes from a folk heritage such as the polka, or is linked to various cultures (e.g., Latin dances come from Central and South America). Social dance is appropriate for learners in sixth grade through high school.

Social dance stemmed from the court dances of the Renaissance. Dancing masters taught dances and social etiquette. The dance forms changed during the 19th century when dancers executed couple dances, which were considered risqué. According to Harris, Pittman, and Waller (1999) there were seven periods since the 1900s. The dances within these periods comprise the foxtrot, Charleston, swing, Latin, rock 'n' roll, country western, and dances from the later part of the 20th century (touch dancing, disco, salsa, swing, Latin, break dance, hip-hop, and international style).

Special Features

The following are specific features of social dance:

- Social dance is a recreational dance form performed by couples.
- Social dances mirror trends and times as well as traditional dances.
- Couple and group interaction is promoted through the dances.
- This dance form is a physical and social outlet for the dancers.
- Social dances mirror the rhythm of the music.

Principles

Movement, choreographic, and aesthetic principles that specifically apply to social dance are shown in the shaded regions of the following icons.

Movement Principles of Social Dance

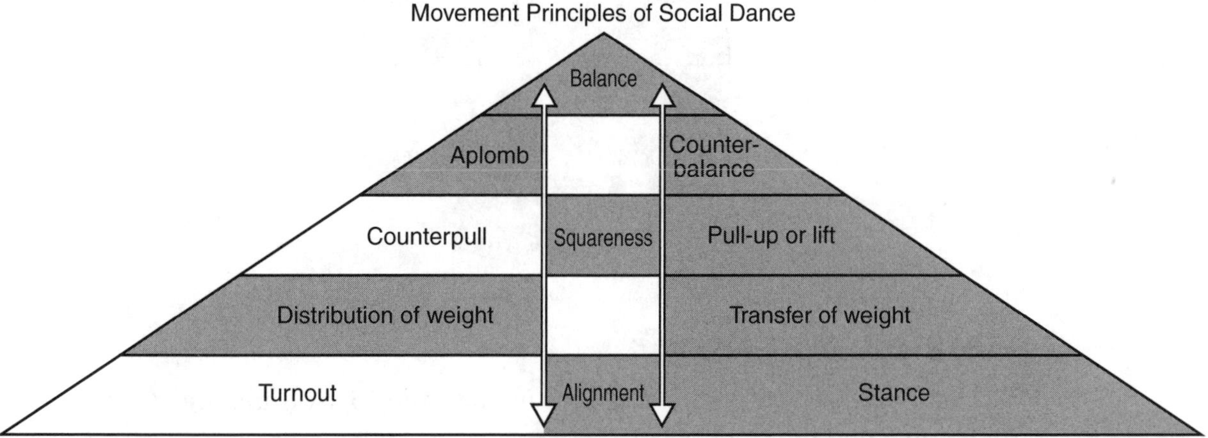

Choreographic Principles of Social Dance

Choreographic elements	Choreographic structures	Choreographic designs	Choreographic devices	Choreographic relationships
Motif Phrase Theme and variation	Simple musical forms • AB (binary) • ABA (ternary) • Rondo • Theme and variation Contrapuntal forms • Canon (round) • Fugue Others • Narrative (story) • Open (free)	Dancer's body shape Dancer's pathway through space Visual design • Symmetrical • Asymmetrical Symbolism • Representational • Abstraction • Distortion Relationship • Unison • Sequential • Successional • Oppositional • Complementary	Repetition Reverse Alter • Addition or subtraction • Directional change • Facing or focus • Level • Dimension • Tempo • Rhythm • Quality or effort action • Positioning • Movement section	Solo Duet Trio Quartet Small and large groups

Traditional Dance Elements

Space	Time	Force	Relationships
Directions Dimensions Levels Shapes Pathways Focus	Duration Tempo	Movement qualities • Sustained • Percussive • Swinging • Suspended • Collapsing • Vibratory	Among body parts Among people Between people and props

Laban's Dance Elements

Space	Time	Weight	Flow
Direct or indirect	Sudden or slow	Light or strong	Bound or free

Effort actions (use space, time, and weight)

• Dab • Flick • Punch • Slash • Glide • Float • Press • Wring

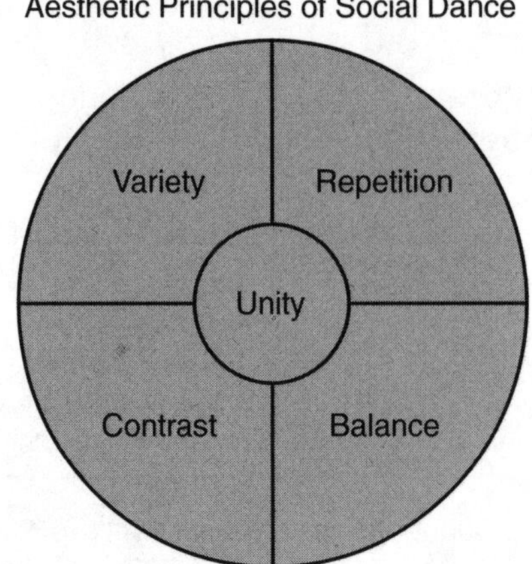

Dances and Steps

The dances covered within this unit include the foxtrot, the waltz, swing, the merengue, and the cha-cha.

The Foxtrot

The foxtrot is an American social dance. The name of the dance came from a star of musical comedy, Henry Fox, who danced a trotting step to ragtime music in the Ziegfeld Follies. The Castles (Vernon and Irene) also influenced and developed the smooth and elegant style of the foxtrot. Originally danced in a 2/4 meter, the foxtrot used the quick one–step. Later the dance evolved into a two–step in 4/4 meter that consists of quick, quick, slow. The speed of the foxtrot varies from slow to moderate to fast.

FOXTROT STEP PROGRESSIONS

When you teach the foxtrot, you begin with simple transfer of weight, forward and back, then move on to more complex foot patterns. Foxtrot step progressions begin with the one–step, then the dance walk, the turn, and finally the foxtrot combinations.

One–Step

All instructions are written for the man (or leader); the woman (or follower) begins with the right foot and *moves backward.*

Count	Footwork	Cue
1	Step (left foot) forward	Quick
2	Step (right foot) forward	Quick
3	Step (left foot) forward	Quick
4	Step (right foot) forward	Quick
1-4	Repeat one–step backward, begin with the left foot	Quick

a

b

Closed position: *(a)* side view, *(b)* back view.

Dance Walk

Count	Footwork	Cue
1-2	Step (left foot) forward	Slow
3-4	Step (right foot) forward	Slow
5-6	Step (left foot) forward	Slow
7-8	Step (right foot) forward	Slow
1-8	Repeat dance walk backward, begin with the left foot	Slow

Turn

Counterclockwise, a quarter turn

Count	Footwork	Cue
1	Step (left foot)	Quick
2	Step (right foot)	Quick
3	Step (left foot)	Quick
4	Step (right foot)	Quick

Slow Turn

Count	Footwork	Cue
1-2	Step (left foot)	Slow
3-4	Step (right foot)	Slow
5-6	Step (left foot)	Slow
7-8	Step (right foot)	Slow

Side Close

Count	Footwork	Cue
1	Step side (left foot)	Quick
2	Together (right foot)	Quick

FOXTROT COMBINATIONS

These combinations use the steps previously taught. The combinations become more rhythmically complex.

Magic Step

Count	Footwork	Cue
1-2	Step forward (left foot)	Slow
3-4	Step forward (right foot)	Slow
5	Step side (left foot)	Quick
6	Step together (right to left)	Quick

Half-Box Progressive

Count	Footwork	Cue
1-2	Step forward (right foot)	Slow
3	Step side (right foot)	Quick
4	Step together (left to right)	Quick
1-4	Repeat half-box progressive backward, begin with the left foot	Slow (1-2) and quick (3 & 4)

Westchester Box

Counts	Footwork	Cue
1-2	Step forward (left foot)	Slow

3	Step side (right foot)	Quick
4	Step together (left to right)	Quick
5-6	Step back (left foot)	Slow
7	Step side (right foot)	Quick
8	Step (left foot) together to right	Quick

Waltz

The waltz originated in central Europe, primarily in Germany and Austria. Inspired by the composers Johann Strauss and his sons, the waltz became popular during the 1840s. This dance has an elegant, swinging quality. The waltz was a part of elegant balls and assemblies in America. This dance caused a scandal because of its use of the closed dance position. The dance is performed in 3/4 meter at a slow, medium, or fast tempo. A Viennese waltz has a fast tempo.

WALTZ STEP PROGRESSIONS

Because the waltz progressions are in 3/4 time, they require the couple to concentrate more on their footwork.

Waltz Step

Count	Footwork	Cue
1	Step (left foot)	Quick
2	Step (right foot)	Quick
3	Step (left foot)	Quick

Dance Walk

Count	Footwork	Cue
1-2	Step (left foot, flat)	Slow or down
3-4	Step (right foot, lift)	Slow, up, or lift (on balls of the feet)
5-6	Step (left foot, lift)	Slow, up, or lift

Box Turn

Counterclockwise or clockwise, an eighth or quarter turn in closed dance position. The turn is initiated on the forward and the back steps.

Count	Footwork	Cue
1	Step forward (left foot, flat)	Slow or down
2	Step side (right foot, lift)	Slow, up, or lift
3	Step together (left foot, lift)	Slow, up, or lift
4	Step back (right foot, flat)	Slow or down
5	Step side (left foot, lift)	Slow, up, or lift
6	Step together (right foot, lift)	Slow, up, or lift

Half-Box Progression

Count	Footwork	Cue
1	Step forward (left foot, flat)	Slow
2	Step side (right foot, up)	Slow
3	Step together (left foot, up)	Slow
4	Step forward (right foot, flat)	Slow
5	Step side (left foot, up)	Slow
6	Step together (right foot, up)	Slow

Hesitation

Count	Footwork	Cue
1	Step forward (left foot)	Quick
2	Touch (right foot)	Slow
3	Hold	Hold

Swing

Through the years, the swing has progressed through a variety of dances such as the West Coast swing, East Coast swing, jive, jitterbug, shag, and lindy hop. The dance is performed in 4/4 time and has many variations that include different partner turns, swing-outs, and couple positions.

LINDY STEP PROGRESSIONS

Lindy progressions include the single, the double, and the triple basic steps.

Single Lindy Basic

The numbers in parentheses indicate an alternative way of counting the step.

Count	Footwork	Cue
1-2	Step (left foot)	Slow
3-4	Step (right foot)	Slow
1	Step (left foot)	Quick
2	Step (right foot)	Quick

Double Lindy Basic

Count	Footwork	Cue
1	Dig (left toe)	Quick or toe
2	Step (left, heel drop)	Quick or heel
3	Dig (right toe)	Quick or toe
4	Step (right, heel drop)	Quick or heel
1	Ball (left, back)	Quick or back
2	Step (right foot)	Quick or step

Triple Lindy Basic

Count	Footwork	Cue
1	Step forward (left foot)	Quick or forward
&	Step (right foot) together to left foot; right foot takes the weight	Quick or together
2	Step forward (left foot)	Slow or forward
3	Step backward (right foot)	Quick or back
&	Step (left foot) together to right foot; left foot takes the weight	Quick or together
4	Step backward (right foot)	Slow or back

Rock Step

Count	Footwork	Cue
1	Step (left foot) slightly behind right heel	Quick
2	Step (right foot) in place	Quick

Dish Rag

The leader and follower join hands. The follower moves to the leader's left (her right). They turn back to back, arching, and return to face each other. To complete this sequence, execute a double lindy.

Turn under, or dish rag.

Arch Out (Semi-Open Position)

The leader does the foot pattern in place as the follower turns under his left arm. She ends facing him, still holding his hand.

Count	Footwork	Cue
1	Dig ball (left foot)	Dig

The leader places his left hand on the follower's waist; he raises his left hand above her and she turns under, facing him.

Count	Footwork	Cue
2	Step (left foot)	Turn or step

The follower pivots on her right foot going clockwise halfway around to face the leader.

Count	Footwork	Cue
3	Dig (right foot)	Dig

The leader and follower dig step (left foot) facing each other in place.

Count	Footwork	Cue
4	Step (right foot)	Step
1	Rock back (left foot)	Rock

Both partners rock back and away on left foot.

Count	Footwork	Cue
2	Rock front (right foot)	Rock

The leader touches his right hand to the follower's left shoulder blade to return her to the semi-open position.

Basic Turn

In the semi-open position, the couple turns clockwise. The leader steps on the left, pivoting a quarter turn on the ball of the foot, finishing the sequence to face a new direction.

Count	Footwork	Cue
1	Dig (ball of left foot)	Dig
2	Turn on the right foot	Turn
3	Dig (ball of left foot)	Dig
4	Step (right foot)	Step
1	Rock (ball of the left foot)	Rock
2	Step (right foot)	Step

Merengue

The merengue, the simplest of the Latin dances, is a Caribbean dance to energetic music. The Haitian style is smooth, whereas the Dominican Republic uses a limping motion. The dance is in 4/4 meter with couples using the closed and open dance positions.

MERENGUE STEP PROGRESSIONS

The merengue is a simple Latin dance. The steps move sideward, forward, and backward. If you step on the right foot, your hip releases to the left and vice versa.

Basic Side Step

Count	Footwork	Cue
1	Step side (left foot)	Quick or side

2	Step together (weight on right)	Quick or together
3	Step side (left foot)	Quick or side
4	Step together (weight on right)	Quick or together

Box Step

Count	Footwork	Cue
1	Step forward (left foot)	Quick or forward
2	Step together (weight on right)	Quick or together
3	Step backward (left foot)	Quick or back
4	Step together (weight on right)	Quick or together

Box Turn

Count	Footwork	Cue
1	Step one-quarter turn counterclockwise (left foot)	Quick or turn
2	Step together (weight on right)	Quick or together
3	Step backward (left foot)	Quick or back
4	Step together (weight on right)	Quick or together

Cross Step

This step begins in the closed position.

Count	Footwork	Cue
1	Step side (left foot), and turn to open position	Quick or side
2	Step forward (right foot), remaining in open position	Quick or forward
3	Step side (left foot), and turn to closed position	Quick or side
4	Step together (weight on right)	Quick or together

Ladder

Count	Footwork	Cue
1	Step side (left foot)	Quick or side
2	Step together (weight on right)	Quick or together
3	Step forward (left foot)	Quick or forward
4	Step together (weight on right)	Quick or together

Cha-Cha

The cha–cha, a combination of the Mambo and American swing, is an old Latin dance that originated in Cuba. It has a light and playful attitude. The cha–cha is danced in 4/4 time with the couples in closed position, face to face, and shine position.

CHA–CHA STEP PROGRESSIONS

The rhythm for the cha–cha is difficult because it crosses over measures.

Basic Footwork

Count	Cue
1	
2	Slow
3	Slow
4	Quick
&	Quick
1	Slow

Back Basic

Partners use either the two hands joined or the shine position. The back basic is used only at the beginning of a dance.

Count	Footwork	Cue
2	Step side (left foot)	Slow or side
3	Step back (right foot)	Slow or back
4	Step forward (left foot)	Quick or forward
	Together (right foot)	Quick or step
&	Step in place (left foot)	Quick or step
1	Step in place (right foot)	Slow or step

Shine position.

Forward Basic
The partners use either the two hands joined or the shine position.

Count	Footwork	Cue
2	Step forward (left foot)	Slow or forward
3	Step back (right foot)	Slow or back
4	Step in place (left foot)	Quick or step
&	Step in place (right foot)	Quick or step
1	Step in place (left foot)	Quick or step

Cross Over
The partners are in the side to side position.

Count	Footwork	Cue
1		
2	Step forward (left foot)	Slow or forward
3	Back to place (right foot)	Slow or place
4	Step in place (left foot), turn to face follower while releasing her right hand	Quick or turn
&	Step in place (right foot), continuing to turn while taking her left hand	Quick or step
1	Step in place (left foot), ending a half turn to face the opposite side, in side to side position	Slow or step

Return to Basic
The partners are in the side to side position. They face right and begin with the inside foot.

Count	Footwork	Cue
2	Step forward (left foot)	Slow or forward
3	Step back in place (right foot), and turn to face partner	Slow or turn
4	Step in place (left foot)	Quick or step
&	Step in place (right foot)	Quick or step
1	Step in place (left foot)	Quick or step

Take both hands off the follower while doing the "quick, quick, quick."

Cha–Cha Chase Half Turn
The leader does one turn ahead of the follower. He begins the turn while she does a basic cha–cha step. On the follower's next forward basic step, she does the turn. After he finishes the turn, he turns with a forward basic step. The follower finishes her last turn to face her partner. The dancers are in shine position.

Cha–cha chase.

Count	Leader's footwork	Cue
2	Step on the left, turning clockwise with both feet halfway around and his back to the follower. The leader looks back at the follower.	Slow
3	Weight is on the right foot	Slow
4 & 1	Step left, right, left in place	Quick, quick, slow
2	Step forward on right foot, turning counterclockwise a half turn, with both feet on the ground, facing the follower's back	Slow
3	Shift the weight on the right foot	Slow
4 & 1	Step left, right, left in place	Quick, quick, slow

Count	Follower's footwork	Cue
2	Step backward on the right	Slow
3	Step forward on the left in place	Slow
4 & 1	Step right, left, right in place	Quick, quick, slow
2	Step forward on the right while turning clockwise halfway around on both feet with her back to the leader	Slow
3	Step on the right foot	Slow
4 & 1	Step on left, right, left in place	Quick, quick, slow

Vocabulary

The vocabulary for social dance covers information about partners, positions, and leading and following rules.

Partners

Social dance is a form that depends on the interaction of two people. There is a subtle communication between these two people as partners. The man is responsible for establishing the rhythm, choosing the step performed, and deciding the direction and how to progress across the floor. As the follower, the woman follows the man's lead by the cues he gives her with his hands.

The social dancer is concerned with the following aspects:

- Footwork: length of step, foot placement, weight distribution
- Rhythm: rhythmic pattern (even and uneven) and meter (2/4, 3/4, and 4/4 time signatures)

Partner Positions

Closed position: See the folk dance unit, page 237.

Open position: See the folk dance unit, page 237.

Semi-open position: See the folk dance unit, page 237.

In the **shine position,** the couple faces each other. The dancers move apart; their elbows are close to the body and wrists move loosely with the fingertips facing the floor (see figure 13.6a).

Inside hands joined and **one hand holds** are terms that describe how partners hold hands. In social dance, the couple may face each other or may have their bodies side to side.

Two hands joined and **two hand holds** refer to couples that hold each other's hands, usually face to face, but may also have their arms in front, to the side, or behind each other (see figure 13.6b).

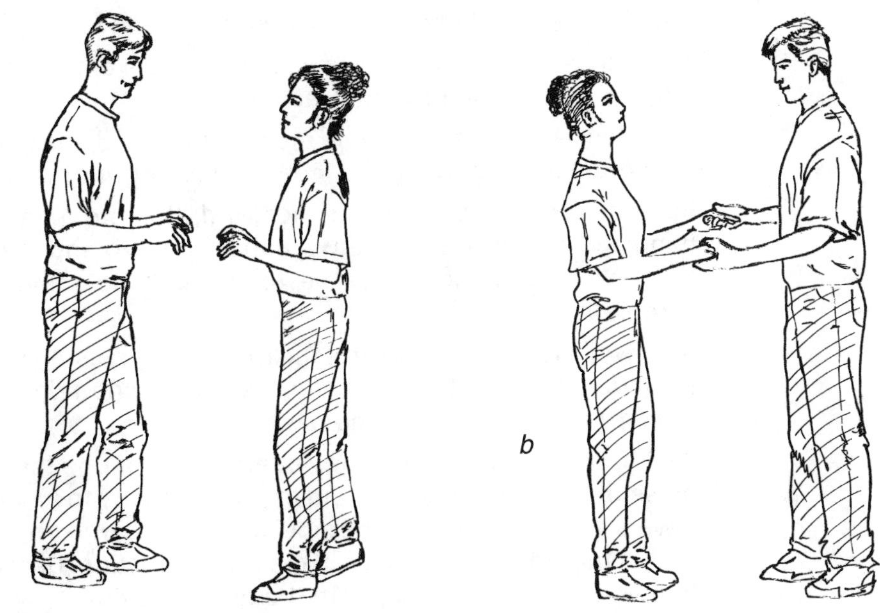

Figure 13.6 Partner positions: *(a)* shine position; *(b)* facing with two hands joined.

Leading and Following

In social dance, the man leads, and the woman follows. Many leads and follows exist; the ones described here are usually covered in beginning social dance.

The man is traditionally the **leader.** He is ready to move using his body as a unit. Having a partner position enables the other dancer to feel supported and confident. He has to know all the cues to lead in specific directions, positions, steps, and variations. Before a new step, the leader uses pressure to lead his partner. During the dance, he is attuned to musical tempo and styles.

- The body moves as a complete entity.
- The weight of the body is forward over the foot.
- The basic partner positions (closed position, semi-open, open) contribute to the support and security of the partner.

According to Harris, Pittman, and Waller (1999), the principles of leading are as follows: (1) Body and arm movements lead the couple in a particular direction, and hand pressure shows a change in position or direction; (2) abrupt body tension demonstrates or warns of various actions (hold, pivot, and dipping action). The following are general rules for the leader:

- Support the partner with confidence.
- Listen to the music.
- Move on the music.
- Begin a step with the left foot.
- Initiate the lead before the new step or direction.
- Start with simple steps and then add variation.

The following are specifics for leading:

- While starting with the first step, the man steps on the upbeat with the left foot with the body moving in a forward direction.
- Moving forward, the man leads the lady with a forward motion; with his right arm, he cues the lady in the correct direction.
- Moving backward, the man uses the pressure of the right hand, bringing the lady forward in the proper direction.
- In closed dance position while moving sideward, the man adds pressure with his right hand, signaling the lady to move right or left.
- In a box turn, his body moves forward, then he gives pressure to his right hand and elbow and pulls toward the right, moving into a forward combination. With a forward pressure to the left, he moves her in a backward combination.
- Also while leading a box turn, the man uses pressure with his right hand and shoulder to direct the turn. He pushes his shoulders forward as he steps forward and backward in the back step.
- To transfer to an open (conversation) position, the man leads with the pressure of the heel of his hand to pivot the lady to an open position. Then he lowers the right elbow to the side, and at the same time his entire body turns so that the lady and man face in the same direction. Reaching his hand slightly higher helps the lady step into the open position.

- When leading the lady into a closed position, the man adds a slight pressure with the right hand, elevating the right arm into the formal beginning position to move the lady to the closed position.
- If the man leads into the side-to-side (parallel) position, he lifts his right arm, turning his partner clockwise an eighth of a turn.
- In the right side-to-side position, the man pulls with the right hand and lowers his right arm. He gently pushes with the left hand, making a slight pivot about a quarter of a turn to his left.
- During a hesitation step, the man leads with a slight pressure of the right hand on the initial step with abrupt change of energy.
- Executing all turns, the man drops his shoulder in the direction he is turning. His upper torso turns before his legs and feet.

The lady is traditionally responsible for **following** her partner and adjusting to the rhythm and style of her dance partner. She maintains a light resistance throughout her body so that the man can easily direct her. The lady's hand keeps contact with the man's upper right shoulder, and she gives a little resistance against his outstretched hand. Here are the general rules for following:

- Stay in time with the man's rhythm.
- Be attentive to the man's lead, but don't anticipate.
- Be responsible for your own weight.
- Arch your back, respond, and move to the hand of your partner.
- Step backward in a straight path with your right foot and give yourself enough room to move in a straight path.
- Keep your feet close to your partner's feet.
- Know the leading cues to specific positions and directions.
- Know social dance steps and some variations.

Reference

Harris, J.A., A.M. Pittman, and M.S. Waller. 1999. *Dance a while: Handbook of folk, square, contra and social dances.* 7th ed. Minneapolis: Burgess.

Selected Resources

Selected resources include social dance texts, music, and videos.

Texts

Harris, J.A., A.M. Pittman, and M.S. Waller. 1999. *Dance a while: Handbook of folk, square, contra and social dances.* 7th ed. Minneapolis: Burgess.

Martin-Schield, M. 1985. *Social dance.* Dubuque, IA: Brown.

Quirey, B. 1997. *May I have the pleasure? The story of popular dance.* London: Dance Books.

Wright, J. 1996. *Social dance instruction: Steps to success.* Champaign, IL: Human Kinetics.

Wright, J. 2003. *Social dance: Steps to success. 2d ed.* Champaign, IL: Human Kinetics.

Music

Alabama. 1986. *Alabama's greatest hits.* New York: RCA Ariola International DCDI-7170.

Jones, W., and A. Hayashi-Jones. 1999. *Salsa.* Thousand Oaks, CA: Compass Music (Life Scape).

Lane, C. 1997. *Let's do ballroom.* Palm Springs: Let's Do It CL117-CD.

White, B. No date. *Betty White selects music strictly for your dancing and listening pleasure: 14 different dances.* Farmingville, NY: Conversa-phone CD-17561.

White, B. No date. *Betty White selects music strictly for your dancing pleasure: Latin dances.* Ronkokoma, NY: Conversa-phone CD 17556.

Wright, J. 1992. *Social dance music set (swing, waltz, cha–cha, fox trot, polka).* Champaign, IL: Human Kinetics.

Videos

Astaire, A. 1998. *Ballroom: The fox, the waltz.* Scottsdale, AZ: Teacher's Video.

Pozo, C. 1996. *Salsa merengue.* Scottsdale, AZ: Teacher's Video.

Pozo, C. 1999. *Learn to dance: The basic lessons.* Scottsdale, AZ: Teacher's Video.

Pozo, C. 1999. *Swing.* Scottsdale, AZ: Teacher's Video.

Regan, V., and D. DeVito. 1999. *You can dance: Cha-cha.* Scottsdale, AZ: Teacher's Video.

Regan, V., and D. DeVito. 1999. *You can dance: Foxtrot.* Scottsdale, AZ: Teacher's Video.

Regan, V., and D. DeVito. 1999. *You can dance: Mambo.* Scottsdale, AZ: Teacher's Video.

Regan, V., and D. DeVito. 1999. *You can dance: Swing.* Scottsdale, AZ: Teacher's Video.

Regan, V., and D. DeVito. 1999. *You can dance: Tango.* Scottsdale, AZ: Teacher's Video.

Regan, V., and D. DeVito. 1999. *You can dance: Waltz.* Scottsdale, AZ: Teacher's Video.

Teten, C. 1998. *Dancetime 500 years of social dance volume I: 15th century through 19th century.* Hightstown, NJ: Princeton.

Teten, C. 1998. *Dancetime 500 years of social dance volume II: 20th century.* Hightstown, NJ: Princeton.

Teten, C. 1999. *How to dance through time: The romantic of mid 19th century couple dances: Waltz, gallop, polka, mazurka.* Hightstown, NJ: Princeton.

Teten, C. 1999. *How to dance through time volume II: The dances of ragtime era 1910–1920.* Pennington, NJ: Princeton.

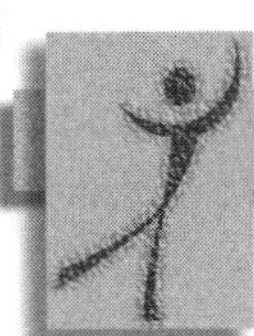

Ballet Dance Unit

Teaching Overview

Psychomotor Objectives

- Execute basic ballet exercises, steps, three or four step combinations, positions, and poses to music.
- Demonstrate the relationship of movement to music (counts, rhythm, tempo, time signature).
- Demonstrate application of movement principles to ballet.

Psychomotor Evaluation

- Performance test of selected ballet exercises, steps, positions, and poses in relation to music, with application of principles.

Cognitive Objectives

- Recognize beginning ballet terminology.
- Translate action words into beginning ballet vocabulary (French terminology).
- Conduct a self-evaluation or peer evaluation of a beginning ballet dance performance.
- Write a dance concert report about a ballet dance performance (technique, choreography, production).

Cognitive Evaluation

- Complete written test of beginning ballet knowledge (exercises, steps, positions, poses, terminology, definitions, history, self-assessment of performance).
- Translation of action words into French terminology or vice versa.
- Write a dance concert report about a ballet performance (technique, choreography, production).

Affective Objectives

- Practice the etiquette for dancers in the ballet class.
- Demonstrate movement confidence and performance attitude.
- Apply corrections to your performance.

Affective Evaluation

- Demonstrate etiquette, movement confidence, and performance attitude; apply corrections to performance.

Teaching Approaches

Ballet allows for many approaches to using the dance content. Following a predetermined syllabus originating from a school or method of teaching with periodic technical examinations enables the student to move from one level of study to the next. An eclectic syllabus drawn from several schools and methods provides a variety of experiences for students.

Specific Teaching Methods

As soon as the students can execute a barre exercise with competency, combine two, then three exercises, such as battement frappé and petit battement sur le cou-de-pied.

FORM 13.13

Scope and Sequence for Ballet

New = N Review = R Performance test = PT

	1	2	3	4	5	6	7	8	9	10	11	12	13	14	15
Definition and history, etiquette, sew tie and elastic on shoes	N														
Center point and flex feet	N		R												
Body alignment at floor and barre; weight distribution	N	R			PT										
Demi-plié, first and second position	N	R	R		PT		R	R							
Battement tendu, front and side	N	R			PT										
Arm positions and preparation	N														
Arm position and foot position preparation	N														
Ballet walks, révérence	N														
Point and flex à la seconde		N													
Demi-plié, third position		N	R				R	R							
Battement tendu, front, side, back		N	R		PT										
Petit battement piqué front, side foot presses		N	R												
Stretches on floor		N		R											
Port de bras, first and second		N													
Center, barre battement tendu		N	R	R											
Battement tendu en croix			N		PT										
Grand battement, front and side (floor)			N	R	PT										
Center, barre petit battement piqués			N	R											
Pas de bourrée			N												
Foot exercises (circling the feet)				N											
Battement dégagés (modified)				N	PT		R								
Rond de jambe à terre (modified)				N	PT										
Coupé at barre and center				N	PT										
Chassé (to side across floor)				N											

New = N   Review = R   Performance test = PT

	1	2	3	4	5	6	7	8	9	10	11	12	13	14	15
Balancé					N	N	R								
Chassé (to front across floor)					N	N									
Grand plié first, second, third position							N	R							
Battement tendu with demi-plié							N	R							
Battement tendu relevé							N								
Rond de jambe à terre (half and full)						N	R								
Rélevé first and second						N	R	R							
Grand battement back, front, side						N									
Retiré devant, derrière						N									
Center battement tendu en promenade						N									
Pas de chat						N									
Battement tendu with rélevé						N	N	R							
Battement dégagé (slow)						N	N								
Port de corps devant							N	R							
Sous-sus							N	R							
Passé en avant, en arrière							N								
At barre arabesque in first and second, en fondu							N								
Center classical body positions							N								
Pas de bourrée with coupé and rélevé							N								
One- and two-step combination							N								
Glissade							N								
Ballet walks with arabesques							N								
Demi-plié and grand position plié fifth								N							
Battement dégagé en cloche							N	N							

(continued)

FORM 13.13 *(continued)*

New = N Review = R Performance test = PT

	1	2	3	4	5	6	7	8	9	10	11	12	13	14	15
Port de corps derrière								N							
Sur le cou-de-pied front and back								N							
Battement frappé (modified)								N							
Grand battement en croix (one hand on barre)								N			R				
Center body positions add second part								N	R	PT					
One, two, and three-step combinations								R							
Demi-plié and grande plié sous-sus and balancé									N	R	R	R			
Combine battement dégagé en cloche									N		R	R			
Rond de jambe à terre with port de corps									N		R	R			
Battement frappé en croix								N			R	R			
Développé front, side, back								N			R				
Sauté (first and second)								N	R						
Adagio: arabesques first, second, third									N	PT	R				
Combination of previous step									N						
Leg swings										N					
Petit battement sur le cou-de-pied (at barre)										N			R		
Battement développé en croix										N		R			
Changement										N					
Petit allegro (3 steps)										R					
Assemblé										N					
Chassé, arabesque										N					
Grande jeté (run, run, grade jeté)										N					
Petit battement (one hand)										N					
Adagio battement développé en croix										N					

FORM 13.13

New = N Review = R Performance test = PT

	1	2	3	4	5	6	7	8	9	10	11	12	13	14	15
Pas de basque (Russian)											N				
Petit allegro three- and four-step combination											N				
Echappé sauté											N	R			
Changement and echappé sauté											N	R			
Barre exercises standard tempo												N			
Battement and petit battement												N			
Adagio: battement développé and arabesques												N			
Temps levé												N			
Piqué en avant												N			
Set barre exercise and steps for testing													R	R	PT

FORM 13.14

Ballet Block Time Plan

Class 1	Class 2	Class 3	Class 4	Class 5
• Rules and etiquette • Body alignment (on the floor) Barre (facing the barre) • Foot positions • Body placement (alignment, weight distribution) • Demi-plié (first and second positions) • Battement tendu (front and side) Center • Pointing the feet and flexing (sitting on the floor) • How to sew elastic on shoes and tie them • Arm positions and preparation • Stage directions • Ballet walks across the floor • Révérance	Barre • Body placement (alignment, weight distribution) • Preparation for barre exercises • Foot exercises: point and flex (side, or à la seconde) • Demi-pliés (first and second, third) • Battement tendus (combine 4 front, 4 front; 4 side, 4 side; teach back) • Petit battement piqués (front, front; side, side) • Foot exercises: press and pedals Center Stretching on the floor (body bends, knee to torso, point and flex with rotation (see Modern Dance) • Port de bras (first and second) • Center barre: battement tendu (4 to side; repeat other side; decrease number of repetitions)	Barre • Demi-pliés (first and second, third) • Battement tendus (en croix) and with demi-plié • Petit battement piqués (en croix and decreasing number of repetitions) Center • Grand battement (lying on the floor: front, side) • Center barre: battement tendu, petit battement piqués (en croix; combine both sides), foot exercises (presses and pedals) • Pas de bourrée (full foot)	Barre • Foot exercises: point and flex (side), circle the foot from ankle, presses and pedals • Battement dégagé (modified) • Rond de jambe à terre (front to side, close first position; back to side, close first position or with pointe tendue) • Coupé at the barre (third position) Center • Stretching on the floor • Grand battements (front, lying on the floor) • Port de bras Center barre: battement tendus (4 en croix, with demi-plié), foot exercises (presses and pedals and petit battement piqués) (4 en croix) • Coupé • Review pas de bourrée flat, add coupé • Chassé (to side across the floor)	Barre Assessment of barre exercises, foot positions, and understanding of principles. Center Center barre: Foot exercises (presses and pedals, battement tendus) (4 en croix both sides) and petit battement piqués (4 en croix) • Coupés • Pas de bourrée (full foot) • Balancé • Chassé (to front across the floor)

FORM 13.14

Class 6	Class 7	Class 8	Class 9	Class 10
Barre • Grand pliés (first and second, third) • Combine battement tendu with demi-plié • Battement tendu relevé (without demi-plié) • Battement dégagé (modified) • Rond de jambe à terre (half circles with pointe tendue) en dehors and en dedans • Relevé (first and second position) • Grand battement (stand facing barre: back, back; then with back to the barre: front, front; side, side) • Retiré devant and derrière Center • Battement tendu en promenade en avant, en arrière • Balancé • Pas de chat	Barre • Combine demi-pliés and grand pliés (first, second, third) • Battement tendu relevé (with demi-plié) • Battement dégagé (slow) • Rond de jambe à terre en dehors and en dedans (slow) • Port de corps (devant) • Relevés (first, second; extend balances) • Sous-sus • Passe (en arrière and en avant, full foot) • Arabesque positions (1, 2, 3, facing the barre) • Arabesque fondu Center • Classical body positions (see part 1)* • One- and two-step combinations of previous steps • Pas de bourrée (with coupé and en relevé) • Glissade • Ballet walks combined with arabesque	Barre Some exercises facing the barre • Demi-pliés and grand pliés (first, second, fifth), add relevé, balances • Combine two: battement tendus with and without demi-plié and battement tendu relevé with and without demi-plié • Battement dégagé en cloche • Port de corps (devant and derrière) • Sur le cou-de-pied position (front and back) • Battement frappé (modified) • Combine relevés and sous-sus; balances • Grand battements en croix (one hand on the barre) Center • Classical body positions (part 1 review and add part 2)* • One- and two-step combinations of previous steps	Barre • Demi-pliés and grand pliés (first, second, fifth) with relevé, sous-sus, and balances • Combine battement dégagé and battement dégagé en cloche • Rond de jambe à terre en dehors and en dedans with port de corps, sous-sus balance • Battlement frappé (slow, en croix) • Développé (front, side, back) • Sauté (first, second positions facing the barre) Center • Practice classical body positions, both sides combined* • Arabesques 1, 2, 3 (combine into an adagio) • Two-step combinations of previous steps: pas de bourrée (with relevé), balancé (with arms), pas de chat, glissade, jeté devant, chassé (side or forward) • Sautés (first and second positions) • Temps levé	Barre • Leg swings • Demi-pliés and grand pliés (first and second, fifth) with port de corps devant and derrière and relevé, sous-sus and balances • Petit battement sur le cou-de-pied (facing the barre) • Battement développé (en croix) • Changement Center • Performance assessment of classical body positions* or selected allegro combinations • Arabesque adagio (first, second, third à terre or en l'air; in combination) • Petit allegro combinations: three steps • Assemblé • Grand Allegro • Chassé, arabesque, sauté • Grand jeté (run, run, grand jeté) • Changements

(continued)

FORM 13.14 *(continued)*

Class 11	Class 12	Class 13	Class 14	Class 15
Barre • Petit battement sur le cou-de-pied (one hand on the barre) • Grand battements en croix (decreasing number of repetitions) Center • Adagio: three arabesques or battement développés en croix • Pas de basque (Russian) petit allegro combinations: three to four steps • Three-step turn • Combine: chassé, arabesque, sauté; repeat other side; run, run, grand jeté; repeat other side • Echappé sauté • Combine changements and échappé sautes	Barre Standard musical tempo for exercises • Combine battement frappé and petit battement sur le cou-de-pied Center • Adagio: battement développés or arabesques • Sauté combinations: changements, échappé sautés, temps levé • Petit allegro combinations • Grand allegro combinations • Piqué en avant	• Set barre and center combinations for performance testing	• Practice set barre and center combinations	• Execute set barre and center combinations for performance test

* *Note:* Teaching the classical body position is an option for a unit of this length.

Part 1: croisé devant, à la quatrième devant, écarté, éffacé, battement tendu à la seconde close fifth front, first port de bras.

Part 2: à la seconde, épaule, à la quatrième derrière, croisé derrière, first port de bras; combine both parts.

This unit is designed for a 50-minute class.

After exploring directional patterns, decrease the number of repetitions of the exercise in each direction. Later practice exercises with level changes (e.g., relevés and fondus). Beginning ballet students should execute exercises and steps at no higher than 45 degrees off the floor to control turnout, alignment, and balance.

Musical Accompaniment

The most common time signatures used in the beginning ballet class are 4/4, 2/4, 3/4, and 6/8. The tempos in the ballet class range from adagio (slow) to allegro (fast) with exercises performed at a slower-than-standard tempo. Petit allegro steps and combinations are often performed in cut time. Cut time refers to performing an exercise or step during a single measure rather than in standard time when a step is generally performed during one count of the measure.

Dance Class Format

The ballet class format has two main sections: the barre and the center. The first part of the class is performed at the barre, which is a railing made of wood or metal and attached to the wall or standing freely as a portable unit. The barre is also the series of exercises the dancer uses to warm up the body and acquire acuity in performing.

The barre exercises and center steps listed in the vocabulary section of the sample unit plan are in the order they are performed at the barre or in the center, not the order in which they are learned. For further information on teaching progressions, see *Teaching Beginning Ballet Technique* (Kassing and Jay 1998). All ballet exercises, steps, positions, and poses use turned-out classical positions of the feet. The beginning ballet student learns the barre exercises facing the barre and with both hands placed on the barre. Later the student performs the exercises with one hand on the barre.

In the beginning ballet class, barre exercises take up the majority of the class time until students learn center steps. Students often return to the barre to learn and practice new steps before attempting them in the center and as part of combinations.

Classroom Considerations

Most concert dance forms have a definite arrangement of the students in class. Everyone must have enough space to move safely. Attire reflects the standard in the field. Classroom etiquette is formal, courteous, and structured.

Safety

Students must have enough space to perform exercises at the barre and combinations in the center and across the floor. The room should be well ventilated and the floor should not be too slippery.

Attire

Dancers in the ballet class wear tight-fitting attire so that the teacher can see the dancers' body lines to make corrections. For female students in the ballet class, traditional attire is tights and a leotard or unitard (a full body suit). Hair should be secured away from the face and neck, and jewelry should be minimal. Male students wear a tight-fitting T-shirt or leotard and tights or unitard. They also wear a dance belt (similar to an athletic supporter) and either a belt or suspenders. More casual clothing, usually for men, is often allowed to make them feel comfortable in the ballet class.

Students wear ballet shoes, which may be canvas or leather; they must fit the feet snugly. Elastic bands, sewn securely (across the instep), secure the shoes. Strings are tied and tucked inside the shoe. Ballet shoes should be worn only inside the dance studio or the performance space so that the soles remain clean.

Classroom Etiquette

When students arrive, they should quietly go to their places at the barre before the beginning of class. If students arrive after the class starts its exercises, you, the teacher, will determine whether the students will join the class. As in any concert dance class, if students arrive late, they must ask your permission to join the class.

During center work, students follow a set pattern for rotating lines. Students who are in the front half of the class separate, move to the sides, and take their places in the back half of the dance class. At the same time, students in the back half of the class walk forward quickly to take their places in the front of the class.

For skills that travel across the floor, students watch their spacing as they move in groups of two, three, or four. Before starting a combination, each group allows adequate time after the previous group, but not so much time that it slows down the class.

The teacher leads the students in a révérence at the end of class, then students applaud the teacher and the musician. In short classes, the traditional reverence is practiced only occasionally.

Beyond Technique Assignments

The following are some suggestions for beyond technique assignments in ballet:

- Perform an alignment self-check before beginning each barre exercise.
- View a performance of a ballet on video and identify steps performed. Write a dance video report about the ballet. Include historical information and describe the choreography and the production.
- Near the end of the unit, practice center combinations. Find a partner and participate in reciprocal teaching: One person performs the combination while the other watches. After the performance engage in dialogue about how the performer might improve his performance; then reverse roles.

Content Overview

The content overview provides the necessary information for teaching the ballet unit.

Definition and History

Ballet has had many different meanings throughout its evolution. This dance form emanated from the court dances performed in various dramatic and musical entertainments produced by Louis XIV of France in the 17th century. Louis XIV was a dancer who elevated ballet from a court amusement to an art; he also established the Academy of Dance to train professional dancers. During the 18th century, ballet moved from the courts into the theater. Male danseurs such as Vestris and the Gardel Brothers dominated this century, and female innovators like Camargo and Sallé made an impression on the art. At the beginning of the century, ballets focused on mythological characters and themes; during the latter part of the century ballets contained more humanistic characters that used both dancing and pantomimes to tell the stories. These *ballets d'action* established the elements of dramatic ballet.

Ballet became an established theatrical dance form by the 19th century. It gained new popularity in the romantic era with the rise of ethereal, sylphlike female dancers poised on the tips of their toes. These female dancers (such as Marie Taglioni, Carlotta Grisi, Fanny Elssler) became the stars of the 19th century, while men continued to direct and choreograph. At the end of the century, the classical era of ballet ushered in entire evenings of story ballets. The female dancers dominated the ballets with their technique and pointe work. Male choreographers created the ballets that have become classics *(Swan Lake, Sleeping Beauty, Nutcracker).*

The 20th century was rich with diverse ballets and choreography that have spanned the world. Choreographers diversified ballet by moving to one-act ballets, abstract ballets, and ballets on contemporary themes. Dancers extended the limits of technique and styles. These experiments led to an amalgamated form: modern ballet that attracted movements and styles from modern dance and other dance forms. Modern ballet is as unique as the choreographer's point of view.

Special Features

The following are specific features of ballet:

- Ballet is a codified, classical dance form with a distinct vocabulary of specific exercises, steps, positions, and poses that have been adopted into or merged with other dance forms.
- The foremost feature of ballet is turnout, the outward rotation of the legs from the hip joints.
- The vocabulary of ballet is expressed in the French language.
- The quality of ballet is to defy gravity with large jumps and turns in the air, to create movements and poses that extend the body's lines, and to move effortlessly to present a quality of supreme control of movement in relation to the music and the role portrayed.

Principles

Movement, choreographic, and aesthetic principles that specifically apply to ballet are shown in the shaded regions of the following icons.

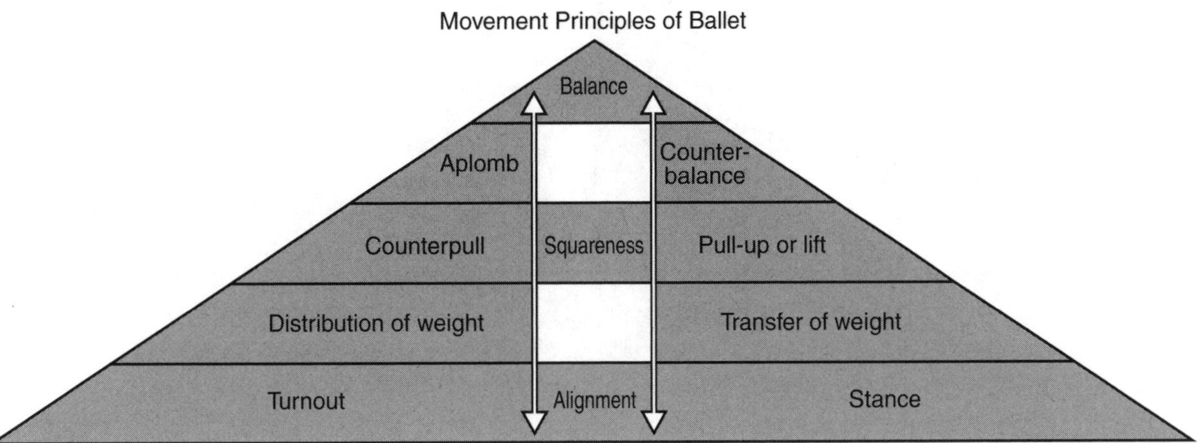

Choreographic Principles of Ballet

Choreographic elements	Choreographic structures	Choreographic designs	Choreographic devices	Choreographic relationships
Motif Phrase Theme and variation	Simple musical forms • AB (binary) • ABA (ternary) • Rondo • Theme and variation Contrapuntal forms • Canon (round) • Fugue Others • Narrative (story) • Open (free)	Dancer's body shape Dancer's pathway through space Visual design • Symmetrical • Asymmetrical Symbolism • Representational • Abstraction • Distortion Relationship • Unison • Sequential • Successional • Oppositional • Complementary	Repetition Reverse Alter • Addition or subtraction • Directional change • Facing or focus • Level • Dimension • Tempo • Rhythm • Quality or effort action • Positioning • Movement section	Solo Duet Trio Quartet Small and large groups

Traditional Dance Elements

Space	Time	Force	Relationships
Directions Dimensions Levels Shapes Pathways Focus	Duration Tempo	Movement qualities • Sustained • Percussive • Swinging • Suspended • Collapsing • Vibratory	Among body parts Among people Between people and props

Laban's Dance Elements

Space	Time	Weight	Flow
Direct or indirect	Sudden or slow	Light or strong	Bound or free

Effort actions (use space, time, and weight)

• Dab • Flick • Punch • Slash • Glide • Float • Press • Wring

Aesthetic Principles of Ballet

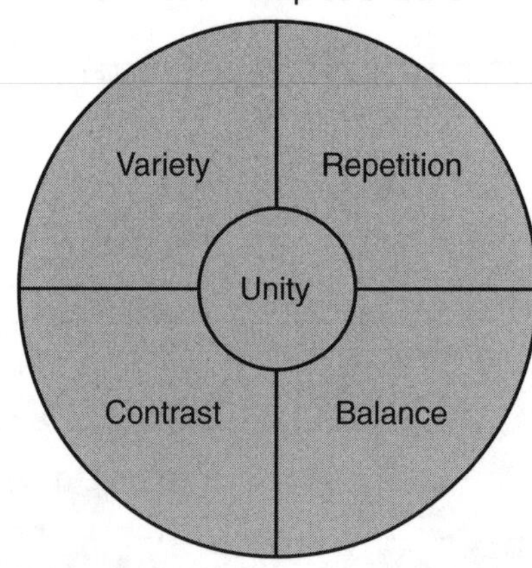

Vocabulary

Ballet shares its vocabulary with other concert dance forms. If you need help learning the ballet pronunciations, refer to *Interactive Beginning Ballet Technique* (Kassing 1999), *Teaching Beginning Ballet Technique* (Kassing and Jay 1998), or another ballet dictionary. (See the "Selected Resources" section at the end of this unit.)

Ballet Positions

Basic positions of the feet are **first, second, third, fourth, fifth,** and **B+** (attitude derrière à terre). In first position, heels are together with legs rotating outward from 90 to 100 degrees. Weight is distributed equally on both feet. In second position, legs are turned out and feet are separated approximately shoulder-width apart. Weight is equally distributed with great toes on a straight line parallel to the front of the body. In third position, legs are turned out with the front foot crossing to the middle of the back foot. Weight is equally distributed on both feet. In fourth position, legs are turned out with one foot in front of the other the length of one foot forward. For the beginning dancer, the fourth position is either forward from first position or third position. The weight is equally distributed, and the hips and shoulders are square. In fifth position, legs are turned out with one foot in front of the other, with the insides of the feet touching. The feet cross with the heel of the front foot to the joint of the great toe of the back foot (Cecchetti), or the heel of the front foot crosses to the tip of the great toe of the back foot (Russian). In either position, weight is equally distributed (Kassing and Jay 1998). In B+ (attitude derrière à terre), the dancer's supporting and working legs are well turned out. Standing on one leg, the dancer bends the other leg at the knee with the foot pointed and the tip of the great toe touching the floor behind the ankle. Female dancers keep the upper legs together. Male dancers separate the legs, with the heel of the working foot touching the back of the ankle of the supporting foot.

Active foot positions are **sur le cou-de-pied, coupé,** and **retiré devant** and **derrière.** See the definitions for these terms in the "Barre Exercises" section of the Vocabulary, pages 310-313.

First and second feet and arm positions.

Third and fifth feet and arm positions.

Fourth feet and arm positions.

Basic arm positions are **preparatory position, first, second, third, fourth,** and **fifth.** Variations are **fourth position en avant** and **demi-seconde.**

Port de bras means the position of the arms. There are first and second port de bras. (See definitions for these terms in the "Center" section of the Vocabulary, page 313.)

Prebarre Exercises

Prebarre exercises warm up the hips, knees and ankles, back, legs, and feet. Foot exercises are point, flex, presses, and pedals.

Barre Exercises

Preparation at the barre is an introduction to exercises and steps. Using port de bras includes change of arm positions and often foot positions, depending on the exercise.

Demi-plié in first, second, third, and fifth positions is a half bend of the legs with both feet remaining on the floor.

Grand plié in first, second, third, and fifth positions is a complete bend of the legs with the heels releasing off the floor after the demi-plié. The grand plié continues down until the thighs are parallel to the floor. On the ascent, the heels return to the floor and the legs straighten. The exception to this is second position grand plié, in which the feet remain in the full-foot position throughout the plié.

The following barre exercises are performed in the following directions: front, to the second (often referred to as *side*), and back. These directions are incorporated into patterns such as **en croix** (in the shape of a cross: front, side, back, and side; or other patterns such as front, back, side, side). The number of repetitions of an exercise decreases from 4 to 2 to 1 as a dancer gains the ability to change directions.

In **battement tendu** from any of the starting positions (first, third, or fifth), the working foot slides from full foot and extends through to a pointed position with the toes remaining on the floor in front, side, or back. From the pointed position, the working foot returns through the foot closing in the starting position. In the tendu to the front, the heel leads the movement so that the foot remains turned out. The toes lead as the foot returns to closed position.

À la seconde, à la quatrième devant, à la quatrième derrière.

Battement tendu with demi-plié is the same exercise as the battement tendu, except when closing into the starting position, both legs are in demi-plié.

In **battement tendu relevé** from fifth position, slide the working foot from full foot, releasing through the foot to a pointed position in front, side, or back. Press the working foot from the toes through to full foot into either fourth or second position. On the return, the working foot stretches to the pointed position, and then slides to the full-foot position to close in the starting position. This exercise is performed in all directions and may be executed with demi-plié on both legs during the press of the working foot into either fourth or second position or at the completion of the exercise. The relevé refers to the extension of the working foot from full-foot to pointed position.

Battement dégagé begins in first, third, or fifth. Slide the working foot from full foot through a pointed position, extending the foot barely off the floor. For the return, the pointed foot touches the floor and slides back to the full-foot position, closing in the starting position. This step is done in all directions.

Battement dégagé en cloche begins in first position or pointe tendu either à la quatrième devant or derrière. Brush the working foot front to back or back to front through first position up to 45 degrees from the floor.

Rond de jambe à terre literally means "round the leg on the ground." From first position, the working foot tendus either to the front or the back. The working foot traces a half-circle on the floor and then brushes to full foot in first position. The rond de jambe à terre is performed eight times, decreasing to four times in both directions: **en dehors** and **en dedans.** En dehors (outward, away from the supporting foot) starts in the front, circling to the back and through first position. En dedans (inward, toward the supporting foot) starts at the back, circling to the front and through first position.

The **port de corps devant** (front), which is a carriage of the body, can be performed forward in two ways: through the hinge position in which the back bends forward at a right angle to the legs, or rolling down and up the spine.

Stand in an aligned position and stretch the body upward and bend forward from the hips through the hinge position (a 90-degree angle of the back to the legs). The back elongates, stretching toward the floor; the legs remain perpendicular to the floor. On the return, the head and back stretch outward and upward, returning to the aligned position; the legs remain perpendicular to the floor. The arm away from the barre complements the bending and straightening actions.

To roll down and up, stand in an aligned position and allow the head to bend forward and continue through the vertebra to the hips. On the return to alignment, begin with the lower spine and retrace the path with the head being the last to return to the vertically aligned position. The arm away from the barre complements the bending and straightening actions.

The **port de corps derrière** (back) begins with stretching on the vertical alignment and beginning the bend backward with the head, through the spine, to the waist. The head initiates the return, retracing the path to the vertically aligned position. The arm away from the barre is usually in fifth position **en haut** (raised above the head). The head may be in either a neutral position facing forward or turned toward the center of the room.

Battement frappé starts with the working foot in the sur le cou-de-pied position (see next exercise). The toes and ball of the foot strike the floor, stretching the foot to a pointed position off the floor and straightening the leg. This is performed in all directions.

Petit battement sur le cou-de-pied starts with the working foot in the sur le cou-de-pied position, which is at the ankle of the supporting foot. The working leg and foot trace an acute angle from in front of the ankle (devant) out to second position, ending behind the ankle (derrière); then it reverses the direction. For the beginning student, this exercise is most beneficial if the toes and ball of the foot maintain contact with the floor and the working leg remains well turned out.

Retiré is an active foot position in which the little toe of the working foot is under the front of the knee or the heel touches behind the back of the knee. In some schools, this position is under the front of, behind, or at the side of the knee. The ability to perform this position with the hips level while maintaining balance on the supporting foot forms the foundation for performing battement développé, arabesques, and other movements.

The **passé** begins in either third or fifth position and moves up the leg to either the coupé or retiré position devant or derrière and then down the opposite side of the leg. When the passé is performed at the level of coupé devant or derrière, it is called low passé.

The **coupé** position is the approximate midpoint of the lower leg, in front of or just under the calf muscle. This position is a petit allegro step and is part of other petit allegro steps.

In **battement développé** starting in fifth position, the working leg moves from full foot to a pointed position through the sur le cou-de-pied position upward along the leg, first to coupé and later retiré. The working foot directs the unfolding of the lower leg to front, side, or back while the thigh supports and maintains the height of the leg. For the beginner, battement développé is executed at 45 degrees, so the working leg raises to coupé.

Grand battement is first performed in devant and seconde while lying on the floor or in devant, seconde, or derrière while standing at the barre. At the barre, standing in alignment, face away from the barre and stretch the arms along the barre for devant and side; face the barre for derrière. From first, third, or fifth positions, brush the working leg and pointed foot into the air to approximately 45 degrees. On the return path, the leg stretches back to pointe tendue and then brushes through the foot, closing in the beginning position.

For **relevé,** stand in first, second, and then fifth position. Demi-plié, then straighten the knees and rise up on the balls of the feet to three-quarter relevé. On the return, stretch to the full-foot position on the floor and into the demi-plié. A number of relevés, usually four to eight, are practiced. Often the sequence ends with a balance en relevé and the arms extending either to second or fifth en haut position.

Sous-sus is a specific relevé in fifth position. Demi-plié and spring to three-quarter relevé. During the sous-sus, the feet either spring or pull together on three-quarter relevé; both legs straighten and one foot crosses in front of the other in fifth position. The springing movement centers the legs under the body.

Center

Center work is the second part of the ballet class. The barre exercises become the components of steps performed in the center. This section of the class includes center practice of barre exercises, port de bras, and new steps and combinations.

Port de Bras

The corners and walls of the dance studio are numbered as **stage directions.** There are two different methods of using stage directions: Cecchetti and Russian (see figure 13.7, a–b).

In the center, the dancer stands in third or fifth position facing a stage direction and executes a **preparation** or port de bras to introduce the combination.

The most often used **port de bras** at the beginning level are first port de bras and second port de bras. **First port de bras** begins with the arms in the preparatory position. Raise the arms to first position, then open to second position. Then return the arms to the preparatory position. **Second port de bras** begins with the arms in the preparatory position. Raise the arms through first position to fifth position en haut. Open and rotate the arms to second position, and close in the preparatory position.

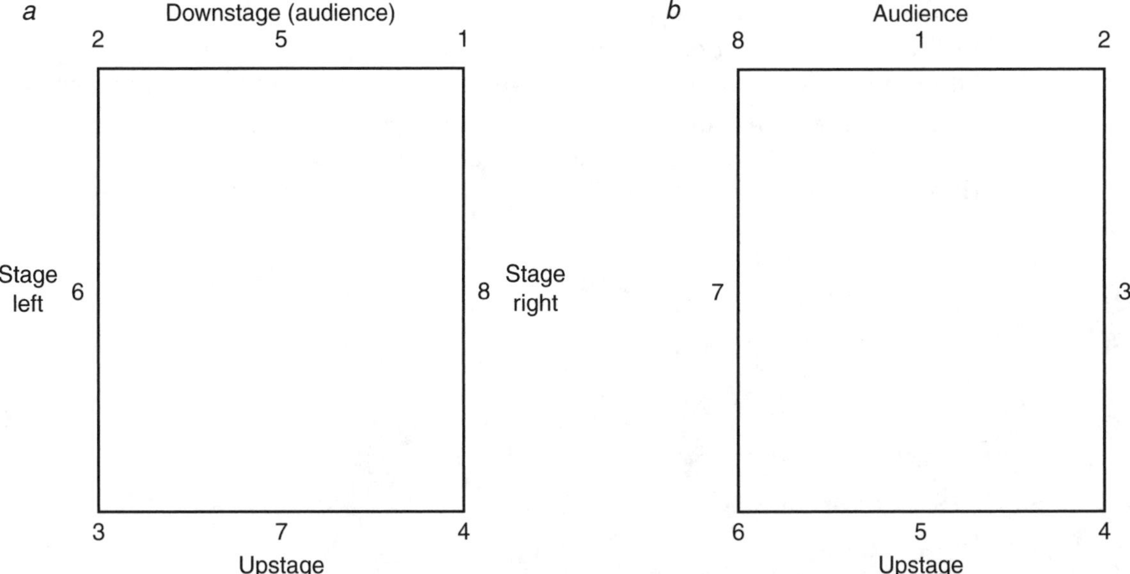

Figure 13.7 Stage directions. *(a)* Cecchetti stage directions. Direction 1: right front corner or downstage right; direction 2: left front corner or downstage left; direction 3: left back corner or upstage left; direction 4: right back corner or upstage right; direction 5: front *(en face),* or facing the audience; direction 6: left wall (or *stage left*); direction 7: back wall (or *upstage*); direction 8: right wall (or *stage right*). *(b)* Russian stage directions.

The traditional structure of the center includes center practice, adagio, preparation for pirouettes, sautés (jumps), petit allegro, and grand allegro steps.

Center Practice

This is a short section of the center work in which students repeat barre exercises, such as battement tendus, battement dégagés, and grand battements.

Battement tendu en croix is a series of battement tendus in the shape of a cross: front (devant); to the seconde, or side (à la seconde); back (derrière); and to the seconde, or side (à la seconde).

Battement tendu en promenade is a series of battement tendus à la seconde, alternating legs. The dancer walks either backward (en promenade en arrière) by closing the working foot in third or fifth position back (derrière), or forward (en promenade en avant) by closing the working foot in third or fifth position front (devant).

Passé en promenade is a series of passés moving in the same pattern as battement tendu en promenade, either backward (en arrière) or forward (en avant).

Adagio

Adagio is a slow, fluid, continuous movement to slow music. Exercises, steps, and poses learned at the barre are then practiced in the center. For the beginning ballet student, the amount of steps performed en l'air (in the air) and on the ground (à terre) is balanced so that the dancer can gain strength. The beginning dancer should not spend more than 8 counts on one leg.

Battement développé front (devant); second (à la seconde); back (derrière); or en croix. (See definition under "Barre Exercises" on page 312.)

Poses in the center are **arabesques** in first, second, and third. They are done separately or together in combination.

For **first arabesque,** stand on the supporting leg (right) in profile to the audience, with the working leg extended behind the body. The body is square and counterbalanced. The right arm extends forward at the height of the forehead; the head points forward with the eyes gazing over the fingertips. The left arm opens out and back of second position. The arms create complementary lines to the extended leg. Variations of first arabesque have slight differences in arm height and placement.

In **second arabesque**, stand on the supporting leg (right), with the left leg extended behind the body. The left arm stretches forward at forehead height; the right arm stretches behind the body. The head tilts to the left with the eyes gazing

First, second, and third arabesques.

Croisé devant (left) and effacé devant (right).

over the fingertips. The arms create complementary lines to the extended leg. Second arabesque may be performed either in profile or to a corner.

In **third arabesque,** stand on the supporting leg (right), with the left leg extended behind the body. Both arms stretch forward; the downstage arm is at shoulder height; the upstage arm is at forehead height. The head focuses between the arms. The arms create a window through which the dancer gazes. Third arabesque may be performed either in profile or to a corner.

Classical body positions are **croisé devant, à la quatrième devant, écarté devant, effacé devant, à la seconde, épaulé, à la quatrième derrière, croisé derrière.** Progressions use the shortened version (**croisé devant, à la quatrième devant, effacé devant, à la seconde, close fifth derrière, first port de bras**; then perform other side) or complete version of all eight classical body positions performed on one side and then both sides. (See photo for examples of croisé devant and effacé devant.) For descriptions of these positions, refer to *Teaching Beginning Ballet Technique* (Kassing and Jay 1998).

Preparation for Pirouettes

Beginning dancers are limited in their ability to perform spinning and turning movements. Students should study and practice the components of the pirouette to refine them.

A **three-step turn (gavotte turn)** is often introduced near the end of the unit. Starting pointe tendue devant with right foot, step to the side en relevé on right foot, do a half turn; step on left foot en relevé and complete the turn, ending facing the front. Step full foot to the side with the right foot, pointe tendue devant with the left foot. The three-step turn alternates to the other side.

Introduction and Transition Steps

Walks, pas de bourrée, and glissade serve as introductions to the adagio steps and poses as well as transitions in both petit and grand allegro combinations.

For **ballet walks,** begin in classical alignment with legs turned out. Walk with the feet pointing and going to full foot beginning with the toe and moving through the heel.

Begin **pas de bourrée** in fifth position with right foot in front. Put left foot in coupé derrière, step left foot en relevé behind right foot, step right foot into first position en relevé, step left foot full foot, with the right foot either returning to front full foot behind or in coupé derrière to begin the pas de bourrée to the other side.

Chassé means to chase. Begin in fifth position with the right foot in front. Demi-plié and slide the front foot to either fourth position front or second position. The other leg pushes the body into the air where both legs and feet extend in a crossed position. Land on the right foot first, then resume fifth position demi-plié.

Begin **glissade** in fifth position with the right foot in front. Demi-plié and dégagé the right leg à la seconde just above the floor. Then immediately push off with left foot so that both legs and feet extend in the air. Land on right foot and quickly slide left foot into the fifth position demi-plié.

Begin **pas de basque** in fifth position facing a corner. Brush the front foot to pointe tendue in second position. While changing direction to the other corner, transfer the weight to the pointed foot, extending the other leg and foot in pointe tendue. Pass through first position. (The arms begin in the preparatory position and pass through a first port de bras and end in second position.) Then slide into fourth position croisé devant (the opposite arm moves from second position through the preparatory position to end third position), with the back foot pointe tendue and close before performing it to the other side.

Sautés (Jumps)

Beginning dancers study and practice basic jumping techniques and jumps first at the barre, then in the center. Each step is executed repeatedly up to eight times; the repetitions are later decreased and two steps may be combined. Sautés can be performed either before the allegro or after the grand allegro section.

From **first position,** jump with both legs from demi-plié to full extension of legs and feet in the air. End in first position. This is usually repeated four to eight times.

From **second position,** jump with both legs from demi-plié to full extension of legs and feet in the air. End in second position. This is usually repeated four to eight times.

From **fifth position,** jump with both legs from demi-plié to full extension of legs and feet in the air. End in fifth position. This is usually repeated four to eight times.

Changement begins in fifth position with right foot in front. Jump with both legs from demi-plié to full extension of legs and feet in the air. The legs change position at the top of the jump and land with the left foot in front in fifth position. The first objective is to extend the legs in first position. Next, extend the legs and keep them in fifth position in the air until they change positions.

A **coupé** is to leap from one leg to the other with the working foot touching the middle of the lower leg either in front or back.

In **temps levé** in fifth position, hop on one foot with the other foot in the coupé position either in front or back.

For **echappé sauté** in fifth position, jump from both legs into second position demi-plié; jump from second position and close in fifth position with the other foot in front.

Petit Allegro

Petit allegro steps are quick, small, and light with ballon (bounce). The beginning ballet dancer generally executes a series of each step to gain technique before combining the step into a combination. Combinations for beginning ballet involve one, two, and three steps. The allegro steps for the beginning dancer include introductory and transitional steps that will link allegro steps into combinations later.

Pas de chat means step of the cat. Start in fifth position with the left foot in front. Demi-plié, lift the right foot to coupé derrière, and spring upward and to the side while lifting the left foot to coupé devant at the same height as the right foot. The left foot closes quickly into fifth position devant. Arms are usually held in fourth position en avant.

Jeté starts in fifth position with the left foot in front. Demi-plié and dégagé the right foot à la seconde. The left leg, in demi-plié, pushes into the air, extending the leg and foot toward the floor. At the top of the air moment, both legs and feet are extended. Land on the right leg with the left foot in coupé derrière. The second jeté begins by brushing the left foot through fifth position demi-plié to dégagé à la seconde. This step alternates from side to side; jeté may be performed as a series of eight or four en promenade, en avant (forward), and en arrière (backward), or combined into petit allegro combinations.

For **assemblé,** start in fifth position with the left foot in front. Demi-plié and dégagé the right foot à la seconde. The left leg, in demi-plié, pushes into the air, extending the leg and foot toward the floor. At the top of the air moment, both legs and feet are extended. Both feet land in fifth position demi-plié with the right foot in front. This step may alternate from side to side, be performed as a series of eight or four en promenade, or combined into petit allegro combinations.

Grand Allegro

Grand allegro steps are large jumps with extended moments in the air. The beginning dancer studies the grand jeté (leap) combined with transitional steps such as running or introductory steps such as the arabesque sauté.

For **grand jeté,** start in B+ position with the right leg in back. Brush the right leg into a grand battement devant, push off the left leg, and extend it while moving forward in the air. Land on the right leg in demi-plié. The back counterbalances and the back leg continues to extend and stretch. The arms move in opposition to the legs. If the grand jeté is initiated with the right leg, then the left arm is forward and remains there until the end of the step. Runs are a good approach to grand jetés for the beginning dancer.

Révérence is the traditional bow performed by male dancers and curtsy by female dancers at the end of the class, followed by applause for the teacher and the musician for dance.

References

Kassing, G. 1999. *Interactive beginning ballet technique* (CD-ROM). Champaign, IL: Human Kinetics.

Kassing, G., and D. Jay. 1998. *Teaching beginning ballet technique.* Champaign, IL: Human Kinetics.

Selected Resources

Selected resources include ballet dance texts, music, and videos.

Texts

Grant, G. 1982. *Technical manual and dictionary of classical ballet.* 3rd ed. New York: Dover.

Grieg, V. 1994. *Inside ballet technique: Separating anatomical fact from fiction in the ballet class.* Pennington, NJ: A Dance Horizon.

Hammond, S. 1993. *Ballet basics.* 3rd ed. Mountain View, CA: Mayfield.

Kassing, G., and D. Jay. 1998. *Teaching beginning ballet technique.* Champaign, IL: Human Kinetics.

Lawson, J. 1979. *Teaching young dancers muscular coordination in classical ballet.* New York: Theatre Arts Books.

Lawson, J. 1984. *Ballet class: Principles and practice.* New York: Theatre Arts Books.

Lawson, J., A. Dowell, and A. Crichamay. 1980. *The principles of classical dance.* New York: Alfred A. Knopf.

Paskevska, A. 1981. *Both sides of the mirror: The science and art of ballet.* 2nd ed. Pennington, NJ: Princeton.

Warren, G. 1989. *Classical ballet technique.* Tampa, FL: University of South Florida Press.

Warren, G. 1996. *The art of teaching ballet: Ten twentieth-century masters.* Gainesville, FL: University Press of Florida.

Music

Boudewyns, D. 1999. *Beautiful music for ballet class.* Chicago: Sky's the Limit.

Howard, D. 1992. *Classics for kids.* Dallas: Bodarc Productions.

Howard, D. 1993. *Ballet music with David Howard.* L.I.C., NY: Roper Records.

Howard, D. 1995. *Ballet music for barre and center: Elementary, intermediate & advanced.* L.I.C., NY: Roper Records.

Howard, D. 1997. *Ballet music for barre and center: Elementary, intermediate & advanced.* L.I.C., NY: Roper Records.

Howard, D., and D. Corbin. 1995. *In the spirit of dance.* Dallas: Bodarc Productions.

Stanford, L. 1983. *More Lynn Stanford: Music for ballet class.* Dallas: Bodarc Productions.

Stanford, D. 1991. *Every dancer.* Dallas: Bodarc Productions.

Videos

Ashley, M., K. McKenzie, and G. Parkinson. *The video dictionary of classical ballet.* Hightstown, NJ: Princeton.

Fllindt, V., and K.A. Jiirgensen. 1992. *Bournonville ballet technique: Fifty enchainment.* Hightstown, NJ: Princeton.

Howard, D. 1986. *Ballet class for beginners.* Hightstown, NJ: Princeton.

Howard, D. 1986. *Ballet class: Intermediate and advanced.* Hightstown, NJ: Princeton.

Howard, D. 1991. *Take a master class with David Howard.* Hightstown, NJ: Princeton.

Kassing, G. 1999. *Interactive beginning ballet technique* (CD-ROM). Champaign, IL: Human Kinetics.

Lowe, M. 1984. *The ballet workout I.* Hightstown, NJ: Princeton.

Lowe, M. 1993. *The ballet workout II.* Hightstown, NJ: Princeton.

Rommett, Z. 1991. *Floor-barre technique I.* Hightstown, NJ: Princeton.

Rommett, Z. 1997. *Floor-barre technique II.* Hightstown, NJ: Princeton.

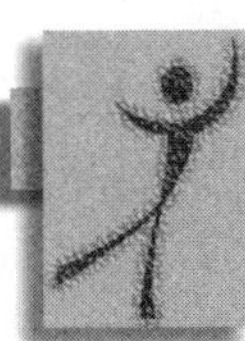

Modern Dance Unit

Teaching Overview

Psychomotor Objectives

- Execute basic modern dance steps and combinations of three to four steps to accompaniment.
- Demonstrate relationship of movement to music (count, rhythm, tempo, time signature).
- Demonstrate application of movement principles of modern dance.

Psychomotor Evaluation

- Performance test of selected modern dance steps and combinations in relation to music, with application of principles.

Cognitive Objectives

- Recognize beginning modern dance terminology.
- Translate a beginning modern dance into movement from oral or written instructions.
- Conduct a self-evaluation or peer evaluation of a beginning modern dance performance.
- Write a report about a modern dance performance.

Cognitive Evaluation

- Complete written test of beginning modern dance knowledge (modern dance technique, terminology, definitions, history, and culture; self-assessment of personal performance).
- Write a dance concert report about a modern dance performance (technique, choreography, production).

Affective Objectives

- Practice the etiquette for dancers in the modern dance class.
- Demonstrate movement confidence and performance attitude.
- Work with the group to refine performance.

Affective Evaluation

- Demonstrate etiquette, movement confidence, performance attitude, cooperation, contribution, and leadership within the group and class.

Teaching Approaches

You can use a variety of teaching approaches for modern dance:

- Implement classes based on your training and experiences.
- Teach modern dance using a syllabus based on a modern dance artist's technique, such as that of Graham, Hawkins, or others.
- Do a theme approach based on a movement motif or phrase, or emphasize a quality or topic.
- Create a loose structure with a moving warm-up and short improvisational problems that may or may not culminate into an extended improvisation in

FORM 13.15

Scope and Sequence for Modern Dance

New = N Review = R Performance test = PT

	1	2	3	4	5	6	7	8	9	10	11	12	13	14	15
Definition and history	N														
Rules and etiquette	N														
Lying on the floor and sitting alignment	N														
Tailor or breathing, bending side	N			R	R				R	R	R				
Long position feet flex and point	N	R		R	R										
Standing: demi-plié parallel first and second	N	R		R	R				R	R	R	R	R	PT	PT
Battement tendu parallel front and side (first and second)	N	R		R	R				R	R	R	R	R	PT	PT
Foot exercise: presses and pedals	N														
Walks across the floor	N				R				R	R	R	R	R	PT	PT
Dance walks high and low	N				R				R	R	R	R	R	PT	PT
Alignment (lying on floor, standing)	N														
Standing bend front, side, and diagonals		N			R										
Sitting long position feet turnout		N			R										
Hook position: knee into torso		N			R				R	R	R	R	R	PT	PT
Hook position: figure eights with legs		N			R										
Roll down and up		N			R										
Demi-plié turned out first and second		N	R	R	R										
Battement tendu turned out front and side		N	R	R	R										
Swing body part, front and back, side to side		N	R		R	R					R	R	R	PT	PT
Walk combination across the floor		N			R										
Sideways grapevine different pathways		N			R										
Lying on the floor: hook position crunches			N	R	R	R	R	R	R	R	R	R	R		
Leg extensions, grand battements			N		R										
On abdomen: cobra			N		R				R		R				

From *Dance Teaching Methods and Curriculum Design* by Gayle Kassing and Danielle M. Jay, 2003, Champaign, IL: Human Kinetics.

FORM 13.15

New = N Review = R Performance test = PT

	1	2	3	4	5	6	7	8	9	10	11	12	13	14	15
On side: développé and enveloppé			N		R				R		R	R		PT	PT
Battement tendu with demi-plié			N		R										
Across the floor: forward and backward walk			N		R							R	R	PT	PT
Triplet steps			N												
Lying on the floor: hook position grand battement				N	R			R		R	R	R	R	PT	PT
Hook position: working on half circle with right leg				N	R										
Hook position: arches (sternum lift)				N	R			R	R	R		R	R	PT	PT
Standing: battement tendu parallel and turnout back				N	R										
Battement dégagé front and side				N	R			R	R	R	R	R	R	PT	PT
Retire front and back				N	R					R					
Twist torso and figure eight with arms				N	R		R			R		R	R	PT	PT
Runs forward and backward across floor				N	R							R	R	PT	PT
Runs leading with various parts of the body				N	R		R	R	R			R	R	PT	PT
Lying on floor: knee to chest diagonals															
Sitting tailor: contraction and release						N	R	R	R	R	R	R	R	PT	PT
Long and straddle: bends						N	R	R	R	R	R	R	R		
Long and straddle: circles, point and flex with knee flexion						N	R					R	R		
Lying on floor: open fourth position						N	R								
Standing: grande plié						N	R			R	R	R	R	PT	PT
Battement tendu relevé						N	R			R	R				
Passé parallel and turned out						N	R								
Front fall						N	R			R	R	R	R	PT	PT
Across the floor: hops, jumps, and prances						N	R			R		R	R	PT	PT
Lying on the floor: log roll								N	R		R				

(continued)

FORM 13.15 *(continued)*

New = N Review = R Performance test = PT

	1	2	3	4	5	6	7	8	9	10	11	12	13	14	15
Sitting: seat spins								N	R	R	R				
Standing: half and full body circles								N	R		R				
Sitting with seat spin combinations								N	R	R	R				
Back falls								N	R	R	R			PT	PT
Across the floor: chassé side, front								N	R	R	R			PT	PT
Jumps								N	R	R	R			PT	PT
Combination jumps, hops, leap runs								N	R	R	R			PT	PT
Sitting in open fourth: spirals									N	R	R				
Coccyx balances									N	R	R				
On knee: standing side falls									N	R	R	R			
Across the floor: gallops									N	R	R			PT	PT
Skips									N		R			PT	PT
Combinations									R	R	R			PT	PT

FORM 13.16

Modern Dance Block Time Plan

Class 1	Class 2	Class 3	Class 4	Class 5
Rules and etiquette • Lying on the floor • Alignment (and sitting) Sitting • Tailor position: breathing and relaxing down (exhale) and aligning (inhale) • Bending to each side and forward, return to aligned position • Long position: pointing and flexing feet (parallel position) Standing • Demi-plié (parallel first and second positions) • Battement tendu (parallel first and second positions), front and side • Foot exercises: presses and pedals Across the floor • Walk naturally • Dance walk • Walk high (en relevé) • Walk low (in demi-plié)	Standing • Alignment (lying, then standing) • Bend forward and side; stretching up, side, front, and diagonals Sitting • Long position: point and flex feet (parallel); repeat (turned out) Lying on back • Hook position: Knee to torso and hold; extend to 90 degrees, stretch into long position on the floor • Hook position: Figure eights with legs Standing • Roll down and roll up to standing aligned position • Review demi-pliés first and second positions (parallel), repeat turned out • Battement tendus front and side • Swings: body parts side to side, front and back Across the floor • Walks: combine different walks • Walks: directions (add sideways, grapevine), pathways	Lying • Hook position: crunches • Leg extension or grand battements On abdomen • Cobra On side • Développés/enveloppés Sitting Standing • Battement tendus and demi-pliés Across the floor • Combine forward and backward walks (full foot, relevé) • Triplet	Lying • Hook position: leg extensions (grand battement) • Hook position: half circles with working leg • Hook position: arches • Hook position: crunches (moving, static); with arches On front of body: sternum lifts Sitting Standing • Battement tendus: parallel and turned out; back • Battement dégagés: parallel and turned out first position; front and side • Retiré (front and back) • Twist and figure eight with arms and torso Across the floor • Run forward; backward; sideward • Run leading with different body parts	Lying Sitting • Review all exercises for selected performance assessment Standing Across the floor • Review walks, runs, swings for selected performance assessment

(continued)

FORM 13.16 *(continued)*

Class 6	Class 7	Class 8	Class 9	Class 10
Lying • Knee to chest and diagonals Sitting • Tailor position: Contraction and release • Tailor, long and straddle: bends and half-circles • Long and straddle: point and flex, add knee flexion; in parallel to turned-out and return • Open fourth position: spiral Standing • Grand plié • Battement tendu relevé Review swings • Passés (parallel and turned out) • Sitting and standing • Front falls Across the floor • Hops • Jumps • Prances	Lying • Log rolls Sitting • Seat spins Standing • Standing: half and full body circles • Sitting with seat spins • Back falls; review front falls Across the floor • Chassés (side, front) • Jumps • Combination of 2 to 3 steps: jumps, hops, leaps, runs, chassés	Lying Sitting • Open fourth: spirals • Coccyx balances Standing • Side falls (from knees) • Kneeling to standing and return • Front falls, back falls, seat spins and standing Across the floor • Gallops • Skips • Combinations: 2 and 3 steps	Lying Sitting Standing Review all exercises forward, backward, and sideward Across the floor Combinations to review work	• Set exercises and music for performance test • Give specific counts for each exercise, combination Center • Review falls to side and various directions • Hinge from the knee Across the floor • Create a 16-count combination using locomotor movements (construct it so that it can be transposed to the other side)
Class 11	**Class 12**	**Class 13**	**Class 14**	**Class 15**
• Rehearse exercises • Review the combination • Students transpose it; practice both sides • Give feedback	• Review the entire set class	• Practice performance test	• Assess each set exercise or combination in groups of three or four students	• Assess set exercises and combination in groups of three or four students • Give personal feedback on performance

the class. This can be done in two or three groups and viewed by the other members of the class.

- Use a body therapy or somatic technique for the warm-up and movement sequences.
- Provide creative projects along with the technical studies.
- Use von Laban's theories and terminology to inspire the class.

Specific Teaching Methods

Modern dance is a concert dance form. Students learn exercises to gain strength, flexibility, coordination, and technique. This dance form presents many steps and concepts for students to explore and develop. A balanced study of modern dance enables students to execute movement correctly and explore their creativity using the elements of the dance. When constructing exercises and combinations, keep track of the variables (direction, level, weight transfer, and balance) that students will encounter. Limit these variables until students gain competency in the work and experience in adding variables into the work.

Learning in modern dance involves working and cooperating in small groups to create a study. In the modern dance class, the students dance as well as serve as audience members. Students must learn to be good audience members and use theater manners even for informal showings in the dance class. Likewise, students in modern dance should experience working with other students cooperatively in small groups to create dance studies or solve movement problems that are performed for the class.

In the modern dance class, the center exercises and combinations consist of movement selected from some of the exercises performed while standing, sitting, or lying on the floor. The bend, stretch, twist, turn, elevate, and fall categories of movement contribute to center combinations. The center work begins with one type of movement performed side to side then progressively adds other movements to the combination. Later locomotor and nonlocomotor steps are included. Some general examples of constructing beginning modern dance center combinations are a starting place for other combinations that move across the floor or extend into short dances:

- Swing forward and back, side to side, and in a figure eight combined with a walk or step in any direction for eight repetitions (decrease repetitions to four, then two).
- Execute falls forward or backward, and connect them with a seat spin and standing up. Or, combine falls with twists and turns.
- Add contractions that twist or connect with falls and rises.
- Begin with a movement motif that runs through the warm-up and into center combinations. For example, the concept of opening and closing may initiate twists, turns, elevation movements, or falls. If you have a limited amount of time in class, incorporate the movements that will be in the center combinations into your warm-up; this will give the dancers more practice in perfecting the movements.

Musical Accompaniment

Musical accompaniment for modern dance includes the following:

- Musician who plays piano, drums, or other instrument and has improvisation skills

- Compact discs, tapes, and records for modern dance
- Eclectic music from New Age, world music, classical, jazz, and contemporary styles

Dance Class Format

The class format for modern dance is as follows:

1. Warm-up
2. Practice of exercises to increase technique and flexibility
3. Slow and fast combinations in the center or traveling across the floor
4. Improvisation or movement studies
5. Cool-down exercises to end the class

Classroom Considerations

Classroom considerations for modern dance class are similar to considerations for other concert dance forms. A student should become aware of his body as it moves through the space and in relation to other bodies. The student should be quiet and respond to the instructor in a respectful manner.

Safety

Because the dancers are barefoot in the modern dance class, the floor should be smooth and free of splinters; it should also not be slippery. Monitor the floor surface to ensure it is clean and disinfected.

Attire

Female students wear a leotard and tights or a unitard. Male students wear tight T-shirts or a leotard with tights. Males also wear a dance belt and belt or suspenders. Other clothes such as T-shirts and pants are also allowed, depending on the teacher's discretion. Jewelry such as dangling earrings, necklaces, and bracelets should not be worn to class because they can impede dancers' safety. It is important for modern dance students to maintain foot hygiene. On some surfaces, dancers wear modern dance sandals to protect their feet.

Classroom Etiquette

Modern dance class etiquette conforms to that of other concert dance forms. (See the ballet dance unit, page 306.)

Beyond Technique Assignments

The following are some suggestions for beyond technique assignments in modern dance:

- Develop an 8- to 16-count combination. Transpose it to the other side and add another 8 to 16 counts to the combination. The length depends on the age group.
- Select three or four exercises and steps from a list and create an 8- to 16-count combination and find musical accompaniment for the combination.

- Create a movement study that explores qualities of movement (se of five) or design symmetrical and asymmetrical elements u transitions, axial and locomotor movements, entrances or exits who are not performing describe the qualities, designs, and other they saw in the study.
- Research a modern dancer or choreographer and present the inforn.ation in an oral report to the class.

Content Overview

The content overview provides the information necessary for teaching the dance unit.

Definition and History

Modern dance includes a broad range of styles that range from a specific technique created by a dance artist to a personal technique that may be a composite built from studying with different artists and teachers.

Begun at the start of the 20th century as a rebellion against the rigid, codified form of classical ballet, a new dance emerged as aesthetic dance. It freed the body, encouraged personal creativity and expression of feelings, and served as a means of communicating physically and psychologically. Artists early in the century used natural movements (bending, stretching, twisting, turning, rising, and falling) and everyday movements (walking, running, leaping, jumping, hopping, skipping, sliding, and galloping). Individual dancers created their own technique and movement vocabularies based on their movement preferences, body shapes, and capabilities as dancers. These dance artists in dual roles of dancer and choreographer provided the substance for this new dance form, which became known as modern dance.

According to dance history authors Kraus, Hilsendager, and Dixon (1991), modern dance has had three distinct eras during the 20th century. The first era spanned the first half of the 20th century. During this time, dance artists and choreographers developed their dance techniques, choreographic forms, philosophies, and aesthetics of modern dance; and they influenced student dancers, teachers, and audiences. The second era encompassed the maturing of artists and companies established after the 1950s. Martha Graham, José Limon, Paul Taylor, Alvin Ailey, and Merce Cunningham codified their techniques preserved through their choreographic works. At the beginning of the 1960s many of these artists, such as Ailey, Alwin Nikolais, and Cunningham, were considered at the forefront of the avant–garde; by the end of the decade they were revered as the mainstream choreographers. The final period of modern dance broke the established artistic and choreographic traditions to experiment with expressing political and social ideas. In this era dance artists expanded their parameters of possibilities by collaborating with performance art and media; exploring tasks; and using minimalist concepts, improvisation, contact improvisation, and environments in their works.

Modern dance is an ever-changing dance form as eclectic as the artists and choreographers that create it. Within one century, the pendulum of change swung from exploration to formal dance forms to experimentation. This constant searching for new ways of expression in modern dance is its lifeblood for the future.

Special Features

The following are specific features of modern dance:

- It is based on the work of artists who devised their own technique, which often developed into codified forms.
- It provides a creative, artistic outlet for expression through movement.
- Movements, techniques, and styles are as eclectic as the choreographer.
- Often the dancer is also the choreographer for the work, which gives a personal perception of a topic.

Principles

Movement, choreographic, and aesthetic principles that specifically apply to modern dance are shown in the shaded regions of the following icons.

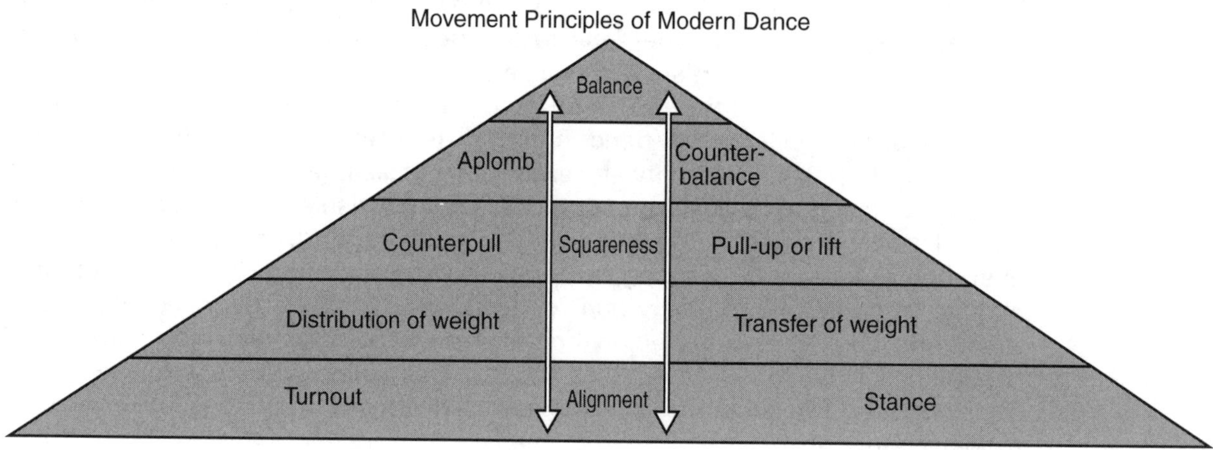

Choreographic Principles of Modern Dance

Choreographic elements	Choreographic structures	Choreographic designs	Choreographic devices	Choreographic relationships
Motif Phrase Theme and variation	Simple musical forms • AB (binary) • ABA (ternary) • Rondo • Theme and variation Contrapuntal forms • Canon (round) • Fugue Others • Narrative (story) • Open (free)	Dancer's body shape Dancer's pathway through space Visual design • Symmetrical • Asymmetrical Symbolism • Representational • Abstraction • Distortion Relationship • Unison • Sequential • Successional • Oppositional • Complementary	Repetition Reverse Alter • Addition or subtraction • Directional change • Facing or focus • Level • Dimension • Tempo • Rhythm • Quality or effort action • Positioning • Movement section	Solo Duet Trio Quartet Small and large groups

Traditional Dance Elements

Space	Time	Force	Relationships
Directions Dimensions Levels Shapes Pathways Focus	Duration Tempo	Movement qualities • Sustained • Percussive • Swinging • Suspended • Collapsing • Vibratory	Among body parts Among people Between people and props

Laban's Dance Elements

Space	Time	Weight	Flow
Direct or indirect	Sudden or slow	Light or strong	Bound or free
Effort actions (use space, time, and weight) • Dab • Flick • Punch • Slash • Glide • Float • Press • Wring			

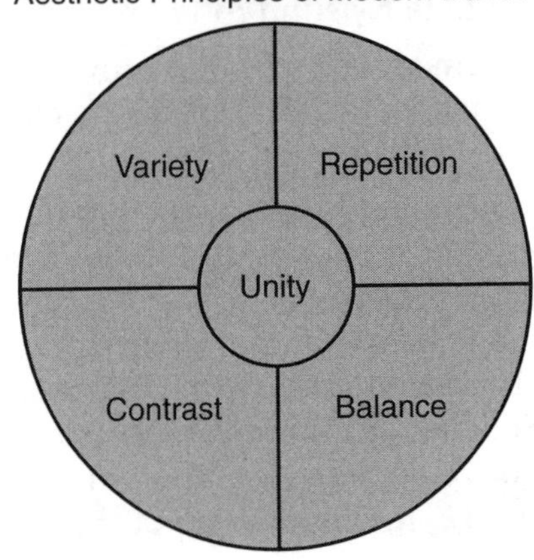

Vocabulary

The vocabulary for modern dance is shared with other concert dance forms.

Dance Skills

Modern dance has two basic types of movement: nonlocomotor (or axial) and locomotor movements. Locomotor movements are addressed in the "Across the Floor" section, page 342.

Nonlocomotor Movements

In **nonlocomotor movements** (also known as axial movements) body parts move around a stationary base. The base could be the feet, knees, buttocks, back, side, or front of the body. Bending, stretching, rising, falling and recovering, twisting, and turning are general categories of nonlocomotor movements.

Bending can be forward, backward, or sideward. The body bends at the neck, the upper back, waist, hips, knees, ankles, and feet. In forward bending, the dancer's range is from a slight bend of the body to a complete folding of the body so that it rests against the legs. In sideward and backward bending, the dancer's range is determined by the flexibility of the muscles on the sides of the body and whether the hips flex when the body bends.

Stretching happens in all directions. The dancer stretches the body parts in all directions: diagonal front, diagonal back, diagonal down, diagonal up, forward low, forward middle, forward high, side low, side middle, side high, back low, and back high.

Rise means to change level upward. It entails moving from lying, sitting, kneeling, plié, standing, or spiraling upward to a higher level on the floor or into the air.

A **fall** changes level downward. It entails moving from a position in the air, standing, kneeling, or sitting to a lower level on the floor. Falls move either fast to slow in a forward, backward, sideward, or spiral pattern.

Recovery is a level change upward and the return from a fall to the floor. The recovery entails moving upward from the end of the fall to the floor back to a sitting, kneeling, or standing position. Similar to the fall, the recovery moves in a straight, diagonal, or spiral path (see *contraction*).

Twist is a turn around an axis. The dancer twists the torso or body parts. These body parts stretch or bend during the twisting movement. Body parts, such as an arm moving in an arc, initiate twisting movements.

A **turn** is different from a twist in that it moves the body as a unit around an axis, such as on the foot, the knees, or hips. Turns can also travel across the floor and through the air.

Some nonlocomotor movements in modern dance occur in other concert dance forms. These extension movements are performed in parallel and turned-out positions. The directions are front, to the side, back, and front and back diagonals. Dancers do these exercises while standing, sitting, and lying. The terms not defined here are found in the ballet unit: demi-plié, grand plié, foot exercises (point and flex, presses, and pedals), battement tendu, battement dégagé, battement tendu relevé, battement développé, and grand battement.

In **battement enveloppé,** the working leg does a grand battement. On the return path, it passes to retiré (front, side, or back), then slides down the leg through the sur le cou-de-pied with the foot pressing into the full-foot position on the floor. This is the reverse of battement développé. Word cues are brush up, in, down.

Leg swings are performed front and back and from side to side crossing and opening. This exercise is performed at various heights while standing and often in a series with a decreasing number of repetitions. The working foot brushes to full foot through first position turned out as it swings. Word cues are front and back, cross and open.

Arm swings, with one arm or both arms, move front to back, side to side, and in a figure eight. This exercise is performed while standing and often in a series with a decreasing number of repetitions. The arm swings can propel the body from side to side or into a spin. Word cues are front to back, back to front, cross to open, and open to cross.

Body swings occur front to back; side to side; in an upper or lower arc; in a circular path; and as an initiative to a fall, spiral, or turn. This exercise is performed while standing and often in a series with a decreasing number of repetitions. Word cues are front to back, side to side, and up.

Contraction is a curving of the torso into a concave shape. The action initiates from the pelvis, the abdominal muscles, the upper chest, or the entire torso.

a

b

Contraction: upper, middle, and whole body. *(a)* Front view, *(b)* side view.

Release returns the body to its starting, straight, or convex position.This action is often a return from a contraction. As the back releases, the upper to middle back arches and the chest expands and extends toward the ceiling.

Tilt shifts the torso off vertical alignment. Often nonlocomotor movements are performed vertical or tilted.The body tilts in all directions during nonlocomotor or locomotor movements. In modern dance, the torso shifts off the vertical axis. As a result, the weight shifts within the foot triangle to accommodate and balance the tilted body shape.

Flexibility Exercises

These exercises stretch parts of the body and increase range of motion. Dancers do flexibility exercises in both parallel and turned-out positions while lying on the floor, sitting, kneeling, and standing. Each of these general positions has variations.

Complementary shapes.

High and low contrasting shapes.

Floor Exercises

Exercises in the lying position use the front, side, and back body facings. The legs extend in first position parallel or turned out and in the long position, where the legs and feet extend along the floor. Or, to provide a more stable base, the supporting leg is in the hook position.

To do the **hook position,** lie on your back with the hips and knees bent. The knees in the parallel position face the ceiling. The feet rest on the floor, placed about 9 inches away from your buttocks. The arms may rest alongside the body or out to the side middle. This is a safe position for exercises on the floor, especially for beginners and people with lordosis and other back problems. To ensure stability of the back and the hips, perform flexibility exercises in the hook position before attempting them with the legs extended. Other flexibility exercises include these from the ballet unit: battement développé and grand battements.

The **knee to torso** (forward and to the side) is a static stretch. Lying on the back with legs parallel and stretched on the floor, gradually draw the knee closer to the chest and hold the position. For this exercise, hold the back of the upper leg when moving it nearer the body. Relax the hip joint, maintain the three natural curves of the back, and reach the hips to the floor. When executing this exercise to the side, the hips remain level and square. The supporting hip and leg remain on the floor. To the side, the working leg is in a diagonal front position. Word cues are keep your back aligned on the floor, clasp your hands behind the thigh, and gently draw the leg into the chest.

For **knees to chest** with diagonals, lie on the back in the hook position. Raise the knees to the middle of the chest. Extend arms to side middle. Keep the back on the floor while the knees move diagonally right and left across the body slowly. This exercise stretches the back and engages the abdominal muscles. In the next progression of this exercise, the legs in parallel move diagonally right or left, then extend in that direction, returning to the middle position with the knees bent into the chest. Repeat to the other side and for the same number of repetitions. Keeping the sides of the leg from falling to the floor increases the use of the abdominal muscles in this exercise. Word cues are up and right and left, or up and left and right.

Leg extensions are another type of floor exercise. Lying on the back, bend the working leg so that the knee is near the chest. Clasp both hands behind the upper leg. Extend the leg upward, then inward toward the body. Continue to stretch and move inward while moving the hands down the leg until you reach the ankle. Release the head off the floor and hold the final position. Attempt to touch your nose to your knee. Word cues: Keep your back aligned on the floor, bend the working leg into the chest, and clasp both hands behind the thigh. Extend the leg upward and inward toward the body. Stretch and move the hands down the leg to just above the ankle. Now release your head off the floor and h-o-l-d that position.

We include leg extension variations in this and the following three paragraphs. Legs extended, slide one leg into the hook position, extend the other leg straight and perpendicular to the floor, then stretch the back to the floor. Word cues are extend up and down.

Figure eights are done while lying on the back. The supporting leg is either extended along the floor or in the hook position. The working leg bends at the hip and knee. It describes a figure eight in front of the body: one direction, then reverse. This exercise frees movement in the hip joint. Word cues: Draw a figure eight in front of your body with your knee four or eight times; now reverse the direction.

Leg circles include half and whole circles. For half circles, the supporting leg extends on the floor in the long position while the working leg extends upward, perpendicular to the floor. The leg opens up and out to second position and then circles down to the long position on or just above the floor. The half circle is performed the same number of repetitions outward and then inward. Word cues are up, out, down. In whole circles, the supporting leg extends on the floor in the long position while the working leg describes a circular path either outward or inward in front of the body. In the circular pattern, the working leg and hip release from the floor on the part of the pattern that crosses the body to the side. The aim is for the working leg to nearly touch the floor on either side of the body near the hands. The working leg extends as high as possible near the head and then opens to the side, returning to the long position. In this exercise, the arms stretch along the floor, palms down at the side middle level. The legs are either in parallel or turned-out position with the feet pointed. Word cues are up, out, down, across, up, out, down.

Coccyx balance is performed while lying on the back. The legs are parallel either extended forward or in the hook position. Lift the head and torso so that the back is at a 45-degree angle off the floor. Then return to the beginning position. There are several levels of difficulty for this exercise. Word cues are up and return. Second level: With the legs in the hook position, lift the head and torso so that the back is at a 45-degree angle off the floor. Raise the feet off the floor so that the lower leg extends parallel to the floor. Word cues are up and return. Third level: Both the body and the extended legs lift off the floor to a 45-degree angle. Both legs and torso are straight and balance on the coccyx bone. Word cues are up and return. During the coccyx balance, both arms extend at the forward middle level with the palms up.

Another type of floor exercises are side exercises, which we describe in this and the following paragraph. Lie on your side. The lower arm is straight, lying on the floor extending under your ear. A variation is the lower arm bends at the elbow with the hand supporting your head. The upper arm bends at the elbow, resting close to the body, with the palm of the hand on the floor in front of the body facing in the same direction as your supporting arm. The following exercises are performed either parallel or turned out: battement développé, battement envéloppé, flex and point, grand battement.

In **leg extensions,** hold the ankle or farther up the leg and then extend it to the side. Or retiré to the side, then press the thigh back so that the leg is bent behind you (in attitude). Keep the knee from falling forward. Word cues are up, retiré, attitude.

There are three common extension floor exercises with the legs in the air. Start by lying on the back, and extend the legs to the ceiling. The legs are perpendicular to the floor. The back remains on the floor and the arms are placed alongside the body or at side middle. In the first exercise, the legs cross at the ankles and exchange places. The legs can be straight or bent slightly; the feet can be pointed or flexed. Word cues are and cross, and cross. In the second exercise, the legs open into a rotated, straddle position in the air. In this position, the dancer grasps the ankles and the body remains on the floor. Word cues are extend, open into straddle, and stretch. In the third exercise, the head lifts off the floor and the arms stretch forward between the legs and hold in this static position. The dancer reaches forward between the legs 16 repetitions. Word cues are extend, open into straddle, reach and return. This exercise aids in flexibility and engages the abdominal muscles. Keep the back on the floor for safety.

We describe lying in the prone position (on the front facing of the body) exercises in this and the following two paragraphs. Arms rest alongside the body or at side middle or side high. The head is in either a neutral position or turned to the side. The head may rest on the back of the hands that rest on top of each other. In this position, the head is neutral or it faces either side. The following exercises are performed either parallel or turned out: battement dégagé, flex and point.

In the **cobra,** hands rest by the side of the chest, and palms are on the floor facing forward with shoulders down. Arms straighten so that the chest releases to the ceiling and then returns to the floor. The legs remain extended, and feet are pointed on the floor. The abdominal muscles engage, pulling upward. The hips may remain on the floor. Word cues are u-p, h-o-l-d, d-o-w-n.

In the **arch,** the front of the body rests on the floor. The arms extend overhead, and palms face downward. Raise one arm upward and place it back on the floor. Raise the other arm and place it back on the floor. Lift one leg and return it to the floor. Lift the other leg and return it to the floor. Raise the right arm and left leg simultaneously and return them to the floor, then the opposite arm and leg. Then lift both arms and legs while the back arches. Return to the floor. Word cues are u-p, h-o-l-d, d-o-w-n.

The exercises in the next two paragraphs involve lying supine, or on the back. The **sternum lift** is a flexibility exercise that begins lying on the back. The legs may be in either the hook position and later extended in the long position. The three curves of the back should be maintained. The chest rises from the sternum, and the back arches. In this exercise, the height of the sternum lift determines the position of the head. This exercise has four levels of progression:

1. Lifting up so that the top of the head remains on the floor (word cues are u-p, d-o-w-n)
2. Lifting higher so that only the palms remain on the floor (word cues are u-p, d-o-w-n)
3. Lifting up higher so that the hands are off the floor (word cues are u-p, h-o-l-d, d-o-w-n)
4. Lifting to an aligned sitting position (word cues are u-p, h-o-l-d, d-o-w-n)

The release for this exercise is when the torso stretches forward over the extended legs.

For **log rolls,** lie on your back on the floor with the arms extended overhead by your ears. The side of the body lifts to initiate the roll to the other side of the body. This exercise is done slowly with minimal movement at first to control the roll and prevent injury and bruising of bony body parts. This is the initial experience in rolling; later rolling is incorporated into falls and spins and combined with other movements. Word cues are r-o-l-l, and r-o-l-l.

To do **crunches,** lie on your back with the legs in the hook position. The head and upper torso form a curve as they lift off the floor to the beginning of the thoracic spine. The body then returns to its original position lying on the floor. The head lifts and the eyes focus on an upper diagonal during the lift off the floor. The arms have progressive positions:

1. Resting on the floor alongside the body
2. Folded across the chest with the elbows bent and resting on the torso
3. Hands placed behind the head with the elbows bent and remaining out to the side
4. One hand behind the head with the other arm stretching forward middle or on a slight upward diagonal
5. Both arms extended forward on an upward diagonal.

If performed correctly, this exercise strengthens the abdominal muscles. If the body rises too high off the floor, the hip flexors (iliopsoas) engage. Word cues are and up, and down.

In **static crunches,** the head and upper torso lift off the floor to the beginning of the thoracic spine. When you reach this position, hold for 16 counts, then return to the beginning position. This exercise is performed for progressively descending numbers of counts (eight, four, two). Both crunches and static crunches are performed forward and to the right and the left sides of the body. By performing these exercises right and left, you engage the oblique abdominal muscles. Word cues are and up, and 2, and 3, and down.

While executing **moving crunches,** reach forward on an upward diagonal on each beat of the music. After each reach, relax for a moment before reaching again. Performing the crunches to the right or left side and forward diagonal engages the oblique abdominal muscles. Word cues are and reach, and reach, and reach, and down. There are other crunch positions, including those in the following list:

- Lie on the floor with the supporting leg in the hook position. The other leg bends at the knee, rotating outward (similar to a passé position) with the outside of the ankle placed on the supporting knee to form a line parallel to the floor. Variation: The supporting foot releases from the floor, and the lower leg lifts slightly and extends parallel to the floor. The other leg bends, rotates outward with the outside of the ankle placed on the thigh of the supporting leg.
- Both legs extend up to the ceiling, perpendicular to the floor, with the knees slightly bent and outwardly rotated.
- Legs fully extend up, perpendicular to the floor, crossed at the ankles with the knees together. In both of these positions, the back remains completely on the floor.

Sitting Positions

In the **sitting position,** the back is aligned perpendicular to the floor with the weight resting on both "sit bones," or ischia. Vertically aligned, the spine stretches upward from the floor toward the ceiling. The shoulders are over the hips and relaxed down into the shoulder girdle. The neck elongates with the head poised on top of the spine. The back may round progressively toward the legs, arch up and back; or it may tilt on a forward or back diagonal. Generally, the arms hang alongside the body, and the hands are on the floor near the body or execute arm movements to complement the exercises. Sitting positions include tailor, butterfly (or frog), inside-out, tailor extended to the toes, extended (long), straddle, and hook sitting position.

In the **tailor position,** sit with the ankles crossed one on top of the other in front of the body and the legs rotated outward and bent at the knees. Feet may be relaxed or pointed.

In the **butterfly (frog),** sit with the soles of the feet together and the knees rotated outward to the side.

For the **inside-out position,** sit with legs rotated outward and bent at the knees with one leg resting inside the other on the floor.

For the **tailor extended to the toes,** sit in the tailor position with the feet pointed, with only the side of the little toes in contact with the floor. The ankles lift off the floor so that the feet do not sickle (turn inward). The lower legs and feet maintain a straight line.

In **extended forward (long)** position, sit with legs extending forward of the front of the body. The feet either are pointed or flexed.

In **on the walk** position, sit in tailor position with the legs turned out, the heels lifted with only the outside of the foot and little toes touching the floor in the flexed position. Then the ankle and toes extend; in the extended position, the heel remains up and the toes are fully pointed on the floor.

Straddle involves sitting with legs open to the sides, or second, position, parallel or turned out, with the feet either pointed or flexed.

The **hook sitting** position has the legs parallel and slightly separated, knees bent at a 90-degree angle with the feet on the floor under the hips about 9 inches away from the hips.

Sitting Exercises

Perform **breathing exercises** while sitting in tailor or inside-out position. Inhale and stretch the body upward on its vertical alignment. On the exhalation, return to the starting position. Wrists rest on the knees. This is an important centering exercise for the beginning dancer and a way to activate breathing, which becomes a part of other exercises. Word cues are inhale and stretch, exhale and relax.

The **body bend forward** exercise is performed in the extended (long), tailor, and straddle positions. The body begins vertically aligned. The back stretches to a flat or straight diagonal front position. Then the back and head round and the body contracts. Starting from the base of the spine, the back unfolds in a sequential manner; the head is the last to arrive before the body returns to the aligned position. The hands are close to the body and relaxed at the sides. Word cues are sitting tall, inhale and bend forward, keeping the back long; round the back; unfold the back beginning from the base of the spine upward until the head returns and back. This exercise reverses beginning with a contraction, goes to a diagonal flat back, and raises to the vertically aligned position. Word cues are contract, stretch long, and return sitting tall.

Variation: Sit in the tailor, inside-out, or the straddle position with the back vertically aligned and the wrists resting on the knees. The torso lifts and then twists diagonally. Then the chest moves into a high release, with the head lifted so that the eyes focus on the ceiling. The exercise finishes in the vertically aligned position. This exercise can begin and end with a contraction. Word cues are lift and twist, release and return.

Lateral body bends start in the tailor or inside-out position. Sit on both sit bones; both hips remain on the floor at all times. The torso bends to the side, keeping the chest open. Place the hand with the palm up and the forearm on the floor in a line with the hip bone. The other arm curves and stretches over the head and in line with the ear. The arm does not cross your line of vision. The head faces forward. The torso remains square throughout the exercise. The torso stretches to the side in the largest arc possible. This exercise progressively diminishes beginning with 16 counts, then 8, 4, 2. Repeat to other side; balance the number of repetitions per sides. Word cues are sitting tall, bend and stretch the arm to the side, and stretch upward back to your alignment.

For **half circles,** bend the torso laterally toward the side forearm with the opposite arm overhead. Then change to a curved body shape, drawing a half circle forward and around to the other side. Both arms are rounded diagonally forward and sweep with the movement. As the torso unfolds laterally at the other side, the forearm is on the floor, palm up, and the opposite arm is overhead. As the body lifts to the aligned position, the arms open to second position with the palms up. Word cues are sit tall and bend and stretch the arm to the side, curve over, open to the other side, and stretch upward back to your alignment.

For **full circles,** bend the torso laterally with the forearm on the floor and the palm up. Perform a complete circle with the torso rounding forward. When you reach the other side, place the palm on the floor diagonally back from the hip, then lift the upper torso to the ceiling. The opposite arm raises over the head and opens out and down to place the forearm on the floor with the palm up in line with the hip. The other arm lifts overhead. In this exercise, instead of placing the forearm on the floor, move the arms in a circular path slightly above the floor. Word cues are sit tall and bend and stretch your arms to the side, round forward, open, and arch.

For **hook position to fourth position sit,** sit in the hook position on the sit bones with thighs next to the chest, the back rounded, and the arms wrapped around the lower legs. As the arms open to second position and the legs open to long, straddle (fourth position) and the back vertically aligns or goes into a high release. Word cues are in and o-u-t, or contract and release.

For **seat spins,** sit in the fourth position (see open fourth position, below) and lift the legs into the hook position off the floor. The action of the legs with the hands pushing off the floor initiates the turn. The turn can be partial or a full turn. The legs end in the other fourth position or another position. Word cues are and t-u-r-n, and hold.

In this and the next five paragraphs, we describe foot exercises that can be done while sitting. Sit in long (extended), straddle position (parallel), or on the walk position (turned out).

In the **point and flex** exercise, the feet point and flex together or alternating feet (one points as one flexes). Word cues are point and flex, or point, and point.

For **leg extension of point and flex** exercises, sit in the long position. Flex both the ankles and bend knees and hips in the parallel position or turned out. Then extend the legs and point the feet. For a variation, one leg extends and the foot points while the other leg bends and the foot flexes. Word cues are flex and extend.

For **point and flex with rotation,** sit in long position with feet in first position parallel. Point both feet, then flex and rotate the legs to first position turned out. Flex in turned-out first position, then rotate legs to parallel first position. Here are other variations of this exercise:

1. Flex and straighten the ankles and the knees.
2. Extend legs and point feet in first parallel position; turn out legs to first position, flex ankles or ankles and knees in turned-out position; rotate into parallel first position flexed (ankles or ankles and knees).

These variations are performed in a series with an equal number of repetitions in each direction. Word cues are point, flex, and (rotate) point, flex.

In **open fourth position with body spiral,** sit with the back leg rotated in and bent at the knee with the entire inside of the leg resting on the floor behind the hip. The forward leg bends with the knee outwardly rotated and the foot on the walk with the heel in line with the navel. In this position, the back hip initiates a spiral movement of the torso. The movement begins with the rotation of the body around itself to the foot on the walk. During this action, the back hip lifts and the front foot on the walk changes to a pointed position. From this position, the hip leads and returns to the floor so that the body returns to its beginning position. During the exercise, the weight shifts from the back hip to the front hip and then returns. Word cues are and up, around, back and down.

On the **second level of open fourth position with body spiral,** arm movements accompany the exercise. The arms begin in a demi-seconde position over the back leg. The head focuses to the side between the arms. As the back hip initiates the spiral movement, the front arm raises to fifth position en haut by the time the dancer has spiraled to the front leg. This arm continues outward to demi-seconde while the other arm rises to fifth position en haut. As the hip leads back to the floor, the arm circles outward so that both arms arrive at demi-seconde when the body returns to its beginning position.

Kneeling Exercises

Kneeling is in the parallel position with the legs next to each other or slightly separated and in line with the hips. The kneeling position may be either low (sitting on the heels) or high (with the thighs extended).

For **kneel sits,** sit in the kneeling position on the heels with legs together and the back vertically aligned. Using the abdominal muscles, raise the body vertically off the heels and sit to the side of the legs. Return to the kneeling position. Repeat to the other side. This is performed in a series. The arms either open from alongside the body to the opposite side from the sit at middle side with a flowing quality, or the arms rise overhead with the arm opening to the side opposite the direction of the sit. Word cues are up and sit.

For **kneeling to hinge position,** sit in the kneeling position on heels. Legs are slightly separated in line with the hips, and the back is vertically aligned. Rise to the high kneeling position, keeping the neck and head, torso, and upper legs as a unit; lean back from the knees. Return to the high kneeling position. Engage the abdominal muscles during the lean. The arms begin along the side of the body and reach forward on the lean back, returning to alongside the body. Word cues are up, and lean; return and down.

For **kneeling to standing,** sit in the high kneeling position with toes flexed under. Place the hands on the floor under the shoulders, fingers facing forward. The back, neck, and head are in a straight line parallel to the floor. Extend one leg back with toes flexed under; lower the body to the low kneeling position on the supporting leg. The back tilts forward and the hands remain under the shoulders. Both the front and back legs share the weight. Engage the abdominal muscles and push upward to a lunge position. The body remains tilted, an extension of the back leg; the arms hang alongside the body. The back leg steps forward to meet the front leg, and the back vertically aligns; arms remain alongside the body. This exercise is then reversed. Word cues are extend the leg back, and up, close, hold and down.

Symmetrical and asymmetrical shapes.

Changing levels, an important foundational skill for the beginning modern dancer, involves moving from a standing position to the floor or from the floor to a standing position. The goal is to make smooth transitions from one level to another.

In **moving from standing to sitting,** step to the side with the right leg and cross the left leg behind with the foot raised off the floor. Keep the weight over the right leg as it demi-pliés; this controls the lowering of the body to the left leg into the kneeling position directly behind the right leg. First the top of the left foot touches the floor, continuing through the lower leg. In the kneeling position, counterpull as the body lowers to a sitting position behind the left leg, which is rotated out and bent at the knee. The right leg flexes at the hip, knee, and ankle with the full foot resting on the floor. During the sit, the body remains aligned, giving the illusion that it is moving vertically down to the floor with the arms extended in second position for balance. Word cues are step, cross, keep your weight on the forward leg as you descend to the floor.

In **moving from sitting to standing position,** reverse the instructions for the move from standing to sitting. Sit behind the left leg that is rotated and bent. Keep the right leg rotated outward and bent at the knee, with the front leg flexed at the hip, knee, and ankle and the full foot resting on the floor. The arms are in second position. The initiative for standing begins with engaging the abdominal muscles and shifting the weight forward to the front leg. Keep the back aligned as the body rises and roll the back leg to a kneeling position. The weight remains over the front leg as it straightens from kneeling to a standing position. Consequently, the back leg straightens too. Word cues are sit tall, engage abdomen, press the weight onto the forward leg, and keep your alignment as you rise.

Falls are executed forward, to the side, backward, or in conjunction with other movements on the floor or while standing.

In a **backward fall,** stand, step forward, and hop. The other leg outwardly rotates, bending at the knee. The ankle touches the back of the knee of the supporting leg (the arms begin alongside the body and rise overhead at the height of the hop; then they return to the side of the body). Keep the weight over the front leg as it demi-pliés, to control lowering the body onto the back leg into the kneeling position, directly behind the front leg. First the top of the foot touches the floor, continuing through the lower leg. In the kneeling position, counterpull as the body lowers to a sitting position behind the back leg, which has rotated out, bent at the knee. The front leg flexes at the hip, knee, and ankle with the full foot resting on the floor. During the sit, the body remains aligned giving the illusion that it is moving vertically down to the floor. Roll back gently, rounding the back until the entire back rests on the floor. The front leg extends with the foot pointed; the back leg remains outwardly rotated, bent at the knee with the ankle touching the back of the knee of the front leg. With the arms alongside the body, the hands control the roll back onto the floor. To return to standing, the body rocks back and then up to a sitting position, continuing into the kneeling position, with the hands giving an initial push. In this position, the front leg pushes up to standing. Word cues are and hop; and down; and r-o-l-l; and forward, push up.

For a **side fall,** stand, step forward, and hop on the right foot; the left leg is parallel, bent at the knee with the ankle touching the side of the knee of the supporting leg. The arms begin alongside the body and rise overhead at the height of the hop. The arms circle to the right, the same side as the supporting leg. Keep the weight over the supporting leg as it demi-pliés, to control lowering the body onto the left leg in the kneeling position, directly beside the supporting leg. First the top of the left foot touches the floor, continuing through the lower leg. In the kneeling position, counterpull as the body lowers to a sitting position and onto the left hip. The right leg flexes at the hip, knee, and ankle with the full foot resting on the floor. The body remains aligned, giving the illusion that it is moving vertically down to the floor. Slide the left arm out to the side along the floor, taking the weight of the body into a lying position on the side. The right upper arm rests alongside the body, bent at the elbow with the palm on the floor in front of the chest. The left leg is parallel, bent at the knee with the foot touching under the knee of the upper right leg that extends long. The right hand initiates the slide off the floor to the low kneeling, sitting position on the left leg. Using this impetus, the front leg pushes up to a high kneel and to a standing position. Word cues are and hop; and down; and s-l-i-d-e; and s-l-i-d-e up, and stand.

For a **forward (Swedish) fall,** stand, step forward, and tilt the body forward until the hands are placed on the floor in front of the shoulders. Keep the weight over the straight front leg to control lowering the body to the floor. The working leg extends back to complete a diagonal line from the shoulders through the foot. As the arms lower the body to the floor, the supporting foot releases so that the toes and ball of the foot remain on the floor. The working leg closes behind the front leg. From this position, roll to a hip, moving the legs into fourth position. Word cues are over, d-o-w-n, roll, and sit.

Standing and Center Exercises

Standing exercises are performed in the center. This section of class blends gaining technique with learning combinations of these exercises.

The leg and foot positions in modern dance use both parallel and turnout (see the ballet dance unit, page 309). In parallel positions the knees must fall directly over the feet, specifically between the second and third toes.

In **first position parallel,** both legs and feet face directly forward of the body. In first position parallel the insides of the feet may touch or they may be slightly separated so that the legs are directly under the hips.

In **second position parallel,** both legs and feet face directly forward of the body. In second position parallel the feet are separated to approximately shoulder width. Knees fall over toes.

The modern variation of the **B+ position** is with the supporting leg either parallel or naturally turned out. The thigh of the working leg touches the supporting leg; the knee of the working leg is bent with the lower leg extending behind and the foot pointed and the toes and metatarsals flexed so that they rest on the floor.

In modern dance **foot positions,** the pointed foot extends from the ankle, which is identical to ballet pointing. Many teachers prefer that the ball of the foot and toes flex to continue the line from the lower leg through the foot; this causes the line of the foot to curve when it is pointed in the air. In the **flexed foot,** the ankle flexes, the heel thrusts forward, and the toes pull up to complete this line.

The **arm positions** emulate many of the ballet positions, or the arms and hands extend straight in various directions (see photos in the ballet dance unit). Other arm positions may be natural movements or specific designs to complement the movement or choreography.

For a **lunge,** stand in first or fifth position and brush the foot along or off the floor and shift the weight either forward, to the side, or backward. The back may remain aligned, tilted, or contracted. The leg accepting the weight away from the body is bent; the supporting leg remains straight. The supporting leg may release from the floor, as does the working leg on its return.

Modified push-ups build arm and chest strength. The front of the body faces the floor. The arms are under the shoulders with the palms on the floor and the fingers forward. Knees are on the floor and under the hips with the body on a diagonal. The arms bend and stretch, lowering the body to about 2 inches off the floor and lifting to full extension of the arms.

Inverted push-ups build arm and chest strength. The back of the body faces the floor, with the arms behind and legs bent in front. Begin in a sitting hook position with arms straight and placed behind your shoulders; wrists are bent and fingertips are directed toward your feet. Raise and lower your body by bending your elbows and keeping your feet on the floor.

The **knee to chest standing** stretch is the same as that on the floor in a lying position. Stand and do the exercise to either the front or side. To the back, begin in first position parallel and bend the working leg; keeping the thigh extended to the floor, fold the lower leg up and hold the lower leg near the ankle.

The following exercises are executed standing in the center. The following exercises are defined in the ballet unit: demi-plié, grand plié, battement tendu (brushes on the floor), battement dégagé (brushes off the floor), battement tendu relevé.

- The **flex and point** is performed at one level or gets progressively higher each time. Word cues are flex and point.
- **Leg swings** are front and back, open and crossed with the back aligned, and later with a contraction. Arms are either in second position or swing in opposition to the leg directions (front and back).
- Practice **passé** in first position parallel or turned out, moving backward and forward (see the ballet dance unit, page 312).
- **Développé** is performed front, side, and back with turn out or in parallel (see the ballet dance unit, page 312).
- **Arabesques** are basically the same as in ballet (see the ballet dance unit, page 314-315).

Across the Floor

After nonlocomotor exercises and flexibility exercises, including center combinations, steps and combinations of locomotor, axial movements, and steps are executed across the floor.

Basic Locomotor Steps

Many locomotor steps listed here are defined in the creative movement and creative dance unit.

- **Natural walk** is heel, ball, toe; it's the walk you use in everyday life.
- The **dance walk** is toe, ball, heel. This is performed in both parallel and turned out (see the ballet dance unit, page 315).
- The **heel walk** moves in parallel position on the heels with the feet flexed and toes pulled back.
- The **high walk** moves on three-quarter relevé either parallel or turned out.
- **Runs** are quick transfers of weight from one leg to another with one leg off the floor.
- **Jumps** move forward, back, to the side, and in a circle; from two feet to two feet; two feet to one foot; one foot to two feet; one foot to one foot (coupé; see the ballet dance unit, page 316).

Contact improvisation.

- A **hop** is a spring off the floor from one foot to the same foot.
- **Prance** changes weight from one foot to the other foot quickly while lifting the working leg off the floor at various heights (ankle, middle of the lower leg, side of the knee). They are performed in parallel position. The body is lifted off the legs. The feet articulate through each position: heel, ball, toe on the push from the floor; then toe, ball, heel on the descent to the floor.
- A **leap** is a transfer of weight from one leg to the other with an air moment in which both legs are off the floor (see the ballet dance unit, page 317; and the jazz dance unit, page 360).
- In the **gallop,** the front foot steps forward, pulling the back foot to it in the air. The step does not alternate feet.
- In the **chassé,** the front foot slides out and the second foot pushes the body into the air with the legs coming together, landing on the second foot; the front foot slides out again for the next chassé quickly (see the ballet dance unit, page 315).
- A **skip** is a step–hop movement but with an extended air moment. The extended air moment is accented.
- In the **triplet** step, step forward onto the full foot in demi-plié (right), step forward onto three-quarter relevé (left foot), step forward onto three-quarter relevé (right foot). The basic triplet moves forward, on a forward diagonal, or in a turn. The arms are in various positions and complement the steps.
- **Grapevine** is a step sideward, and the other foot crosses either in front or back, followed by another side step. The step usually ends with one foot touching the ball of the foot at the instep of the supporting foot. This allows the step to reverse (see the folk dance unit, page 242).
- The **three-step turn** is a step to the side, step, half turn, step, half turn around yourself; then step, touch or point (hold so that you can repeat the step to the other side). You can perform this step either in full-foot or en relevé (see the ballet dance unit, page 313).

- In **paddle turns,** step on full-foot in demi-plié. This is one supporting and pivoting foot. Touch the ball of the other foot near the supporting foot. This foot pushes. Alternate step, ball, step, ball while turning (see the folk dance unit, page 242).

Other Components

The other components in beginning modern dance are the same as those in creative movement and creative dance. See **qualities, effort actions, dynamics, design,** and **choreographic structure** in the creative movement and creative dance unit, pages 220 and 221.

Reference

Kraus, R., S.C. Hilsendager, and B. Dixon. 1991. *History of dance in art and education.* Englewood Cliffs, NJ: Prentice Hills.

Selected Resources

Selected resources include modern dance texts, music, and videos.

Texts

Cheney, G. 1989. *Basic concepts in modern dance: A creative approach.* 3rd ed. Princeton, NJ: Princeton.

Cohan, R. 1986. *The dance workshop: A guide to fundamentals of movement.* New York: Simon & Schuster.

Duffy, N. 1982. *Modern dance: An adult beginner's guide.* Englewood Cliffs, NJ: Prentice Hills.

Furst, C., and M. Rockefeller. 1981. *The effective dance program in physical education.* West Nyack, NY: Parker.

Hawkins, A. 1988. *Creating through dance.* 2nd ed. Princeton, NJ: Princeton.

Kraus, R., S.C. Hilsendager, and B. Dixon. 1991. *History of dance in art and education.* Englewood Cliffs, NJ: Prentice Hills.

Lockhart, A.S., and E.E. Pease. 1982. *Modern dance building & teaching lessons.* 6th ed. Dubuque, IA: Brown.

Minton, S.C. 1984. *Modern dance: Body & mind.* Denver: Morton.

Minton, S.C. 1989. *Body & self: Partners in movement.* Champaign, IL: Human Kinetics.

Penrod, J., and J. Plastino. 1990. *The dancer prepares: Modern dance for beginners.* 3rd ed. Mountain View, CA: Mayfield.

Perces, M.B., A.M. Forsythe, and C. Bell. 1992. *The dance techniques of Lester Horton.* Pennington, NJ: Princeton.

Poll, T. 1977. *Complete handbook of secondary dance activities.* West Nyack, NY: Parker.

Pomer, J. 2002. *Perpetual motion: Creative movement exercises for dance and dramatic arts.* Champaign, IL: Human Kinetics.

Redfern, B. 1982. *Concepts in modern education dance.* London: Dance Books.

Schurman, N. 1972. *Modern dance fundamentals.* New York: Macmillan.

Sherbon, E. 1990. *On the count of one: The art, craft, and science of teaching modern dance.* 4th ed. Pennington, NJ: A Cappella Books.

Music

Bennett, G. 1997. *Music for bipedal movement.* Toronto: TTG Music Lab.

Mortilla, M.D. 1997. *Music piano improvisation.* Vol. I. Santa Barbara, CA: Mid-Life Crisis.

Stanford, L., and D. Hochoy. 1990. *Music for contemporary dance class.* Dallas: Bodarc Productions.

Videos

Cheney, G. 1995. *Journey through dance.* Hightstown, NJ: Princeton.

Cunningham, M. 1985. *Cunningham dance technique: Elementary level.* New York: Insight Media.

Cunningham, M. 1987. *Cunningham dance technique: Intermediate level.* New York: Insight Media.

Forsythe, A.M., and M. Parces. 1990. *Lester Horton technique: The warm-up.* Hightstown, NJ: Princeton.

Gutelius, P. 1989. *Contemporary dance training: Off center step into modern dance I.* Hightstown, NJ: Princeton.

Hackney, P. 1989. *Contemporary dance training: Off center step into modern dance II.* Hightstown, NJ: Princeton.

Limon, J. 1988. *Jose Limon technique.* New York: Insight Media.

Solomons, G., and R. Solomons. 1995. *Anatomy as a master image.* Hightstown, NJ: Princeton.

Stodelle, E. 1992. *Doris Humphrey technique.* Hightstown, NJ: Princeton.

Jazz Dance Unit

Teaching Overview

Psychomotor Objectives

- Execute beginning jazz dance vocabulary, isolations, steps, and combinations of three to four steps to music.
- Demonstrate relationship of movement to music (count, rhythm, tempo, time signature, and polyrhythms).
- Demonstrate application of principles to jazz dance.

Psychomotor Evaluation

- Performance test of selected jazz dance steps and combinations in relation to music, with application of principles.

Cognitive Objectives

- Recognize beginning jazz dance terminology.
- Translate a beginning jazz dance into movement from oral or written instructions.
- Conduct a self-evaluation or peer evaluation of a beginning jazz dance performance.
- Write a dance concert report about a jazz dance performance (technique, choreography, production).

Cognitive Evaluation

- Complete written test of beginning jazz dance knowledge (jazz dance steps, terminology, definitions, and history and culture; self-assessment of personal performance).
- Write a dance concert report about a jazz dance performance (technique, choreography, production).

Affective Objectives

- Practice etiquette for dancers in the jazz dance class.
- Demonstrate personal movement confidence and performance attitude.
- Work with the group to refine the performance.

Affective Evaluation

- Demonstrate etiquette, movement confidence, performance attitude and cooperation, contribution, and leadership within the group and class.

Teaching Approaches

Jazz serves as an excellent introduction to dance. It is constantly changing and evolving and is influenced by the music of the times. You can also use a specific technique, such as those of Matt Mattox, Luigi, Gus Giordano, or Joe Tremaine, to train students.

Specific Teaching Methods

To hold the interest of the students, be aware of new trends in both jazz music and dance. Continue to study jazz dance and use popular music in the classroom. Dancers relate to this type of dance because it reflects their era, music, and culture.

FORM 13.17

Scope and Sequence for Jazz Dance

New = N Review = R Quiz = Q Review for test = RT Performance test = PT

	1	2	3	4	5	6	7	8	9	10	11	12	13	14	15
Definition and history of jazz dance	N														
Attire and etiquette	N														
Isolations: head, shoulders, ribs, hips	N	R	R	R	R	R	R	R	R	R	R	R	RT	PT	
Demi-plié: parallel, turned out, first, second	N	R	R	R	R	R	R	R	R	R	R	R	RT	PT	
Battement tendu: front, side	N	R	R	R	R	R	R	R	R	R	R	R	RT	PT	
Foot pedals	N	R	R	R	R	R	R	R	R	R	R	R	RT	PT	
Leg swings: front, side	N	R	R	R	R	R	R	R	R	R	R	R	RT	PT	
Stretches: body, hamstrings, arms	N	R	R	R	R	R	R	R	R	R	R	R	RT	PT	
Sitting: straddle, long position, crunches	N	R	R	R	R	R	R	R	R	R	R	R	RT	PT	
Jazz walks	N	R													
Step, touch	N	R													
Cross, touch; cross, ball–change		N													
Modified push-ups		N	R	R	R	R	R	R	R	R	R	R	RT	PT	
Sitting long position: flex and point feet		N	R	R	R	R	R	R	R	R	R	R	RT	PT	
Toe heel; heel toe walks		N													
High and low jazz walks, hip walks			N	R	R	R									
Heel, bend			N	R	R	R									
Step, ball–change			N	R	R	R									
Battement développé				N	R	R	R	R	R	R	R	R	RT	PT	
Relevé walk; step, relevé passé				N			R								
Step–hop				N			R								
Step, relevé passé pivot turn					N		R								
Three-step turn					N										
Inverted push-up					N	R	R	R	R	R	R	R	RT	PT	

(continued)

From *Dance Teaching Methods and Curriculum Design*
by Gayle Kassing and Danielle M. Jay, 2003, Champaign, IL: Human Kinetics.

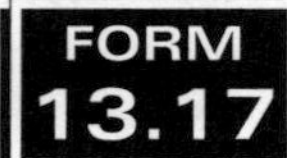

FORM 13.17 *(continued)*

New = N Review = R Quiz = Q Review for test = RT Performance test = PT

	1	2	3	4	5	6	7	8	9	10	11	12	13	14	15
Chest lift					N	R	R	R	R	R	R	R	RT	PT	
Pas de bourrée						N	R	R				R			
Step, kick; kick, ball–change						N		R							
Run, run, leap							N		R						
Stag leap							N		R						
Vertical jump								N		R					
Jazz terminology											Q				
Jazz square								N				R			PT
Jazz slide									N			R			
Jazz half split									N			R			
Contraction										N	R	R	R	PT	
Paddle turn										N					
Pike jump										N	R				
Tuck jump										N	R				
Performance combination											R				PT
Warm-up											R			PT	

FORM 13.18

Jazz Dance Block Time Plan

Class 1	Class 2	Class 3	Class 4	Class 5
• Define jazz dance • Relate history • Talk about attire, etiquette, warm-up • Isolations: head, shoulder, ribs, hips • Demi-plié: turned out, parallel, first, second • Battement tendu: front, side • Foot pedals • Leg swings • Floor stretches: body, hamstrings, arms • Sitting: straddle, long position • Lying on floor crunches: center • Jazz walk • Step, touch	• Warm-up • Review • Isolation • Demi-plié • Battement tendu • Foot pedals • Leg swings • Stretch • Sitting • Long position • Cross, touch • Cross, ball–change • Lying on floor: Modified push-ups Jazz walks Step, touch Toe–heel walks Heel–toe walks	• Review • Warm-up • Standing • Floor • Sitting • Lying on floor • Across the floor • Low jazz walks • High jazz walks • Heel–bend hip walks • Step, ball–change	• Warm-up • Add • Battement développé • Across floor Relevé walks Step, relevé passé Step–hop	• Warm-up • Add • Inverted push-up • Chest lift • Step, relevé passé • Three-step turn • Pivot turn
Class 6	**Class 7**	**Class 8**	**Class 9**	**Class 10**
• Warm-up (add arms) • Pas de bourrée • Step, kick; kick, ball–change • Review Low and high jazz walks Step, ball–change	• Warm-up • Run, run, leap • Stag leap • Teach Two-step combination with learned vocabulary • Review Relevé walks Step, relevé passé Step, relevé passé pivot	• Warm-up Increase number of repetitions • Vertical jump • Paddle turn • Jazz square • Review Step, kick Kick, ball–change Run, run, leap	• Jazz slide • Jazz half split • Teach three- or four-step combinations • Review • Stag leap • Vertical jump	• Warm-up Increase speed contraction Pike jump Tuck jump • Review Jazz square Jazz slide

(continued)

FORM 13.18 *(continued)*

Class 11	Class 12	Class 13	Class 14	Class 15
• Review • Warm-up • Teach • Performance combination • Review • Contraction pike jump • Tuck jump	• Review • Warm-up • Discuss criterion for performance • Review combination • Quiz over jazz terminology	• Review warm-up and combinations OR • Students devise combination in groups of four (select music, steps, after viewing a jazz dance video)	• Performance test on warm-up OR • Rehearse own combination with your group	• Performance test on combination

The dance form often makes a social statement about society and what is happening in it.

Musical Accompaniment

Musical accompaniment for jazz dance includes compact discs and tapes of popular music and jazz music from a specific era or from musical theater.

Dance Class Format

The class format for jazz dance is as follows:

1. Warm-up and isolations
2. Practice of exercises to increase technique and flexibility
3. Standing and floor exercises
4. Slow and fast combinations in the center or traveling across the floor (step combinations, turns, elevation steps)
5. Cool-down exercises to end the class

Classroom Considerations

Classroom considerations for jazz dance class are similar to those for other concert dance forms. A student should become aware of his body as it moves through the space and in relation to other bodies. The student should be quiet and respond to the instructor in a respectful manner.

Safety

The dance classroom should be large enough to accommodate students as they do combinations with several big locomotor steps and jumps. Students must be aware of their spatial needs, especially when performing kicking movements, fast-moving steps, and big jumps through the space with other dancers. Floors should not be too slippery, but the surface should have the right texture to accommodate sliding movements.

Attire

Male students wear a tight T-shirt or leotard and pants or tights, or unitard and a dance belt. The male student wears either a belt or suspenders. Female students wear a leotard and tights or clothing in which the teacher can see the line of the body. Hair should be secured away from the face to keep it out of the eyes. Jewelry such as dangling earrings, necklaces, and bracelets should not be worn to class for safety reasons.

Students usually wear jazz shoes, which are leather lace-up oxfords with full suede or split rubber soles. Other types of jazz footwear are soft boots and ballet shoes.

Classroom Etiquette

In the jazz dance class, students conform to concert dance class etiquette. They remain quiet and courteous to the dance teacher.

Beyond Technique Assignments

The following are some suggestions for beyond technique assignments in jazz dance:

- View a videotape of a musical or a music video, or see a performance and write a report on the performance.
- View several styles of jazz dance and compare and contrast these styles.
- Research and write a paper; present your findings to the class with examples of these styles.
- View two different musicals choreographed by two different people or from different eras. Give an oral presentation that describes and analyzes the choreographic differences and similarities between the two choreographers' styles and musicals.
- Form a small group with other students and use selected beginning jazz dance vocabulary to create a jazz dance and perform it for the class.

Content Overview

The content overview provides the necessary information for teaching the jazz dance unit.

Definition and History

Jazz dance is a hybrid form of dance that has its roots in African American, Afro-Cuban, Haitian, and Hindu (East Indian) cultures and dance. This dance form incorporates ballet and modern dance movements and is a part of musical stage dance.

The origin of jazz stems from the rhythms and movement of African Americans. Their musical outlets (church hymns, brass bands, spirituals, and blues) influenced the development of jazz dance and music. Throughout the 20th century these art forms paralleled each other. Jazz is an ever-changing and evolving means of expression that mirrors the life and times of the people within each decade.

With the 1920s came the Charleston, Black Bottom, and Castle Walk. In the 1930s, jazz was a strong influence on the movies with dancers such as Ginger Rogers and Fred Astaire and the producer Busby Berkeley. During this time, Dixieland jazz, followed by big bands and boogie, became popular, performed by such celebrated musicians as Duke Ellington, Louis Armstrong, Glenn Miller, and Artie Shaw. In the 1940s on the Broadway stage, Jerome Robbins and George Balanchine united classical and contemporary dance. Also in this decade, Jack Cole developed a jazz form that blended dance moments from the cultures of Asia (especially Hindu), Latin America, and Harlem. The 1950s brought the birth of rock 'n' roll along with various social dances such as the Stroll, Chicken, and Hully Gully. The 1960s brought an age of rebellion with dances like the Monkey, Pony, and Frug. In the 1970s disco dance reigned with the advent of dances like the Bus Stop, the Hustle, and the Bump. The 1980s brought punk rock, slam dancing, and break dancing; again, these dances stemmed from popular social dances. The famous musical theater choreographers Bob Fosse and Michael Bennett heightened the interest of dancers and audiences to jazz dance. In the 1990s, hip-hop evolved from rap music.

Jazz dance is an American dance form that is as popular as its music. This dance form has influenced Broadway shows, musicals, and music videos. Those credited with creating various jazz styles are Jack Cole (East Indian influence), Matt Mattox (percussive), Luigi (lyrical), Gus Giordano (natural form and body movement), and Bob Fosse (minimal and sensual). Dance students and choreographers will often study a specific style or use an eclectic approach.

Special Features

The following are specific features of jazz dance:

- Dancers use isolated movements of various body parts while performing steps in place or through space.
- Jazz dance has percussive, lyrical, and fluid qualities.
- The isolations and movements use syncopation and polyrhythms.
- Jazz dance synthesizes popular dances, mores, and music of the time period.

Principles

Movement, choreographic, and aesthetic principles that specifically apply to jazz dance are shown in the shaded regions of the following icons.

Movement Principles of Jazz Dance

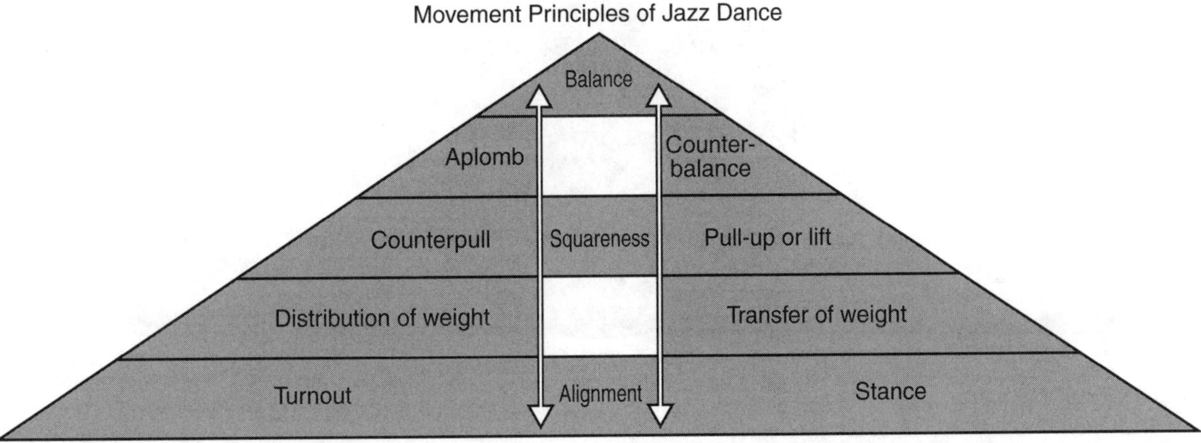

Choreographic Principles of Jazz Dance

Choreographic elements	Choreographic structures	Choreographic designs	Choreographic devices	Choreographic relationships
Motif	Simple musical forms	Dancer's body shape	Repetition	Solo
Phrase	• AB (binary)	Dancer's pathway through space	Reverse	Duet
Theme and variation	• ABA (ternary)	Visual design	Alter	Trio
	• Rondo	• Symmetrical	• Addition or subtraction	Quartet
	• Theme and variation	• Asymmetrical	• Directional change	Small and large groups
	Contrapuntal forms	Symbolism	• Facing or focus	
	• Canon (round)	• Representational	• Level	
	• Fugue	• Abstraction	• Dimension	
	Others	• Distortion	• Tempo	
	• Narrative (story)	Relationship	• Rhythm	
	• Open (free)	• Unison	• Quality or effort action	
		• Sequential	• Positioning	
		• Successional	• Movement section	
		• Oppositional		
		• Complementary		

Traditional Dance Elements

Space	Time	Force	Relationships
Directions Dimensions Levels Shapes Pathways Focus	Duration Tempo	Movement qualities • Sustained • Percussive • Swinging • Suspended • Collapsing • Vibratory	Among body parts Among people Between people and props

Laban's Dance Elements

Space	Time	Weight	Flow
Direct or indirect	Sudden or slow	Light or strong	Bound or free

Effort actions (use space, time, and weight)

• Dab • Flick • Punch • Slash • Glide • Float • Press • Wring

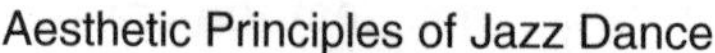

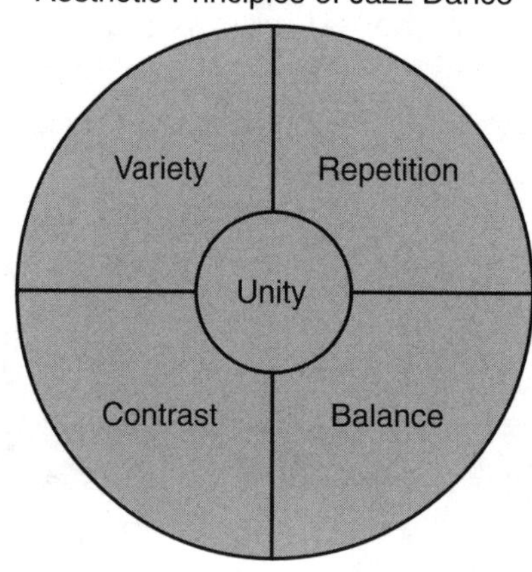

Vocabulary

The vocabulary for jazz dance is shared with other concert dance forms.

Foot, Arm, and Hand Positions

In jazz dance, the foot positions are the same as in modern dance and ballet. The arms and hands in jazz dance are similar yet contain specific stylistic differences.

Foot Positions

First position is parallel and turned out.

Second position is parallel and turned out.

Fourth position is parallel and turned out.

Third and fifth positions are turned out.

See the modern dance and ballet units for definitions of the following foot positions:

- Demi-plié and grand plié
- Full foot
- Three-quarter relevé

Neutral (left) and jazz (right) hands.

Forced arch is when the foot is in three-quarter relevé with the knee bent.

Arm and Hand Positions

Jazz arms are usually straight to give the dancer a long, extended line. The following positions are basic.

- **Second position** is out to the side and slightly below the shoulder.
- In the **overhead position**, both arms stretch up in a V position with the shoulders down.
- In **opposition,** one arm stretches forward and the other to second position approximately at shoulder height, or one hand overhead and the other in second position.
- **Hands on hips** is with hands low on the hips where the torso joins the legs; hands can be placed flat in front or with thumbs behind.
- In the **arms bent in front of chest position,** arms are parallel to the shoulders with elbow to the side and fingertips almost touching.

In **jazz hands,** the palms are flat with the fingers stretched wide apart. A jazz hand variation is with the palms flat and the fingers stretched but close together. In jazz hands, the palms may face up, down, or forward. Other hand positions (such as fists, a relaxed hand or wrist, or ballet hands) relate to specific styles.

Jazz Dance Technique

The jazz dance exercises, steps, and combinations are presented in the general order of the class.

Warm-Up

Isolations involve moving individual or multiple body parts while other parts remain still or move in a different way.The head, shoulders, rib cage, arms, hands, hips, knees, and feet are the parts that can move in isolation.

The **head** begins centered; it focuses directly forward to the audience.

- Head turns to one side or the other in a straight path.
- Head moves up; eyes focus diagonally up.

Shoulder isolations.

- Head moves down; eyes focus outward, downward, or on a diagonal.
- Head tilts downward with the ear in line with the shoulder.
- Head moves in a half circle, beginning with a turn to the side, down, and to the other side.

Shoulders begin in a neutral or centered position. The shoulders are down and square to the front of the room.

- **Shoulder shrugs** involve rapidly raising and lowering the shoulders.
- **Shoulder raises** involve lifting the shoulders to under the ears and dropping into the neutral position.
- In **shoulder isolations,** shoulders move forward, center, back, and center.
- In **oppositional shoulder lifts,** one shoulder moves up as the other moves down; then they reverse positions.

The **rib cage** lifts off the hips, but it is not expanded. The rib cage isolations begin in a neutral (centered) position. Place the hands on the hips with elbows out to the side.

- **Side-to-side isolations** move from center, to side, to center, to side in a straight line. Next, do the isolations without stopping in the center position.
- **Front-to-back isolations** move from center, to front, to center, to back, to center in a straight line. Next, do these isolations without stopping in the center position.
- Combine the side-to-side and front-to-back ribcage isolations. Reverse the directions.
- Another directional isolation begins in the central position, moves forward, side, back, and center; then forward, other side, back, and center. This exercise may begin from the back, reversing the directions of the isolation sequence.

Hip isolations are generally performed in demi-plié for stability and complete isolation of the hip movements. The hips are centered and vertically aligned with the tailbone dropping downward to the floor. Perform these exercises in parallel position.

- **Side-to-side hip isolations** begin in a neutral (centered) position.
- **Side pulses** are quick thrusts to the side; they can also be done to the front and back.
- **Hip lift isolations** move one hip upward, shortening the space between the ribs and the hips, and return to center. These hip lifts are later performed through the center.
- **Forward and back hip isolations** move forward, center, back, center in a straight line. This isolation reverses beginning from the back.

Standing Exercises

See the ballet dance and modern dance units for definitions of the following exercises.

- **Demi-plié** is in parallel, turned out, in first, second, and fifth position.
- **Battement tendu** is in parallel position and turned out, to the front and side.
- **Battement tendu with demi-plié** is in parallel and turned-out position.
- **Battement dégagé** is in turned-out and parallel positions, to the front and side.
- **Foot pedals** are in parallel and turned-out first position.
- **Battement développé** is in parallel and turned-out positions.
- **Stretches** happen with the arms and body reaching upward, sideward, downward, and on diagonals.
- **Pulses** are quick stretches and releases of arms reaching upward, front, to the side, and on the diagonal.
- **Leg swings** are to the front, side, and back through first position.
- **Contractions** (see the modern dance unit, page 330) occur in the shoulders, waist, hips, or in the whole torso.

Floor Work

Crunches increase abdominal strength. They are done to the front and side while lying on the back with knees bent. (See the modern dance unit, pages 335-336.)

Modified push-ups: See the modern dance unit, page 342.

Inverted push-ups: See the modern dance unit, page 342.

Butterfly stretch: Sitting with soles of the feet together, hold the ankles and let the body round forward, keeping the buttocks on the floor.

Body bend forward stretch: See the modern dance unit, page 337.

Body bend forward stretch in straddle: See the modern dance unit, page 337.

Knee to torso stretch (hamstring stretch): See the modern dance unit, page 333.

Sternum lift: See the modern dance unit, page 335.

In the **jazz split (half split),** kneel on one knee, turned out. Extend the other leg forward in parallel position. Keep the shoulders and hips square over the front leg, and keep the back straight. Slide the front leg forward, slowly stretching the body toward the floor. Place one hand on either side of the front leg as it slides. Let the back lower leg rotate inward, lowering the hips toward the floor. The goal is for the hips to rest on the floor in the jazz split, or half split, position. Later this exercise can be attempted with arms up.

Center and Across the Floor

This section of the class includes walks, step combinations, turns, and extension steps.

Jazz Walks

There are many types of jazz walks.

In the **walk,** the heel hits the floor first, and the step rolls through the ball of the foot and the toes. The arms work either in opposition or are held along the sides of the body. Word cues are out, out.

In the **dancer's walk,** the legs and feet are turned out from the hips. The toes contact the floor first, then the ball, then the heel. The entire body moves as a unit when walking either forward or back. Word cues are walk, walk.

In the **toe–heel walk,** the legs are parallel. Walk by placing the ball of the foot and then the heel on the floor. Word cues are toe, heel.

In the **heel–toe (or heel–bend) walk,** the heel touches the floor and rolls through the foot to the toes while the knee bends in demi-plié simultaneously. Word cues are heel, toe.

The **relevé walk** takes the full body weight on the toes and ball of the foot while the legs remain straight. Word cues are up, up.

In **step, relevé passé,** step on the ball of the foot (relevé) and lift the other foot to the side of the knee with the foot pointed. The legs and feet are in either turned-out or parallel position. Word cues are step, lift.

Step, relevé passé pivot is a variation of step, relevé passé. Do the step, relevé passé, then pivot an eighth, quarter, or half turn and step (fall lightly) full foot. Word cues are step, lift, pivot, fall.

In **low jazz walk,** the working leg and foot extend forward, accepting the weight through the toe, ball, and heel with the supporting leg in demi-plié. The back leg extends behind the body. The body remains in the low level as the dancer moves across the floor. Word cues are low, low.

In the **hip walk forward,** the hip lifts and extends, then shifts the weight to the working leg. The foot presses into the floor and the knee bends on the front diagonal to the body. The hip walk is also performed to the side. Word cues are hip, lift, down.

In the **hip walk backward,** the hip lifts and extends, then shifts the weight to the working leg. The foot presses into the floor and the knee bends on the back diagonal to the body. Word cues are hip, lift, down.

Vegas walk (sugars), is performed in parallel position on relevé. Step forward, crossing the other foot on relevé. Repeat with the other foot. This walk is also performed backward. Word cues are twist, twist.

In the **L.A. walk,** move the hip side and step side simultaneously; then step, crossing the other foot in front. Word cues are side, across.

Step Combinations

In **step, touch,** step on one foot, touch the floor (front, side, or back) with the other foot. Do not place weight on the foot that touches. Word cues are step, touch.

In **cross, touch,** step over one foot to the side and touch the other foot to the side. Word cues are cross, touch.

For **step, ball–change,** step right foot forward on full foot, then transfer weight briefly onto the ball of the left foot behind the right foot, then step full foot on the right foot either front or side. Repeat to other side. Word cues are step, back, front.

For **cross, ball–change,** step left foot over right foot. The weight transfers briefly to the ball of the right foot; then step on the left foot, taking the weight. Repeat to the other side. Word cues are cross, ball–change.

In **step, kick,** step on one foot and kick the other leg from the knee. Word cues are step, kick.

In **kick, ball–change,** kick from the knee with one leg and step on the ball of the foot, behind the other foot; then step on the other foot. Word cues are kick, ball–change or kick, step, step.

For **pas de bourrée in place,** cross right foot on full foot or relevé in front or back of left foot; step left foot to the left side on relevé, and step right foot on full foot in demi-plié. This step can be done on full foot or with relevés. Word cues are cross, side, front.

For **side pas de bourrée,** cross right foot behind left foot, step left foot to the left side on relevé, and step crossing right foot in front of the other foot. Word cues are back, side, front.

For **pas de bourrée turns,** cross right foot behind left foot; step on left foot and do a counterclockwise quarter, half, or full turn. Complete the turn by placing the right foot in front. This is an outward turn. Word cues are turn back, side, front.

For **jazz square,** step forward on right foot; then the left foot crosses over the right foot. Step back with the right foot, and step to the left side with the left foot. The arm moves in opposition to the working foot, or the arms move from side to side in opposition to the feet. Word cues are forward, cross front, back, side.

In **jazz slide step,** step (back or side) in demi-plié (lunge); slide the other leg. The sliding leg is straight and turned out, and the foot is pointed. The body leans toward the supporting leg (back or side). The arms are on diagonal, parallel to the line of the straight leg. Word cues are slide, out.

Jazz layout.

Turns

For **paddle turn step,** step back on the ball of the foot while the front leg and foot steps and rotates around the supporting foot. The ball of the foot acts as a pivot. The turn is performed for eight, two, and four counts. Word cues are back, front.

In **three-step turn,** step out to the side; the other foot steps forward with a half turn to face the opposite direction. Then the first foot completes the turn to end facing front with the other foot either touching the side or front of the full foot or pointing to the side. Word cues are step out, turn, turn and touch; or out, half turn, half turn, touch.

In **step pivot turn,** step and do a quarter, half, or three-quarter turn while the other foot rises to the ankle or to the side of the knee in parallel position. This may also be broken into a step, then turn. Word cues are step, pivot or step and pivot.

For **pirouette,** turn on one foot with the other foot raised in various positions (to the ankle or knee, parallel or turned out). The supporting foot is on full foot, on relevé, or in demi-plié; or the pirouette is combined with a jump. The pirouette does a one-quarter, one-half, three-quarter, or a full revolution. It ends in a foot position or an open position with the weight distributed unequally. Word cues are turn and down.

Elevation Steps

Vertical jump starts in demi-plié. Jump from both feet and stretch legs in the air. The legs are straight and perpendicular to the floor. Both arms begin parallel to the side, raise alongside the ears, and return to the side of the body on the landing. Word cues are plié, jump.

Arch jump begins in demi-plié. Jump into the air with the body straight and both legs straight; point feet. At the top of the jump, arch the upper back (under the shoulder blades) and stretch the legs behind the body. The body returns to alignment and lands in demi-plié. Word cues are plié, arch, plié.

Pike jump starts in parallel position demi-plié. Jump with both legs extended. At the top of the jump, the torso bends at the waist and the legs are in front, almost forming a V shape if viewed from the side. During the jump, the arms rise from the sides of the body in a parallel path so that at the top of the jump they are slightly diagonally forward of the body. Word cues are plié, pike, plié.

Tuck jump begins in demi-plié. Jump with both knees raised and near the chest, feet pointed. Torso is aligned in the air and for the landing. Word cues are plié, tuck, plié or land.

For **step–hop,** step on one foot and hop; the other foot is in a parallel or turned-out position at the ankle, on the side, in front, in back of the knee, or in front or back of the body. Word cues are step, hop.

The **leap** in jazz dance differs from the grand jeté in ballet. The air moment is often parallel to the floor. The jazz leap can be executed front and side. The standard position for the arms is in opposition to the working leg; if the right leg extends forward, the left arm is in front and the right arm is in side position. Arms may be in a variety of positions. Word cues are and leap.

In the **stag leap,** the front leg extends; at the top of the leap, the knee bends and the thigh lifts near the torso. The back leg remains extended in the air during the leap. Word cues are plié, lift, plié.

For **hitch kick,** kick right leg in front, then kick the left leg in front in succession. Land in demi-plié on the right leg; the left leg remains extended in front. In this step, the legs are straight to perform a scissoring action. Word cues are kick, kick, down.

Jazz step–hop.

Jazz leap.

Selected Resources

Selected resources include jazz dance texts, music, and videos.

Texts

Cayou, D.K. 1981. *Modern jazz dance.* Palto Alto, CA: National Press.

Cohan, R. 1986. *The dancer workshop: A guide to fundamentals of movement.* New York: Simon & Schuster.

Giordano, G. 1978. *Anthology of American jazz dance.* Evanston, IL: Orion.

Giordano, G. 1992. *Jazz dance classes: Beginning through advanced.* Pennington, NJ: Princeton.

Hatchett, F., and N. Gitlin. 2000. *Frank Hatchett's jazz dance.* Champaign, IL: Human Kinetics.

Kraines, M., and E. Pryor. 2000. *Jump into jazz.* 4th ed. Palo Alto, CA: Mayfield.

Kriegel, L.P., and K. Chandler-Vaccaro. 1994. *Jazz dance today.* St. Paul: West.

Lane, C. 1983. *All that jazz and more: Complete book of jazz dancing.* New York: Leisure Press.

Lihs, H. 1991. *Jazz dance.* Boston: American Press.

Wydro, K. 1981. *The Luigi jazz dance technique.* Garden City, NY: Doubleday.

Music

The best of hip hop. 1992. Hollywood: Priority Records P27053.

Boyer, V.J. 1981. *Dancin.* Long Branch, NJ: Kimbo Educational.

Demarco, R. 1988. *New York jazz.* Dallas: Bodarc Productions BOD 87-10.

Nossen, S. 1965. *Modern class: Beginner's class.* New York: Statler.

Videos

Andree, K. 1996. *Steppin' out with a star.* Hightstown, NJ: Princeton.

Benson, S. 1996. *The jazz man.* Hightstown, NJ: Princeton.

Coombes, A. 1989. *The jazz workout.* Hightstown, NJ: Princeton.

Giordano, G. 1984. *Jazz dance class with Gus Giordano.* Chicago: All Night Moving Pictures.

Lane, C. 1994. *Christy Lane's funky freestyle dancing.* Hightstown, NJ: Princeton.

Lane, C. 1994. *Christy Lane's more funky freestyle dancing.* Hightstown, NJ: Princeton.

Luigi. 1988. *The master jazz class.* Hightstown, NJ: Princeton.

Luigi. 1988. *The master style & technique.* Hightstown, NJ: Princeton.

Rizzo, B. 1993. *Bob Rizzo's jazz class for kids.* Hightstown, NJ: Princeton.

Rizzo, B. 1996. *Jazz-a-matazz: Hot routines for jazz, lyrical, funk.* Hightstown, NJ: Princeton.

Rizzo, B. 1996. *Jazz for kidz.* Hightstown, NJ: Princeton.

Youngblood, B. 1996. *Party time.* Hightstown, NJ: Princeton.

Tap Dance Unit

Teaching Overview

Psychomotor Objectives

- Execute basic tap dance steps, three- or four-step combinations, and dances to music.
- Demonstrate application of principles to tap dance.
- Without music, identify and perform basic tap steps that produce various sounds.
- Demonstrate the relationship of movement to music (count, rhythm, tempo, time signature).

Psychomotor Evaluation

- Performance test of selected tap steps: sounds, breaks, combinations and dances in relation to music (count, rhythm, tempo, time signature), application of principles.

Cognitive Objectives

- Recognize beginning tap dance terminology.
- Translate a beginning tap dance into movement from oral or written instructions.
- Conduct a self-evaluation or a peer evaluation of a beginning tap dance performance.
- Write a dance concert report about a tap dance performance (technique, choreography, production).

Cognitive Evaluation

- Complete written testing of beginning tap dance knowledge (steps, terminology, definitions, history and culture; self-assessment of personal performance).
- Write a dance concert report about a tap dance performance (technique, choreography, production).

Affective Objectives

- Practice etiquette for dancers in the tap dance class.
- Demonstrate personal movement confidence and performance attitude.
- Work with the group to refine performance.

Affective Evaluation

- Demonstrate etiquette, movement confidence, performance attitude and cooperation, contribution, and leadership within a group and class.

Teaching Approaches

Tap dance is a dance form for people of all ages.The preschool child performs movement songs that include simple tap dance skills and creative tap, which incorporates specific steps into a dance. In high school dance programs, tap dance is a popular course that provides an additional outlet for students who have studied tap dance in a dance studio.Tap dance is performed in many musical theater productions and variety shows.

FORM 13.19

Scope and Sequence for Tap Dance

New = N Review = R Review for test = RT Performance test = PT

	1	2	3	4	5	6	7	8	9	10	11	12	13	14	15
Definition and history of tap dance	N														
Attire, etiquette, and safety	N														
Articulation of heel, ball of foot	N														
Ankle, full foot, flex, point, and circle foot	N	R	R	R	R	R	R	R	R	R	R	R	R	RT	
Step-stamp toe, heel drops, toe and heel digs	N	R	R	R	R	R	R	R	R	R	R	R	R	RT	
Toe taps, brush (front and back)	N	R	R	R	R	R	R	R	R	R	R	R	R	RT	
Shuffle, shuffle stamp	N	R	R	R	R			R			R			RT	
Shuffle, step with clap	N	R	R	R	R										
Flap, step		N	R	R		R			R			R		R	
Brush, hop, step		N	R	R		R				R			R	R	
Shuffle, step (front, side, back)		N	R	R		R									
Step, ball–change			N	R		R				R			R	R	
Waltz clog single step, shuffle, ball–change				N	R	R	R	R	R	R	R	R		RT	PT
Waltz clog double, flap, shuffle, ball–change				N	R	R	R	R	R	R	R	R		RT	PT
Waltz clog triple, shuffle, step, shuffle, ball–change					N	R	R	R				R		RT	PT
Three flaps, ball–change					N	R	R	R			R	R	R		PT
Shuffle, hop; shuffle, hop, step							N	R				R		RT	
Shuffle stamp; step, shuffle, ball–change							N	R				R	R		PT
Shuffle, heel drop, step									N		R	R		RT	
Flap, shuffle, hop; flap, heel drop									N			R	R		PT
Buffalo: single, double, triple									N		R	R		RT	
Soft shoe essence: single, double, triple										N		R	R		PT
Pivot step										N	R	R		RT	
Buck time step: shuffle hop (wait) step, brush front, ball–change, break: shuffle, hop, step, flap, ball–change											N	R	R	R	PT

FORM 13.20

Tap Dance Block Unit Plan

Class 1	Class 2	Class 3	Class 4	Class 5
• Define tap dance • Tap dance history • Attire, etiquette, and safety • Warm-up • Articulation of ankle and foot, ball of foot, toe and heel • Tap exercises: full foot; flex; point; circle foot; stamp; step; toe and heel drops; toe and heel dig; toe taps; brush (front and back); shuffle; shuffle, stamp; shuffle, step, clap	• Review (barre) • Warm-up of ankle, foot, toe, ball of foot • Flap, step • Brush, hop step • Shuffle step (front, side, back) • Review • Shuffle • Shuffle, stamp • Shuffle, step with clap	• Review • Warm-up (barre) • Step, ball–change • Flap • Shuffle • Brush, hop, step • Shuffle (front, side, back)	• Review • Warm-up • Waltz clog (single) *step, shuffle, ball–change* • Waltz clog (double) *flap, shuffle, ball–change* • Flap • Shuffle • Brush, hop step • Shuffle (front, side, back) • Shuffle, stamp • Shuffle, step with clap	• Review • Warm-up • Waltz clog (triple) *shuffle, step shuffle, ball–change* • Three flaps, ball–change • Review • Waltz clog (single and double)
Class 6	**Class 7**	**Class 8**	**Class 9**	**Class 10**
• Review • Warm-up (in center) • Waltz clog (all) • Single • Double • Triple • Flaps • Shuffle • Combination	• Warm-up (in center) • Review • Waltz clog *three flaps, ball–change* *shuffle, hop, shuffle, step* *shuffle, stamp*	• Warm-up (in center) • Shuffle, hop, shuffle, hop, step • Shuffle stamp • Step, shuffle, ball–change	• Warm-up (in center) • Shuffle, heel drop, step • Flap, shuffle hop • Flap, heel drop	• Warm-up (in center) • Soft shoe essence Single *step, brush, ball–change* Double *flap, brush, ball–change* Triple *shuffle, step, brush, ball–change* *(entire combination step, brush ball–change; step, brush, ball–change; brush ball–change; brush, ball–change)* • Pivot step

(continued)

FORM 13.20 *(continued)*

Class 11	Class 12	Class 13	Class 14	Class 15
• Warm-up • Buck up *shuffle, hop (wait), step, brush front, ball–change* • Break *shuffle, hop, step* *flap, ball, change* • Review • Shuffle step, shuffle, ball–change • Pivot step • Buffalo *shuffle, heel drop, step*	• Warm-up • Review • All dance steps	• Warm-up • Go over steps and dance types for test • Establish criteria for evaluation • Brush, hop, step • Flap, shuffle, heel drop • Buffalo • Waltz clog • Buck time step • Soft shoe essence	• Review all steps and exercises for performance test	• Warm-up • Performance test • Waltz clog, soft shoe essences, time step and break • Various steps

Creative tap uses a story with action words. The dancers mimic the words usi tap sounds. For example, the children stamp down the stairs and shuffle across the street.

Specific Teaching Methods

Start the tap class in a chair, on a low bench, or at the barre. This helps students to focus on the use of the feet and the sounds each movement makes. Balance becomes an issue when you begin to move one foot while you are standing on the other.

Teach the step without the music, then later add the music to the steps. Use words, such as "shuf-fle, step," to mimic the sounds made by the taps; say the syllables in the rhythm of the step.

Musical Accompaniment

Musical accompaniment for tap dance includes CDs, records, and cassettes of different genres of music: soft shoe, military, waltz clog, buck time step and other time steps, ragtime, hip-hop, show tunes, and popular standards (such as "Tea for Two," "East Side, West Side," "Carolina in the Morning," "Colonel Bogey March").

Dance Class Format

The dance class format for tap dance is as follows:

1. Warm-up at the barre or in the center
2. Practice of exercises and steps to increase technique and flexibility
3. Slow to fast combinations in the center or traveling across the floor and learning dances (routines) to gain performance qualities and styles that will enable dancers to choreograph routines
4. Cool-down exercises to end the class

Classroom Considerations

Dancers in the tap class must be aware of the space in which they move. Students must be quiet and attentive to the instructor. The students should be able to move in the attire they choose for dance class.

Safety

Tap safety is a primary concern. Some tap shoes are sold with the taps attached. If the shoes and taps are sold separately, have a professional shoemaker attach the taps. Regardless of whether the tap shoes have single or double taps, the nails that hold the tap to the shoes should allow the tap to produce the sounds, yet ensure that the tap does not fall off the shoes.

The floor is another important concern for the tap dancer. Slippery floors and tap shoes don't mix. Make a floor check before starting a tap class.

Attire

Students should wear attire that allows them to move comfortably. Males wear a shirt with shorts or pants. Females can wear a leotard and tights or a shirt with shorts or pants.

Males and females can wear oxford-style tap shoes with low heels. Females may wear tap shoes with ribbon ties or another fastening. High-heeled shoes with ıckles are more appropriate for the more advanced tap dancer. Tap dancers ould wear tights or socks so that they don't get blisters.

lassroom Etiquette

ıdents remain silent and keep their feet still when listening to the teacher and ıen other groups are dancing. Before leaving the dance classroom, dancers ..ould remove tap shoes so that they do not disturb other people in the building.

Beyond Technique Assignments

The following are suggestions for beyond technique assignments in tap dance:

- Create a tap conversation with a partner: One person makes a "tap statement." The other person may "agree" and replicate the sounds or "disagree" and make another statement. (This is similar to a question and answer in music.)
- Create a tap dance on a new theme or in a different style to different music than is normally used in tap dance.
- Take a combination and expand it to form a dance. The teacher can create a combination, and groups of students can each add a section to create a dance.
- View one or more tap dance movies from the 1940s and 1980s; compare and contrast the dancers' styles and how the tap dances were part of the movie.
- Do an oral or written report on one or more tap artists.
- Create a tap dance in the style of a particular tap artist.

Content Overview

The content overview provides the necessary information for teaching the tap dance unit.

Definition and History

Tap dance, considered an American dance form, is a theatrical and concert dance form that has its roots in African American, Native American, English, and Irish culture. Tap dance blends the Irish jig and clog dancing, American soft shoe, and African-American-based steps. Tap styles include shuffle, syncopated buck, wing, and styles from other cultures and eras.

Africans who were brought to the United States as slaves were forbidden to use drums, so they developed percussive sounds such as stomps, claps, rasps, and bones to accompany their dancing. An 18th-century African American performer, William Henry Lane (with the stage name of Juba), became popular in the United States. Abroad, he performed dances composed of syncopated rhythms. In the 19th century, minstrel shows became popular and their dancing influenced many American and European stage dancers. In the last quarter of the century, dancers performed competition dances and other styles of tap dances on both the variety and vaudeville stages.

By the 20th century tap dance gained even more popularity with the birth of ragtime and jazz. In the 1920s, dancers in New York's Harlem nightclubs stole steps from one another at the Hoofers' Club. Many famous African American tap dancers, such as Bill "Bojangles" Robinson and King Rastus Brown, came to this club to perform. Robinson's trademark style was his upright posture, his clear tap sounds, rhythmic swing, and time steps. Later, dancers such as John Bubbles expanded the genre of rhythm tap, while Charles ("Honi") Coles had a lyrical style that contrasted Bubbles' traveling and fast, turning footwork. Coles and his partner, Charles ("Cholly") Atkins, excelled in their tap improvisations.

In the 1940s Gene Kelly and Fred Astaire made tap dance popular in the movie musicals. In the 1980s, tap dancing was an important part of musical theater in such works as *42nd Street* and *A Chorus Line.* Dancers such as Paul Draper, Donald O'Connor, and Dick Van Dyke were featured artists on stage and screen. Each of these dancers created a personal style of tap. Paul Draper combined ballet and tap dance. Fred Astaire created a cool, sophisticated quality that blended ballroom and jazz dance with tap dance. Gene Kelly's style incorporated athleticism into the ballet, jazz, and ballroom dance he mixed with tap dance.

Female tap dancers appeared on stage and screen with male partners or as soloists. Eleanor Powell created her own style of tap dance. Debbie Reynolds, Ginger Rogers, Ann Miller, and other female stars danced their way into America's heart in the movie musicals.

Gregory Hines, known for his dancing roles in *Cotton Club, White Nights,* and *Tap,* gave tap dance a new resurgence in the movies. In the 1990s, new tap companies such as Tap Dogs, movies such as *Tappin',* and musicals such as *Juba* and *Bring in 'da Noise, Bring in 'da Funk* have reinforced the popularity of tap dance.

Special Features

The following are specific features of tap dance:

- Tap dance uses rhythm and sound mixed with movement.
- The dance form has styles based on popular music from different eras and musicals.
- Tap dance combinations most often begin on the 8 count of the measure before or the "&" ("and") before the 1.
- Tap dance enables a person to express feelings. Attitude, musicality, and style are part of its performance attributes. Individuality, improvisation, and creativity became the hallmarks of accomplished stage tap dancers, or "hoofers." They are said to have a balance of vitality and "cool."
- Tap dance enhances students' ability to listen, count, move, and to replicate progressively complicated sounds and foot movements. The sounds produced by the feet become a part of the accompaniment.

Principles

Movement, choreographic, and aesthetic principles that specifically apply to tap dance are shown in the shaded regions of the following icons.

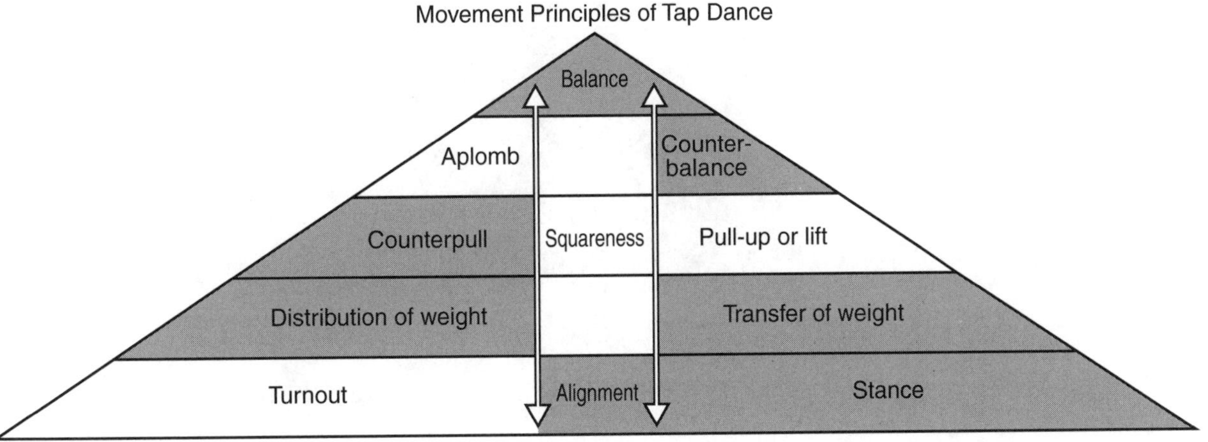

Choreographic Principles of Tap Dance

Choreographic elements	Choreographic structures	Choreographic designs	Choreographic devices	Choreographic relationships
Motif Phrase Theme and variation	Simple musical forms • AB (binary) • ABA (ternary) • Rondo • Theme and variation Contrapuntal forms • Canon (round) • Fugue Others • Narrative (story) • Open (free)	Dancer's body shape Dancer's pathway through space Visual design • Symmetrical • Asymmetrical Symbolism • Representational • Abstraction • Distortion Relationship • Unison • Sequential • Successional • Oppositional • Complementary	Repetition Reverse Alter • Addition or subtraction • Directional change • Facing or focus • Level • Dimension • Tempo • Rhythm • Quality or effort action • Positioning	Solo Duet Trio Quartet Small and large groups

Traditional Dance Elements

Space	Time	Force	Relationships
Directions Dimensions Levels Shapes Pathways Focus	Duration Tempo	Movement qualities • Sustained • Percussive • Swinging • Suspended • Collapsing • Vibratory	Among body parts Among people Between people and props

Laban's Dance Elements

Space	Time	Weight	Flow
Direct or indirect	Sudden or slow	Light or strong	Bound or free

Effort actions (use space, time, and weight)

• Dab • Flick • Punch • Slash • Glide • Float • Press • Wring

Aesthetic Principles of Tap Dance

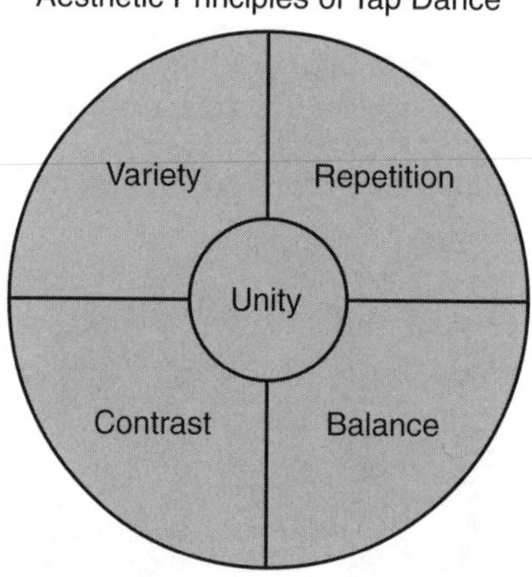

Heel dig, toe dig, and toe tip.

Vocabulary

Tap dance shares its vocabulary with other concert dance forms.

Tap Dance Skills

The basic skills of tap dance include footwork, rhythm, sound techniques, and arm movements.

- **Footwork** is the articulation of the feet: moving toes, ball, heel, ankle, full foot, and tip of the foot.
- **Rhythm** occurs in producing tap sounds while moving on the beat; moving on the "&," "a," and the "&" before the measure; creating sounds to counterpoint the music; using syncopated sound accents with toes, heels, hand claps, snaps, and slaps on the body.
- **Sound techniques** use single sound, double sounds, three sounds, hand claps, snaps, slapping the body, and multiple sounds in various rhythms.
- **Arm movements** provide balance and line to the dancer's performance, complement body and leg movements of a specific style of tap dance, remain below shoulder height, extend the arm completely or move it in succession.

Steps and Combinations

The steps listed are basic tap dance vocabulary, followed by examples of variations or progressive combinations. Most of the steps alternate to the right and left sides. They are often practiced in a series for seven times, ending with a stomp or a break to change to other side. In beginning combinations, a step is performed alternatively seven or three times, followed by a break before going on to the next combination.

Step is a transfer of weight to the full foot with a lighter sound than a stomp.

Count	Footwork	Cue
1, 2, 3, 4	Step (right), step (left), step (right), hold.	Step, step, step, hold

Count	Footwork	Cue
1, 2, 3, 4	Step (right), step (left), step (right), clap (hands).	Step, step, step, clap
1, 2, 3, 4	Step (right, left, right), hop (right).	Step, step, step, hop

Toe drop occurs in the transfer of weight to the toes and ball of foot, before the heel drop.

Heel drop occurs in the transfer of weight to the heel, after the toe drop.

In a **heel dig,** the heel strikes the floor quickly and releases.

Count	Footwork	Cue
1, 2	Step (right), heel dig (left).	Step, heel dig
1, 2, 3, 4	Step (right), step (left), step (right), heel dig (left).	Step, step, step, heel dig

Toe dig (diagonal view).

In a **toe tap,** the toes and the ball of the foot touch the floor and release quickly. This is an exercise performed in a series to increase ankle flexibility.

In a **toe tip,** the tip of the shoe strikes the floor sharply as an accent before quickly releasing from the floor.

In a **toe dig,** the toes strike the floor and quickly release off the floor.

Stamp occurs when the full foot hits the floor and quickly releases. This is done repeatedly with same foot or alternating feet.

Stomp occurs when the full foot hits the floor and accepts the weight. The sound is strong and decisive. This step alternates feet.

In a **brush,** the working foot is raised off the floor. The toes and ball of the foot brush the floor and continue off the floor. Brushes are executed forward and backward. When performed together, they maintain their distinct and separate sounds.

Count	Footwork	Cue
1 &	Brush front (right), step (left); repeat other side; do in a series.	Brush front, step
1 &	Brush back (right), step (left); repeat other side; do in a series.	Brush back, step
	Brush forward, backward (right), step (left); repeat other side; do in a series.	Brush forward and backward, step
1 & 2	Brush (right), hop (left), step (right); move forward or backward.	Brush, hop, step
1 & 2 &	Brush forward, backward (right); toe tap (right), step (right). Repeat other side; do in a series.	Brush forward, brush backward, toe tap, step

a

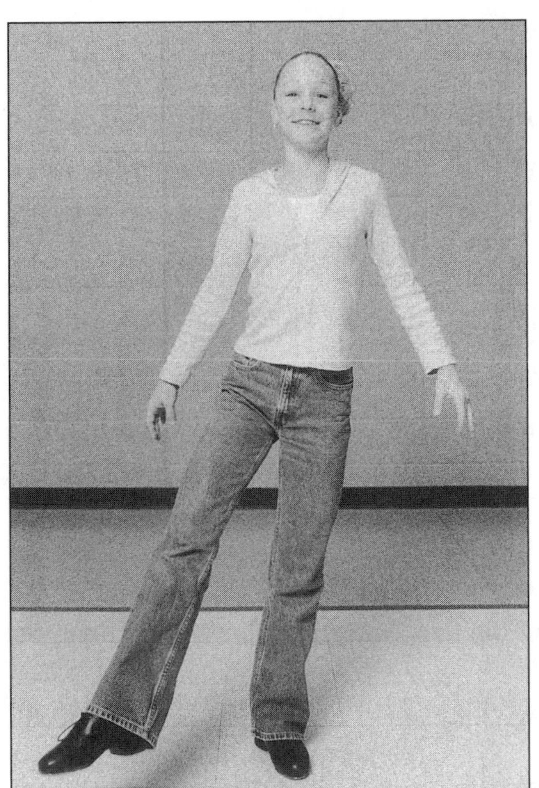

b

Brush the foot *(a)* out in front of the supporting leg and *(b)* across the front of the supporting leg.

Shuffle is a brush of the toes and ball of the foot forward and back quickly to join the sounds. Saying the step as "shuf-fle" illustrates the sounds.

Count	Footwork	Cue
1 & 2	Shuffle (right), step (right).	Shuffle, step
1 & 2	Shuffle (right), heel drop (left).	Shuffle, heel drop
& 1, 2 & 3, 4	Shuffle (right), heel drop (left), brush back (right), toe (right), heel drop (right).	Shuffle, heel drop, brush back, toe, heel drop
1 & 2	Shuffle (right), stamp (right).	Shuffle, stamp
1 & 2	Shuffle (right), leap (right).	Shuffle, leap
1 & 2	Shuffle (right), hop (left).	Shuffle, hop
1 & 2 &	Shuffle (right), hop (left), step (right) moving forward or backward.	Shuffle, hop, step
1 & 2	Shuffle (right), heel drop (right).	Shuffle, heel drop

In **ball-change,** the toes and ball of the back foot briefly take the weight behind the front foot on the "&." The front foot steps in place on the count.

Count	Footwork	Cue
1 & 2	Step (right), ball (left), change (right).	Step, ball-change
& 1 & 2	Brush (right), step (right), ball (left), change (right).	Brush, step, ball-change
& 1 & 2	Shuffle (right), ball (right), change (left).	Shuffle, ball-change

For **flaps,** brush with and step onto the ball of the foot. This step alternates feet and is performed moving forward and back.

Count	Footwork	Cue
& 1	Flap (right), step (left).	Flap, step
& 1, 2	Flap (right), heel drop (right) moving forward or backward.	Flap, heel drop
& 1 & 2	Flap (right), ball (left), change (right).	Flap, ball–change
& 1 & a 2	Flap (right), shuffle (left), hop (right).	Flap, shuffle, hop
& 1 & 2 & 3 & 4	Flap (right), shuffle (left), hop (right), step (left). Three flaps (right, left, right), ball (left), change (right).	Flap, shuffle, hop, step, flap, flap, flap, ball–change
1 & 2 & 3	Step (right), shuffle (left), ball (right), change (left).	Step, shuffle, ball–change

Waltz clog single

Count	Footwork	Cue
& 1 & 2 & 3	Step (right), shuffle (left), step (right), step (left).	Step, shuffle, step, step (ball–change)

Waltz clog double

Count	Footwork	Cue
& 1 & 2 & 3	Flap (right), shuffle (left), step (right), step (left).	Flap, shuffle, step, step (ball–change)

Waltz clog triple

Count	Footwork	Cue
& 1 & 2 & 3	Shuffle step (right), shuffle (left), step (right), step (left).	Shuffle, step, shuffle, step, step (ball–change)

Soft shoe single essence

Count	Footwork	Cue
1 & a 2	Step (right), brush (left), ball front (left), change (right).	Step, front, ball–change

Soft shoe double essence

Count	Footwork	Cue
1 & a 2	Flap (right), brush (left), ball front (left), change (right).	Flap, brush, ball–change

Soft shoe triple essence

Count	Footwork	Cue
& a 1 & a 2	Shuffle, step (right), brush (left), ball front (left), change (right).	Shuffle, step, brush, ball–change

The **buffalo** step is a combination of three movements: leap (right), shuffle (left), step (left) with the right leg bent and the foot in front of the supporting leg. This step is performed to the side.

Soft shoe essence.

Buffalo step.

The **time step** is a series of steps performed in combination that alternates in a series, ending with a break to begin the series again on the other side. Time steps progress from simple to difficult with the addition of sounds and footwork. For this unit, the single time step is included.

Buck time step

Count	Footwork	Cue
8 & 1, 2 & 3 &	Shuffle (right), hop (wait), step (right), brush front (left), ball (right), change (left).	Shuffle, hop, hold, step, brush, ball–change

Break

Count	Footwork	Cue
8 & 1, 2 a 3 &	Shuffle (right), hop (left), step (right), flap (left), ball (right), change (left).	Shuffle, hop, step, flap, ball–change

In tap dance, a **break** is a transition to change weight or direction or connect combinations. The following are basic breaks:

- Stomp
- Flap, clap
- Shuffle, hop, step
- Ball–change

The following are turns used in tap dance:

- **Pivot:** Step (right), ball (left), and turn a half turn.
- **Paddle:** Step (right), touch the toe (left) to the side, and continue these two steps while moving in a circle around yourself.
- **Three-step turn:** See the ballet dance unit, page 315.
- **Buzz step:** See the folk dance unit, page 242.

Specialty steps in tap dance include steps from other dance forms, such as balancé and pas de bourrée.

Selected Resources

Selected resources include folk dance texts, music, and videos.

Texts

Hoctor, D. 1971. *Graded exercises for tap dancing.* Waldwick, NY: Dance Records.

Marx, T. 1983. *Tap dance: A beginners guide.* New Jersey: Prentice-Hall.

Shipley, G. 1974. *The formation of tap technique.* Self-published.

Sutton, T. 1986. *Tap along with Tommy: A technique guide for tap dance teachers.* Vol. 1, 2, and dictionary. Decatur, GA: Weslock Circle.

Music

Bassing, J.A., and J. Matthew. 1993. *Music for tap class and choreography.* Dallas: Bodarc Productions.

Bassing, J.A., and L. Stanford. 1992. *Music for tap class.* Dallas: Bodarc Productions.

Collins, B. 1982. *Tap technique: Elementary & intermediate.* L.I.C., NY: Roper Records.

Dorame, S. 1990. *Tap dance.* Paris, France: Arion.

Kimble, B., and S. Randall. 1967. *Modern tap dancing.* Long Beach, NY: Kimbo Educational.

Videos

Brown, R., and C. Green. 1972. *Tap dance.* New York: Insight Media.

Cramer, L. 1995. *The tap dictionary.* Hightstown, NJ: Princeton.

Cunne, C. 1995. *Celtic feet.* New York: Insight Media.

Dee, D. No date. *Tap technique: Beginning level.* Los Angeles: Al Gilbert, Stepping Tones Records.

Draper, P. 1997. *Paul Draper on tap.* New York: Insight Media.

Hines, G. 1995. *About tap.* New York: Insight Media.

Hoctor, D. 1987. *Tap dancing technique: Basic beginner through advanced exercises.* Hightstown, NJ: Princeton.

Lawton, S. 1997. *Rhythm style and tap.* Hightstown, NJ: Princeton.

Omickel, A. 1997. *Dance: New York tap.* Hightstown, NJ: Princeton.

Rizzo, B. 1998. *Funky rhythm tap.* Hightstown, NJ: Princeton.

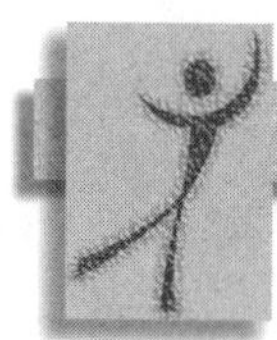

Aerobic Dance Unit

Teaching Overview

Psychomotor Objectives

- Execute various exercises, dance steps, combinations, and line dances to music.
- Demonstrate relationship of movement to music (count, rhythm, tempo, time signature).
- Demonstrate the application of aerobic dance principles.

Psychomotor Evaluation

- Complete performance test of aerobic dance exercises or dance routines (steps, line dances performed to the music).

Cognitive Objectives

- Describe the various steps and exercises of aerobic dance.
- Calculate target heart rate zone according to the Karvonen formula.
- Apply the various fitness principles related to aerobic dances.
- Assess personal aerobic fitness by charting the heart rate during each class throughout the semester.

Cognitive Evaluation

- Complete written test of the principles of aerobic dance and related concepts and benefits.
- Calculate target heart rate range.

Affective Objectives

- Practice the etiquette for dancers in an aerobic dance class.
- Demonstrate personal movement confidence.
- Work with a partner or group.

Affective Evaluation

- Demonstrate etiquette, movement, confidence, responsibility, and cooperation in the class.

Specific Teaching Methods

As an instructor in the aerobic dance class, you will demonstrate a step or combination completely at the appropriate tempo. Initially, teach the step or combination at a slow tempo and then gradually up to tempo. The students master the movements through repeated practice. Demonstrate the next step, and the students practice it; then add it to the first step, and so on. These steps form a combination or a complete dance, and the degree of difficulty increases throughout the week or unit.

Ask a student to demonstrate the movement after you teach it. The student who knows the exercise or routine can come to the front of the class so that you are free to provide feedback to the other students. This prevents wear and tear on your own body and helps to involve the students in the teaching and learning process.

FORM 13.21

Scope and Sequence for Aerobic Dance

New = N Review = R Performance test = PT Hand in = HI

	1	2	3	4	5	6	7	8	9	10	11	12	13	14	15
History and purpose of aerobic dance	N														
Take pulse and heart rate, resting heart rate	N														
Appropriate dress	N														
Format of class	N														
Assess physical condition	N														PT
Walk/run	N														PT
Push-ups, curls	N														PT
Sit and reach (flexibility) test	N														PT
Karvonen formula	N														PT
Journal	N														HI
Warm-up: head		N	R	R	R	R			R	PT					
Demi-plié with arms		N	R	R	R	R			R	PT					
Shoulder roll, hips		N	R	R	R	R			R	PT					
Lunges		N	R	R	R	R			R	PT					
Arm circles		N	R	R	R	R			R	PT					
Arm		N	R	R	R	R									
Strengthening: curls (static)		N		R	R	R		R	PT						
Push-ups		N		R	R	R		R	PT						
Aerobic: step and together, step touch (side, back, front)		N		R	R	R		R	PT						
Abdominal curls			N	R	R	R		R	PT						
Reaches			N	R	R	R									
Aerobics: Charleston, (walks) apart bend bend			N	R	R	R									
Step, heel, hoop skirt jump			N												
Cool-down: reach side to side, bend pull out and in			N	R	R	R		R	PT						

(continued)

From *Dance Teaching Methods and Curriculum Design*
by Gayle Kassing and Danielle M. Jay, 2003, Champaign, IL: Human Kinetics.

FORM 13.21 *(continued)*

New = N Review = R Performance test = PT Hand in = HI

	1	2	3	4	5	6	7	8	9	10	11	12	13	14	15
Floor side leg lifts, abdominals			N	R	R	R		R	PT						
Rock forward-backward				N	R	R									
Three-step turn				N	R	R									
Cool-down: leg lifts—back				N	R	R		R	PT						
Abdominal twist (obliques)				N	R	R		R	PT						
Warm-up: add arms (up and down, side to side)						N		R	PT						
Strengthening: repetitions						N		R	PT		R	R	R	R	
Crunches with leg crossed at the knee						N		R	PT		R	R	R	R	
Inverted push-ups						N		R	PT		R	R	R	R	
Aerobic: cha–cha						N				R					
Break, can-can runs						N				R					
Knee lift, double and single						N				R					
Grapevine						N				R					
Cool-down: demi-plié second						N	R	R	PT						
Leg lifts on floor on different body facings						N	R	R	PT						
Warm-up: rotate palm-up-down						N		R	PT						
Strengthening increase 8 to 16						N		R	PT						
Aerobic: dance square step										R					
Step out, across step out, behind										R					
Cool-down, pull together						N		R	PT	R					
Lunge combination						N		R	PT	R					
Criteria/checklist								N	PT	R					
Warm-up: increase tempo										N	R	R	R	R	
Strengthening: increase repetition and tempo										N	R	R	R	R	R

FORM 13.21

New = N   Review = R   Performance test = PT   Hand in = HI

	1	2	3	4	5	6	7	8	9	10	11	12	13	14	15
Demi-plié first, second										N	R	R	R	R	R
Sitting on floor: legs parallel, body relaxed										N					
Soles of feet together										N					
Aerobic: step ball–change (different wall)											N	R	R	R	
Schottische: 2 step touch, 3 rock and hold											N	R	R	R	
Step, chug, step front and behind											N	R	R	R	
Rock forward, backward side to side											N	R	R	R	
Touch across											N				
Step, kick, together											N	R	R	R	
Three-step turn											R				
Take home quiz														HI	
Dance routine													R	PT	
Criteria													N		
Posttest															PT

FORM 13.22

Aerobic Dance Block Time Plan

Class 1	Class 2	Class 3	Class 4	Class 5
• History and purpose of aerobic dance • Learn to take pulse and heart rate • Attain resting heart rate • Appropriate dress • Format of class • Assess according to ACSM* Walk or run Push-ups Curls Sit and reach (flexibility) test • Karvonen formula with resting heart rate • Keep a journal of heart rate and how you feel that day	• Begin with warm-up • Head turns side to side • Head tilts side to side • Demi-plié with arm curls, flex and extend arm circles • Shoulder rolls (forward and backward) • Hip isolations (side to side, forward-back circle) • Lunge forward • Lunge side • Arm circles • Arm swing • Strengthening • Abdominal curls static • Push-ups modified • Aerobic: step, together, step, touch step; touch side to touch side; forward and back	• Review all warm-ups • Add difficulty • Lunge combination • Arm swing • Abdominal curls • Reaches • Run down from sitting • Aerobic • Charleston • Charleston walks • Apart, bend, bend • Step hit heel • Hoop skirt jump • Cool down • Reach side to side bend • Pulls out and in • Floor • Side leg lifts • Abdominals	• Review • Add 10 arm reps • Aerobic section • Charleston • Combination review and add • Rock forward and rock backward • Three-step turn • Single knee lift • Cool-down • Review • Add • Leg lifts on back with one knee bent • Abdominal twist	• Review • Warm-up • Review faster • Aerobics • Review everything • Increase speed • Cool-down, review all

*ACSM = American College of Sports Medicine

FORM 13.22

Class 6	Class 7	Class 8	Class 9	Class 10
• Review • Warm-up • Add arm to movement (up, down, side to side) • Strengthening • Add more repetitions, use more complex and/or different exercise, crunches with leg crossed at knee and inverted push-up • Aerobic dance: Cha–cha Break Can–can runs Knee lifts, double and single Grapevine • Cool-down • Review • Add second position • Demi-plié • Exercise on floor, leg lifts on different body facings	• Alert to performance exercise exam • Review • Warm-up • Rotate palm up and down during movement • Strengthening • Increase repetition 8 or 16 times • Review aerobic dance: Add square step Step out across Step out behind • Cool-down and review • Pull together, lunge combination • Floor work review	• Review the warm-up, strengthening, and cool-down exercise • Stress criteria of each exercise • Checklist for each exercise	• Performance exam: Warm-up strengthening and cool-down exercises	• Review • Warm-up increase tempo • Strengthening • Increase repetition and tempo • Aerobic dance review from 6th and 7th class • Cool down flexibility review • Demi-plié 1st and 2nd • Floor setting • Leg parallel and body relax • Relax with soles of the feet together

(continued)

FORM 13.22 *(continued)*

Class 11	Class 12	Class 13	Class 14	Class 15
• Review • Warm-up • Strengthening review • Aerobic dance: step ball change (use different wall as the front) each time Schottische Step touch 2 × and rock 3 × hold Step chug Step front and behind	• Review • Warm-up • Strengthening review • Aerobic dance: Add Rock forward-backward, side to side, Touch across Step kick together 3 step turn • Give take home quiz • Calculate Karvonen formula with resting heart rate • Briefly discuss benefit of aerobic dance	• Review • Warm-up • Strengthening review • Aerobic dance review • Rehearse aerobic dance routine • Give criteria of assessment • Knowledge • Rhythm • Execution • Poise • Overall • Cool-down	• Shorter warm-up and strengthening exercises • Test aerobic dance	• Post assessment • Sit and reach or flexibility test—ACSM • Push-ups • Curls • Walk, run • Turn in journal • Quiz

Student leads line dance.

Construction of Choreography

Do the combinations while facing forward (usually toward a mirror in the gym or studio). When the class is comfortable with the quarter turn toward each wall (front, side, back, and side), do half turns facing front, back, front, and back. For this type of directional change, line dances are appropriate because the intensity and pace increase and the combinations are fun and easy to remember.

Dance steps that travel forward, backward, and side to side are easier on the joints than steps that move in place. When moving through space, you place one and one-half times your body weight on your joints; while moving in place, you place four times your body weight on your joints. Work to achieve a balance of nonlocomotor and locomotor steps.

Musical Accompaniment

Aerobic dance classes use recorded music available on tape and CD format. Many tapes and CDs are geared toward dance fitness classes. Often dance fitness CDs include listings of beats per minute for each piece of music; this helps you increase and decrease the intensity of the workouts. Use music that inspires and incites the dancers to move and has a strong and countable beat. Different dance forms use various types of music from different eras, such as country western, classical, rock, swing, hip-hop, and rap.

Dance Class Format

The format for the aerobic dance class is similar to that of other dance forms, but the goal is to increase aerobic fitness (cardiovascular endurance) and gain strength and flexibility in all parts of the body.

Warm-Up Exercises

The class begins with a warm-up that covers the entire body. This warm-up consists of stretching exercises that can progress from the head to the feet or from the feet to the head. The flexibility exercises help students develop greater range of motion to prevent injury. To save time, you can warm up several parts of the body simultaneously. The warm-up varies from 5 to 10 minutes depending on the length of the class. Teaching and learning the warm-up may take a while, but once students learn the procedures, they can perform the series quickly.

Static stretches lengthen a muscle when it is relaxed. Gravity helps the muscles to stretch—the weight of your body facilitates the muscle to stretch. Hold a stretch 15 to 30 seconds or 16, 24, or 32 counts. These exercises need to be done at the beginning and end of class. Ballistic stretches are forceful in nature and work the stretch reflex response, which makes the muscle contract and may increase muscle tension. After the muscles are fully warmed, ballistic stretches are safe to perform.

Strengthening Exercises

This section, which lasts about 5 to 10 minutes, may also follow the aerobic section. The focus is on increasing muscular strength and endurance with the use of modified push-ups, inverted push-ups, abdominal crunches, leg lifts, and other floor work. Be sure to engage all major muscle groups, and use all opposing muscle groups:

- Chest (pectoralis major) and upper back (trapezius, latissimus dorsi)
- Abdomen (rectus abdominis, internal and external obliques, transverse abdominis) and lower back (gluteus maximus and medius)
- Thighs (quadriceps: medial, intermediate, and lateral vasti; rectus femoris) and hamstrings (semitendinosus, semimembranosus, biceps femoris)
- Inner thighs (adductors: longus and magnus) and outer thighs (abductors)
- Calves (gastrocnemius) and shins (tibialis anterior)
- Anterior upper arms (biceps brachii) and posterior upper arms (triceps brachii)

Crunch exercise.

Push-up exercise.

Use and strengthen opposite pairs equally; this decreases the risk of injury and places equal wear on the joints. Also use a variety of exercises to strengthen and tone the muscles.

Perform movements in a slow and controlled manner to strengthen the muscles. This type of movement is an isometric muscular contraction, which works against gravity and uses tension throughout the entire muscular contraction.

Aerobic Exercises

The aerobic section follows the strengthening section, depending on who teaches the class. As the instructor, you will teach on the move. The students keep moving by marching in place when you demonstrate a step or combination. Line dances (which exist in social, folk, country western, and party dance forms) are appropriate for aerobic dance classes. Line dances consist of a series of simple, repetitive dance steps that travel forward, backward, and side to side. Usually the dances have 32 to 64 counts, and steps are repeated two to four times for 4, 8, or 16 counts.

The aerobic section varies from 12 to 30 minutes. The length of the aerobic section increases as students become more advanced. During this portion students take pulse readings to see whether they are working within their target heart rate zones.

Cool-Down Exercises

The final section is the cool-down, which lasts 5 to 10 minutes and consists of gradually slowing movement, stretching, and strengthening exercises for the legs, back, arms, and abdomen. During the cool-down, students bring their heart rates down to at least 120 beats per minute.

Cautions

In aerobic dance, the following exercises are not recommended:

- Full sit-ups stress the iliopsoas and may cause lower back pain.
- Hurdler stretches overuse the medial ligament in the knee of the back leg.
- Head rolls cause injury to the cervical vertebrae.
- Extreme flexion of the head (back and down) hyperextends the muscles of the neck.
- Two-legged lifts increase strain on the lumbar region of the spine.
- Fast rotation at the waist places pressure on the lumbar region and upper back.
- Forward flexion of the hip joint may cause an extreme stretch of the hamstrings, hyperextension of the knee, and pressure on the lower back.

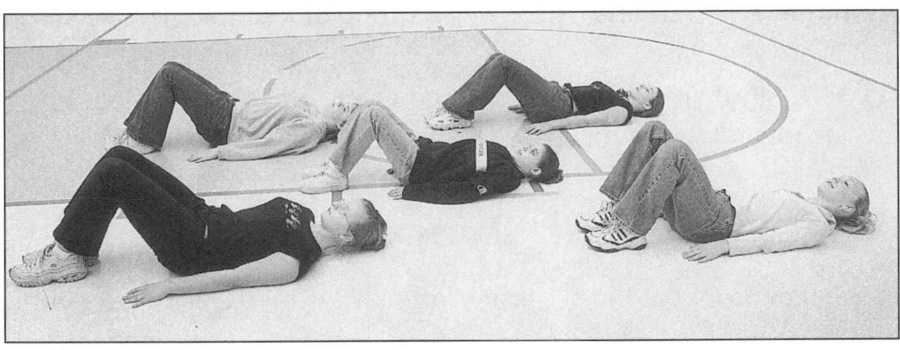

Hook position.

- Donkey kicks may cause injury to the lumbar spine and hamstrings.
- Abdominal work in a cycling position may cause pain in the lumbar region if the stomach muscles are weak and the lower back muscles are tight.
- Ploughs (lying on the back with the legs raised up and over the head) place too much pressure on the neck and may overstretch the cervical spine because most of your weight rests on your neck.

Classroom Considerations

Dancers need adequate space to move in the aerobic dance class. The space should have a sprung flooring or be covered with vinyl flooring. Mirrored walls are ideal because students can check their placement and see your movements in the mirror. Students wear comfortable clothing that allows the teacher to see their body positions. Dancers need to be respectful toward the instructor and cooperative with other students in the class.

Safety

The aerobic dance space should be adequately lit, well ventilated, and free of obstacles and clutter. A sprung floor of wood or vinyl, or a suspended floor (not concrete), helps keep dancers injury-free.

Attire

Clothing should be comfortable and absorbent. Women can wear a unitard or bike pants or shorts and a sports bra top, or leotard and tights. A sports bra provides the extra support that women need during aerobic exercise. Men wear a T-shirt and bike shorts or shorts with an athletic supporter. Aerobic shoes and socks are required.

Classroom Etiquette

Everyone in the class should have fun. As the teacher, you must make sure students hear your instructions so that the students perform the movements correctly. Talking is not appropriate; if students have questions, they should raise their hands.

Beyond Technique Assignments

The following are suggestions for beyond technique assignments in aerobic dance:

- Perform an aerobic dance to various types of music.
- Create your own aerobic line dance with a group of four people.
- Teach an exercise or step.
- View aerobic dance videos and assess their safety and appropriateness.
- Research, read, and report on an article related to dance and fitness.

Content Overview

The content overview provides the necessary information for teaching the aerobic dance unit.

Definition and History

Aerobic dance is a fitness activity that uses rhythmic danc
on fitness, cardiovascular endurance, muscular strengt
flexibility. This form also uses large muscle movement an
exercises from all dance forms. Students do dances individu
involves a series of steps that are simple and fun; dancers also sh
wall to another during a dance. The steps are usually combined into a se
16, 32, or 64 counts. Repetition of the steps and exercises keeps either the fee
other body parts continuously moving. If the steps are difficult, dancers will lose pace and consequently slow down or stop, which defeats the purpose of aerobic dance.

Aerobic dance exercise (commonly known as *aerobics*) stems from the research of Dr. Kenneth Copper in 1968, who found that prolonged rhythmic exercise increases an individual's aerobic capacity. *Aerobic* refers to any activity that uses continuous, rhythmic movement of the large muscles. In 1972, Jackie Sorenson created an exercise form that uses vigorous dance exercise and steps with musical accompaniment. Aerobic dance has altered many people's fitness regimes because it became an alternative to running and other activities and became a fun way to exercise. The different levels are high impact (both feet are off the ground), medium impact (the ball of one foot is on the ground), and low impact (one foot always remains on the ground).

Special Features

The following are specific features of aerobic dance:

- It lowers resting heart rate.
- It decreases blood pressure.
- It aids in preventing osteoporosis.
- It increases delivery of oxygen to cells.
- It enlarges muscle fiber and enhances muscular strength.
- It maintains flexibility around the joints.
- It improves circulation to the heart.
- It decreases the risk of coronary disease.
- It lowers cholesterol in the blood.

Principles

Movement, choreographic, and aesthetic principles that specifically apply to aerobic dance are shown in the shaded areas of the icons on pages 390-391.

Students need to know proper form, training effect, and exercise principles to help them understand and get the most out of aerobic dance. Alignment is the proper position of body parts during specific exercises. Training effect is the physiological result of exercise on the body; this concept comprises the exercise principles of specificity, overload, reversibility, duration, intensity, and frequency.

Alignment

Correct body alignment is an essential part of any dance form. Keep your shoulders down and back, directly over your hips. Hold your head erect. Keep your abdominal muscles engaged during all movements. The knees should be lifted but not locked. Try to maintain the three natural curves in the back (cervical, thoracic, and lumbar)

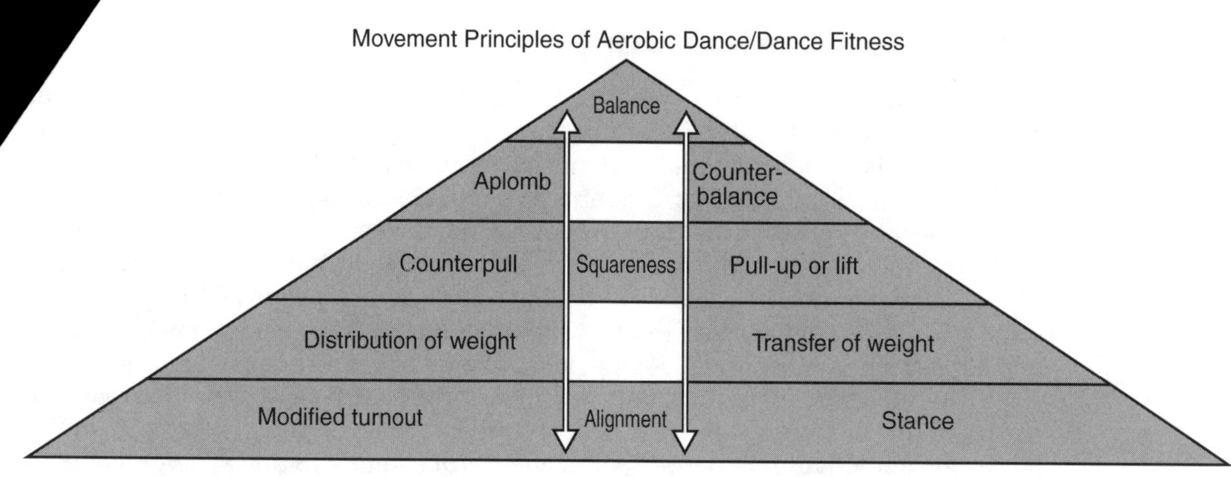

Choreographic Principles of Aerobic Dance/Dance Fitness

Choreographic elements	Choreographic structures	Choreographic designs	Choreographic devices	Choreographic relationships
Motif Phrase Theme and variation	Simple musical forms • AB (binary) • ABA (ternary) • Rondo • Theme and variation Contrapuntal forms • Canon (round) • Fugue Others • Narrative (story) • Open (free)	Dancer's body shape Dancer's pathway through space Visual design • Symmetrical • Asymmetrical Symbolism • Representational • Abstraction • Distortion Relationship • Unison • Sequential • Successional • Oppositional • Complementary	Repetition Reverse Alter • Addition or subtraction • Directional change • Facing or focus • Level • Dimension • Tempo • Rhythm • Quality or effort action • Positioning • Movement section	Solo Duet Trio Quartet Small and large groups

Traditional Dance Elements

Space	Time	Force	Relationships
Directions Dimensions Levels Shapes Pathways Focus	Duration Tempo	Movement qualities • Sustained • Percussive • Swinging • Suspended • Collapsing • Vibratory	Among body parts Among people Between people and props

Laban's Dance Elements

Space	Time	Weight	Flow
Direct or indirect	Sudden or slow	Light or strong	Bound or free

Effort actions (use space, time, and weight)

• Dab • Flick • Punch • Slash • Glide • Float • Press • Wring

Aesthetic Principles of Aerobic Dance/Dance Fitness

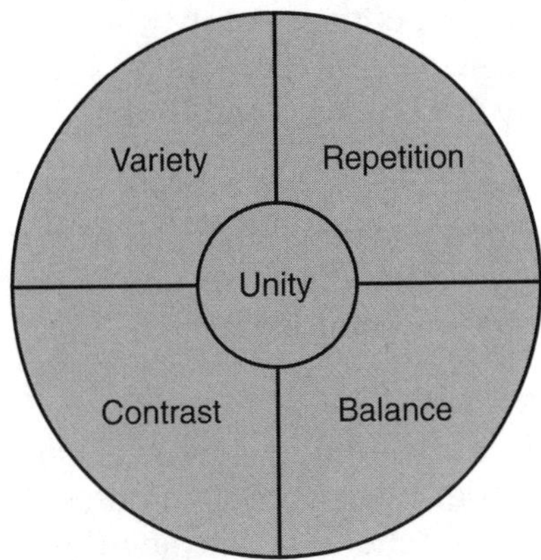

as the tailbone drops and the spine lengthens. Muscles should go through a full range of motion in flexibility exercises. A moderate speed is safe; if the movement is too fast, this heightens risk of injury to the joint.

Training Effect

The American College of Sports Medicine (ACSM) recommends 20 to 60 minutes of aerobic exercise, three to five times per week, to develop a training effect of increased cardiorespiratory fitness. A training effect occurs when you work within 60 to 90 percent of your maximum heart rate, also known as your target heart rate zone. It is important to monitor your heart rate during exercise to determine whether you are working within your target heart rate range (THR). Heart rate reserve (HRR) is calculated with the Karvonen formula, which uses your resting heart rate (RHR) as a baseline. Take the following steps to measure your RHR: After you wake on two or three consecutive mornings, relax for a few minutes, find your radial or carotid pulse, and take a count for one minute. The average of the two or three mornings is your RHR. To figure your THR using the Karvonen formula, begin with the predicted maximal heart rate (MHR), which is 220 minus your age. Next, subtract the RHR from the MHR; this is your HRR. Then multiply the percentages (as decimals) for the upper (90 percent) and lower (60 percent) limits by the HRR. Finally, add your RHR to these numbers.

Karvonen Formula

220 − 20 (age) = 200 (MHR) − 70 (RHR) =
130 (HRR) × .60 (lower limit) = 78 + 70 (RHR) = 148.
220 − 20 (age) = 200 (MHR) − 70 (RHR) =
130 (HRR) × .90 (upper limit) = 117 + 70 (RHR) = 187.
The target heart rate range is from 148 to 187 bpm.

Specificity

Select exercises that pinpoint specific muscle groups that you want to tone. This is the principle of specificity. For example, if you want to tone the leg muscles, you would do lunges, relevés, leg lifts, and pliés.

Overload

During each class, gradually increase the degree of difficulty by adding more steps or exercise repetitions so that dancers perform slightly beyond their comfort zone.

Through this principle of overload, the class is able to monitor progress and become stronger; consequently, this enhances the training in the class. Monitor the heart rate at least three times during the class. This enables the students to see whether they are working within their target heart rate.

Reversibility

Just as your body has the ability to adapt to physical demands placed on it, it also has the ability to lose the gains you have made through a lack of activity. In short, if you don't use it, you lose it.

Duration

Duration refers to the length of time of each bout of exercise. The length of an aerobic dance class varies from 40 to 60 minutes. The class has three to four parts depending on the instructor's choices. This includes the warm-up (stretching or strengthening exercises), the aerobic section (line dances and other dance steps), strengthening exercises, and cool-down (flexibility exercises and abdominal and leg work).

Intensity

During the class each dancer works within her target heart rate zone, which is from 60 to 90 percent of her maximal heart rate. Dancers monitor themselves throughout the class by taking their pulse either at the neck or wrist for six seconds and multiplying by 10 or by counting the number of heartbeats per minute.

Frequency

This refers to the number of exercise bouts per week. To gain a training effect, each dancer must work in his target heart rate range for at least 20 minutes three times per week.

Vocabulary

Dance steps are used in the aerobic section of the class. Line dance steps are also incorporated into this dance form.

Line Dance Steps

Step, touch starts with the feet together. Step side (left), touch; step side (right), touch; step forward, touch; and step backward, touch. Word cues are step, touch.

The **touch** is a step that doesn't take the weight. Touch front, touch side, touch back, step side; reverse. Use different combinations:

- Two touches in front, two to the side, two to the back. Touch to the side and transfer the weight.
- One touch in front, one in back, one in front, step in place, and shift weight.

Line touch step variation starts with feet together. Touch front, touch side, touch back; then step, step, step in place. Repeat to the other side. Word cues are touch front, side, back, step.

Step, together, step, touch begins with the feet together. Step left foot to the side, then bring right foot together with the left foot; step side left, touch right foot on floor. Do step, together, step, touch to the opposite side or step forward, together; step forward, touch; step backward, together; step backward, touch. Word cues are step, together, step, touch.

Schottische (see the folk dance unit, page 241) can be performed sideward, forward, and backward. Word cues are step, step, step, hop.

In **rock forward and rock backward (rock step),** step forward on right foot and lift other foot; step backward on left foot and lift right foot. Word cues are rock, rock.

In **grapevine step,** step right foot to the side and cross the left foot over the right in front. Step side right and touch with the left foot to the right. Reverse and step to the left; cross the right foot in back. Step side left and touch with the right foot. Word cues are side, cross, side, touch. This is a slight variation of the grapevine step described in the folk dance unit, page 242.

In the **touch across,** touch foot to side, then step across; touch side, then across. Word cues are touch, across.

In **across, touch,** step forward and step across and touch with opposite foot. Word cues are across, touch.

For **box step,** step out to the side, step across, step back, step back two more times. Repeat, then step side to side three times and hold; reverse. Word cues are step, cross, step back, step back.

For **rock step,** step, touch and lean forward; step, touch, lean backward, rock, rock, hold. Word cues are step, touch and lean, step, touch and lean, rock, rock, hold.

Three-step turn: See the jazz dance unit, page 360.

For **step, ball–change,** step right foot forward on full foot, then transfer weight briefly onto the ball of the left foot behind the right foot, then step full foot on the right foot either front or side. Repeat to other side. Word cues are step, back, front. For variations, do four step, ball–changes to front wall; four to right side wall; four to the back wall; and four to side wall. Then do two front, two side, two back, two side; one front, one side, one back, one side.

For **step chug,** step on one foot and scoot forward on the same foot.

For **step scuff,** step on one foot and brush the heel of the opposite foot.

Aerobic Dance Steps

Apart bend begins with the feet together in parallel first position. Jump apart to second position, then bring feet together; do two knee bends and pause. Keep arms in a low V position. Word cues are apart, together, bend, bend.

Arm swings begin in second position. Arms are down and slightly in front of the body. Swing both arms to the right and upward in a semicircle. Reverse. Bend knees at the beginning of the swing and straighten at the height of swing. Word cues are bend, swing.

A **break** starts with feet in parallel first position. Jump upward with the feet together. Arms are parallel with the body and the elbows are bent. Fingers point upward. Then bring the arms downward before starting the next jump. Word cues are slow jump, slow jump, quick jump, quick jump.

Can–can runs start with feet together and ready to move forward. Lift one leg up slightly forward; lean backward. Leap on alternate feet four times. Then lean the body forward as you lift the leg slightly backward and off the ground. Leap on alternating feet four times. Perform four or eight runs: four back, four forward, two forward, two back. Circle arms in front of the body or clasp hands behind buttocks or clap hands on each run. Word cues are 8 forward and backward, 4 forward and backward, 2 forward and backward.

Cha–cha basic starts with the feet together with the weight on the left foot. Rock forward onto the right foot, then rock back on left foot; step right foot next to left foot, step left foot in place, step right foot in place. Rock backward onto left, then rock forward onto right foot; step left foot next to right foot; step right in place, step left in place. Word cues are front, back step, step, step; back, front step, step, step.

Charleston starts with the feet together in parallel first position. Step forward on the left foot; point right foot in front. Step back on the right foot; point left foot in back. Step front on the left. Arms swing in opposition to the feet right, left, right, left every time a foot moves. Word cues are front step, touch front; back step, touch back.

Charleston walk begins with the feet together. Step forward with heel of right foot and bend right knee slightly. Step forward with heel of left foot and bend left knee slightly. Word cues are step, bend, step, bend.

Circle arms start with arms at shoulder level to the sides. Move both arms in small circles clockwise, then counterclockwise. Use one arm or alternate right and left arms. Circle each arm forward toward the front of the body, forward overhead, and backward (in a backstroke). Perform at a moderate tempo.

Circle arms and swing starts with feet in second position parallel. Sway body and swing arms to right (bend knees at beginning of swing and straighten at height of swing). Swing arms to left. Make a complete circle right with an arm swing. Word cues are swing, circle up, and around.

Cross side runs begin with the feet together. Leap to the right side; left foot crosses over and takes the weight. Repeat two more times, then leap to the right side and touch left foot to the right foot. Repeat to the left side. Word cues are leap across, leap across, leap across, leap and touch.

Dancing skip starts with the feet together and knees relaxed. Step forward on right foot, then hop on right and extend left leg low in back. Step forward on left foot, then hop on left foot and extend right leg to back (arm swing alternates with opposite arm and leg). Skip is an uneven step. Word cues are and skip, and skip.

Flapper lunges start with feet together in parallel first with knees relaxed. Step wide to right on the right foot and bend both knees. Pull right foot back into left. Repeat, then reverse. Palms move up and down at wrists. Word cues are step out together or side together.

Forward hop, backward hop starts with the feet together and arms down at sides. Step forward on right foot and hop on right; extend left leg back. Step back on left foot, hop left with right leg extended forward. Swing arms forward and back. Word cues are hop forward, hop backward.

Half breaststroke starts with the feet in second position. Left hand is on waist and right hand is in front of chest with elbow held up to shoulder level, palm away from the chest. Bend right knee and rock to right; do breaststroke with right arm. Rock to left and bend left knee. Word cues are rock, bend, and pull arms.

Half-knee bends begin with the feet together. Bend knees and stretch the calves. Keep the heels on floor. Word cues are bend and stretch. This is also a demi-plié in parallel position.

Hit your heel starts with the feet together and arms down. Hop or step on left foot; hit right heel with the right hand (knee bends and foot slightly kicks to the back). Do the combination three times turning to left, alternating feet; then step and bring feet together. Word cues are step, hit heel; step, hit heel; step, hit heel; step, together.

Hoop-skirt bounce starts with feet approximately hip-width apart. Jump three times, turning clockwise. Then jump three times counterclockwise. Arms circle

Leg kick with clap.

outward, then arms circle inward, respectively. Word cues are hop, hop, hop, pause.

Leg kick starts with feet together. Kick right leg out in front, then bring right foot back to floor and bend together. Kick out left, then bend together, alternating legs. Keep hands on hips. Word cues are kick, bend; kick, bend.

Single knee lifts begin with the feet together and the arms at sides. Raise knee as high as possible and slap the knee. Then lower the knee and bring both feet together. Word cues are knee lift, together.

Double knee lifts start with the feet together and arms at sides. Raise right knee, lower right knee. Raise right knee again. Transfer the weight and reverse. Can be done with a slap on each knee. Word cues are knee lift, knee lift, other side.

Jump forward and backward starts with the feet together. Bend and jump forward; arms come up to chest. Bend and jump back; arms slap thighs. Word cues are jump forward; bend and jump.

Bend kick starts with feet together. Bend and kick the leg across the body in front or back. Reverse, arms at shoulder level. Word cues are bend, kick across or behind.

Lunge forward starts with the feet together. Lunge forward by bending the right knee and stepping the right foot forward. Simultaneously bring the arms overhead. While the feet are together, the arms will pull down by your sides. Reverse. Word cues are lunge forward, together.

Lunge combination begins with the feet together in first position parallel. Do lunge forward on the right leg, together to the left foot, then forward on the left leg, together to the right foot; and then lunge side (to right foot) to side (together to left). Word cues are lunge forward, together; forward, together; backward, together; backward, together.

Point step begins with the feet together. Hop or step on the left foot while pointing the right foot forward; jump together or step together. Hop or step on the right foot and point left foot forward; jump together or step together. Arms are in opposition to the feet. Word cues are hop, point; or step, point.

Lunge side to side starts with feet together in parallel or turned-out first position. Lunge to right side, bend right knee. Return to starting position. Repeat on left side. Word cues are lunge out, together.

Polka step (heel and toe slide) starts with the feet together. Hop on left leg, touch right heel to front. Hop on left leg, touch right toes across left foot (flex right knee).

Side lunge.

Repeat this action twice. Heel, toe, heel, toe, slide the right foot two times to the right. Step together. Reverse. Arms move upward (and downward) to the left and right diagonals at the same time; on slide, arms are at shoulder level. Word cues are heel, right toe; heel, right toe; slide, slide, step together.

Posture walks begin with the feet together and arms at side. Hold body in alignment with abdomen pulled in, tailbone down, shoulders back and down. Keep head neutral. Walk lightly first with ball of foot and drop to heel and bend knee. Arms swing in opposition. Word cues are ball, toe, bend.

Push down, pull up starts with the feet in parallel second position. Knees bend and straighten while the palm of the hand pushes down, bending at the wrist, and then the palm bends upward at the wrist and pulls up. Place hands in front of chest with fingers touching, palms down, elbows out at shoulder level. Push hands down to floor while keeping the chin up. Pull hands up with elbows straight (two counts up and two counts down). Word cues are down and up.

Reaches side to side starts with feet in turned-out second position with arms held out to sides at shoulder level. Reach as far as you can to the right and bend the right knee. Shift the weight side to side. Reverse. Word cues are reach side to side.

Rocking horse starts with the right foot extended forward. Rock forward on right with the right knee flexed and the left leg extended back. Rock back on left foot with the left knee flexed and the right leg extended forward. Bring arm forward and backward; reverse. Word cues are front, back, front hold and back, front, back hold.

Rocking side to side starts with feet in parallel first position. Rock to the right with right knee flexed and left leg extended and pointed to left side. Reverse direction. Word cues are rock right, rock left.

Single shoulder rolls start with the feet comfortably apart and arms down at sides. Rotate right shoulder up and down and around in a continuous motion. Reverse. Word cues are up, back, and around or up, forward, and around.

Side kick starts with the feet together and the body facing front. Kick left leg straight to side, hopping on right foot. Reverse. Arms swing overhead from side to side. Word cues are kick, hop.

Step and cross starts with the feet together and weight on the left foot. Step to right side on right foot; cross left foot over right foot and repeat two more times and step touch. Knees are bent; arms swing low to right on step and low to left on cross over. Word cues are out across; out across; out across; step, touch.

Step behind left starts with the feet together and the knees relaxed. Step to the side on right foot, step left behind, step right to side, step left behind, step right to side, and step touch left.The arms swing to the right as the left foot touches to right foot. Word cues are side, behind; side, behind; side, behind; step, touch.

Side leg raise starts on the floor lying on the right side. Right arm extends along floor under the head and left hand is on floor in front of you for support.The left leg bends as if you are sitting in chair. Raise the right leg to the side and keep your foot flexed; lower it. Word cues are side lift and lower.

Side bend starts with the feet in second and the arms at the sides. Bend the body to the left. Stretch high with right arm and hold for three counts. Support body with left hand on hip. Move back to the center and repeat on other side. Word cues are stretch out, hold.

Second position demi-plié starts with the feet shoulder-width apart and slightly turned out. Do demi-pliés with knees in line with toes; go down on counts one and two and up on counts three and four. Word cues are down, up.

Slide begins with the feet together. Step right foot to the right; slide left foot to meet the right foot. End on left. Slide seven times, then jump with feet together. Reverse. Word cues are slide, together.

Train step starts with the feet together. Step forward on left foot and draw the right foot to the left foot. Repeat three times to the left; on the fourth time, step, touch, reverse. Arms move from the waist on the first step and to the waist on the second. Word cues are or step, draw; step, touch.

Rope pulls begin with the feet in wide second position (turned out). Arms are at shoulder level straight out to the left. Step and bend right knee while pulling arms across the body, ending at left. Reverse. Move as if you are pulling a rope. Word cues are step out, pull; step out, pull.

Selected Resources

Selected resources include dance fitness texts, music, and videos.

Texts

Bishop, J. 1999. *Fitness through aerobics.* 4th ed. Needham Heights, MA: Viacom.

Brick, L. 1996. *Fitness aerobics.* Champaign, IL: Human Kinetics.

Cotton, R.T. 1993. *Aerobics instructor manual:The resource for fitness professionals.* San Diego: American Council on Exercise.

Mazzeo, K. 1992. *Aerobics the way to fitness.* Englewood, CO: Morton Publishing Company.

Polley, M. 1983. *Dance aerobics two.* Mountain View, CA: Anderson World Books.

Music

Clark, L. 1987. *Hooked on classics.* Plymouth, MN: K-tel International, MU 6113.

Low impact aerobic program. 1988. Minneapolis: National Dance Exercise Instructors Training.

Mega hit disco, Vol 10. 1991. Hollywood: Priority.

The NDEITA aerobic workout I. 1990. Minneapolis: NDEITA.

The NDEITA stretch, tone, & relaxation. 1990. Minneapolis: NDEITA.

The NDEITA stretch, tone, & relaxation, Vol 2. 1991. Minneapolis: NDEITA.

The new aerobic workout. 1989. Minneapolis: National Dance Exercise Instructors Training (cassette).

Poly Gram Records. 1995. *Instant party disc.* Los Angeles: Rhino.

Videos

Lane, C. 1992. *Line dancing.* Westlake Village, CA: Brentwood Home Video.

Lane, C. 1993. *Hot new line dances.* Westlake Village, CA: Brentwood Home Video.

Lane, C. 1994. *More funky freestyle.* Westlake Village, CA: Brentwood Home Video.

Lane, C. 1996. *Learn the dances of the 50's and 60's.* Palm Springs: Let's Do It.

Lane, C. 1996. *Learn the dances of the 70's.* Palm Springs: Let's Do It.

Lane, C. 1996. *Learn the dances of the 80's.* Palm Springs: Let's Do It.

Leight-Hart, C. 1990. *Switching gears: How to go from high to low.* San Diego: IDEA.

Nies, E. 1995. *MTV grind workout: Hip-hop aerobic.* New York: Sony Music Video.

Stretch, tone and relaxation. Vol II. 1991. Minneapolis: NDEITA.

CHAPTER

14

Culminating Curriculum Portfolio

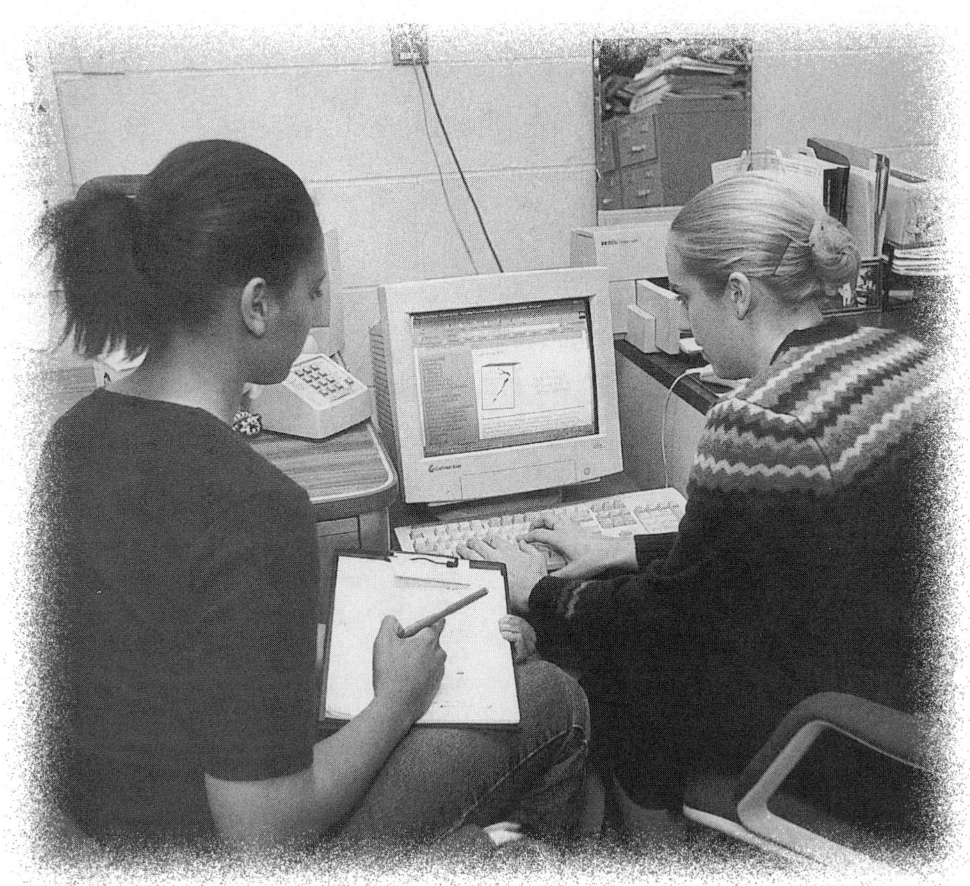

As a dance instructor interviewing for a job in public education, you must prove that you can do the job. You will gain an edge over competing candidates if you present a curriculum portfolio at your interview; this will give the prospective employer insight into your knowledge of dance content, your organization skills, and your ability to put theory into practice. This chapter will guide you in creating a model for dance curriculum portfolio for a public education setting.

By now, you have learned how to do all the parts of the curriculum portfolio assignment. The curriculum portfolio contains five sections. The first two sections are descriptions that specify the environment and the learner. The last three sections comprise the content for a dance curriculum. The unit plans make up a one-year program that meets state or National Dance Standards.

Depicting the Teaching Environment

The first section of the portfolio is a description of the teaching environment (educational level, department, and number of faculty; see chapter 7), population (grade and skill levels; see chapter 7), length of class, number of class meetings per week, and length of unit (see chapter 9). Include the type of facilities and equipment (see chapter 6) and the kind of instruction and teaching styles used in the department (see chapter 5). This section relates the mission of the department to the curriculum model with a rationale for including dance in the department (see chapter 9).

In the narrative, indicate the purpose of dance in the department as an art form; a mode of physical fitness; or an aesthetic, cultural, or interdisciplinary form of education. Address the community values so that curriculum development parallels the values of the community (see chapter 7). Finally, write your philosophy of dance (see chapter 6). Try to keep each of these parts no longer than one or two paragraphs.

Describing the Learner

The second narrative section relates to the learner. When analyzing the learner, consider the characteristics, needs, and appropriate activities for that age, skill level, and grade (see chapters 4 and 7). The school environment influences what you will teach. These factors help you to determine the dance content knowledge. Select the appropriate dance forms (recreational, concert, creative, dance fitness) for the learners and the environment. Using the cross-disciplinary knowledge categories (see chapter 2), gather the information (history, definition, and other supportive knowledge of the dance form; see chapter 8) that you think the students will learn in each of the units. Decide on the specific dance content (elements, exercises, steps).

Selecting Dance Content for Each Unit Plan

In the third section of the curriculum portfolio, organize the dance content for the unit plan for each dance form. Write the objectives for each unit in the cognitive, psychomotor, and affective domains; relate each objective to the state or National Dance Standards. Create a scope and sequence, listing all content in the unit and the order in which you will teach it. Next, write the block time plan, a day-to-day plan of what you will teach, review, and assess throughout the unit. (See chapters 9, 10, and 11.)

Devising Learning Experiences for the Dance Form

In the fourth section, devise the learning experiences for the dance form content before creating the lesson plans. The learning experiences support the learner, the environment, and the dance content; they also focus on dancing, dance making; and dance appreciation. Use a top–down or bottom–up strategy in developing a unit (see chapter 12). In this section, describe two types of assessment tools: a performance rating scale or a rubric and a written test for each of the units (see chapter 10).

Writing the Lesson Plans

The fifth section is writing the lesson plans (see chapter 11). After developing the learning experiences, draft two lesson plans for each unit with behavior objectives that relate to the National Dance Standards. Use the dance form content and its appropriate class format and include progressions, cues, imagery, teaching styles, and management strategies. Select the musical accompaniment for the various sections of the class. Be thorough and detailed. Finally, write a one-year dance program; include a one-paragraph rationale for the order of your units.

To make your culminating portfolio project ready for presentation, collect your work and put it into a three-ring binder. Label the parts and include a title page and table of contents.

Epilogue

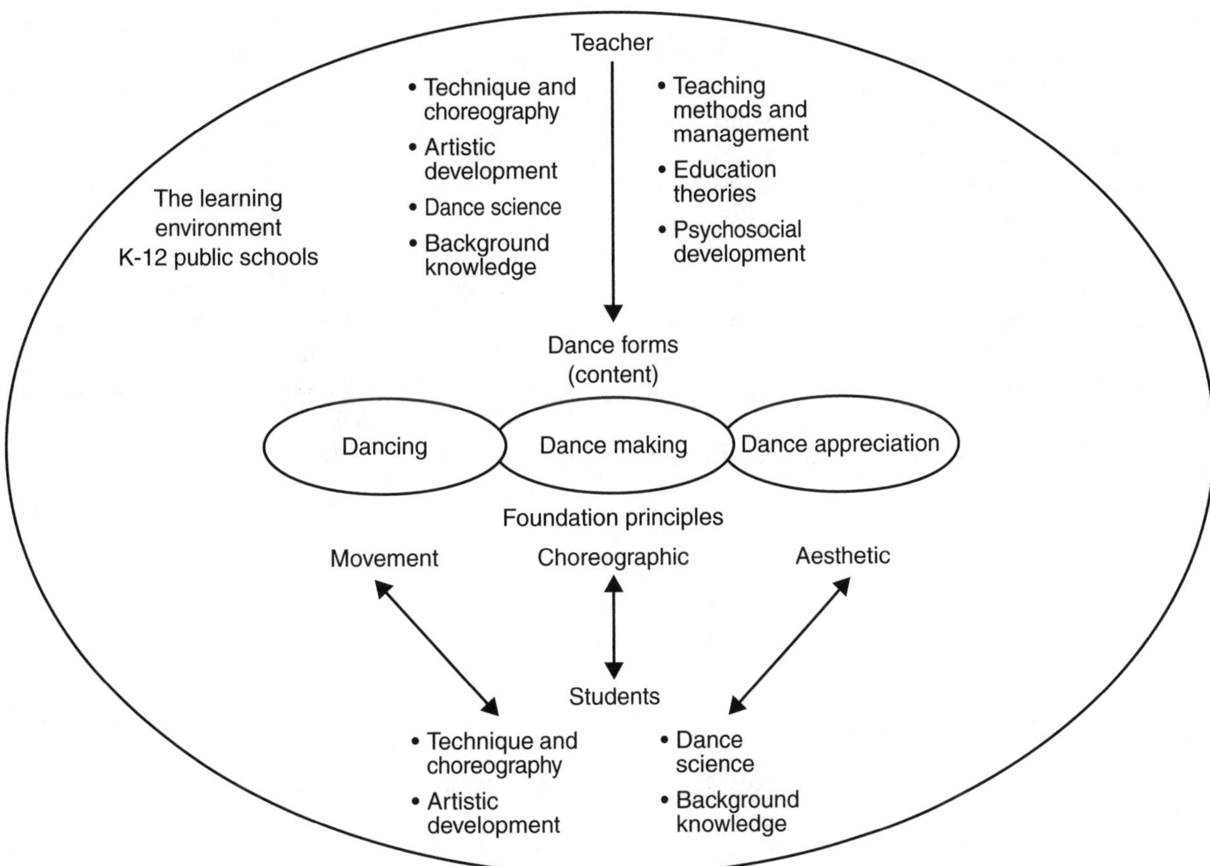

The complete teaching and learning process model.

When you participate in dance classes, you learn a great deal more than exercises, steps, and dances. You develop personal attributes and skills that easily transfer to other academic disciplines and jobs and function as important life skills. These skills, both physical and mental, seem to happen effortlessly because of the intricate coordination that takes place when you initiate them. The following are some of the qualities you acquire from participating in dancing, dance making, and dance appreciation:

- Self-esteem, positive body image, and self-confidence
- Concentration
- Movement confidence
- Kinesthetic awareness and muscle memory
- Visual acuity (seeing and replicating)
- Auditory acuity (hearing and understanding music)
- Ability to articulate concepts, principles, and skills to others

These skills nourish the physical, emotional, and spiritual aspects of your education, experience, and performance as a dancer and dance teacher.

Teaching dance is the art of facilitating learning and guiding students through dancing, dance making, and dance appreciation. You not only present and explain the information in a logical and expeditious manner, but you also manage the situation to provide effective and efficient learning. In this role, you demonstrate various teaching strategies appropriate for the needs, interests, and maturity of the learners and the objectives of the program. The dance educator has many various roles and responsibilities. You have or will acquire a professional identity supported by behaviors and qualities that are associated with the dance and education profession. You will fulfill the roles of teacher, mentor, choreographer, director, curriculum planner, and evaluator.

The teaching and learning process model is now complete (see figure on page 403); we have explored all of the parts.

If you are a dance education student, you have had the time to think, research, experiment, organize, and write what you plan to teach and how you plan to teach it. Often in a job situation, you don't have as much time to plan as you would like. As a new dance educator, your experiences and philosophy will become a part of planning, teaching, and designing a curriculum. The information in this book is a ready reference and perhaps a way for you to extend yourself into new areas of dance.

The future is exciting for dance and dance education. As teachers who have taught dance and prepared students to teach dance in public schools, we share our knowledge and experiences with others. We have had an exciting and fascinating journey through dance and education. We hope to inspire you in your teaching and love of dance so that you can impart and inspire your generation and future generations of dancers and dance educators. Your students teach you and you influence so many students . . . Reggie, Scott, Maureen, Joel, Ann, Robin, Mary, Jeffi, Dave, Sally, Becca, Marissa, Demetri, Steve, Lee, Lauren, Becky, Barb, Anna, Andy . . . ?

Who will you influence? . . . It's your turn.

Appendix

FORM A.1

Dance Unit Rubric

Student name: ______________________ Class: __________ Date: ________

Either put a ✓ in the most appropriate column for the student's performance or write notes in the selected box.

	Description of characteristics		
Selected objectives for psychomotor domain	**Beginning (1)**	**Developing (2)**	**Excellent (3)**
	Executes some *(select one or more items from the following list or use your own)* movements, exercises, steps, combinations, or dances correctly some of the time and integrates some components, such as • movement principles, • style, and • transitions in relation to the music for a somewhat technically correct and budding artistic performance.	Executes most *(select one or more items from the following list or use your own)* movements, exercises, steps, combinations, or dances correctly most of the time and integrates • movement principles, • style, and • transition in relation to the music for a technically correct and maturing artistic performance.	Executes all *(select one or more items from the following list or use your own)* movements, exercises, steps, combinations, or dances correctly and with precision all of the time and integrates all components, including • movement principles, • style, and • transitions in relation to the music for an exceptionally technical, maturing, artistic, and seamless performance
Perform aerobic dance • exercises *(list them)*, • steps *(list them)*, and • routines *(list them)*.			
Perform selected recreational dance form (______________) • footwork *(list them)*, • figures *(list them)*, • steps *(list them)*, • partner positions *(list them)*, • formations *(list them)*, • combinations *(list them)*, and • selected dances *(list them)* with application of principles.			

(continued)

FORM A.1 (continued)

	Description of characteristics		
	Beginning (1)	**Developing (2)**	**Excellent (3)**
Perform creative movement and creative dance movements—locomotor and non-locomotor *(list them)* • activities, with music, in relation to other dances and props; • application of concepts; and • creation of a dance to meet appropriate criteria for the activity.			
Perform selected concert dance form (_________________) • exercises *(list them),* • steps *(list them),* • combinations *(list them),* and • dances *(list them)* in relation to music with application of principles.			

FORM
A.2

Dance Unit Rubric

Student name: ______________________ Class: ____________ Date: _________

Either put a ✓ in the most appropriate column for the student's performance or write notes in the selected box.

	Description of characteristics		
Selected objectives for affective domain	**Beginning (1)**	**Developing (2)**	**Excellent (3)**
	Some of the time demonstrates full participation, cooperation, leadership, and a professional attitude toward the work in the class and respect for fellow classmates and the teacher.	Most of the time demonstrates full participation, cooperation, leadership, and a professional attitude toward the work in the class and respect for fellow classmates and the teacher.	All of the time demonstrates full participation, cooperation, leadership, and a professional attitude toward the work in the class and respect for fellow classmates and the teacher.
Demonstrate aerobic dance • etiquette, • participation and contribution, • movement confidence, • responsibility, and • cooperation and leadership within class.			
Demonstrate selected recreational dance form • etiquette, • participation and contribution, • movement confidence, • performance attitude, and • cooperation and leadership within class.			
Demonstrate creative movement and creative dance • etiquette, • participation and contribution, • movement confidence, and • cooperation and leadership within class.			
Demonstrate selected concert dance form • etiquette, • participation and contribution, • movement confidence, • performance attitude, and • and cooperation and leadership within class.			

FORM A.3

Dance Unit Rubric

Student name: ______________________________ Class: _______________ Date: __________

Either put a ✓ in the most appropriate column for the student's performance or write notes in the selected box.

	Description of characteristics		
Selected objectives for cognitive domain	**Beginning (1)**	**Developing (2)**	**Excellent (3)**
	Completes written test or assignment with at least 70 percent accuracy.	Completes written test or assignment with at least 80 percent accuracy.	Completes written test or assignment with at least 90 percent accuracy.
Written testing of aerobic dance demonstrates students' knowledge of • dance skills *(list them),* • principles related to concepts *(list them),* • benefits, • self-assessment, and • personal journal entries.			
Written testing of selected recreational dance form (____________________) demonstrates students' knowledge of • dances *(list them),* • dance skills *(list them),* • terminology (definitions and history), • self-assessment, and • translation of written or oral instructions of dance performed to music.			
Written or oral testing of creative movement and creative dance demonstrates students' knowledge of • dance skills *(list them),* • terminology, • definitions, and • translations of the teacher's instructions.			

From *Dance Teaching Methods and Curriculum Design* by Gayle Kassing and Danielle M. Jay, 2003, Champaign, IL: Human Kinetics.

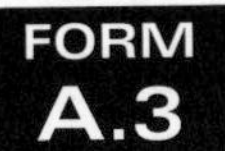

FORM A.3

	Description of characteristics		
	Beginning (1)	**Developing (2)**	**Excellent (3)**
Written testing of selected concert dance form (________________) demonstrates students' knowledge of • dance skills *(list them)*, • terminology, • definitions, • translation of written or oral instructions, and • written dance concert or video report			
	Prepares and presents oral presentation that demonstrates incomplete research from few sources; lack of synthesis of content, use of few presentation techniques to control content; and little or no integration of visual, audio, or performance materials that are all presented in a manner demonstrating little organization and presentation techniques.	Prepares and presents oral presentation that demonstrates adequate research from several sources; some synthesis of content, use of several presentation techniques with a majority of control of content; and partial integration of visual, audio, or performance materials that are all presented in a manner demonstrating a majority of organization and presentation techniques.	Prepares and presents oral presentation that demonstrates in-depth research from many sources; synthesis of content, use of presentation techniques with expert control of content; and complete integration of visual, audio, or performance materials that are all presented in a manner demonstrating organization and presentation techniques in a concise, articulate, and poised manner.
Oral presentation on aerobic dance demonstrates students' • research; • content knowledge; • organization; • presentation techniques (eye contact, attire, length of presentation); and • integration of visual, audio, or performance materials.			

(continued)

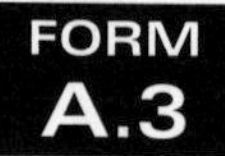

FORM A.3 *(continued)*

	Description of characteristics		
	Beginning (1)	**Developing (2)**	**Excellent (3)**
Oral presentation on selected recreational dance form (_________) demonstrates students' • research; • content knowledge; • organization; • presentation techniques (eye contact, attire, length of presentation); and • integration of visual, audio, or performance materials.			
Oral presentation on creative movement and creative dance demonstrates students' • research; • content knowledge; • organization; • presentation techniques (eye contact, attire, length of presentation); and • integration of visual, audio, or performance materials.			
Oral presentation on selected concert dance form (____________) demonstrates students' • research; • content knowledge; • organization; • presentation techniques (eye contact, attire, length of presentation); and • integration of visual, audio, or performance materials.			
	Rarely calculates training heart rate correctly.	Most often calculates training heart rate correctly.	Always calculates training heart rate correctly.
Written or technique testing in aerobic dance demonstrates proper calculation of target heart rate.			

	Description of characteristics		
	Beginning (1)	**Developing (2)**	**Excellent (3)**
	Conducts inadequate self-assessment and then applies few of the findings to personal performance.	Conducts nearly accurate self-assessment and then applies at least half of the findings to personal performance.	Conducts a precise self-assessment and then consistently applies the findings to personal performance
Self-assessment in aerobic dance demonstrates students' knowledge of • dance skills *(list them)* and • principles related to concepts *(list them).*			
Self-assessment in selected recreational dance form (_________) demonstrates students' knowledge of • dances *(list them),* • dance skills *(list them),* • terminology (definitions and history), and • translation of written or oral instructions of dance performed to music.			
Self-assessment in creative movement and creative dance demonstrates students' knowledge of • dance skills and dances *(list them),* • terminology, • definitions, and • translations of the teacher's instructions.			
Self-assessment in selected concert dance form (____________) demonstrates students' knowledge of • dance skills *(list them),* • dances *(list them),* • terminology, • definitions, and • translation of written or oral instructions.			

(continued)

FORM A.3 *(continued)*

	Description of characteristics		
	Beginning (1)	**Developing (2)**	**Excellent (3)**
	Following the dance concert or video report format, the written report provides few facts and performance details and a cursory analysis of the performance, which create an incomplete pictorial analysis report of the dance performance.	Following the dance concert or video report format, the written report provides accurate facts with some performance details and analysis of the performance, which create a passable pictorial analysis report of the dance performance.	Following the dance concert or video report format, the written report provides precise facts with some performance details and analysis of the performance, which create an exceptional pictorial analysis report of the dance performance.
Written report on an aerobic dance video provides • facts, • performance details, • analysis, and • a review of components.			
Written report on the selected recreational dance form (__________) performance provides • facts, • performance details, • analysis, and • a review of components.			
Written report on creative movement and creative dance performance provides • facts, • performance details, • analysis, and • a review of components.			
Written report on selected concert dance form (______________) performance provides • facts, • performance details, • analysis of choreography, and • a review of components.			

Index

About the Authors

Gayle Kassing

Gayle Kassing and **Danielle M. Jay** have taught dance technique and pedagogy, dance methods, and curriculum design in dance teacher education preparation programs in both physical education and fine arts departments for more than 25 years. Many of their former students are now professionals in K–12 dance education programs.

Drs. Kassing and Jay have helped write state curriculum guidelines and dance teacher certification tests and have presented nationally on teaching methodologies. The two have coauthored one previous book, *Teaching Beginning Ballet Technique.* Dr. Kassing—a former publications director for the National Dance Association (NDA)—is the media author of *Interactive Beginning Ballet Technique,* an interactive multimedia CD-ROM for students. Both have received Outstanding Young Women of America awards from the Outstanding Young Women of America Program. Both authors hold PhDs in dance and related arts and belong to the NDA and National Dance Education Organization. Dr. Jay has served on the committee that selects the NDA Dance Educator of the Year award.

Dr. Kassing lives in Champaign, Illinois, where she is an acquisitions editor in Human Kinetics' division of Health, Physical Education, Recreation and Dance. As a professional dancer, she performed ballet, modern dance, and musical theatre. Dr. Kassing has taught dance in university physical education and fine arts departments and elementary public magnet schools. She administered university dance and fine arts programs and was a Florida Artist in Residence for two terms. She has conducted dance workshops in public schools for state departments of education, in graduate programs, and for professional organizations. In her free time, Kassing enjoys spending time with her family and close friends, walking, reading, and traveling.

Dr. Jay is a professor of dance education at Northern Illinois University. A student of ballet since the age of three, she has studied with Margaret Craske and Celene Keller at Jacob's Pillow; with David McLain, David Blackburn, and Oleg Sabline at the University of Cincinnati; and with Grace Thomas, a soloist with the Radio City Ballet. Dr. Jay lives in Sycamore, Illinois; her favorite leisure-time activities include spending time with her relatives and close friends, reading, and choreographing.

Danielle M. Jay